Ius Gentium: Comparative Perspectives on Law and Justice

Volume 100

Ius Gentium is a book series which discusses the central questions of law and justice from a comparative perspective. The books in this series collect the contrasting and overlapping perspectives of lawyers, judges, philosophers and scholars of law from the world's many different jurisdictions for the purposes of comparison, harmonisation, and the progressive development of law and legal institutions. Each volume makes a new comparative study of an important area of law. This book series continues the work of the well-known journal of the same name and provides the basis for a better understanding of all areas of legal science.

The *Ius Gentium* series provides a valuable resource for lawyers, judges, legislators, scholars, and both graduate students and researchers in globalisation, comparative law, legal theory and legal practice. The series has a special focus on the development of international legal standards and transnational legal cooperation.

Richard Hyland

Common Law Judging and the Great Tradition

Springer

Richard Hyland
Rutgers Law School
Camden NJ USA

ISSN 1534-6781 ISSN 2214-9902 (electronic)
Ius Gentium: Comparative Perspectives on Law and Justice
ISBN 978-3-032-02306-3 ISBN 978-3-032-02307-0 (eBook)
https://doi.org/10.1007/978-3-032-02307-0

This Springer imprint is published by the registered company Springer Nature Switzerland AG
The registered company address is: Gewerbestrasse 11, 6330 Cham, Switzerland

For Rivka, who asked at dinner one evening
As we looked out over the Golden Horn,
'I don't mean to be too gloomy, Daddy,
But what will happen to these ideas when you're gone?'

We do not abandon the concept of the ideal crystal
when we learn that nature never offers one.

— John Archibald Wheeler

We aim at the infinite and when our arrow falls
to earth it is in flames.

— Justice Holmes

Acknowledgments

Alabamians: Sherri Brackin, Grant Brown, Joe Ealum, Serena Ealum, Steve Garrett, Henry Gilmore, Frank Hickman, Andria McCormick, Frank McGuire, Mary Rogers Poole, Edna Thomas, Bob Watson, Jerry Watson, Nathan Watson, June Williams, Tripp Winters

Archivists: Alex Boucher, Doug Brown, Christopher Carter, Lorraine Madway, Joohi Patel, Courtney Pinkard, Alison Thurman, Sarah Wharton

Editors, Publishers, Agents: Luke Adams, Doreen Anderson, Kate Brauning, Chris Calhoun, Elizabeth Demers, Alex Flach, William Frucht, Jonathan Galassi, John Gillespie, Stephen Gutierrez, Ahmed Hegazi, Harley Hightower, Wendy Lochner, Carol McGeehan, Richard Pine, Maria Sosnowski, Alex Star, Sam Stark, Anja Trautmann, Daniel Waterman

Family, Friends: Rivka Hyland, Sharka Hyland, Marty Schlesinger

Foresters: J. Travis Bryant, Frank Corley, Billy Cruse, Ryan Daniels, Tom Evans, Peter McGowin, Steve Stewart

Institutions: Rutgers Law School (financial support for research and book production)

Lawyers: Ginny Childs, Derek Crawford, Pete Hamilton, Quintina Harrington, Mike McMahon, Calvin Poole III, Alden Webb, Ren Werrenrath III

Librarians: Sebastian Hierl, Sarah Lerner, Megan Miller, Jeanne Pavy, Connie Phelps, Charlotte Schneider, Nancy Talley, Genevieve Tung, Johannah White

McGowin Family: Eleanor Adams, Mary Alice Beck, Keville Larson, Stallworth Larson, Mason McGowin, Norman McGowin III, Vivian McGowin

North Carolinians: Sam Ballard, Jr., Antonio Blue, Gorham Bynum, Will Carr, James Carsto, Abbie Covington, Sadie Crawford, Sam Davis, John Hutchinson, Tommy LeGrand, Anette McNeil, Dorothy Miller, Percy Miller, Loletta Palmer, Mechelle Preslar, Benny Sharpe, Kim Sharpe, Dale Strong, Alicia Taylor

Readers: Mary Alice Beck, Steve Beck, Brian Bix, David Bradley, David Carlson, Katie Eyre, Jay Feinman, Michael Fischl, Jane Ginsburg, Pat Gudridge, Phil Harvey, Stacy Hawkins, Mike Macnair, Jim Maxeiner, Crescente Molina, Emily Osborn, John Osborn, Dennis Patterson, Calvin Poole III, Gerry Postema,

Benjamin Salvatore, Joe Sampson, Matt Shapiro, Jim Snipes, Allan Stein, Alec Walen, Lynn West

Research Assistants: Derek Gretkowski, Gina Lombardo, Christian Pirri, Arden Walker

Scholars: Eric Arnesen, Rachel Barney, Chistoph Bezemek, Jamie Boyle, Naomi Cahn, Ed Dwyer, Wolfgang Ernst, Noah Feldman, Werner Gephart, Martin Häublein, Sukaina Hirji, Bernhard Koch, Andrew Kull, Arthur Laby, David Lemmings, Johannes Meier, Susan Meyer, Paul Nail, David Perkins, John Oberdiek, Sebastian Omlor, Florence Roisman, Lawrence Scaff, Kim Scheppele, Hilary Sigman, David Trubek, Geoffrey Watson, Jim Whitman, Hans Wilke

Statisticians: Mingshi Cui, Yulin Li, Minge Xie (of the Rutgers Office of Statistical Consulting)

Webb Family: Janice Webb Hammond

Contents

Part I
Introduction

Chapter 1
The Common Law

How do common law judges decide cases? That simple question has no simple answer. For guidance, we might look to the opinions that judges write to explain their decisions, but they will usually disappoint us. Judges rarely explain how they arrive at their solutions. To understand the process, we will have to look elsewhere. I am going to suggest that we read a few memorable books together.

Pre-legal Understanding

I have regularly taught a seminar about some of these books. The problem with the course is that the vision they present contradicts so thoroughly the usual story, particularly as it is taught in the American law school classroom, that students reject it out of hand when I present it at the beginning of the term. The only method I have found to convince my students to suspend their disbelief long enough to take these ideas seriously is to explore with them the process by which these thoughts emerged over the past couple of centuries.

Students come to law school with a clear idea of legal method. They believe that cases are decided by locating the applicable rule and applying it to the facts. This method seems so obvious that those starting law school do not ask about alternatives. If we are not applying rules, we are not doing law. And yet their method is *pre-legal*. And I say that even though many lawyers and law professors share this view. 'The theory that rules decide cases seems... to have fooled... judges' and 'even those skillful and hard-bitten first-hand observers of judicial work: the practitioners.'[1]

The shared premise of the books that we will discuss is that this view has nothing to do with how cases are decided. Yet it is not helpful to tell students on the first day

[1] Llewellyn (1934), p. 7.

R. Hyland, *Common Law Judging and the Great Tradition*, Ius Gentium: Comparative Perspectives on Law and Justice 100,
https://doi.org/10.1007/978-3-032-02307-0_1

that everything they think they know about law is mistaken. Since law students must learn the rules, it makes sense to begin with what they are willing to study.

As students memorize rules and arrange and re-arrange their outlines, sometimes using oversized paper with great creativity, they occasionally suspect that something is wrong. The same legal question is posed in two cases with similar facts, and yet the cases come out differently. Students then typically decide that one of the cases represents the rule and the other the exception. But even the exceptions do not hold. Exceptions are then made to exceptions, and in the end they record a Ptolemaic system of cycles and epicycles on their inventive maps of the law. There was nothing wrong in practice with ancient astronomy, and the Greeks were able to find their way to Alexandria by charting the stars. In the same way, students are able to do well on their exams and pass the bar on the basis of their imagined legal method.

Irreconcilable Views

At some point, though, students grow beyond that understanding. They have in their minds two incompatible visions of law, and they are looking for a way to reconcile the contradiction. In one, the law consists of an intricate structure of complex rules that are interpreted and accommodated as cases are decided. In the other, judges follow their personal sense of justice. The first is a vision of a rigorous system with right and wrong answers, the second an intuition that anything goes. Both are possible interpretations of the judicial opinions that students study by the hundreds in law school. As they search for an alternative, some join my seminar on Roman law, while others take my course on these demanding books. Because the classical Roman jurists were common lawyers too, both courses offer a similar message. The pages ahead present my understanding of their collective wisdom.

Studying law is much like learning to ride a bicycle. When teacher and student are not exceptionally daring and able, they start with training wheels. Training wheels have nothing to do with riding a bike, but they solve a problem. A beginning cyclist must gain a sense of steering, braking, and balance, but not everyone can learn them at the same time. Training wheels solve the challenge of balance while the focus is on the mechanical skills. Once balance becomes second nature, the training wheels come off.

Common Premise

The books we are about to discuss disagree with each other about nearly everything. What they share is little more than a thought from Holmes: 'General propositions do not decide concrete cases.'[2] When my daughter was ten, she asked what I teach my

[2] *Lochner v. New York*, 198 U.S. 45, 76 (1905) (Holmes, J., dissenting).

students, and that is what I told her. The insight struck her as obvious. 'Otherwise,' she said, 'monkeys could do it.' Many who have studied American law may be more reluctant to accept the idea—and uncomfortable with the further thought that a method not involving the application of rules could provide the foundation for any legal system, let alone for the common law. I will try to show that this is indeed the common assumption of the books we will examine—and also why it is right. But right now I am interested in a different thought. Only if we accept this insight can we see the unnerving question hiding behind it: if the rules alone do not decide the cases, how then are cases decided?

Judicial Opinions

As we discussed earlier, it seems that we should be able to learn how cases are decided by studying the opinions that judges write to explain their decisions. Unfortunately, the court's analysis cannot teach us how it is done, and that is because 'only by happenstance will an opinion accurately report the process of deciding.'[3] A majority opinion has other tasks:[4] it shows that the decision follows precedent, reassures the losing party that its arguments have been heard, and addresses issues that troubled fellow judges.[5]

Why not then simply call up a judge and ask? Because judges rarely volunteer more information about a decision than they include in the opinion. If they were to admit that the rules did not compel the result, it might provoke an appeal. Besides, the process is both so complex and so intuitive that there is no reason to believe that judges themselves are aware of all the factors that influence their decisions. 'They tend to parrot an official line about the judicial process (how rule-bound it is), and often to believe it, though it does not describe their actual practices.'[6] Whatever the reason, 'pitifully little of significance has been contributed by judges regarding the nature of their endeavor.'[7] And yet we will soon find that we have a lot to learn from a few of our great judges.

Challenges

If, as our books explain, the common law does not decide cases by applying rules, it will eventually have to respond to two challenges.

[3] Llewellyn (1960), p. 56.

[4] Id., p. 131.

[5] Id., pp. 26, 132.

[6] Posner (2008), p. 2.

[7] Frankfurter (1954), p. 233.

To begin, there is 'an underlying and pervasive principle of law that like cases should be treated alike.'[8] If judges are allowed to dodge the rules, how can we be sure that all litigants are receiving the same treatment?

There are also political difficulties. Judges are appointed by the executive or subject to infrequent elections after restricted campaigns. We would therefore expect them to leave lawmaking to the elected bodies and simply follow established case law. But in fact, as we will see, judges revise and even reject precedent to reach what they consider to be the appropriate result. Are they then not exceeding the proper scope of judicial power? 'If the precedent just does not conform to modern conditions, its overruling is a legislative act.'[9]

We will have to respond to these concerns, but that is not the half of it. We will also have to explain how a legal system can decide cases without applying pre-existing rules—in fact, without applying anything at all—and yet still count as a legitimate exercise of judicial power. 'Judges make up the common law as they go along, yet common law decision-making is a lawlike activity.'[10]

Questions of Fact, Questions of Law

Let us begin by clearing up a common misunderstanding. Lawyers often talk about how a judge decided a case, but in practice judges do not work alone. The law distinguishes between two types of questions—questions of fact and questions of law—and judges are in principle responsible for answering only one of them.

Questions of fact relate to the events that led to the dispute—what happened in the world outside the courtroom. Whether the defendant ran a red light is a question of fact. Questions of law usually involve the interpretation of a rule, whether found in a statute, an administrative regulation, a judicial opinion, or a contract. If the facts are not in dispute, determining whether a claim is barred by the statute of limitations is a question of law. Characterizing any particular question as one or the other can be difficult, and even judges complain about 'the vexing nature of the distinction.'[11] We can ignore most of these difficulties.

And yet the distinction is important. At trial, questions of fact are often resolved by a jury, and once the facts are established, they are generally not questioned on appeal. Questions of law are decided by the court—which means by a judge or a panel of judges—but for these questions the appellate court is not bound by the trial judge's answer. When lawyers ask about how a case was decided, they are often thinking of how the judge decided the questions of law, and particularly the central legal question—the *issue* or the *question presented.*

[8] Hart and Sacks (1994), p. 147.

[9] Posner (2008), p. 83.

[10] Id., p. 277.

[11] *Pullman-Standard v. Swint*, 456 U.S. 273, 288 (1982).

But there is a caveat. Lawyers may instead mean something else entirely. They may want to know what the judge ordered the parties to do in the real world—to pay damages, perform the contract, or return a benefit received. In other words, the question about how a case was decided might refer either to how a rule was interpreted or to the practical consequences for the parties. We will soon see why it makes sense to examine these aspects separately.

Precedent

Common law cases are generally governed by *precedent*—a rule or principle abstracted from earlier cases, whether decided by the same or a different court. But how can a particular decision by a particular judge in a particular case generate a general rule?

Lawyers often say that a case stands for a particular proposition, which we call its *holding*. The holding is the answer to what we have just learned to call the *issue*, the main legal question in the case, and we would expect to find that proposition in the opinion. And yet in its most important sense, it is often not there. What will ultimately count as the holding is the meaning that will later be attributed to the case: 'Just in proportion as a case is new and therefore valuable, no one, not even the judges, can be trusted to state the *ratio decidendi* [legal rationale].'[12]

The proposition a case stands for is refined over time. For recent decisions, we create a placeholder by imagining 'the minimum rule... necessary to explain the outcome.'[13] Once a court has decided a number of similar cases, the principle that is able to explain the majority of those cases becomes a general rule.

Paradox

The rules that emerge from the precedents have a gravitational attraction that my students usually cannot resist. They forget about the facts, extract the rules, and apply them to the hypotheticals. And yet even as they do, they sense an uncomfortable paradox. The opinions assure them that questions of law are resolved by *applying* the governing legal rules, which means taking account only of the *legally relevant facts*. Nevertheless, as they try to make sense of the decisions, they notice that judges often take into account facts that the applicable rule does not mention, 'facts outside the reports, facts closer to life, the facts our courts so very often know—and so rarely say anything about.'[14]

---

[12] [Holmes] (1871a), p. 539.

[13] Landes and Posner (1976), pp. 249–250.

[14] Llewellyn (1930b), p. 320.

Actually, the problem is worse than it seems. The rules play only a minor role in deciding cases. That is because the jumble of conflicting rules and principles found in the law is incapable of deciding anything. But I am getting ahead of myself, and at this point that suggestion is needlessly provocative. And yet it is already worth noting that we will have to hold two contradictory approaches in mind. We will see how courts, as they reason from precedent, often limit their discussion to facts and factors that the previous cases designated as determinative. At the same time, the books we are about to read will explain why rules alone cannot decide cases and that judges also take account of many other concerns.

Common Law

We will limit our discussion to the *American common law*. To get a sense of this way of thinking about law, it is useful to begin by comparing it to the *civil law*, the common law's great rival.[15] The civil law tradition includes legal systems that trace their origin to the *Digest*, a kind of legal codification compiled in the early sixth century in Constantinople by the legal advisors to the Roman emperor Justinian.[16] The foundation of the civil law is an *authoritative text*—like the *Digest* or the codes—that jurists interpret and apply to resolve disputes. When the civil law's related approaches are considered as a single tradition, it is the dominant legal system in the world today.

The *common law* arose from legal practice in the English royal courts after the Norman Conquest (1066), was elaborated by the courts sitting in Westminster, and then transplanted to the British colonies.[17] As a rule of thumb, some version of the common law often governs today in countries in which English is an official language. In contrast to the civil law, the common law has *no authoritative text*. Common law judges decide cases by referring to earlier cases—their decisions are based on judicial precedent. Some fields of American law are still governed by precedent—including the laws of contract, tort, and restitution that we will soon explore. Some judicial rulings have become so firmly established that they help lawyers anticipate how judges will decide future cases. These we can treat as the *rules* of the common law.

Each common law system is distinct, and the American version is perhaps the most distinct of all, for it has turned an approach devoted to precedent into a dynamic force, one that restlessly generates new ideas and novel institutions.[18]

---

[15] For an introduction to the civil law, see Merryman and Pérez-Perdomo (2019).

[16] For an introduction to the *Digest*, see Nicholas (1962), pp. 38–45. For the classical jurists, see id., pp. 28–36.

[17] For an introduction to the common law, see Samuel (2023).

[18] See Wiegand (2021), pp. 142–147; Wiegand (1991), pp. 236–245.

Private Law

The common law forms a part of the *private law*, which with the criminal law and the public law, is one of the three main fields of a modern legal system. In general, though the same courts decide disputes in all these fields, they involve 'differences in the content of the material, the intellectual approach, and the technique of adjudication.'[19]

The private law focuses on disputes between those the law considers to be persons—physical individuals, of course, but also collective bodies such as partnerships and companies. The private law is vast. It governs important events from birth to death, from who gets custody of the child in divorce to who should inherit under a will.

Some fields of the private law that were long governed by the common law have now been codified by statute, such as in the Uniform Commercial Code, which we will explore a little later and that I will call the UCC or the Code. Courts often treat the Code and those other statutes as they do precedent. When 'a statute has been in existence for a few years its meaning and its effect can be determined only by reading the decisions construing it, not by reading the statute.'[20] As a result, the 'system of case law... is the dominant American system even in primarily statutory fields.'[21]

Notable Books

We are about to discuss what a dozen books have to say about how judges reach their decisions. Which books should we consider?

The notion of *classics* often refers to works written in the distant past by writers whose perspective it may seem the world has long since overtaken. Whatever of value they may offer may appear not to be worth the effort it would take to reconstruct it. The notion of a *canon* of these books seems especially problematic—and that is because the criteria for inclusion are increasingly difficult to justify.

The noteworthy books of the common law resemble the Western canon in some respects but not in others. They too have generally been written by a restricted part of the population, though there is greater diversity among the more recent authors. And these books too surrender their secrets only to those who are willing to reread them. The difference is that there is no alternative. No other books offer anything like the insight that these books provide into the common law.

There are about two dozen books that might seriously claim to be included in our discussion. Everyone agrees on three of them—those by Blackstone, Holmes, and

[19] Frankfurter (1923), p. 910.

[20] Corbin (1914), pp. 236–237.

[21] Posner (2008), p. 210.

Cardozo—three books that are in dialogue with each other.[22] We will include those three books and complete the list with works that continue the dialogue.

Great Tradition

I believe that these books, together with a few others like them, depict the essence of the common law and form what I would like to call the *great tradition*. The great tradition, like all traditions, is a conversation over time. To be part of it, a book must rise to the level of the discussion and grasp the gravity of the questions presented, the subtlety of the answers proposed, and the burning need for resolution. Books that belong to a tradition transform it. Those that merely comment on it or summarize it do not. The great tradition lives by continual renewal—by the constant recombination of customary understanding and present concern. It reexamines the past, disrupts the present, and points the way to the future.

When I call this tradition *great*, I have in mind the notion of greatness described in two different works of literary criticism, each of which took for its title *The Great Tradition*.[23] The tradition I have in mind is morally serious—it sees clearly the dilemmas we face. It is honest, grounded in accurate observation and reliable reporting. It is authentic, animated by a pressing interest in life, especially contemporary life. The tradition has a passion for detail, which it uses to test what has long passed for truth. And yet it also has an inner sense of purpose. Its books seem objective, real. They step off the page and into our lives.

Not many books rise to this challenge. Many lack the vigor of purpose needed to understand what is at stake. They cling to isolated observations and fail to perceive an all-embracing pattern. The lessons of the past have not sunk in deeply enough to shape their conception. As a result, they do not fully realize either their own promise or that of the tradition. Books from the great tradition show us something we had not previously imagined. Others leave us asking whether our time might have been better spent.

History and Philosophy

Both history and philosophy have had a lot to say on the topics we are about to discuss. I want to explain why we will generally not consult them this time around.

Historians teach that no text can be properly understood until it is contextualized. We understand a text by learning about the discussion that it was a part of and how it was hoping to influence the debate. More background is always better, and a

[22] See Blackstone (2016); Holmes (2009); Cardozo (1921b).

[23] Leavis (1948); Hicks (1935).

deeper understanding requires serious involvement with the life of the mind at the time. A historian would expect a genuine effort to contextualize each of the books we discuss.

I will disappoint the historians. I start from a different premise. Little about our discussion depends on knowing the intellectual or cultural challenges our writers confronted or following their dialogue with their contemporaries. We are interested instead in the dialogue that each book is having with earlier books in the same tradition. We want to know what each book makes of its predecessors and what later authors in the tradition make of it.

Legal philosophers who are thinking of joining our journey will have in mind a question I have so far ignored. Philosophers distinguish between *descriptive* and *normative* claims and are unhappy until they understand which game is being played. Does the tradition describe how judges *in fact* decide cases or do our books explain instead how judges *ought* to go about their work? The question is justified, but my answer will not satisfy them: the discussion combines description and value judgments to form a different category.

We will not try to describe how any one judge actually reaches a decision, let alone how all of them do. There is no reason to think that all judges approach cases in the same way, or even that the same judge uses a single method when deciding different cases. Our books portray instead the existential dilemma of judging.

Our discussion also does not attempt to tell judges how they should decide cases. In fact, our books rarely discuss whether a particular case was rightly decided. They instead take the decisions as they find them. This may seem a conservative bias, but as we will see, it is anything but. We will accept their viewpoint to get to their unsettling insights, which lie elsewhere. These books also shy away from abstract concepts and are particularly careful 'to avoid any intrusion of issues about the nature or content of justice.'[24]

Kessler's Approach

To understand how these books create something new, I suggest that we consult the work of Friedrich Kessler (1901–98),[25] the professor with whom I was lucky enough to study contract law in Berkeley some fifty years ago. Kessler taught as Sterling Professor at the Yale Law School until 1970, then retired and moved to the Bay Area. He was widely admired as a scholar and remembered with affection by generations of students. Kessler's approach is the thread that we will follow as we try to

[24] Llewellyn (1960), p. 59.

[25] For Kessler, see Collins (2022); Black (2009b); Graham (2002), pp. 796–802 (citing archival sources); Joerges (1995); Kronman (1995); McNulty (1995); Priest (1995); Gilmore (1975); and in German, Stiefel and Mecklenburg (1991), pp. 59–60. For correspondence by and about Kessler between 1933 and 1944, see Emergency Committee.

find our way out of the labyrinth in which we find ourselves as soon as we ask how common law judges decide cases.

A central feature of Kessler's method was that he generally did not criticize the decisions. Instead, he asked us to assume that judges usually have good reasons for deciding cases as they do. He did not expect us to accept all the reasoning we find in the opinions. Instead, he wanted us to see that the ultimate decision—where the loss should fall, who should receive the benefit—usually seemed reasonable in light of the situation. Kessler was typically untroubled when a court's reasoning struck him as flawed.[26] As his friend Llewellyn put it, 'Here is the case whose reasoning is wretched, grotesque. Yet how of the outcome, on the *facts*—was it not rather sane?'[27] We will adopt Kessler's premise—partly because we have little alternative. The opinions give us only the barest sketch of the facts, which leaves us in no position to second-guess the result. More importantly, if the common law's decisions were often unconvincing, the system itself would be a problem. Yet the common law is widely regarded as a successful method for resolving disputes.

Like Kessler, our books do not tell us how to recognize a correct decision. But do they at least suggest a preferred method? Is there a metarule by which we can determine which factors courts should consider, which to disregard, and in case of conflict, which should carry more weight? Without some means of orientation, we seem to be left with a conceptual muddle that cannot possibly be called law. And yet the books we will discuss are unconcerned with these questions. To the extent they are normative, our texts are normative at the next level up. They suggest that we remove the blinders imposed by precedent and look more closely at the facts and at the many factors that come to mind as we think about the events that led to the dispute.

If Kessler was not interested in discussing with us whether the cases were rightly decided, what was he after? He wanted us instead to come up with the best argument for each side. He assumed, as I do, that a good legal argument can be made on both sides of any serious case—not on both sides of any legal issue, but rather globally for each of the parties. Kessler was not innovating. Llewellyn had already explained that 'in any case doubtful enough to make litigation respectable the available authoritative premises... are at least two, and... the two are mutually contradictory as applied to the case at hand.'[28]

If each party can usually come up with a meaningful legal argument, why do some cases nonetheless seem unproblematic? A decision appears effortless when the judge, after weighing the arguments, concludes that the obvious precedent also offers the best solution. But the arguments on both sides are always there. With few exceptions, any result a common law court prefers can be convincingly anchored in

[26] 'The court overlooked section 1 of the *Restatement*. This observation is not meant to criticize the soundness of the result reached by the court.' Kessler (1975), p. 1072 note 39 (discussing *Hoffman v. Red Owl Stores, Inc.*, 133 N.W.2d 267 (Wis. 1965)).

[27] Llewellyn (1960), p. 397.

[28] Llewellyn (1931e), p. 1239.

the law. This is what Llewellyn described as 'the extraordinary leeway which our legal system allows in the particular case for reaching *either* result contended for, and for reaching either of those results "*under law*."'[29] Kessler and Llewellyn learned this lesson from Arthur Corbin, who argued that the cases provide 'authority for both sides of almost any question.'[30] If these three great students of the common law are right, then even easy cases are not straightforward. When the lawyers are doing their jobs, the judge will usually be deciding against a convincing legal argument.

In Kessler's contracts class, the discussion continued until we constructed the best arguments for each side. Once the case became undecidable, we moved on. Kessler never expressed an opinion about whether a decision was correct. Deciding cases was not his job—or ours.

Open Minds

Judges take a different tack. They assume that some decisions are better than others and that one is the best of all. They want to find the result that is right for these parties and this dispute, for this legal system and this society, all while satisfying whatever constraints they impose on themselves—everyone should get a fair shake, the world should be made a better place.

And yet even when we agree on the relevant factors, we cannot instruct a judge how to balance those factors or which decision is the right one. Finding the best solution is a task that each judge must face alone. As unsettling as this may seem for a legal system based on precedent, it is a permanent feature of the human condition. As we search for our path in life, we ask many people for advice, but in the end we are working with our own criteria, and the decision is always only our own.

What then can we suggest to our judges? The lesson of the books we will read is an approach rather than a method: they should keep an open mind. The tradition's principal *ought* is that judges should question their oughts; they should work to overcome their limits and expand their creativity. Each case presents a new challenge and calls for a specific solution—'In some degree, every new case is a case "of first impression."'[31] These are normative claims, but not of the kind we typically encounter in the law: they loosen the limits that we have long thought necessary to impose on judging.

---

[29] Llewellyn (1940a), p. 591.

[30] Corbin (1914), p. 246.

[31] C[orbin] (1938), p. 1352.

Visionaries

The books we are about to read represent a tradition that is neither purely descriptive nor straightforwardly normative. It offers instead thoughts about what judging is and what it might become. In this sense, these books are best understood as part of a tradition of visionary thought. Though they often begin by reading cases, they ultimately develop a picture of social order, responsibility, and freedom. That is why they endure. Each of these books is visionary on its own, but together they read like chapters in an ongoing effort to reimagine the possibilities of the common law.

Plato's *Republic*

The *Republic*[32] of Plato (c. 424/423–348/347 BC)[33] so closely resembles the books of the great tradition that we may want to include it as an honorary member.

As Socrates and his friends began their discussion, Thrasymachus offered his account of justice: it is whatever serves the interests of the powerful.[34] We think it is just to obey the law, he argued, and yet the law is made by those who rule, and they shape it to their advantage. His definition of justice may seem absurd, and yet it is not totally unfamiliar—entering law students also typically believe that judges should just apply the statutes that our politicians have enacted.

As Socrates pushed past this position, he faced a question similar to the one that the great tradition addresses: if simply applying the law does not necessarily lead to appropriate results, where do we look for guidance? Both the *Republic* and the great tradition respond to that question with portraits of an exemplary polity. The vision that emerged from the Socratic discussion is wild, crazy, and beautiful. It offers an alternative perspective to allow us to see the world anew. The great tradition also expresses a vision, and though it differs from the one described in the *Republic*, it shares something of its spirit and is every bit as instructive, imaginative, and thrilling.

---

[32] Plato (2004).

[33] For Plato, see Waterfield (2023).

[34] Plato (2004) 338b9–c2, p. 15. For Plato's Thrasymachus, see Barney (2017); Anderson (2016). For the historical Thrasymachus of Chalcedon (fl. 427 BC), see White (1995), especially pp. 321–322. For bibliography about the Thrasymachian definition of justice, see Anderson, p. 172.

References

Anderson M (2016) Thrasymachus' sophistic account of justice in Republic i. Ancient Philosophy 36:151–172
Barney R (2017) Callicles and Thrasymachus. In: Zalta E (ed) The Stanford encyclopedia of philosophy. https://plato.stanford.edu/archives/fall2017/entries/callicles-thrasymachus/
Black B (2009b) Kessler, Friedrich. In: Newman R (ed) pp 315–316
Blackstone W (2016) Commentaries on the laws of England, Prest W (ed), 4 vols. Oxford University Press, Oxford
Cardozo B (1921a) A Ministry of Justice. Harvard Law Review 35:113–126
Cardozo B (1921b) The nature of the judicial process. Yale University Press, New Haven
Collins H (2022) Professor Friedrich Kessler (1901–1998). In: Goudkamp J, Nolan D (eds) pp 253–275
Corbin A (1914) The law and the judges. Yale Review 3:234–250
C[orbin] A (1938) The common law of the United States. Yale Law Journal 47:1351–1353
Frankfurter F (1923) Twenty years of Mr. Justice Holmes' constitutional opinions. Harvard Law Review 36:909–939
Frankfurter F (1954) Some observations on the nature of the judicial process of Supreme Court litigation. Proceedings of the American Philosophical Society 98:233–239
Gilmore G (1975) Friedrich Kessler. Yale Law Journal 84:672–682
Goudkamp J, Nolan D (eds) (2022) Scholars of contract law. Hart, Oxford
Graham K (2002) The refugee jurist and American law schools, 1933–1941. American Journal of Comparative Law 50:777–818
Hart H, Sacks A (1994) The legal process: Basic problems in the making and application of law, Eskridge W, Frickey P (eds). Foundation, Westbury
Hicks G (1935) The great tradition: An interpretation of American literature since the Civil War. International Publishers, New York
[Holmes O] (1871a) Review of Brightly, A digest of the decisions of the federal courts, from the government to the present time. American Law Review 5:539
Holmes O (2009) The common law. Harvard University Press, Cambridge
Joerges C (1995) Demos vs. ethnos in private law: Friedrich Kessler and his German heritage. Yale Law Journal 104:2137–2143
Kessler F (1944) Natural law, justice and democracy—some reflections on three types of thinking about law and justice. Tulane Law Review 19:32–61
Kessler F (1975) Some thoughts on the evolution of the German law of contracts—a comparative study: Part I. UCLA Law Review 22:1066–1082
Kronman A (1995) My senior partner. Yale Law Journal 104:2129–2132
Landes W, Posner R (1976) Legal precedent: A theoretical and empirical analysis. Journal of Law & Economics 19:249–307
Leavis F (1948) The great tradition: George Eliot, Henry James, Joseph Conrad. G. W. Stewart, New York
Llewellyn K (1930b) A modern law school. Columbia University Quarterly 22:316–327
Llewellyn K (1931e) Some realism about realism—responding to Dean Pound. Harvard Law Review 44:1222–1264
Llewellyn K (1934) The constitution as an institution. Columbia Law Review 34:1–40
Llewellyn K (1940a) On reading and using the newer jurisprudence. Columbia Law Review 40:581–614
Llewellyn K (1960) The common law tradition: Deciding appeals. Little, Brown, Boston
McNulty J (1995) A student's tribute to Fritz Kessler. Yale Law Journal 104:2133–2136
Merryman J, Pérez-Perdomo R (2019) The civil law tradition: An introduction to the legal systems of Europe and Latin America, 4th edn. Stanford University Press, Stanford

Newman R (ed) (2009) Yale biographical dictionary of American law. Yale University Press, New Haven
Nicholas B (1962) An introduction to Roman law, Metzger E (ed). Oxford University Press, Oxford
Plato (2004) Republic, Reeve C (trans). Hackett, Indianapolis
Posner R (2008) How judges think. Harvard University Press, Cambridge
Priest G (1995) Contracts then and now: An appreciation of Friedrich Kessler. Yale Law Journal 104:2145–2151
Samuel G (2023) Common law. In: Smits J et al (eds) Elgar encyclopedia of comparative law, vol 1. Edward Elgar, Cheltenham, pp 317–326
Stiefel E, Mecklenburg F (1991) Deutsche Juristen im amerikanischen Exil (1933-50). Mohr Siebeck, Tübingen
Waterfield R (2023) Plato of Athens: A life in philosophy. Oxford University Press, New York
White S (1995) Thrasymachus the diplomat. Classical Philology 90:307–327
Wiegand W (1991) The reception of American law in Europe. American Journal of Comparative Law 39:229–248
Wiegand W (2021) Americanization of law: Reception or convergence? In: Friedman & Scheiber (eds) Legal culture and the legal profession. Routledge, New York, pp 137–152

Chapter 2
The Consideration Doctrine

If we are going to explore the great tradition, we will need a case, and I have one in mind. It is a decision that I have been trying to understand since my first semester in law school, the one that first made me suspect that rules alone do not decide cases. Many readers will agree with the court's result, even though it is difficult to anchor the decision convincingly in the law.

Let us begin with the rule that the court was trying to find its way around—the consideration doctrine.

World of Exchange

The consideration doctrine is the balance wheel of the law of contract, which itself is the mainspring of the private law. And yet many argue that the rule has no purpose, and some of its corollaries strike almost everyone as misguided. Here is one way of stating the rule: *No promise is enforceable at law unless it is part of a bargain.*

For a promise to be supported by consideration, there generally has to be an exchange. If you agree to buy my bicycle for $50, we make two promises. You promise to pay the price, while I promise to deliver the bicycle. Each promise provides consideration for the other. Consideration is therefore often defined as *what is bargained for and given in exchange*.[35]

As Kessler's friend Arthur Corbin put it, no legal system can afford to enforce just 'any old promise.'[36] Common law courts are easily convinced to enforce promises that

[35] See Restatement (Second) of Contracts § 71 (1981).

[36] Kessler et al. (1986), p. 37 (quoting Corbin).

R. Hyland, *Common Law Judging and the Great Tradition*, Ius Gentium: Comparative Perspectives on Law and Justice 100,
https://doi.org/10.1007/978-3-032-02307-0_2

are part of an exchange, and they are correspondingly reluctant to enforce gratuitous promises—like the promise to make a gift.

Consideration is not the only limit, for courts are also reluctant to intervene in bargains among friends or family members.[37] If you and I agree to go for a walk this weekend, and when the time comes I prefer to stay home, no court will grant you a remedy. Though the law of contract has a wide reach, it is helpful as a first step to think of contract law as providing the rules that govern exchange in the marketplace.

Familiar Difficulties

The consideration doctrine is a chestnut of the first year of law school because it invites irritating hypotheticals. Those difficulties arise most sharply when there are good reasons to enforce a promise but the doctrine seems to stand in the way. The question then is what a court should do. The so-called *firm offer puzzle* is a familiar example. Suppose you and I negotiate. I offer you an appealing deal worth millions and give you a month to think it over. You will of course expect me to keep my offer open. Nothing in contract doctrine, however, requires me to do so. A firm offer is typically binding only if the promise to keep it open is itself turned into a contract—an *option contract*—supported by separate consideration.[38] We might, for example, agree that you will pay a nominal fee—maybe $10—for the privilege of having the month to decide.[39] If we do not make that separate agreement, I remain free to revoke the offer at any time before you accept it.[40] The Restatement tries to soften this result by suggesting that a firm offer should be binding as long as a consideration is stated, even if it is never paid.[41] But this raises an obvious question: in a multimillion-dollar transaction, why should a return promise of $10 matter—especially if everyone understands that the money will never change hands? It is concerns like these that have led some scholars to argue that some subsidiary promises should be enforceable without consideration.[42]

Kessler would have abolished the consideration doctrine. And yet even if we were to get rid of it, he understood that we would not escape the problem it was meant to address. 'An abolition of the consideration doctrine in toto would still

---

[37] Restatement (Second) of Contracts § 21 comment c (1981).

[38] See id. § 87.

[39] For a similar option contract, see *Fundamental Long Term Care Holdings, LLC v. Cammeby's Funding LLC*, 985 N.E.2d 893 (N.Y. 2013).

[40] *Finzio v. American Steel Export Co.*, 183 N.Y.S. 317, 319 (N.Y. App. Div. 1920).

[41] Restatement (Second) of Contracts § 87(1) and comment c.

[42] See Farber and Matheson (1985), p. 931.

leave us with... the difficult task of finding the line of demarcation between enforceable and nonenforceable promises.'[43]

World of Gift

The consideration doctrine makes a contribution when the time comes to draw the boundary to contract's neighbor, the law that governs gift promises. A promise to make a gift is not part of an exchange, and it is therefore not supported by consideration. As a result, the law—at least in principle—will not enforce it.[44] If I promise to make you a present of my bicycle, a court will usually not help you if I change my mind. Without something more—either a formal writing, proof that the promise was serious and unequivocal, or reliance by the promisee—gift promises are usually not legally binding. Why is that?

We live in two worlds: the world of exchange and the world of gift. Each has its own rules and its own enforcement mechanisms. We speak both languages and move easily between the two. Gift giving is often an aspect of social relationships. If you are invited to a wedding, you know the unwritten rules: bring a present or, if need be, take up to a year to send it along.[45] And you also know that the bond will slacken if you neglect the gift. We set gifts apart by the way we wrap them and by what we say when they are delivered.

A gift should be appropriate. If the rapport has cooled since a gift promise was made, it may make little social sense to complete the gift, and no sense at all for a court to enforce the promise. The common law is not skilled at appreciating these subtleties of feeling. The law therefore tries to stay out of it when gifts are promised in social situations, though it is sometimes willing to enforce other gift promises, like those made to charitable foundations.[46]

As a general rule, the law enforces promises only when it has a good reason to do so. We now know that there are often good reasons for it not to enforce gift promises, and we will soon learn why there are instead good reasons to enforce promises that are part of market exchange. Since the law enforces some promises and not others, it needs a principle to distinguish between the promises it will enforce and those it will leave without a remedy. Any general benchmark would have to be modified to fit the different situations but as a general approach, the consideration doctrine makes as much sense as any other—'it does fit most normal cases in life [and] gives trouble only on the fringes.'[47]

---

[43] Kessler (1954a), p. 164.

[44] See Hyland (2012) para. 693, p. 338.

[45] See [Sprague et al.] (2003), p. 262.

[46] See Restatement (Second) of Contracts § 90(2) (1981).

[47] Llewellyn (1931f), pp. 742–743.

Equity

I have put off as long as I could our discussion of a curious feature of the common law, and that is its split personality. One of the two souls that lives within its breast is called *equity*. The other (confusingly) is *law*. We talk about cases, remedies, and doctrines *at law* and contrast them with those *in equity*.[48] These are two largely separate and self-contained legal systems that share little and often compete with one another. Each has a different understanding of the role of law in society, and each has generated an intricate web of enforceable rules. The two systems govern many of the same fact situations and, when consulted, produce conflicting results. No clear principle determines when one set of rules should be preferred to the other. In many cases, the judge chooses the rule that achieves the desired result.

Equity is the creation of the Court of Chancery, that murky Dickensian realm where the Lord High Chancellor sat Satan-like 'with a foggy glory round his head,' as lawyers 'mistily engaged in one of the ten thousand stages of an endless cause, tripping one another up on slippery precedents, groping knee-deep in technicalities, running their goat-hair and horse-hair warded heads against walls of words, and making a pretence of equity with serious faces.'[49]

And yet, since equity offers considerable flexibility when the time comes to tailor remedies to a challenging situation, it is one of the common law's great assets—'probably the most important and certainly the most astonishing of English contributions to legal thought.'[50] Still today, equity provides tools a court may use to circumvent rigid legal rules. If the common law had not been leavened with equity's flexibility, it would likely have become unworkable and might well have ceded its place to Roman law. 'Equity,' Maitland believed, 'saved the common law.'[51]

Though the common law's split personality may seem odd, it is easy to see that conflicting rules can give judges additional resources to justify their results. 'Our open system of rules and counter-rules has enabled its great judges to be creative and occasionally daring.'[52]

Promissory Estoppel

To see how equity can contribute, let us return for a moment to our statement of the consideration doctrine: *No promise is enforceable at law unless it is part of a bargain.* Tucked inside that sentence is an inconspicuous phrase that we have not yet

[48] For a history of equity, see Baker (2019), chap. 6, pp. 105–125; Maitland (1936), lectures 1–2, pp. 1–22.

[49] Dickens (1996), chap. 1, p. 14.

[50] Milsom (1981), p. 82.

[51] Maitland (1893), p. 496.

[52] Kessler (1954a), p. 168.

discussed—*at law*. The consideration doctrine applies at law but not in equity. When a court sits in equity, it is not worried about finding a bargain. It is looking instead for *reliance*. If the promisor expected the promisee to rely, if the promisee did rely, and if reliance was reasonable, then a court may enforce the promise, even without a quid pro quo.[53]

You are having coffee with a friend at your favorite café, distractedly thumbing through travel magazines, when your friend notices that you have stopped thumbing and are staring longingly at a photo of the Eiffel Tower. You would love to take in Paris, but you are always so busted. Your friend is elated about an unexpected work bonus, one that can easily cover your trip, and she promises to spring for your airfare and hotel. You buy a ticket, reserve a cute room on the Left Bank, and spend a glorious week exploring museums and taking frequent coffee breaks. Only when you get home do you hear the devastating news: while you were away, your friend succumbed in a hiking accident. She had promised to pay for your trip, but she is no longer around. Do her executors owe you? They do if a court would enforce the promise. Because your friend was not looking for a bargain, there was no consideration. And yet equity may come to the rescue. Your friend expected that you would rely on her promise. You did rely, and your reliance was reasonable. A court sitting in equity might decide that you have a good claim.[54]

The reliance principle applies to all sorts of promises, even to those outside the domain of market transactions, including gift promises and those made to friends and family. The doctrine's real benefit is how little reliance it sometimes takes to satisfy a court. The equitable doctrine we are discussing is known as *promissory estoppel*.

References

Baker J (2019) An introduction to English legal history, 5th edn. Oxford University Press, Oxford

Dickens C (1996) Bleak House [1853], Bradbury N (ed). Penguin, London

Farber D, Matheson J (1985) Beyond promissory estoppel: Contract law and the 'invisible handshake.' University of Chicago Law Review 52:903–947

Hyland R (2012) Gifts: A study in comparative law, [rev edn]. Oxford University Press, Oxford

Kessler F (1954a) Arthur Linton Corbin—a tribute. Yale Law Journal 64:164–168

Kessler F et al (1986) Contracts: Cases and materials, 3rd edn. Little, Brown, Boston

Llewellyn K (1931f) What price contract?—an essay in perspective. Yale Law Journal 40:704–751

Maitland F (1893) Outlines of English legal history, 560–1600. In: Maitland F (1911) 2:417–496

Maitland F (1911) The collected papers of Frederic William Maitland, Fisher H (ed), 3 vols. Cambridge University Press, Cambridge

Maitland F (1936) Equity: A course of lectures, Chaytor A, Whittaker W (eds) Brunyate J (rev), 2nd edn. Cambridge University Press, Cambridge

Milsom S (1981) Historical foundations of the common law, 2nd edn. Butterworths, London

[Sprague L et al] (2003) Bride's book of etiquette, rev. edn. Perigee, New York

[53] Restatement (Second) of Contracts § 90(1) (1981).

[54] See *Devecmon v. Shaw*, 14 A. 464 (Md. Ct. App. 1888).

Chapter 3
Moral Consideration

You pick up the tab for dinner. As we part company on the sidewalk outside the restaurant, I say that the next time is on me. A couple of months later, we dine again at our favorite table. When the server brings the check, you look at me. I suggest we split it.

Was my sidewalk promise supported by consideration? Since this is a social engagement, a court would ordinarily not enforce it, but it is still good practice to ask the question.

Reciprocation

If you do me a kindness and I want to preserve the relationship, I have no choice but to return the favor—as my mother used to put it, we don't return a cake pan empty. Perhaps the promise I made as we parted was my way of responding to the fact that you kindly paid for dinner. Is a promise to reciprocate for a prior good deed supported by consideration?

If I intended to reciprocate for your earlier generosity, there was no exchange. Because your performance was in the past, it would be what the common lawyers call *past consideration*,[55] and past consideration is usually no consideration. A promise counts as consideration only if it is bargained for and given in exchange for an act to be performed in the future.[56]

If I intended to reciprocate, could equity solve the problem? I intended for you to rely on my promise, and if you did rely when you joined me again for dinner, I may

[55] Restatement (Second) of Contracts § 71 comment a (1981).

[56] *Sager v. Basham*, 401 S.E.2d 676, 677 (Va. 1991).

R. Hyland, *Common Law Judging and the Great Tradition*, Ius Gentium: Comparative Perspectives on Law and Justice 100,
https://doi.org/10.1007/978-3-032-02307-0_3

be bound as a matter of promissory estoppel. And that would be the case even if you were relying as much on the chance for good conversation as on the prospect of a free meal.

Moral Obligation

There is still more to the consideration question. When I offered to buy our next dinner, I might not have been thanking you for the last one—I might instead have wanted to make sure there would be a next one. 'If you join me again for dinner, I promise to take care of the bill.' There is a bargain, and therefore consideration.

And I might also have been bargaining for something else. Since gratuitous services have to be reciprocated, when I let you pay the first time, I incurred a social obligation to return the favor. That obligation was not legally enforceable, but it was still an obligation. What I am calling a *social obligation* the law calls a *moral obligation*, and that seems fine. When looked at in this way, my sidewalk promise may have been doing more work than I first realized. I might have been suggesting something like this: 'I will pay for our next meal together if you agree that my invitation satisfies my moral obligation to reciprocate for your kindness.' We might then ask whether your promise provides consideration for my promise—*moral consideration*, we would call it. In the world of social relationships, my debt to you still hung in the air, and you were expecting that I would soon reciprocate. The satisfaction of a moral obligation is in this sense a pending matter and not past consideration at all.

As for the law on the question, pretty much everyone agrees that when the moral obligation once existed as a legal obligation, a subsequent promise to retire the debt is supported by consideration. For example, even though the statute of limitations has run on a creditor's claim, the moral obligation to repay the debt remains, and the debtor is bound by a subsequent promise to satisfy it.[57] Moral obligation serves as consideration in other situations as well,[58] and some jurisdictions have included moral obligation in their statutory definitions of consideration.[59]

The question remains open, however, for the intriguing case of rescue. A rescuer saves a person in distress, a promise is later made to compensate the rescuer, and that promise is breached. Everyone agrees that the beneficiary owes a moral debt to the rescuer, and the courts generally begin by asking whether that moral obligation should count as consideration. To answer that question, we will want to explore the consideration doctrine further and also to ask why we enforce contracts to begin with. We will whirl through theories and insights, and before we know it we will be floating on a magic carpet over inky seas and bewitching landscapes. It is more fun each time I do it. Time to begin.

---

[57] See Restatement (Second) of Contracts § 82 (1981).

[58] See *Park Falls State Bank v. Fordyce*, 238 N.W. 516 (Wis. 1931).

[59] See, e.g., Cal. Civ. Code § 1606 (West 2024); Okla. St. Ann., tit. 15, § 107 (West 2024).

Three Cases

In contemporary American law, we generally discuss the intriguing relationship between moral consideration and rescue by comparing three decided cases, each as captivating as it is challenging. We will now take a first look at them. One of the three stands out and suggests itself as a vehicle for further discussion.

Today, we know more about the facts of these cases than the courts presented in their opinions.[60] We will take a look at the expanded context a bit later,[61] but for present purposes we will accept the facts as we find them stated in the opinions.

Mills v. Wyman

In February 1821, Levi Wyman was returning from a sea voyage abroad when, without resources, he fell seriously ill in Hartford, Connecticut.[62] Levi was 25 years old and no longer living with his father, Seth (the defendant), whose home was located some distance away in Massachusetts. Daniel Mills (the plaintiff) cared for Levi for two weeks. When Seth learned that Mills was assisting his son, he wrote to Mills and promised to compensate him. Mills sent Seth the bill, but his care had ended by the time Seth sent off his promise. Seth did not pay, and Mills sued.

Was Seth's promise binding? As the jury interpreted Seth's letter, he was promising to pay for the services that Mills had already rendered to his son. Of course those services were what we have been calling past consideration. But what about Seth's moral obligation to Mills?

Chief Justice Parker wrote the opinion for the Massachusetts Supreme Judicial Court. Though Parker found Seth's refusal to pay the bill disgraceful, his court refused to enforce Seth's promise. A moral obligation cannot serve as consideration in these circumstances. Why not? Because performance of Seth's promise should be left to his 'interior forum'—the tribunal of Seth's individual conscience. Why? 'Great interests of society' suggest that the law should not intervene. Which interests? Parker did not elaborate.

Harvard's Dean Langdell included Parker's opinion in his contracts casebook, which was also the first law school casebook, as Kessler did in his.[63] And yet it is hard to know whether the case is still good law. The only other American cases I have found on the question are the two that we are about to examine.

Because judicial precedent is sparse, we might look for guidance to the Restatement (Second) of Contracts. The Restatements are an influential but unofficial effort to synthesize the law of contracts. Courts often cite the Restatement,

---

[60] For findings about the three cases, see Danzig and Watson (2004).

[61] See below, chap. 17.

[62] *Mills v. Wyman*, 20 Mass. (3 Pick.) 207 (1825).

[63] See Langdell (1871), pp. 367–371; Kessler et al. (1986), pp. 523–526.

though its provisions become law only when adopted by the courts or the legislature.

The Restatement (Second) confirms the result in *Mills* and presents the case as an illustration of the rule that a promise to compensate for past benefit is not binding:

> A gives emergency care to B's adult son while the son is sick and without funds far from home. B subsequently promises to reimburse A for his expenses. The promise is not binding under this Section.[64]

Harrington v. Taylor

Our second case arose in January 1945 in Hamlet, North Carolina. After Lee Taylor assaulted his wife, she sought refuge at the home of her friend, Lena Harrington.[65] Lee was allowed inside Lena's home the next day and assaulted his wife again. She defended herself by hitting Lee with an axe and knocking him down. As he lay dazed on the floor at her feet, she swung the axe toward him and 'was on the point of cutting his head open or decapitating him while he was laying on the floor.'[66] Lena saved Lee's life by reaching for the axe, but it struck her hand and left it badly mutilated. Lee later made an oral promise to pay for Lena's loss but managed only a small down payment. Lena sued Lee for breach of contract. The trial judge decided the case as Justice Parker decided *Mills*: he dismissed the complaint on the ground that Lee's promise was not supported by consideration.

The Supreme Court of North Carolina affirmed: a 'humanitarian act of this kind, voluntarily performed, is not such consideration as would entitle her to recover at law.'[67]

Webb v. McGowin

We now come to the last of our rescue cases.[68] This is the case that first made me wonder about the role that rules play when judges decide cases.

In the summer of 1925, when Joe Webb was working at the W.T. Smith Lumber Company in Chapman, Alabama, he was asked to clear the upper floor of mill No. 2. He pushed a heavy piece of pine to the edge of the deck, and tipped it over. At the same moment, he noticed J. Greeley McGowin standing just below. If Webb had done nothing, the falling block might have injured or even killed McGowin. Though

[64] Restatement (Second) of Contracts § 86 comment a, illus. 1 (1981).

[65] *Harrington v. Taylor*, 36 S.E.2d 227 (1945).

[66] Id.

[67] Id.

[68] *Webb v. McGowin*, 168 So. 196 (Ala. Ct. App. 1935), *writ denied*, 168 So. 199 (Ala. 1936).

Webb could have stayed where he was and simply released the block, he made a split-second decision to hang on and try to maneuver it in the air. Though he succeeded in protecting McGowin, Webb was seriously injured in the fall. He broke his right arm and leg, tore off the heel of his right foot, and became unable to work for the rest of his life. A month later, McGowin promised to pay Webb $15 every two weeks for the rest of Webb's life. Payments began immediately and continued for more than eight years, until a month after McGowin died. At that point, McGowin's executors stopped the payments, and Webb sued. The trial court dismissed Webb's complaint on the grounds that McGowin's promise was not supported by consideration. Webb appealed.

If McGowin's promise formed a contract, his obligation to Webb would be enforceable and his executors would have to continue payment.[69] If there was no contract, disbursements from McGowin's estate would have to stop.

Congress had not yet enacted a national system of social security, and at the time the federal government provided neither retirement nor disability benefits. As a result, workers injured in the workplace relied chiefly on assistance from the state workers' compensation funds that their employers underwrote. Though the compensation remains far from adequate, payment is automatic and, as part of the grand bargain, workers are generally not allowed to sue their employers in tort for the injury. Alabama was one of the last states to pass a workers' comp law, which it did in 1919. Since that law was in effect at the time of Webb's injuries, one of the mysteries of the case is the relationship between Webb's comp benefits and the promised pension. We will delay this discussion until we are able to learn more about the facts. For the moment, we will assume that Webb's right to support depended on whether McGowin's promise formed a contract. How should we rule?

Options

I can guess what you are thinking: '*We have already done this.*' McGowin owed Webb a great moral debt, but the promise to declare a moral obligation satisfied does not serve as consideration for a promise to compensate a rescuer. Great social interests, as Justice Parker put it, prohibit courts from enforcing these promises.

Maybe McGowin's promise can be enforced in equity. Did Webb reasonably rely? Webb was relying in a colloquial sense, since those biweekly payments kept Webb and his family going. But in a legal sense, since Webb's heroic act preceded McGowin's promise by a month, the one was not induced by the other. If McGowin's promise had convinced Webb to retire or dissuaded him from looking for another job, maybe equity could enforce it, but there is no mention of reliance in the facts, and without reliance, equity cannot act.

---

[69] *In re Murphy's Estate*, 71 P.2d 6, 12 (Wash. 1937).

What if we forget about contract for a moment and think of McGowin's undertaking as a gift promise? McGowin fulfilled his promise for eight years, and there is every reason to believe that he would have continued the payments if he had lived. Could a court order the gift to continue? The law does not allow it.[70] Once McGowin was gone, no one could make a gift in his name.[71]

It is easy to get tangled up in technicalities and forget about the human drama. Let us put the consideration doctrine aside for a moment and ask an even more difficult question: how should the case come out? Joe Webb risked his life in an emergency to save a fellow human being and is permanently incapacitated. McGowin promised Webb a lifelong pension and paid it regularly for more than eight years. The payments can continue only if McGowin's promise was supported by consideration. And yet on these facts, there was no bargain.

But wait a minute. Why should the dignity of Webb's family depend on whether McGowin's promise was supported by consideration? Where does the consideration doctrine come from and why does it have the right to stand in the way here? If the law does not yield to our sense of mercy, why do we keep it around?

When we come to something complicated in the law, it is understandable to wish for an immediate answer. It is entirely human to want to put difficulties in the rearview mirror, but that may not be the best approach. There are lawyers who can get to the root of a thorny problem in an instant, but there are not many of them. For the rest of us, the only resource we have—and it is also the only one we need—is time. If you happen to have some right now, let us indulge ourselves.

Stakes

For the next minute or two, please put this book aside, sit back in your chair, close your eyes, and allow your mind to think about whether you would enforce McGowin's promise. As you feel yourself pulled in one direction or the other—or perhaps both—notice what is doing the pulling. If you feel yourself forming a view, ask which reasons are persuading you.

Let me say why this matters. The books of the great tradition that we are about to read offer unfamiliar—and sometimes unsettling—ideas about how judges decide cases. Those ideas are much easier to grasp if you have had the chance to watch your own thinking as you decide a case. To take advantage of what lies ahead, all you will need is the experience you are about to have. I will now pause. Please take a minute or two and think about the case.

---

[70] Hyland (2012) para. 308, p. 179.

[71] Id., para. 311, p. 180, para. 876, pp. 412–413.

Pull of the Facts

My seminar on the great tradition is limited to twenty students, and I put these same questions to them. The results have been surprisingly constant. If all students are present and voting, seventeen or eighteen of them decide for Webb—even though they are not able to explain their decision. The best they can do is to point to one of the facts—Webb's heroic act, the promise, the eight years of payment. The two or three students who go the other way know exactly why. They take rules seriously and feel strongly that judges should disregard their personal sense of right and wrong and just follow the law.

The questions I ask of them—and asked of you—are not trick questions, and yet there is a trick to them. The trick is that it does not matter how you decide. All that matters is once to have had the experience of deciding a case. That experience demonstrates that we often have a decision in mind before we read the briefs or hear oral argument.

I do not want to claim too much for this experiment, for we have as yet only a preliminary conclusion. We do not yet understand clearly why we want to decide the case the way we do, and we also have no legal reasoning to support it. I want to decide the case for Webb, but the problem with the consideration doctrine is hovering just offstage. I spend time with the facts because I know that the law points in the wrong direction, and I hope that they will help me locate a legal argument that can get me to the result I prefer. The law is always already there, but for the moment chiefly as the obstacle I need to overcome.

My conclusion is preliminary in other ways as well. Though I think I know how I want the case to come out, I am not completely convinced, not even today. It is the fact of my decision, strangely, that opens me to opposing argument. Once I realize that the case is difficult, I want to know how others argue and decide it. I would welcome a powerful argument that I have overlooked, even if it were to change my mind.

The *pull of the facts*—'the instinctive reactions of the judges'[72]—is a basic truth of case adjudication in the common law and a central assumption of the great tradition. 'A judge often has a strong sense of which way a case should be decided,'[73] a '*sensation*, if that be all it is, that somehow "cases like this ought to be dealt with in this way."'[74]

I am not sure that we will ever learn why the pull emerges as it does. It is 'a quick judgment without a conscious weighting and comparison of the pros and cons' that perhaps suggests 'a capability for reaching down into a subconscious repository of knowledge acquired from one's education and particularly from one's experiences.'[75]

---

[72] Corbin (1937), p. 456.

[73] Posner (2008), p. 63.

[74] Llewellyn (1940b), p. 1359.

[75] Posner (2008), p. 107.

Because judging often begins not with a rule but 'with a conclusion more or less vaguely formed,'[76] the authors of the great tradition agree that rules are not the central feature of judicial reasoning. If a rule confirms the judge's intuition, the judge will cite the rule and permit—or even promote—the implication that the rule decided the case. However, when a judge's preliminary conclusion deviates from precedent, common law judges do not surrender. They instead get creative and look for an alternate construction: 'When the law's commands seem to conflict with their notion of a just outcome—they choose between giving in and pressing on in search of a plausible argument to the contrary.'[77]

When a rule gets in the way, we usually ask whether we want to make an exception. The factors that come to mind as we ask that question often determine the outcome. Or to be more precise, the law in any case reflects how an experienced jurist sees those concerns. Due to their training and experience, lawyers may be better able to recognize which evidence is relevant and reliable and which is not.

Now that we have had a chance to experience the process in action, we can give some thought to how we want to use the term *law*. For our purposes, the law consists of the factors that we take into account when we consider whether to make an exception. The rules we find in statutes, regulations, judicial precedent, and contracts, are merely factors. Deciding a case does not mean—does not *ever* mean—simply applying a rule. Cases are not decided by applying anything to anything else. The discussion often starts not with a rule but with a sense of the right result.

It may now be easier to understand why law students do best when they do not think of law as a table of rules and exceptions. Rules and exceptions have to be learned, but they are not the law. The law is not found in codes or case reports, or in any books at all. The law is found in the arguments that arise as we think about the facts of the cases. Our job is to discover the place inside where we do law and begin to map it.

If we want to know how judges reach their decisions, the direct path is to watch the process unroll inside us as we think about facts and arguments. That place inside is the great tradition's starting point. It is also its endpoint, though by the time we reach our final cadence we will have seen it elaborated to a point of exquisite awareness.

Webb on Appeal

If you decided the case in favor of Joe Webb, it may not surprise you to learn that the Alabama Court of Appeals agreed with you. It reversed the decision of the trial court and remanded the case for trial.

---

[76] Frank (1930), p. 108.

[77] Fischl (2001), p. 781.

The court's decision is easy to endorse but difficult to explain. The appellate opinion did not challenge the wisdom or validity of the consideration doctrine. Instead, it found consideration on the basis of *moral consideration*, the little-used exception we discussed earlier. As far as I can tell, this is the only modern American case—and quite possibly the only case in the history of the common law—to apply this exception to a promise made to reciprocate for a rescue attempt.

Let us reconstruct the appellate court's reasoning. The judges started from the proposition that, by saving McGowin from death or serious bodily injury, Webb bestowed on McGowin a significant material benefit. Because he accepted and retained that benefit, McGowin was morally obligated to pay for it. By promising to compensate Webb, McGowin transformed the moral obligation into a legal duty. The eight years of payment confirmed that the pension offered the appropriate level of compensation.

In support of its conclusion, the court cited decisions from courts in Alabama and elsewhere in which moral consideration was held sufficient to enforce a promise. In none of those cases, however, were the promises intended to compensate for a compassionate act like rescuing a human being from danger.

Let us set aside for the moment the fact that the *Webb* court struggled to find authority for its decision. There is a more serious difficulty: once we look closely, its argument begins to unravel.[78] To see why, it helps to start with a simple point—I am not required to pay for every benefit I receive. If I return to the law school parking lot after a day in my office and discover that, in my absence and without my knowledge or request, a student has washed, waxed, and detailed my car, I may feel surprised, pleased, and grateful, but I am not obligated to compensate the kind soul who invested the time. The issue was put crisply in the nineteenth century by Charles Pollock, Chief Baron of the Court of Exchequer: 'Suppose I clean your property without your knowledge, have I then a claim on you for payment?'[79] The answer was clear: 'One cleans another's shoes; what can the other do but put them on?' Why is that? 'The benefit of the service could not be rejected without refusing the property itself.'[80]

Let us add a few facts to make my car hypothetical look more like *Webb*. Suppose I locate the generous person who washed my car and promise to pay for making my car shine? Does that promise transform any moral obligation I might have had into a legal one? That depends on whether my promise was supported by consideration—such as might be implied from a prior request. Does my promise mean that I would have requested those services? Not really. My promise would express my gratitude and a desire to set things right. But it would not suggest that I would have requested the service in the first place. My promise manages a fait accompli; it does not suggest an agreement.

---

[78] 'Almost every word of this opinion is wrong as it proceeds with unassailable logic from its faulty premise to its foregone conclusion.' Burnham (2018), p. 962 (discussing *Webb v. McGowin*).

[79] *Taylor v. Laird* (1856) 25 L J Ex 329, 332 (Pollock, CB, in colloquy).

[80] Id. See also Wade (1966), pp. 1198–1199.

Of course, saving a human being from death or serious bodily injury is different. After the rescue, McGowin surely stood in Webb's debt. But what kind of obligation was that? We would not know how to measure it or how to translate it into a price. The court wrote of compensating Webb for his services, but Webb was not rendering services in any ordinary sense. He was acting heroically, and an act like that resists calculation. If the two of them had somehow been able to pause and talk about the question before the rescue, would they have agreed on a price? McGowin would surely have wanted to be saved. But would he have asked a mill worker to risk his life? And would he have offered to pay for the service?

I believe that we have not properly understood McGowin's promise if we characterize the relation between a rescuer and a grateful beneficiary as an exchange. It seems especially strained to reconstruct the promised pension as McGowin's attempt to compensate Webb for his heroic act. Compensation suggests valuation, and it is not clear what is being valued here. I do not think that the amount of McGowin's promise was meant to reflect either the market value of Webb's services or their value to McGowin. The contractual approach does not seem to work. It may be more reasonable to see McGowin's promise in a different light—he was responding to one grand gesture by making another.

Our three rescue cases arise from the gift economy rather than the market. Courts generally do not enforce such promises. 'However much the defendant should be impelled by common gratitude... a humanitarian act of this kind, voluntarily performed, is not... consideration.'[81] This was also the law in Alabama at the moment *Webb* was decided, for the Alabama Supreme Court had expressly approved the holding in *Mills v. Wyman*.[82] Though *Mills* was—and remains—good law in Alabama, the appellate court did not cite it or try to distinguish it from *Webb*.[83]

John Marshall

In his concurrence to the appellate decision, Judge William Samford (1866–1940) acknowledged that strict application of the consideration doctrine would prevent Webb from recovering. He found the path to the result he sought in a sentence from John Marshall (1755–1835):[84] 'I do not think that law ought to be separated from justice, where it is at most doubtful.'[85] Marshall was the visionary judge who established a constitutional role for the federal judiciary and at the time he wrote these

[81] *Harrington v. Taylor*, 36 S.E. 2d 227, 227 (N.C. 1945).

[82] See *Kenan v. Holloway*, 16 Ala. 53, 58–59 (1849).

[83] The Alabama Supreme Court rejected the estate's petition for review but, in a brief opinion, expressed agreement with the appellate court's solution. *Webb v. McGowin*, 168 So. 199 (Ala. 1936).

[84] For Marshall, see Smith (1996).

[85] *Webb v. McGowin*, 168 So. 196, 199 (Ala. Ct. App. 1935) (Samford, J., concurring) (quoting *Hoffman v. Porter*, 12 F. Cas. 304, 305 (C.C.D. Va. 1824) (No. 6577) (Marshall, Circuit Justice)).

words was Chief Justice of the United States. Judge Samford believed that the requirements of justice were apparent in Webb's case. I have always been sorry that Judge Samford did not take the time to elaborate, but it does not matter. We will see how far we can get on our own.

As I have reread the appellate opinion over the years, I have come to think that the invocation of Marshall is the essence of the decision. Even when we know how a case should be decided, we sometimes need someone with the Chief's stature to remind us that courts abuse their mandate if they let technicalities get in the way.

Marshall was not writing for the United States Supreme Court but was instead sitting as a circuit judge in Virginia and deciding a claim for breach of the covenant of good title in a conveyance of real property. The claim would have failed under established law, but Marshall believed that, since justice was with the plaintiff, the law should not stand in the way.

It is surprising that Marshall's pronouncement has not with the years become a master key to unlock the door to otherwise unreachable solutions, an abracadabra to legitimate any purportedly just decision, however unsupported by case law. As far as I can tell, only one other court has cited Marshall's sentence, and curiously it was also to provide authority for a holding that moral consideration was sufficient to support a promise.[86]

Webb Today

Is *Webb* still good law? The decision seems to contradict the holding in *Mills*, which was approved by the Restatement (Second). And yet the same Restatement section that endorsed *Mills* also recommended *Webb*.

> A saves B's life in an emergency and is totally and permanently disabled in so doing. One month later B promises to pay A $15 every two weeks for the rest of A's life, and B makes the payments for 8 years until he dies. The promise is binding.[87]

The Restatement's drafters affirmed *Mills* as a bedrock of the consideration doctrine. They also believed that *Webb* was rightly decided, so they approved it as well. Though they did not try to distinguish the two cases, one possible distinction suggests itself. In *Webb*, the benefit of the compassionate act ran to McGowin, the promisor; in *Mills*, the direct benefit ran not to the promisor but to his son. Harvard's Dean Langdell, whom we will soon meet, thought this difference decisive: 'The subsequent promise was not available [as consideration], because the services were not rendered to the defendant, but to his son.'[88]

---

[86] See *Drake v. Bell*, 55 N.Y.S. 945, 947 (N.Y. Sup. Ct. 1899). Samford's paragraph closely parallels the opinion in the case by William Jay Gaynor (1849–1913). For Gaynor, see Pink (1931).

[87] Restatement (Second) of Contracts § 86 comment d, illus. 7 (1981).

[88] Langdell (1880) no. 74, p. 94.

It may be worth noting that Langdell and his wife had no children.[89] I mention that because many parents would find it difficult to understand why saving the promisor might count as consideration while saving his child would not.

For now, it is enough to observe that the Restatement offers no account of how both *Mills* and *Webb* can be rightly decided.

References

Ames J (1909) Christopher Columbus Langdell. In: Lewis W (ed) (1909), pp 465–489

Burnham S (2018) *Webb v. McGowin*: The perils of 'result-oriented' jurisprudence. In: Arnow-Richman R et al (eds) The best and worst of contracts decisions: An anthology, pp 961–964. Florida State University Law Review 45:887–1020

Corbin A (1937) Recent developments in the law of contracts. Harvard Law Review 50:449–475

Danzig R, Watson G (2004) The capability problem in contract law: Further readings on well-known cases, 2nd edn. Foundation, New York

Fischl M (2001) It's conflict all the way down. Cardozo Law Review 22:773–796

Frank J (1930) Law & the modern mind. Brentano's, New York

Hyland R (2012) Gifts: A study in comparative law, [rev edn]. Oxford University Press, Oxford

Kessler F et al (1986) Contracts: Cases and materials, 3rd edn. Little, Brown, Boston

Kimball B (2009) The inception of modern professional education: C. C. Langdell, 1826–1906. University of North Carolina Press, Chapel Hill

Langdell C (1871) A selection of cases on the law of contracts. Little, Brown, Boston

Langdell C (1880) A summary of the law of contracts, 2nd edn. Boston, Little Brown

Lewis W (ed) (1909) Great American lawyers, vol. 8. John C. Winston, Philadelphia

Llewellyn K (1940b) The normative, the legal, and the law-jobs: The problem of juristic method. Yale Law Journal 49:1355–1400

Pink L (1931) Gaynor, the Tammany mayor who swallowed the tiger: Lawyer, judge, philosopher. International Press, New York

Posner R (2008) How judges think. Harvard University Press, Cambridge

Smith J (1996) John Marshall: Definer of a nation. Henry Holt, New York

Wade J (1966) Restitution for benefits conferred without request. Vanderbilt Law Review 19:1183–1214

[89] Kimball (2009), p. 314; Ames (1909), p. 475.

Part II
Disintegration

Chapter 4
Predictability (Weber)

When I wrote that Kessler was my teacher, I was making it up. I mean, I was mostly making it up. The Kessler I have lodged in memory is largely a figment of my imagination. I was one of 'the happy few who had the good fortune to study their contract law with Kessler,'[90] and as I attended his classes, I could not take my eyes off him. But we spoke only a few times, and I never had lunch with him, or even coffee.

Friedrich Kessler

After Kessler retired from Yale and moved to the Berkeley Hills, he taught one class a year at the Berkeley Law School—a first-year course in contracts. I was one of about a hundred students in the course. He called on me twice, both memorable occasions, and at the end of the year gave me a good grade, though not an outstanding one. I attended every class, but I understood almost nothing of what Kessler was teaching. After taking the final exam, I threw into the wastebasket the several notebooks in which I had taken nearly verbatim notes for two semesters. I would now gladly trade a month's salary to have them back.

The little I understood of Kessler's approach I pieced together during the discussions that followed his classes. As the scheduled session ended, some of my classmates gathered close around him at the front of the large lecture hall, usually the same students, and they kept the discussion going, often for as long as another hour, in the otherwise empty classroom. Those students held advanced degrees in various academic fields and discussed the material with passion and brilliance. I sat down behind them in the first row and listened. On a few occasions, when I thought I

[90] Gilmore (1975), p. 678.

R. Hyland, *Common Law Judging and the Great Tradition*, Ius Gentium: Comparative Perspectives on Law and Justice 100,
https://doi.org/10.1007/978-3-032-02307-0_4

understood enough to ask a question, I waited until the others had gone, followed Kessler into the hall, and spoke with him briefly as he walked back to his office. At the end of our conversations, he usually had a book recommendation for me. I did not read those books, though I carefully noted their titles in the notebooks that I later discarded. As a first-year law student, I barely had time to read the cases assigned for the next day.

Kessler spoke English 'with a flavor of the Continent,'[91] and for the first couple of weeks I could not understand his German accent. But that did not bother me. I could not get enough of him, that aged German scholar with well-thinned hair, bright eyes, and a tickled grin. Even on a late summer morning in the Bay Area, he was dressing for an Ivy League classroom, at ease in his tweed jacket, striped tie, and sweater vest. I relished watching him lift his watch from the lectern and, as a standard part of our discussions, offer it to us for sale. Whenever someone asked a question, his eyes opened wide and he smiled. Then he offered a sentence or two, usually ending with an ironic twist. He was having a great time.

I was taken with him and with the culture he represented, the world of Weimar that he was so obviously still inhabiting. I was watching him in our classroom a month into the term, enchanted but uncomprehending, when I heard myself whisper aloud the words that changed my life: '*I want to be like him.*' No one had ever affected me like that. In those first weeks, while I was reading cases that I did not understand and listening to discussions that baffled me, I decided to become a law professor. After watching Kessler teach, I have never wanted to do anything else.

Kessler's Casebook

Still today, fifty years later, I try to imitate Kessler in the classroom. I never lecture. I try not to talk at all. But as wonderful as my students are, they often get stuck, and since I worry that they may not be able to unstick themselves, I lend them a hand. I kick myself each time I do, but I feel in the moment that, if I can just clear up that one difficulty, they will find the rest of the way on their own. After teaching the same courses for decades, I have learned to define each concept in a single sentence. I provide this information as background so we can spend our class time on the challenging questions, but that is not how they see it. They take my definitions as wisdom and write them down. They even ask me to repeat the phrasing. The implication, when I indulge them, is that we are not equals. My thoughts matter more than theirs. Kessler never explained. Though I understood almost nothing he said in class, the lesson I took from watching him converse with us for a year was that he considered me to be a worthy discussion partner.

When I was first hired to teach law, I chose to teach contracts—and to teach it, of course, from the casebook that Kessler edited together with Grant Gilmore and

[91] McNulty (1995), p. 2133.

Tony Kronman.[92] My goal was modest. I was not burning with the ambition to become a great contracts scholar. I was merely hoping one day to understand what Kessler had wanted me to take from his class. Though I have taught from his casebook for several decades, I still puzzle over the cases each time they come up. For many years, I grasped nothing of Kessler's message. And yet the collection of cases was so captivating that I refused to abandon it.

I was struggling with the question that Kessler's casebook poses but does not answer: how do common law judges reach their decisions? The book juxtaposes cases that, though they share similar facts and pose the same question of law, nonetheless come out differently. As a student, I tried to reconcile them. But whenever I managed to produce a workable rule, the next case proved me wrong. Each time one of my classmates tried to explain a case, Kessler's eyes twinkled as he pointed to some fact that the proposed theory could not accommodate. 'That's beautiful, beautiful, Mr. Smith; fancy footwork—but you couldn't be wronger.'[93] The common law became an incoherent jumble, and Kessler never tried to make sense of it. 'The law student, applying the process of inductive reasoning to the collections of cases which were now being set before him, could arrive only at chaos.'[94] That is how Gilmore described the casebooks assigned when he was a law student, and those words apply just as fully to the casebook he put together with Kessler. 'It is no wonder that after a few months the student is in a maze of uncertainty. Are there no controlling "rules of law"? Why doesn't the instructor tell us?'[95] Without a method and a grand vision, no one would devote a career to teaching in a field that was as much of a mess as contract law seemed to be, and without a solid foundation Kessler would not have permitted himself his ironic observations. Maybe he did not want to deprive us of the pleasure of resolving the mystery for ourselves. The matter became critical when I started teaching the course. My students wanted answers, but I had no answers, and also no clever irony. I eventually remembered the books that Kessler recommended. The secret was in those books. I still recalled some of the titles.[96]

Most of those who resolve to confront the challenge that these books present do so because they have come to feel an urgent need to know how judges synthesize existing case law to reach their decisions. But these books do not answer that question, and they also do not explain which question they are addressing. That is why pretty much everyone who picks up most of these books soon puts them back down. But I had to keep reading. The recommendations came from Kessler. They were the

---

[92] Kessler was the lead author of three successive editions of a contracts casebook: Kessler and Sharp (1953); Kessler and Gilmore (1970); Kessler et al. (1986) (with Gilmore and Kronman). The pedagogical stance identified by Kaplan in his review of the first edition remained characteristic: the book 'tells the student all; all, that is to say, except the answers to the baffling problems raised by the separate chapters in each part.' Kaplan (1954), 1039.

[93] McNulty (1995), p. 2136 (quoting Kessler in class).

[94] Gilmore (1963), p. 650.

[95] Corbin (1964), p. 185.

[96] For Kessler's discussion of some of these books, see Kessler (1988).

only clue I had to the conundrums in his casebook, which I had to discuss with my students three mornings a week. I was hoping that I would one day no longer have to admit that I had no idea how the cases fit together.

Berkeley Hills

After teaching law for nearly a decade, I reread the article that Kessler wrote with his research assistant, Edith Fine, on the topic of *culpa in contrahendo*.[97] The title refers to the notion of fault in the process of contracting, and the article offers a virtuoso comparative study of the legal issues that arise during contract negotiation. The topic falls between the stools of tort and contract law, and legal systems understandably have trouble with it. American and German courts begin from different theoretical premises and, as might be expected, construct idiosyncratic doctrinal structures. And yet, since the pressure of commerce everywhere makes itself felt, the practical results are often analogous—'the similarity in the structure of Western commercial and industrial society' is often enough to overcome 'the powerful influence of tradition.'[98] My own comparative research convinced me that Kessler was overstating his case. More typically, the underlying theoretical premises are able to hold their own, even against what seem to be practical necessities, and developed legal systems, even on similar facts, often reach different results.[99]

As I pondered Kessler's thesis, I began to wonder how he came to this idea. He studied law and economics in Tübingen, Munich, and Marburg, then passed his state exam and earned his doctorate in Berlin. The chance to argue cases before the mixed arbitral tribunals established after World War I encouraged his interest in foreign law,[100] and soon Ernst Rabel (1874–1955),[101] a founder of modern comparative law, enlisted him to specialize in American law at the Kaiser Wilhelm Institute, where he worked with Max Rheinstein (1899–1977),[102] who would become one of America's great comparatists.

When, I noticed in a Rheinstein essay the same misleading idea that I had found in Kessler's *culpa* article,[103] I concluded that they had it from Rabel. I searched through Rabel's work, but it was not there. I was making photocopies one summer afternoon at Rabel's old institute, now in Hamburg, when Stefan Riesenfeld

[97] Kessler and Fine (1964).

[98] Id., p. 408.

[99] See Hyland (2012) para. 102–161, pp. 63–102; Hyland (1996).

[100] Telephone conversation with Friedrich Kessler (Dec. 18, 1984). For the mixed arbitral tribunals, see Isidro and Hess (2019).

[101] For Rabel, see Graham (2002), pp. 811–812; Rheinstein (1956).

[102] For Rheinstein, see Graham (2002), pp. 795–796; Caspar et al. (1978); and in German, Duden (1969).

[103] See Rheinstein (1955), p. 147.

(1908–1999),[104] the German refugee who taught me property law, paused to ask what I was working on. Since Riesenfeld had known Rabel, I explained the idea and asked whether Kessler and Rheinstein had borrowed it from their mentor. Riesenfeld smiled, amused that anyone could be as misinformed as I always seemed to be. '*Rabel war ein viel zu guter Romanist*,' he said, Rabel was far too competent as a scholar of Roman law ever to have had such a thought.

The professional association of American law professors was scheduled to meet that winter in San Francisco. Kessler, then in his nineties, was still living on Michigan Avenue in the Berkeley Hills. I called, mentioned that I was a former student, and asked whether I could come by for a chat. He pretended to remember me and agreed. On the last morning of the conference, I took a cab across the Bay Bridge. The young nurse who answered the door was not pleased. She would allow me an hour with my teacher but not a minute more. I went out to sync watches with the cabby.

Kessler was waiting for me in the living room in a baby blue terrycloth bathrobe. He was otherwise unchanged. The nurse's strict time limit disrupted my composure and caused me to abandon what I had learned from my stint among European intellectuals—the preference for indirection and the delight in effortless conversation. I foolishly dispensed with preliminaries and immediately summarized the idea that was troubling me, then asked Kessler what had led him to that conclusion. As always a European gentleman, Kessler was stunned that I would begin a conversation without first catching up a little, especially since we had not communicated for quite a while. But he took it in stride. He looked at me for a few moments and reflected. Then he told me that he did not recognize the idea and that he also did not know where I could find it.

My heart sank. I would now never solve the mystery. I looked at my watch. Ten minutes had passed. I relaxed. I would never see Kessler again. I still had fifty minutes with the scholar who had changed my life and to whom I had just demonstrated my lack of civility. I asked how he was doing. The law school library had recently collected his essays, and he took me to the bookshelves in his bedroom to show them to me. The burlap curtains were drawn, but enough sunlight penetrated the loose weave on that January morning that I had no trouble examining the books. I thought he meant that the university press had republished his writings. Instead, Kessler had asked the law school librarian to arrange reprints of his published papers in chronological order and bind them together. Since the essays had appeared in journals in different countries over the course of several decades, the pages were of different shapes and sizes. Kessler took down each of the four volumes, thumbed through it lovingly, then handed it to me. I had read the articles he published in American law journals, but I had not realized he was still publishing in Europe.

We sat on the bed and chatted for a while, then walked back into the living room. The wide windows looked out over the university below, the bay beyond, and the

[104] For Riesenfeld, see Graham (2002); and in German, Drobnig (1999); Stiefel and Mecklenburg (1991), pp. 66–67.

famous bridges. Our time together was coming to an end. I felt a pang of regret. I looked out to check for the cab.

'It comes from Weber,' he said.

I looked back at him. What?

'That idea you mentioned earlier,' he said. 'It comes from Weber.'

'Max Weber?'

'Yes. It's in my casebook. Don't you remember?'

What did he mean? I knew every word in his casebook.

He walked over to the shelves in the dining area and came back with the book. After flipping through a few pages, he turned it around, handed it to me, and pointed to a footnote in the introduction.[105] The quotation seemed to have nothing to do with the thought I had asked about.

'You see,' Kessler said, 'Weber believed that capitalism can work well in both civil and common law systems.'

I looked up at him. As we had been chatting, this ninety-year-old man had reformulated my question, located it in the context of his work, and remembered its source.

'I was studying in Tübingen when Weber decided to come out of retirement. I spent a year in Munich listening to his last lectures.'

The cab was waiting at the bottom of the steps. The nurse joined us in the living room. She did not need to insist. I shook hands with Kessler for the last time. He smiled his amused smile and thanked me for my visit. I managed to say that it was great to see him again. In the seconds that remained, I wanted to explain how much it meant to me that I had been fortunate enough to be his student, but the words did not come. Instead, I shook his hand again and rushed down the steps to the taxi. The sun sparkled off the water as the cab hurried across the bridge to the airport. There were sailboats in the bay, white specks on the bumpy gray waves.

Weber believed that the common and civil laws were very different, and so the text Kessler quoted in the footnote did not fully reflect Weber's view. Kessler had spent his career trying to demonstrate that the two legal systems were more similar than Weber believed. I stared out the window as the cab sped on. As a young man, as a beginning law student, Kessler found his way to Weber's last lectures, those he was giving in retirement. When I was a young law student, I attended Kessler's last classes, those he too was teaching in retirement. In my scholarly writing, I had been trying to show that Weber was right to suggest that the two systems were different and that Kessler's criticism was overdrawn.

When we begin, we see the world through our teacher's eyes. We eventually question that view and try to come up with something better. It has probably gone back and forth like that since the dawn of human time. Weber, Kessler, and I are but links in a long tradition. It is the tradition that counts. The challenge is to remain worthy of it.

[105] See Kessler et al. (1986), p. 8 note 31 (quoting Weber (1978), vol. 2, p. 890).

Reading

We are about to read a few difficult texts together. The common law, as an intellectual construct, lives chiefly in these books. We find in them much of what we know about how common law courts decide cases. Our difficulty is that much of their meaning is tucked away in the spaces between the sentences, in the steps that are taken for granted. We are trying to read the text that is printed in invisible ink between the lines.

One thing slowly becomes clear: these books treat the question, rather than the answer, as the basic form of knowledge. They suggest that questions open the mind, and that what matters most is the inquiry itself. That is because the questions that we most would like to resolve may not have final answers. But even here, the books do not make things easy. And that is because they rarely state the question they are addressing. Instead, they assume it. All of them are confronting the same challenge—which is why they speak to one another, across time, more than they speak to the rest of what is written today about American law. Our task is to work our way into their conversation, for it is virtually impossible to appreciate what any one of them is doing without seeing how it responds to the others.

If the journey through these texts is maddening, why bother with it? There is only one reason. I am guessing that there are few other sets of books that, when read together, provide as profound an introduction to a complex field of human endeavor as these do to the common law. One exception is surely the mosaic of passages from the classical Roman jurists that are collected in Justinian's *Digest*. But those texts are even more difficult, especially because we do not have the works as those jurists wrote them. In the end, the common law books we are about to discuss are among the most challenging texts I have read, and also among the most rewarding.

We will not be able to do justice to any of these books. We will take from each of them only a thought or two—the thoughts that I think best connect them to the tradition we are trying to understand. We will borrow a few sentences and see whether we can assemble a meaningful paragraph. Because much of the insight is conveyed through their distinctive voices, we will read these authors directly and largely on our own. Commentary may sometimes be helpful, but for our purposes it tends to get in the way.

Finally, let us approach each book with a single goal: to see what we can learn from it. All of these books can be criticized. But if we read only to convince ourselves that we know more than their authors, I would not find the exercise worth the candle. We will focus on the vision, which twinkles as we read. Once we locate the radiance, we will leave the rest to the scholars.

Max Weber

Max Weber (1864–1920)[106] remains 'the towering figure in modern sociology,'[107] a field he co-founded at the turn of the twentieth century. 'No other social scientist explored so many subjects with a mind so restless and rich.'[108] He studied bureaucracy, political legitimacy, economic organization, the nature of knowledge, ethics, and religion. The only major work that Weber published during his lifetime, *The Protestant Ethic and the Spirit of Capitalism*,[109] has been called 'sociology's "most famous" work.'[110] In 1904, Weber lectured at the Congress of Arts and Sciences in St. Louis and then for three months toured the eastern part of the country from New England to the Deep South.[111]

Munich Lectures

At the end of his life, Weber came out of retirement to accept invitations to lecture, first at the University of Vienna and then, during the academic year 1919–1920, at the University of Munich. The lecture cycle for Spring 1920 was entitled *General Theory of the State and Politics (Sociology of the State)*.[112]

As Weber began to lecture, political upheaval was haunting Europe.[113] The Bolsheviks had overthrown Russia's provisional government a couple years earlier, and the brutal civil war was still raging. The Irish Republicans were waging a guerrilla war against the British, while a Soviet regime was first briefly declared in Hungary. An uprising in Berlin led to the assassination of the revolt's leaders, while a few months later a Soviet Republic was first briefly established in Munich and then brutally suppressed. Weber's first lecture had to be postponed for a week as his students fought to suppress a worker uprising in the Ruhr.[114]

---

[106] For Weber, see Radkau (2009); Ringer (2004); Diggins (1996); Mitzman (1985); Mommsen (1984); Bendix (1977); Weber (1975), and in German, Kaesler (2014); Kaube (2014).

Citations are to standard English translations where available and otherwise to the critical edition of Weber's collected works, the Max Weber-Gesamtausgabe (MWG).

[107] Coser (1985), p. xxv.

[108] Diggins (1996), p. xi.

[109] Weber (2012).

[110] Scaff (2011), p. 211.

[111] For Weber's travels, see Scaff (2011), pp. 11–180.

[112] Weber (2009) (MWG III/7) (translation).

[113] This paragraph is drawn partly from Brown and MacDonald (1981), pp. 86–87, 93.

[114] Hübinger (2009), p. 43.

Weber's lectures attracted young scholars who were destined to play very different roles a couple of decades later.[115] Carl Schmitt (1888–1985)[116] developed a formidable political theory and was soon to join the Nazi Party. Hans Frank (1900–1946),[117] who was put in charge of the *Generalgouvernement* in German-occupied Poland, including its four Nazi extermination camps, was tried and executed at Nuremberg. Carlo Mierendorff (1897–1943),[118] a writer and Social Democratic politician, was arrested and jailed under the Nazi government and later joined the military resistance against Hitler. And as we know, Kessler too attended Weber's lectures.

Legitimate Authority

In that frenzied political climate, Weber chose to lecture on the topic of *authority* (*Herrschaft*). The question was why we obey the law—'the basic situation which exists when Jones says "Go," and Smith goes.'[119] We may think it natural to follow the law, but Weber looked at legal obedience differently. Whenever we obey a social rule or conform our behavior to what society expects, the social order can count that as a success. Obedience must be produced, and to produce it government officials must convince us that their rules are legitimate. Historically, the governed have considered governments to be legitimate for three different reasons.[120]

Bureaucratic systems are governed by a professional bureaucracy. They act rationally to promulgate laws and regulations that are realistically formulated to achieve beneficial social ends. *Traditional* authority remains loyal to ideas and procedures inherited from the past. Because the common law turns to custom and precedent to decide cases, Weber thought of it as an aspect of traditional society. In moments of crisis, a leader with rare personal magnetism may secure *charismatic* authority and use it to transform social values. If the government is working well, whatever its basis, even citizens who do not agree with all its norms will still find the system legitimate. 'We obey the law not necessarily because we think that the law is right, but because we think it right to obey the law.'[121]

---

[115] For a description of the audience and the lecture cycle, see Hübinger (2009), pp. 1, 44, 47–51.

[116] For Schmitt, see Mehring (2014).

[117] For Frank, see Schenk (2006).

[118] For Mierendorff, see Albrecht (1987).

[119] Llewellyn (1940b), p. 1356 note*.

[120] For Weber's explanation of the three types of authority, see Weber (1978), vol. 1, pp. 212–254; Weber (2019), pp. 338–389 (translated from the MWG). For the discussion of the topic in Weber's 1920 lecture, see Weber (2009), pp 74–113.

[121] Kessler (1941), p. 107 (quoting MacIver (1926), p. 154); see also Kessler (1944), p. 41.

Germany's Challenge

Weber's audience was eager to learn whether Germany could save itself from social disorder and political radicalism. For centuries, Germany had been governed by traditional authority, but now that the Kaiser had abdicated, it was the moment for Germany to shift from traditional to bureaucratic authority. The Weimar Constitution, promulgated the previous summer, established Germany's first republican government, and its first elections were scheduled for June 1920, a month into the semester. The political campaign was in high gear as Weber was speaking.

The challenge was to manage the transition from tradition to legality without a detour through charismatic authority. Many suspected that the republican experiment would fail, since authoritarian political parties were actively subverting the Republic from both sides. The previous year, Weber had predicted that an Age of Reaction would soon break over the country, 'a polar night of icy darkness and harshness,' and suggested that no one could know how many of those then present would still be alive when that night began to recede.[122] In his Munich lectures, and using only the conceptual language of political sociology, Weber suggested the nature of the contemporary political crisis, clarified the stakes and the risks, proposed a practical solution, and revealed his sense of foreboding. It was a remarkable performance.

Sociology of Law

Weber devoted much of his life to a major theoretical work that remained unfinished at his death, a book that has come to be known as *Economy and Society*.[123] It would be unfair not to note at the outset that Weber's style is difficult —'elephantine involuted awkwardness,' as Llewellyn described it.[124] Each sentence poses challenges, and some are insuperable. We begin our discussion by examining a brilliant but disjointed section of Weber's magnum opus known in English as *The Sociology of Law.*[125] Even in its fragmentary state, Weber's study is probably the greatest work of comparative law ever written.

The idea of beginning a discussion of the common law with a text by Max Weber deserves some explanation. Weber's university training was in law, but he was trained in the civil law, the common law's opposite number. And yet his *Sociology* draws on the work of Blackstone and Maitland, two authors central to the great tradition, and it was in America that the value of Weber's work was first

---

[122] Weber (2004), pp. 92–93.

[123] Weber (1978).

[124] Llewellyn (1931d), p. 904 note 7.

[125] Weber (1978), vol. 2, pp. 641–900.

recognized.[126] Karl Llewellyn, for example, considered Weber's *Sociology of Law* to be 'the one superb publication directly on the whole field.'[127]

Weber is particularly important to us because he shared the great tradition's provocative premise: in the common law, the rules alone do not decide the cases. Since this idea remains controversial, it is encouraging to find it endorsed by a renowned social scientist, maybe the greatest who ever lived. And because he shared this view with our other authors, there is no difficulty welcoming Weber's book into the great tradition.

There is yet another reason to begin with Weber. The fact that Weber understood the common law does not mean that he approved of it. He thought the common law inferior to the civil law, and particularly to the great civil code promulgated at the end of the nineteenth century in Germany.[128] As a system of adjudication, Weber found the common law *irrational*—by which, he meant that it is more primitive than a system that rigorously applies its rules.[129] Weber believed that cases should be decided solely by applying rules to facts. He elaborated the view in detail and provided it with a compelling justification. His is the challenge to which the great tradition attempts to respond. Since our authors agree that the common law does not follow Weber's method, our task will be to justify a process that is not rational in a Weberian sense. Grant Gilmore, one of our most perceptive authors, described the challenge this way: 'It is not all that easy to understand how a nonlogical system can, on any theory, qualify as a system of law.'[130]

Irrationality

When Weber labeled the common law irrational, he did not mean to offend. He meant only that traditionalist institutions like the common law can be legitimate even though they do not rationally pursue social goals. A judge who follows precedent is adhering to custom rather than searching for a meaningful solution to a social problem. The common law is not rational because it does not have to be.

And yet the common law's lack of logic worried Weber, for he believed that it made for unpredictable decisions. Unpredictability is an odd criticism to make of an institution rooted in tradition. Nothing should be more predictable than a system that relies on long-established custom. But Weber was right: custom as a source of norms is inherently unstable. For one, since custom is often unwritten, different judges will understand it differently. And even when they all agree, the agreement

[126] Neumann (1953), p. 22.

[127] Llewellyn (1940b), p. 1355 note*.

[128] For the German Civil Code (BGB), see Zimmermann (2012).

[129] Weber (1978), vol. 2, pp. 654–658. For Weber's concept of rationality, see Kronman (1983), pp. 72–95.

[130] Gilmore (1975), p. 680.

will last only until society takes another step forward. Customary systems do not have tools for solving new problems. When circumstances change, gaps arise, and judges must fill them. Judges adopt different approaches, case results vary, and confusion reigns.

Weber's Revenge

The great tradition responds by offering a different account of how judges decide cases. Our books found that the legal norms Weber championed also do not point to a single solution in each case. If our authors are right, no legal system can achieve predictability by following Weber's advice. And yet Weber will have the last word, for his is a question to which the common law is still trying to respond: what makes common law decisions legitimate?

In a typical lawsuit, at least one party leaves the courtroom unsatisfied. When the losing party asks why the ruling went the other way, how should the lawyer respond? If the common law were an element of traditional society, the lawyer would remind the client of our reverence for judges and the need to follow the wisdom of our ancestors. But in fact when lawyers console their clients, that is not what they say. They explain instead that the decision-maker applied general rules designed to achieve important social goals. In other words, they try to convince their clients that the common law is rational.

At that moment, Weber takes his revenge. We do what we can to convince our students, our clients, and ourselves that common law judges decide cases by applying precedent, even though we know that they also take other factors into account. We believe that the common law is meaningful, but when pressed, we blushingly admit that we cannot describe how its thought process works. Every time I discuss a case in the classroom, I ask myself whether to present it as the application of a rule or whether we should instead explore the complex constellation of factors that influenced the outcome. The legitimacy of a system based on judicial precedent depends on the first, while success in law practice hinges on the second. Some colleagues move seamlessly between these contradictory visions. I do not.

No one doubts—especially not Max Weber—that the common law is one of the world's great legal systems. At the same time, those who have best understood it know that they cannot explain how it works. The greatness of the great tradition lies in its attempt to justify a legal system whose rationality it cannot demonstrate. This predicament shapes the books we are reading and explains why few still consult them. Not many readers will devote time to impenetrable books that unsuccessfully try to answer a question that no one wants to ask. To write well about the common law means to accept that its weirdness is of its essence. Kessler and Weber were trained outside the common law and thus appreciated that it is both great and strange.

The renowned lawyer and legal scholar Frederick Mann (1907–1991),[131] who was educated in the civil law before he began to practice law in England, eventually concluded that the common law 'is largely a lie.'[132] The common law judge asks who deserves to win, 'who has the merits,' and then finds legal sources to justify the intuitive result. After losing a case before Lord Denning (1899–1999),[133] English Master of the Rolls and perhaps the great English judge of modern times, Mann asked him how he reached his decision. 'There was no merit in your man's case,' Lord Denning replied. Mann objected that he had not been asked to present argument about ultimate merit. 'We see through all this—we do not need an argument on merit,' the great judge replied. Many will feel a bit queasy on hearing Lord Denning's response. Our project here is to eliminate the guilty conscience that we experience when we discuss case outcomes in this way. We want to learn from the great tradition how common law judges can take many factors into account and still confer legitimacy on their work.

Lawmaking and Law Finding

Weber's is a simple idea of great beauty. For him, the law consists of two fundamentally different activities—*lawmaking* and *law finding*—and a rational legal system enforces a rigorous division of labor between the two.[134]

Lawmaking creates general rules to address specific social problems. This is the work of Congress, state legislatures, county and municipal governments, and regulatory bodies. Judges do not participate in lawmaking—they do not make law. They are instead engaged in law finding: they locate the applicable rule, apply it to the facts, and decide the dispute. They have no discretion about which rules to apply or how to interpret them. Weber was thinking of the code-based civil law rather than the common law, a legal system in which the judges themselves elaborate the rules. To recast Weber's thought for the common law, we might say that a rational common law judge announces rules of general applicability—rules like the consideration doctrine—and then applies them in subsequent cases without modification. Weber found the common law irrational because it takes other facts and factors into account. As Arthur Corbin explained, a judicial decision often depends on the court's convictions 'as to policy, welfare, justice, right and wrong,' including 'notions [that] are often inarticulate and subconscious.'[135] If common law judges rely on their sense of right and wrong as they decide cases, and if rational judges

[131] For Mann, see Mann (2021).

[132] Id., pp. 226–227.

[133] For Lord Denning, see Burrell (2011); Denning (1981).

[134] Weber (1978), vol. 2, pp. 653–658.

[135] Corbin (1917), p. 206.

must remain unaffected by such concerns, we can agree with Weber that the common law is not rational in his sense.

Arthur Corbin

Since Corbin's name has now come up a couple of times, this may be the moment for an apology. Arthur Corbin (1874–1967),[136] for most of his long career a professor at the Yale Law School, was one of the tradition's most eloquent exponents and the first to draw clear lessons from the opinions of Holmes and Cardozo, both of whom we will soon meet. Corbin and Kessler were friends—'My life,' Kessler wrote, 'has been immeasurably enriched by close and constant contact with him over the last twenty years'[137]—and Corbin tutored both Llewellyn and Gilmore. Corbin transmitted his groundbreaking understanding of common law method with such authority, subtlety, and humor that our tradition should probably be called *Corbinian*.

If I had had more pages, I would have presented the one-volume edition of his grand treatise on the law of contract,[138] the work that Gilmore described as 'the greatest law book ever written.'[139] In a couple of sentences from his introduction, Corbin summarized the insights I hope we will soon reach on our own: 'The law does not attempt the realization of every expectation that has been induced by a promise.... The expectation must be one that most people would have; and the promise must be one that most people would perform.'[140] To report, as I must, that I have not been able to include a chapter on Corbin is like saying that there is no room for Homer in a book about epic. But my reading of Blackstone, Holmes, and Cardozo is (I hope and believe) so Corbinian in spirit, and the Corbinian understanding so richly embroidered by Llewellyn and Gilmore, that Corbin's approach will be our constant companion.

Applying the Law

A Weberian judge *applies the law to the facts*. What does that mean? The process seems obvious only until you are asked to describe it. Since this seemingly self-evident method is the one the great tradition defines itself against, we should make clear at the outset what it would mean for a common law court to follow it.

---

[136] For Corbin, see Klass (2022); Black (2009a); Swan (1964).

[137] Kessler (1967a), p. 886.

[138] Corbin (1952).

[139] Gilmore (1974a), p. 57.

[140] Corbin (1952), p. 2.

In its traditional conception, judicial decision-making involves two steps: the judge first locates the applicable rule and then applies it to the facts of the case. These two steps are known as *classical legal reasoning*. When stated in this way, though, the procedure is missing its central premise, which is this: *there is no third step*. Once the first two steps are complete, the court must stop work. This unspoken limitation defines classical legal reasoning. Common law judges also locate the applicable rule and ask how it relates to the case before them, but that does not end their reflections. Instead, they usually examine a host of other factors before settling on their conclusion.

Sam and Rupert

Let us practice Weber's method by working through a celebrated hypothetical,[141] the story of a homeless person that Samuel Williston (1861–1963),[142] a Harvard legal scholar, recounted in his contracts treatise. To honor both Williston and our homeless person, we will call our wanderer Sam. On an icy winter's day, Sam knocks at the front door of a large home on an extensive estate. When Rupert, the wealthy owner, comes to the door, Sam asks for a handout. Rupert takes a long look at his visitor. Instead of reaching for his wallet, Rupert tells Sam that the coat in the window of the clothing shop in town is on sale for $100. If Sam walks over there, he can have the coat on Rupert's credit. Sam imagines himself in his new threads as he walks the mile into town. He arrives, tries on the coat, and says he will take it. Rupert, however, has called ahead to tell the haberdasher not to go through with the transaction.

Sam is crushed and after a couple of days consults a legal aid lawyer. The lawyer asks what Sam would like to achieve with his lawsuit. Sam wants the coat. Would Sam be happy with $100? He could then spend it as he liked. Sam agrees. The lawyer calls Rupert to request payment. Rupert responds with something unprintable and hangs up.

Classical legal reasoning does not tell the judge how to resolve the dispute. It instead provides the pathway that judges follow as they think through the case. Its purpose is to ensure that legally relevant factors are taken into account—and in a meaningful order. The trailhead is always a remedies provision—in the common law, that means a cause of action. The lawyer has to find a legal claim that authorizes the judge to award the remedy the client is seeking. Sam's lawyer is now looking for a cause of action that authorizes the judge to award money damages to Sam.

This started as a panhandle. In response, Rupert promised Sam that he could have the coat if he took a walk and picked it up. Rupert's statement looks like a conditional gift promise—Rupert promises to buy Sam the coat, if Sam fulfills the

---

[141] See Williston (1920), vol. 1, § 112, pp. 232–233.

[142] For Williston, see Rakoff (2022); Farnsworth (2009); Williston (1940).

condition by strolling over and taking delivery. If we construct Rupert's statement as a conditional gift promise, Sam may well lose—we will come back to this question in just a moment. The rule is that informal gift promises, with or without conditions, are not enforceable at law.[143] If we apply this rule, Rupert's promise was not binding, and he therefore had the right to revoke.

Sam's lawyer may next consider suing Rupert in contract. As we have discussed, the first element of the cause of action for breach of contract is proof that a contract was formed. Formation itself has several elements, including, as we know, consideration. But we first typically examine two other elements of formation—*offer* and *acceptance*. Sam's lawyer will have to prove that Rupert offered to enter into a bargain and that Sam accepted Rupert's offer.[144] Each of these elements has a legal definition. An offer may be defined as a manifestation of a willingness to enter into a bargain so made that the offeree is justified in believing that an acceptance will form a contract.[145]

The first step in classical legal reasoning is to find the governing law, and Sam's lawyer has now located it. The second is to identify the legally relevant facts and decide whether they provide factual support for the elements of the cause of action. Can we find in Rupert's statement the elements of an offer? To get the ball rolling, here is Rupert's sentence as a proposition: 'Take a walk to the clothing store, Sam. If you do, you can have the coat in the window on my credit.'

One thing we are (perhaps surprisingly) not concerned about is what Rupert was thinking as he made that statement. The common law of contract is rarely interested in anyone's actual thoughts. 'A contract has, strictly speaking, nothing to do with the personal, or individual, intent of the parties.'[146] A court will hold that Rupert's statement was an offer if a reasonable person, standing in Sam's shoes, would have understood it as an invitation to enter into a bargain.[147] The legal meaning of Rupert's statement may thus be something that Rupert did not intend and that Sam did not understand.

To a Weberian judge, it would be obvious that no reasonable panhandler would have believed that Rupert was offering to pay him $100 to take a walk. Rupert's sentence was a gift promise—and in principle not enforceable at law. We have now achieved a technically unobjectionable solution. If we follow the method of classical legal reasoning, we are likely to decide against Sam on his contract claim—and not think further about the facts.

Sam's lawyer might then think of suing in promissory estoppel. Rupert intended for Sam to rely on his promise, Sam did rely, and Sam's reliance was reasonable.

---

143 See *Williams v. Ormsby*, 966 N.E.2d 255, 259 (Ohio 2012) (quoting *Carlisle v. T & R Excavating, Inc.*, 704 N.E.2d 39, 43 (Ohio Ct. App. 1997); *Stelmack v. Glen Alden Coal Co.*, 14 A.2d 127, 128–129 (Pa. 1940) (quoting Williston's hypothetical of the homeless person).

144 See Restatement (Second) of Contracts § 17(1) (1981).

145 Id. § 24.

146 *Hotchkiss v. Nat'l City Bank*, 200 F. 287, 293 (S.D.N.Y. 1911) (Hand, J.).

147 See Restatement (Second) of Contracts § 200 comment b; *Real Est. Loan Fund Or. Ltd. v. Hevner*, 709 P.2d 727, 731 (Or. Ct. App. 1985).

The problem is the remedy. The Restatement allows the court to limit the remedy to what is needed to prevent injustice.[148] While legal scholars argue that promisees like Sam should recover only the value of their actual reliance, it seems that the judges have a different idea, for they often grant the full value of the promise.[149] If Sam manages to get the value of the coat, then good for him. If the court decides instead to award only reliance damages, Rupert would only owe compensation for the harm Sam suffered by taking his walk. I cannot think of an objective way to calculate that harm, so my guess is that Sam would then not recover in equity.

I would be disappointed if the court rejects Sam's claims in both law and equity. From the beginning I have felt pulled in Sam's direction. Rupert could simply have refused Sam's request for a handout and instead politely sent him on his way. What was the point of making the promise and then revoking it? Perhaps Rupert was worried that Sam might make a scene. The promise might then have occurred to Rupert as a way to get Sam off his property. If so, there was a bargain after all: Rupert offered Sam the coat in exchange for Sam's implicit promise to move on. Or maybe Rupert sent Sam on a wild goose chase to make sure that he did not come calling again. If Rupert was already planning to revoke as he made the promise, that might be fraud,[150] but on these facts, that is only speculation. In any case, Rupert's call to the clothier humiliated Sam. The wealthy should not treat the unhoused like that. This was some kind of double cross. I would like to teach Rupert a lesson by making him pay for the coat, a solution that has the added benefit that Sam would then have something to keep him warm. To get to that result, all I have to do is decide that Rupert's statement was an offer.

A common law judge would have a choice. If the court felt that Rupert's gesture was essentially a gift promise and that courts should not get involved in gratuitous transactions, it would follow the precedent that denies enforcement to gift promises—all while lamenting that the court had no alternative. If instead the court wanted to teach Rupert a lesson, it might find instead that Sam likely understood that Rupert made the promise to get Sam to move on. There would then be bargain and remedy. A common law judge in Sam's case could choose between two reputable legal arguments—and could decide the case either way.

And yet if we leave things there, we have failed to cover the waterfront. For even if Rupert's statement was a gift promise, Sam might still win. Despite the longstanding view that gift promises are not enforceable at law, it seems that judges now regularly enforce such promises when they are seriously intended and unequivocal.[151] In other words, a common law judge who felt the tug in Sam's direction could choose among several helpful legal theories.

---

148 Restatement (Second) of Contracts § 90(1) and comment d (1981); *AgReliant Genetics, LLC v. Gary Hanstra Farms, Inc.*, 213 N.E.3d 1087, 1098–1099 (Ind. Ct. App. 2023).

149 See Yorio and Thel (1991), pp. 129–151.

150 See Restatement (Second) of Contracts § 171(2), together with comment b and illus. 4 (1981); *Mississippi Power Co. v. Bennett*, 161 So. 301, 306 (Miss. 1935).

151 See Kull (1992), p. 40.

Let us put Sam's case aside for now. It was only for practice anyway. And yet I think it shows how far common law method roams from the Weberian ideal.

Rationality

At this point, Weber may seem like the curmudgeon who shakes his head when kids ride their bikes on the sidewalk. But that is only because we have not yet found our way to the heart of his critique of the common law. Weber classified legal systems according to their degree of rationality. That will sound highly abstract—until we feel it bite.

Weber understood rational activity as *purposive action*—action unaffected by emotion or factual error.[152] Action is irrational, in contrast, when we yield to affective motives—when we are provoked by rage or exuberance. Weber thought that judges act irrationally when they take ethical, emotional, or political concerns into account.[153] In his view, a legal system is rational only when it leaves no room for a judge's personal evaluation and decides solely on the basis of legal logic. That is why judges should not have the discretion to fill gaps or choose between conflicting rules. The civil law was long thought to represent the gold standard of this vision, especially as it was elaborated by German conceptual jurisprudence at the end of the nineteenth century.[154]

Case adjudication too is purposive action—which means it is rational when it pursues suitable ends by adequate means. Though Weber did not talk about the proper ends of judicial decision-making, I think we can reconstruct his thought. He would have begun, I think, by pointing out that the pursuit of justice is not a reasonable goal for case adjudication.[155] Notions of justice are rooted in emotional commitments that are too variable to serve as a rational objective. The goal also cannot be to construct a legal structure proper for market activity. Even economists cannot agree on which legal choices best facilitate commerce, and as we know from the passage from Weber that Kessler quoted in his footnote, market exchange easily adapts to a variety of legal systems.[156]

---

152 Weber (1978), vol. 1, pp. 9, 24–25.

153 Id., vol. 1, pp 6–7; vol. 2, pp. 656–657.

154 And yet the German Civil Code does not correspond to Weber's notion of gaplessness. Soon after it took effect in 1900, courts and legal scholars began to fill its gaps and expand its provisions. See Zimmermann (2001), pp. 53–105.

155 Weber (1978), vol. 2, pp. 759–760.

156 Kessler et al. (1986), p. 8 note 31 (quoting Weber (1978), vol. 2, p. 890); see above, p. 44 note 105. The *legal origins thesis* argues that the common law is better suited to govern the market. See Michaels et al. (2009).

Personal Freedom

In my view, Weber believed that case adjudication was meant to offer a solid foundation for personal freedom. Since we are free only if we can avoid unwanted government interference, especially in the form of judicial process,[157] freedom means making it possible for individuals to predict how the cases will come out. Law finding therefore functions best as an automated process, one that 'can be counted upon, like a machine.'[158] Weber's critics got him right when they compared his method to a generous slot machine—litigants insert facts along with a fee, and a decision pops out along with a flawless opinion.[159]

This is where that abstract notion of rationality shows its teeth. If the purpose of deciding cases is to guarantee a realm for human freedom, and if that goal requires a predictable legal system, then the common law may be in trouble. The books of the great tradition recognize the problem and try to rise to the challenge, but as far as I can tell, they do not provide a convincing response. If the common law has an answer, it is found in the thrust of the tradition through time. We will have to construct the response on our own, and for a running start, it may be useful to explore Weber's concept of freedom a little more closely.

A legal system has a choice to make every time it decides a case. It can reinforce coherence by following system logic, or it can risk inconsistency by taking other factors into account. As Weber himself recognized, the logically predictable response may solidify the conditions for human freedom, but it may also buttress inequality and fail to achieve substantive justice.[160] The more logic, the more abstract human freedom, but at the same time the less sensitivity to evolving conditions and the greater distance from reasonable expectations.[161]

Weber came down firmly on the side of freedom and concluded that a legal system must entirely remove itself from life. The law must be structured as a formal system of rigorous conceptual purity and administered by judges trained to focus exclusively on the rules and instilled with the calling to decide cases by applying them. The judge is there to assure predictability, not to do justice. As for a legal system's other possible goals, let the legislature do its job.

---

[157] Weber (1978), vol. 2, p. 811. See also Cohen (1933), p. 592.

[158] Weber (1927), pp. 342–343.

[159] Weber (1978), vol. 2, p. 886.

[160] Id., vol. 2, pp. 812–813.

[161] Id., vol. 2, p. 855.

Free Law

As Weber was writing, and as he well knew, Germany's free law movement (*Freirechtsschule*) was pointing out the flaws in his argument. The free legal thinkers argued that general propositions are too abstract to produce unique results in individual cases.[162] Gaps and overlaps are inevitable, judges will have to choose between acceptable legal arguments, and they will then have no choice but to weigh the equities.[163] To Weber, the free law thinkers were promoting irrational decision-making similar to what he found in the common law. As a skilled social scientist, Weber understood that even non-logical legal systems offer advantages. The common law responds more quickly to the changing demands of social justice and more easily adjusts its solutions to reasonable expectations. And yet Weber continued to believe that unpredictability was too high a price to pay for additional flexibility. Why was that?

Four Stages

On one of the most cited pages in his book, Weber offered a history lesson: the law becomes predictable as it subjects itself to reason.[164] Biblical societies asked prophets and oracles to decide their cases. Those decisions eventually became embedded in customs, analogies, and precedents—and that evolutionary moment was preserved in traditional systems like the common law. Early modern systematizers organized customs into logical structures, which their rulers then enacted into law. But it was not until the nineteenth century that scholars decided to create a scientific legal system. They abandoned the language of lived experience and formulated the rules in terms of abstract concepts. The German Civil Code represented the culmination of that evolution, exemplary both in rationality and predictability. From that viewpoint, the common law appeared to be a curious fossil, a web of conflicting case law reported in archaic terminology. Weber was open to almost every variety of human experience, but he could not abide confusion.[165] A legal system that defies description was never going to win his heart.

---

[162] For the free law movement, see Schmidt (2016); Herget and Wallace (1987).

[163] Weber (1978), vol. 2, pp. 886–887.

[164] Id., vol. 2, p. 882.

[165] 'Personally I am of the opinion that nothing is too "pedantic" if it is useful for the avoidance of confusions.' Weber (1949), p. 20.

Webb v. McGowin

When we get to *Webb v. McGowin* in my contracts class, I ask a student to stand and recite the facts, we take a quick vote, and those who agree with the decision are tasked with explaining why the case was rightly decided. We are by then several weeks into the term, and the students understand the question, but perhaps some clarification may be helpful here. I do not expect them to discuss whether the decision represented the best interpretation of Alabama law at the time. I am also not interested in learning how the case would come out if the same facts were to present themselves today. Instead, I am asking the students to explore what occurs to them as they ponder the facts and the relevant legal doctrine. They always respond appropriately. They describe the arguments that come to mind and explain which of them they find convincing. The question is whether we want to make an exception to the consideration doctrine to accommodate the facts of the *Webb* case. To those who believe that we should, I put a few additional hypotheticals to explore whether they would be willing to live with the consequences of whatever exception they are proposing.

As we conclude each of our discussions here, we will ask what the text we have just examined has to contribute to our thinking about *Webb v. McGowin*. We will usually not be interested in how the authors themselves might have decided the case, for we do not know enough about their lives and thoughts to answer that question. We will focus instead on the book we have read and ask what it has added to our understanding of judicial decision-making.

Weber's book teaches the importance of classical legal reasoning. We begin with the elements of the cause of action for breach of contract. When we come to the requirement of consideration, we ask whether McGowin's promise was part of an exchange. Since Webb performed his heroic act before McGowin made his promise, McGowin's promise could not have induced Webb's act. For classical legal reasoning, that ends the discussion. While some of us may be tempted to consider other factors—Webb's selfless act, his disability, McGowin's regular payment—Weber's book asks us to resist that temptation. Those factors might be useful if we were trying to do justice, but justice is not our goal. We are after predictability, and that entails a dispassionate application of the accepted rules of contract formation. If we follow Weber's advice, there is no contract, and we would refuse to enforce McGowin's promise.

We are in Weber's debt. He has confirmed that we badly misapprehend the common law approach if we think of it as applying law to facts. We may not be satisfied with his substantive answer to our principal case, but we can no longer avoid his challenge: if precedents alone do not decide our cases, what does?

References

Albrecht R (1987) Der militante Sozialdemokrat: Carlo Mierendorff 1897 bis 1943: eine Biografie. Dietz, Berlin

Bendix R (1977) Max Weber: An intellectual portrait, new edn. University of California Press, Berkeley

Black B (2009a) Corbin, Arthur Linton. In: Newman R (ed), pp 128-129

Brown A, MacDonald C (1981) On a field of red: The Communist International and the coming of World War II. Putnam, New York

Burrell I (2011) Lord Denning, the century's greatest judge, dies at 100. Independent (23 Oct)

Casper G et al (1978) Max Rheinstein. University of Chicago Law Review 45:511–518

Cohen M (1933) The basis of contract. Harvard Law Review 46:553–592

Corbin A (1917) Offer and acceptance, and some of the resulting legal relations. Yale Law Journal 26:169–206

Corbin A (1952) Corbin on contracts: One-volume edition. West, St. Paul

Corbin A (1964) Sixty-eight years at law. Kansas Law Review 13:183–196

Coser L (1985) Preface. In: Mitzman, pp xxv–xxviii

Denning [A] (1981) The family story. Butterworths, London

Diggins J (1996) Max Weber: Politics and the spirit of tragedy. Basic Books, New York

Drobnig U (1999) Stefan A. Riesenfeld, 8. Juni 1908 – 17. Februar 1999. Rabels Zeitschrift für ausländisches und internationales Privatrecht 63:405–408

Duden K (1969) Max Rheinstein — Leben und Werk. In: von Caemmerer E et al (eds) Ius Privatum Gentium: Festschrift für Max Rheinstein. Mohr Siebeck, Tübingen, pp 1–14

Farnsworth E (2009) Williston, Samuel. In: Newman R (ed) pp 593–594

Gilmore G (1963) For Wesley Sturges: On the teaching and study of law. Yale Law Journal 72:646–654

Gilmore G (1974a) The death of contract. Ohio State University Press, Columbus

Gilmore G (1975) Friedrich Kessler. Yale Law Journal 84:672–682

Goudkamp J, Nolan D (eds) (2022) Scholars of contract law. Hart, Oxford

Graham K (2002) The refugee jurist and American law schools, 1933–1941. American Journal of Comparative Law 50:777–818

Herget J, Wallace S (1987) The German Free Law Movement as the source of American legal realism. Virginia Law Review 73:399–455

Hübinger G (2009) Einleitung (pp 1–39) and Editorischer Bericht (pp 43–62). In: Weber M (2009)

Hyland R (1996) Comparative law. In: Patterson D (ed) A companion to philosophy of law and legal theory (Blackwell Companion to Philosophy). Blackwell, Cambridge, pp 184–199

Hyland R (2012) Gifts: A study in comparative law, [rev edn]. Oxford University Press, Oxford

Isidro M, Hess B (2019) International adjudication of private rights: The Mixed Arbitral Tribunals in the peace treaties of 1919–1922. In: Erpelding M et al (eds) Peace through law: the Versailles Peace Treaty and dispute settlement after World War I. Nomos, Baden-Baden

Kaesler D (2014) Max Weber: Preuße, Denker, Muttersohn: Eine Biographie. C. H. Beck, München

Kaplan B (1954) Review of Kessler and Sharp (1953). Yale Law Journal 63:1039–1044

Kaube J (2014) Max Weber: Ein Leben zwischen den Epochen. Rowohlt, Berlin

Kessler F (1941) Theoretic bases of law. University of Chicago Law Review 9:98–112

Kessler F (1944) Natural law, justice and democracy—some reflections on three types of thinking about law and justice. Tulane Law Review 19:32–61

Kessler F (1967a) Arthur L. Corbin. Yale Law Journal 76:886

Kessler F, Fine E (1964) *Culpa in contrahendo*, bargaining in good faith, and freedom of contract: A comparative study. Harvard Law Review 77:401–449

Kessler F, Gilmore G (1970) Contracts: Cases and materials, 2nd edn. Little, Brown, Boston

Kessler F, Sharp M (1953) Contracts: Cases and materials. Prentice-Hall, New York

Kessler F et al (1986) Contracts: Cases and materials, 3rd edn. Little, Brown, Boston

Kessler F (1988) Metamorphosen im amerikanischen Vertragsrecht. Juristenzeitung 43:109–116
Klass G (2022) Professor Arthur Linton Corbin (1874–1967). In: Goudkamp J, Nolan D (eds), pp 201–227
Kronman A (1983) Max Weber. Stanford University Press, Stanford
Kull A (1992) Reconsidering gratuitous promises. Journal of Legal Studies 21:39–65
Llewellyn K (1931d) Review of Frankfurter, Mr. Justice Holmes. Columbia Law Review 31:902–905
Llewellyn K (1940b) The normative, the legal, and the law-jobs: The problem of juristic method. Yale Law Journal 49:1355–1400
MacIver R (1926) The modern state. Oxford University Press, London
Mann F (2021) Life and cases: Manuscript of an autobiography, Ernst W (ed). Bonn University Press, Bonn
McNulty J (1995) A student's tribute to Fritz Kessler. Yale Law Journal 104:2133–2136
Mehring R (2014) Carl Schmitt: A biography, Steuer D (trans). Polity, Cambridge
Michaels R et al (2009) Symposium on legal origins. American Journal of Comparative Law 57:765–876
Mitzman A (1985) The iron cage: An historical interpretation of Max Weber. Transaction Books, New Brunswick
Mommsen W (1984) Max Weber and German politics, 1890–1920, Steinberg M (trans). University of Chicago Press, Chicago
Newman R (ed) (2009) Yale biographical dictionary of American law. Yale University Press, New Haven
Neumann F (1953) The social sciences. In: Neumann F et al (eds) The cultural migration: The European scholar in America. University of Pennsylvania Press, Philadelphia, pp 4-26
Radkau J (2009) Max Weber: A biography, Camiller P (trans). Polity, Cambridge
Rakoff T (2022) Professor Samuel Williston (1861–1963). In: Goudkamp J, Nolan D (eds) (2022), pp 175–200
Rheinstein M (1955) Review of Lawson, A common lawyer looks at the civil law. Stanford Law Review 8:138–147
Rheinstein M (1956) In memory of Ernst Rabel. American Journal of Comparative Law 5:185–196
Ringer F (2004) Max Weber: An intellectual biography. University of Chicago Press, Chicago
Scaff L (2011) Max Weber in America. Princeton University Press, Princeton
Schenk D (2006) Hans Frank: Hitlers Kronjurist und Generalgouverneur. Fischer, Frankfurt am Main
Schmidt K (2016) Law, modernity, crisis: German free lawyers, American legal realists, and the transatlantic turn to 'life,' 1903–1933. German Studies Review 39:121–140
Stiefel E, Mecklenburg F (1991) Deutsche Juristen im amerikanischen Exil (1933-50). Mohr Siebeck, Tübingen
Swan T (1964) Professor Arthur L. Corbin: Creator of the present-day Yale Law School. Yale Law Journal 74:207–208
Weber M (1927) General economic history, Knight F (trans). Greenberg, New York
Weber M (1949) The methodology of the social sciences, Shils E, Finch H (trans, eds). Free Press, New York
Weber M (1975) Max Weber: A biography. Wiley, New York
Weber M (1978) Economy and society: An outline of interpretive sociology, Roth G, Wittich C (eds), 2 vols. University of California Press, Berkeley
Weber M (2004) The vocation lectures, Owen D, Strong T (eds), Livingstone R (trans). Hackett, Indianapolis
Weber M (2009) Allgemeine Staatslehre und Politik (Staatssoziologie) (Unvollendet) (Mit- und Nachschriften 1920), Hübinger G, Terwey A (eds) (MWG III/7). Mohr Siebeck, Tübingen
Weber M (2012) The Protestant ethic and the spirit of capitalism, Kalberg S (trans). Routledge, New York
Weber M (2019) Economy and society: A new translation, Tribe K (ed, trans). Harvard University Press, Cambridge

Williston S (1920) The law of contracts, 4 vols. Baker, Voorhis, New York
Williston S (1940) Life and law: An autobiography. Little, Brown, Boston
Yorio E, Thel S (1991) The promissory basis of Section 90. Yale Law Journal 101:111–167
Zimmermann R (2001) Roman law, contemporary law, European law: The civilian tradition today. Oxford University Press, New York
Zimmermann R (2012) The new German law of obligations: Historical and comparative perspectives. Oxford University Press, Oxford

Chapter 5
Social Expectation (Blackstone)

It is 1832 as the movie opens—John Ford's *Young Mr. Lincoln*—and a covered wagon is pulling into the New Salem town square. John T. Stuart (1807–1885),[166] Whig candidate for the state legislature, is speaking from the wooden veranda of a country store, dressed in tails on a summer's day. He concludes his stump speech and introduces his understudy, a certain Abe Lincoln (1809–1865).[167] Abe, wearing homespun and suspenders, is leaning back in his chair, his feet propped up on the railing, sanding a board. He rises unhurriedly, bashfully recaps his political program, asks for the vote of his fellow townspeople, and then finds his way to the covered wagon to greet the travelers. The family is headed out west and has stopped by the store to buy shirt flannel. All they have to trade is a barrel with a few old books. Abe's face lights up. Books! He tells them to go inside and take what they need. He unloads the barrel, reaches inside, and comes up with a bound volume. It is Blackstone's *Commentaries*.

The scene dissolves to a view of the grassy bank of the nearby Sangamon River. Abe is lying on his back, his feet resting high up on the trunk of a gnarled oak, and he is reading Blackstone. He places the open book on his chest and recalls what he has just learned. Law: the rights of persons and the rights of things. Wrongs: violations of those rights. 'By Gee, that's all there is to it. Right and wrong. Maybe I ought to begin to take this up serious.'

---

166 For Stuart, see Angle (1928).

167 For Lincoln, see Donald (1995).

R. Hyland, *Common Law Judging and the Great Tradition*, Ius Gentium: Comparative Perspectives on Law and Justice 100,
https://doi.org/10.1007/978-3-032-02307-0_5

Farewell to His Muse

William Blackstone (1723–1780),[168] English barrister, legal scholar, Tory politician, and judge, is remembered today as the author of his four-volume *Commentaries on the Laws of England* (1765–1769).[169] We turn now to Blackstone because, though he never traveled to America, it was in America that his book had its great and far-reaching influence.[170] Holmes, Weber, and Cardozo were all thinking of Blackstone as they wrote. No earlier English jurist had anything like Blackstone's impact on American law.

To understand Blackstone's project, we might begin with *The Lawyer's Farewell to his Muse*, a poem that Blackstone wrote as a young man and continued to revise until it was published anonymously a decade later in the best-selling English poetry anthology of the eighteenth century.[171] Blackstone began the piece by recalling for his muse the moments they had shared, versifying in the pastoral mode: 'How blithesome were we wont to rove/By verdant hill and shady grove.' And yet when the time came to choose a profession, law prevailed over poetry, and Blackstone knew that the goddess would disapprove: 'The wrangling courts and stubborn law,/ To smoke, and crowds, and cities draw.' To persuade her, he described the inspiring discovery he had made in that disagreeable setting. The poem is about Blackstone's vision of the common law—which is also the subject of his *Commentaries* and the reason we still read his work.

Blackstone had caught a glimpse of Poetry's sister, the goddess Justice, standing radiant amidst wearisome prose and legal discord. Like the ancients, Blackstone thought of Justice as a woman—at times a queen, at others a 'venerable maid'—and her resplendent genius illuminated those dusty pages, 'Where mixed, though uniform, appears/The wisdom of a thousand years.' Just visible behind the opaque words in the opinions is a majestic realm where 'parts with parts unite/In one harmonious rule of right, and countless wheels distinctly tend,/By various laws, to one great end.' The great end of the English common law is to reveal the spirit of the English people, which had already come into its own centuries earlier. In that land, 'mighty Alfred's piercing soul/Pervades and regulates the whole.'

---

[168] For Blackstone, see Prest (2008), Lockmiller (1938).

[169] Citations to the different editions of the *Commentaries* have traditionally been standardized by reference to the *tenth* edition (1787)—the familiar *star pages*. See Alschuler (1996), p. 3 note 4. The recent Oxford edition, however, uses marginal references to the *first* editions of the four volumes. See Blackstone (2016); Orth (2020), p. 127. Citations here are to the Oxford edition, its marginal page numbers indicated by a white star (☆).

[170] Wickersham (1924), p. 576.

[171] Prest (2008), pp. 57–61. For the text of the poem, see Blackstone (1763).

Commentaries

Blackstone became a barrister at Middle Temple, but since he 'was born outside the enchanted circle of governing families in eighteenth-century England,'[172] he had neither patronage nor client recommendations and soon abandoned practice to pursue an academic career. A few years later, the jurist Charles Viner left funds to Oxford to underwrite the teaching of the common law—for the first time at an English university—and Blackstone became Oxford's first Vinerian Professor. Blackstone lectured for about a decade before turning his lectures into his *Commentaries*. He left Oxford to take up a judgeship, first briefly on the Court of King's Bench, and then for the remainder of his career on Common Pleas.

Blackstone's book is 'a great luminous readable treatise on English law as a whole.'[173] The only earlier attempt to survey the entire common law was the book by Justice Henry de Bracton (1210–1268).[174] But Bracton described the common law before it got serious about case law. He also wrote in Latin and was deeply influenced by Roman law.[175] Though Blackstone borrowed heavily from his predecessors, he had no real model, and his task was especially challenging—the common law at the time existed in the form of a few scholarly commentaries, conflicting maxims in law and equity, and centuries of unruly case law, much of which was in Law French and difficult to locate.

Reception

Lawyers in the American Colonies welcomed the *Commentaries*—which is surprising, given that Blackstone favored the Stamp Act and opposed the American Revolution.[176] The book's first American edition was quickly snapped up when publication began in 1771, and by the eve of the Revolution, nearly as many copies had been sold in North America as in England.[177] Aside from the Bible, no other book played such a significant role in the creation of America's institutions.[178] 'In the first century of American independence, the *Commentaries* were not merely an approach to the study of law; for most lawyers they constituted all there was of the law.'[179]

---

[172] Lockmiller (1938), p. 1.

[173] Holdsworth (1932), p. 266.

[174] Bracton (1968–77). For Bracton, see Tubbs (2000), pp. 7–21; Holdsworth (1938), pp. 16–24.

[175] Pollock and Maitland (1968), vol. 1, p. 207. For the influence of Roman law on Bracton's treatise, see Güterbock (1866).

[176] Alschuler (1996), pp. 4–19.

[177] Burke (1775), p. 26.

[178] Boorstin (1958), p. [iii] (Preface to the Beacon Press edition).

[179] Boorstin (1996), p. 3.

The *Commentaries* were of interest even to those American readers who had not studied jurisprudence. A list of 831 subscribers prefaces the fourth volume of the first American edition.[180] In addition to lawyers, judges, law students, and the notables one would expect—John Adams, John Jay, other signers of the Declaration of Independence, framers of the Constitution, and those prominent in the life of the early Republic—the list includes farmers, merchants, cabinet-makers, booksellers, printers, military officers, tavern-keepers, a minister, a history professor, a steel manufacturer, a surgeon, a shoemaker, and a comedian, as well as several public libraries.[181]

Blackstone put his vision onto the page with such charm and grace that, two and a half centuries later, it continues to captivate. He described the common law in elegant prose inspired by an Enlightenment quest for understanding and provided it with a meaningful structure. The common law makes sense in those pages, even to those who have not studied law, and perhaps for the first time. The English historian Frederic Maitland found there 'an artistic picture of the laws of England such as had never been drawn of any similar system.' As a result, 'no nation but the English had so eminently readable a law-book, and it must be doubtful whether any other lawyer ever did more important work than was done by the first professor of English law.'[182]

Public Lecture

A brief note about form. Blackstone's *Commentaries*, like many of the texts we will read from the great tradition, were originally delivered as lectures to a live audience. We might begin by asking why the form of the public lecture seems to suit a discussion of the common law.

Lectures can convey a sense of the author's voice, even to those who read the text years—or centuries—later. Lectures may also offer untested theories and the excitement of fresh ideas. Both the personal connection and a sense of adventure are characteristic of the common law, which exists less as a set of principles than as a living conversation. Some of our books first appeared in other literary forms—the class handout and the personal journal—that share the common law's dialogic nature and its penchant for constant re-evaluation.

---

[180] Blackstone (1771–72), vol. 4, pp. [ix]–[xxx].

[181] See Wickersham (1924), p. 576. The list indicates the subscriber's profession.

[182] Maitland (1902), p. 116.

Reason

Even today, the common law exists chiefly as a jumble of precedent occasionally formulated in archaic concepts. The civil law, in contrast, offers system and universality, and even some English lawyers have preferred it to the common law: 'A wise prince would banish this barbaric stuff and receive in its stead the civil law of the Romans.'[183] Blackstone had studied the civil and canon laws at Oxford, and he too was impressed. No one was more thoroughly persuaded of 'the general excellence of [the civil law's] rules, and the usual equity of its decisions.'[184]

And yet Blackstone was convinced that the English should keep to their common law. One reason for writing the *Commentaries* was to shelter the common law from the intellectual storm that we now call the French Enlightenment and its devotion to abstract reason.[185] 'Soon after Blackstone's death, the French Revolution was to show where men might go when they were led by "proud Reason" alone.'[186]

Blackstone thought of the common law as 'that antient collection of unwritten maxims and customs.'[187] Because those customs and traditions were no more than local solutions to social needs, Blackstone feared that they would likely not survive if put to the test of abstract rationality. The historian Daniel Boorstin (1914–2004)[188] explained Blackstone's thinking: 'If "proud Science" were to sit in judgment on law, the stability of the legal system might be no more.'[189]

Custom

Solutions dictated by reason have a lot going for them. They convey a sense of objectivity and balance that suggests they are universally applicable. The problem is that law itself remains stubbornly local. Each society generally has its own law, and our efforts to unify the private law across cultures, however inspiring, have difficulty achieving actual uniformity.[190]

---

183 Maitland (1901a), p. 7 and note 11 (summarizing the views of Reginald Pole (1500–1558)).

184 Blackstone (2016), vol. 1, p. ☆5.

185 Boorstin (1996), p. 118.

186 Id., p. 19.

187 Blackstone (2016), vol. 1, p. ☆17.

188 For Boorstin, see Finley (2011).

189 Boorstin (1996), p. 24.

190 See Schwenzer (2014), p. 103 ("It is still … extremely hard work to achieve even a basic level of uniformity in the application and interpretation of the CISG"), discussing U.N. Convention on Contracts for the International Sale of Goods, Apr. 11, 1980, S. Treaty Doc. No. 98-9 (1983), 1489 U.N.T.S. 3.

The social customs that Blackstone found at the root of the common law may lack logic, and yet they seem to work. 'If the customs are observed, they must be good customs in the sense of well suited to the people who observe them.'[191] Customs speak to the peculiar and the local,[192] while reason points instead to an elusive ideal. The distinction of the common law is that it is 'nothing else but custom, arising from the universal agreement of the whole community.'[193]

Essential institutions often arise first in society and are only later shaped by law. 'There was already in operation a practice of making and keeping promises, and a live expectation that promises would be kept, or the law of contract would never have been thought of.'[194] A legal institution is 'built according to the mould of the life it finds already being lived.'[195]

Freedom Again

So then which makes better law: abstract reason or the situated wisdom embodied in custom? This is the question that Weber put to us as we were starting out, and it is the one that we are still trying to answer. We know Weber's view: judges must follow reason if they are to foster predictability. Since common law judges often base their rulings on custom, their decisions, Weber argued, are not predictable, and citizens in common law jurisdictions are not free.

But Blackstone was about to turn the tables on Weber. The English are free, he argued, precisely due to their common law. 'And indeed it is one of the characteristic marks of English liberty, that our common law depends upon custom; which carries this internal evidence of freedom along with it, that it probably was introduced by the voluntary consent of the people.'[196] The essential relationship between the English and their laws made England a land—'perhaps the only one in the universe'—in which political and civil liberty is the goal of the constitution.[197] Civil law rules, in contrast, were imposed as edicts by those who stood above the people and often disdained them: 'What is pleasing to the prince has the force of law.'[198] Reason usually means someone else's reason, and if we are talking law, it means a particular lawgiver's understanding of what is best for society. Solutions that emerge from social experience usually allow more freedom than rules shaped by an

[191] Pocock (1975), p. 15.

[192] Whitman (1991), p. 1327.

[193] Blackstone (2016), vol. 1, p. ☆460.

[194] Llewellyn (1923), p. 27.

[195] Id.

[196] Blackstone (2016), vol. 1, p. ☆74.

[197] Id., p. ☆6.

[198] Id., p. ☆74 (quoting Dig. 1.4.1 (Ulpian, Inst. 1) (in Latin)).

autocrat's whim: 'It is not to be expected from human nature, that *the few* should be always attentive to the interests and good of *the many*.'[199]

It seems for all the world that after reading Weber, Blackstone decided to join issue with him. It is easy to snooze during a debate about which of two legal systems is more rational, but that was not the question that set them off. Weber and Blackstone were each claiming that the other's legal system was incurably despotic. This matters now, and not just to lawyers.

Acolytes

A little more than a century after publication, the *Commentaries* gained a major ally. It was James Coolidge Carter (1827–1905),[200] 'perhaps the most respected appellate advocate in the nation,'[201] after whom Harvard's professorship of general jurisprudence is named. While Blackstone considered 'established custom as *one* of the foundations of the common law,' Carter wrote, 'he should have made it the only foundation.'[202] Judges decide cases by 'affixing the public mark and authentication upon customs and rules already existing, or struggling into existence, in the habits of the people.'[203]

Corbin too agreed with Blackstone's description of custom as the heart of the common law: 'Most legal rules and legal duties are grounded in the prevailing mores of a people and in nothing else.'[204]

Ian Macneil, whom we will meet toward the end of our discussion, also concluded that the law's function is to reflect society's own thinking. 'This function of law is to tell society what is most important' among its 'diffuse sea of custom and social practices.'[205]

Blackstone and his acolytes distinguished custom as *practice*—what is usually done—from custom as *standard*—the 'actually held ideal of what the proper line of actual behavior should be.'[206] Blackstone's followers were not, or at least not typically, holding up a looking glass to what society *does*. They were instead trying to grasp social views about how we *ought* to comport ourselves in particular situations. 'A court is not an inert mirror reflecting current mores but an active participant in the enterprise of articulating the implications of shared purposes.'[207]

199 Blackstone (2016), vol. 3, p. ☆379.

200 For Carter, see Rabban (2013), pp. 27–31; Miller (1909).

201 Grossman (2002), pp. 577–578.

202 Carter (1907), p. 78.

203 Carter (1890), p. 766.

204 Corbin (1952), p. 324.

205 Macneil (1980), p. 94.

206 Llewellyn and Hoebel (1941), p. 275.

207 Fuller (1978), p. 378.

Blackstonian Custom

How are judges supposed to access a culture's sense of what is appropriate? Blackstone thought that judges should begin with precedent: 'Judicial decisions are the principal and most authoritative evidence, that can be given, of the existence of such a custom as shall form a part of the common law.'[208] The case reports are there to show how our forebears resolved similar disputes. 'In plotting our course, the best we have to go by is some knowledge of where we have come from.'[209] And yet precedents may at times be inadequate, misguided, or wrong. Judges then do not hesitate to turn from precedent, to look instead to the customs embedded in social life, and to formulate them as a rule.

These Blackstonian insights remain still today the touchstone of the great tradition. And yet I do not want to claim too much for them. There are also other dynamics in play, some of which we will soon have the chance to explore. The common law has concerns of its own and may at times insist on a rule that does not accord with social expectation. And yet at times judicial concerns may prove inconvenient, and when they do, common law courts may choose to retreat. The world of gift that we were just exploring offers a striking example. To make it easy to recognize the rightful owner, judges long refused to validate gifts that had not been delivered.[210] But donors and donees regularly disregarded the rule, and the judges have now adopted the emerging custom.[211] This back and forth between judicial concern and social expectation represents 'the attempt to frame rules which will fit with a minimum of friction into the mechanism of ordinary life.'[212]

In sum, whatever agenda judges may be pursuing, they are always also trying to grasp what the rest of us, on our good days, would expect—the norms implicit in social life. This is the remnant of Blackstone's understanding that survives in today's common law and that I will refer to as *Blackstonian custom*: generalizations are 'continually to be tested and re-examined in the light of the sources from which they are drawn: the customs, business practices, feelings and opinions... the prevailing mores of the time and place.'[213]

Undue Unfairness

This would be the moment to offer an example of social expectation. But these customary thoughts usually do not express themselves as general rules until a specific situation calls them to mind. And yet we might recognize one notion that often

[208] Blackstone (2016), vol. 1, p. ☆69.

[209] Gilmore (1974a), p. 4.

[210] See Hyland (2012) para. 864–884, pp. 407–417.

[211] See id. para. 885–888, pp. 417–420.

[212] Mechem (1926–1927), p. 365.

[213] Corbin (1962a) §1331, vol. 6, p. 358.

arises when we think about contract disputes. It goes by different names and definitions—*fair exchange*, *equivalence*, *balance*, *mutuality*, *equality in exchange*.[214] As an element of morality, the concern is part of the classical theory of corrective justice[215]—'performances exchanged ought to be equal in value so that neither party is enriched at the other's expense.'[216] As a social expectation, it is less precise—perhaps more like what Llewellyn called the policy 'against undue unfairness.'[217] Most of us would question a deal that lacks a minimum of reciprocity. As it was getting late one evening, my wife rushed into the room where our six-year-old was watching television and told her she would be back in a few minutes to turn off the program. 'Do we have a contract?' my wife asked hurriedly. The little girl did not immediately see how she would benefit. 'Where's the contract?' she asked.

When the two performances are seriously out of proportion, the bargain does not serve its social purpose, and most of us assume that the law will not enforce it—or that it will rebalance the scales before it does. This 'felt need for some balance'[218] is the customary foundation for the consideration doctrine and underlies other contract doctrines as well—from validity (mistake, duress, and unconscionability) to excuse (impossibility, impracticability, and frustration of purpose). This bundle of intuitions expresses the 'sanely seen needs of the country' and has 'been strong enough again and again and again to break through what may have looked like adverse doctrine, and to find expression in decision.'[219] Courts 'have developed a whole series of semi-covert techniques for somewhat balancing these bargains.'[220]

Oracles of the Law

Judges have to translate these intuitions into decisions. How do they do that? How can mere mortals grasp unarticulated social norms with the precision needed to decide cases—especially since our implicit social understanding is not only always evolving but also contested? That is a good question. In fact, it is another way of putting the dilemma that we have been investigating from the beginning: since rules alone do not decide cases, what resources do judges use to reach their decisions?

Let us shift focus for a moment to the common law jury. Juries find facts. Did the defendant run a red light? Was the offeree's acceptance timely? But some questions of fact are as malleable as questions of law—such as the duty of good faith and fair

[214] See Gordley (2023), pp. 47–100 (fair exchange); Zamir (2007) (equivalence); Llewellyn (1941a), p. 871 (balance, mutuality); Gordley (1981) (equality in exchange).

[215] See Weinrib (2012), pp. 56–83.

[216] Gordley (1981), p. 1655.

[217] Llewellyn (1941a), p. 872.

[218] Id., p. 870.

[219] Id., pp. 875–876.

[220] Llewellyn (1939), p. 702.

dealing that is implied in every contract.[221] In some states, the jury is instructed to find that the duty was breached if the defendant acted 'in a manner that a reasonable person would regard as unfair.'[222] How do jurors answer such nebulous questions? We do not know exactly, but they do not seem to have much trouble with it. They talk things over until they reach a consensus about the minimum standard of conduct they would expect in a particular situation. Since there are enough jurors to temper the idiosyncrasies that any one of them may bring to the discussion, the verdict generally gives a good idea of social expectation at a particular time and place. This is Blackstonian custom at work.

To capture the mysterious nature of the process, Blackstone described judges as 'living oracles.'[223] He was thinking of the Pythian oracle at Delphi, who, after finding her way into a trance, was able to channel the wisdom of Apollo.[224] As common law judges put on their robes, they also don a second, oracular self. At that moment, they experience 'a felt pressure to become a something more and better, more responsible, more dispassionate, more restrained, more careful, even wiser, than [their] mere unrobed self.'[225]

Webb v. McGowin

Can the *Commentaries* help us with *Webb v. McGowin*? We can easily guess how Blackstone himself would have decided the case on the Court of Common Pleas. *Webb* would have come before him on a *writ of Assumpsit*,[226] the ancestor of the modern cause of action for breach of contract. Mr. Justice Blackstone would likely have found McGowin's promise lacking in consideration and refused to enforce it. 'A CONSIDERATION of some sort or other is so absolutely necessary to the forming of a contract, that a *nudum pactum* or agreement to do or pay any thing on one side, without any compensation on the other, is totally void in law; and a man cannot be compelled to perform it.'[227]

But the customs that the *Commentaries* describe point in a different direction. They show that the English Church, together with hospitals and almshouses, long provided relief to the poor. When Henry VIII (1491–1547)[228] dissolved the

[221] Restatement (Second) of Contracts § 205 (1981).

[222] See, e.g., Alaska Pattern Jury Instructions—Civil 24.15A Breach of Covenant of Good Faith and Fair Dealing—Commercial Transactions (Revised 2022), https://courts.alaska.gov/CVPJI/index.htm#24.

[223] Blackstone (2016), vol. 1, p. ☆69.

[224] See Broad (2006).

[225] Llewellyn (2008), pp. 172–173.

[226] For the writ of Assumpsit, see below, p. 96.

[227] Blackstone (2016), vol. 2, p. ☆445.

[228] For Henry VIII, see Wooding (2015).

monasteries in the sixteenth century,[229] Parliament required financially able householders to contribute to those who were unable to work.[230] Those with resources who refused to participate were first exhorted, then referred to the bishop, then to the justices, and if they remained obstinate, they were imprisoned.[231] Blackstone concluded that English society took seriously the task of providing for the poor: 'For there is no man so indigent or wretched, but he may demand a supply sufficient for all the necessities of life, from the more opulent part of the community, by means of the several statutes enacted for the relief of the poor.'[232]

Blackstone was exaggerating, for the legislation actually repressed the able-bodied poor and did not provide suitably even for those who could not work. But what matters is Blackstone's sense of social responsibility. Early in the twentieth century, American society too began to acknowledge its obligations. By the time the Alabama courts decided *Webb*, the U.S. Supreme Court had upheld the constitutionality of workers' compensation laws, and the states had enacted a variety of plans.[233]

At the moment, the history of the English poor laws will seem too remote to contribute meaningfully to our thinking about *Webb*, but like everything else we are learning, we will continue to keep it in mind. The hardest thing to accept about the common law is that no single rule, custom, or maxim ever decides a case.

Trial Lawyers

For nearly three decades, I worked on commercial matters as appellate counsel to Bill Brown (1940–2015),[234] an inspired trial lawyer who practiced in Miami, Florida. Those were some of my most rewarding experiences in the law. And yet Bill and I did not agree about how judges decide cases. Bill often took a case because language in a contract or a statute made it 'a sure winner.' I loved working with him, and so I smiled and nodded, but I was worried. If our best argument was to point to a sentence or two, I was pretty sure that we were going to lose. Bill had no patience for jurisprudential debate, so we never took the time to discuss the question. In the briefs I wrote for him, I included the language that he thought would win the case for us, but I also tried to present the facts and the law in a way that I hoped would convince the judges that deciding for our client was the right thing to do. I did not tell Bill what I was doing, and he never had time to read my paper before he filed it.

[229] For the dissolution of the monasteries, see Clark (2021).

[230] Beier (1983), pp. 23–29; Snyder (2003), p. 49 and note 96.

[231] Beier (1983), pp. 23–24.

[232] Blackstone (2016), vol. 1, p. ☆127.

[233] *N.Y. Cent. R.R. Co. v. White*, 243 U.S. 188 (1917) (constitutionality). For the controversies surrounding enactment, see Witt (2004). For the state statutes, see Johnson (2022).

[234] For Brown, see 'William Joseph Brown,' *Miami Herald,* Mar. 18, 2015, p. B5; LaBrecque (1987), pp. 51–66, 83–84.

Bill had a warm, big-hearted soul. He slapped me on the back when we won, always with a knowing smile. 'See,' he said, 'the court followed the law after all.' He taught me the most important thing I know about trial work—you have to celebrate your victories. There are surprisingly few in a career, and often many years pass between them. These celebrations may involve tender cuts of dry-aged beef consumed together with mature bottles of complex vintages. Ties are loosened, collars unbuttoned, suit jackets slipped off, and there is much ribbing and laughter. The meal is enjoyed around a large table dressed in white linen at exclusive locales that I otherwise never have the occasion to frequent.

There was of course no celebration if we lost. Losing stings, especially for lawyers who have worked on a case for years and have, most of the time, done fine work. The hurt lasts, especially the feeling of having let the client down, and the nagging suspicion that perhaps there was something more we could have done. But even losing did not change Bill's mind, even when the judges disregarded the language that he was counting on. 'Judges have their own agendas,' he used to say. 'Even if you have the best case in the world, you still only have an eighty percent chance of winning.'

To console him in those difficult moments, I assured him that we did the best we could with the case we were given. I said it, and I meant it. Yet what I wanted to say (but of course never did) was that he should read Blackstone. The *Commentaries* have helped me survive the pain of defeat, moments so demoralizing that perhaps only those who have experienced them can appreciate the smart. Blackstone taught that the judge is not there to write commentary on a legal text. The job of the common law judge is to understand what is needed to resolve the dispute and to anchor that result in the law. Social expectation often outweighs even the clearest language and the best lawyering.

References

Alschuler A (1996) Rediscovering Blackstone. University of Pennsylvania Law Review 145:1–55

Angle P (1928) One hundred years of law: An account of the law office which John T. Stuart founded in Springfield, Illinois, a century ago. Brown, Hay and Stephens, Springfield

Beier A (1983) The problem of the poor in Tudor and early Stuart England. Methuen, London

Blackstone W (1763) The lawyer's farewell to his muse. In: Dodsley R (ed) A collection of poems in six volumes. By several hands, vol. 4. J. Hughs, London, pp 224–228

Blackstone W (1771–72) Commentaries on the laws of England, 5 vols. Robert Bell, Philadelphia

Blackstone W (2016) Commentaries on the laws of England, Prest W (ed), 4 vols. Oxford University Press, Oxford

Boorstin D (1958) The mysterious science of the law. Beacon Press, Boston

Boorstin D (1996) The mysterious science of the law. University of Chicago Press, Chicago

Bracton H (1968–77) On the laws and customs of England, Woodbine G (ed), Thorne S (trans), 4 vols. Belknap Press, Cambridge

Broad W (2006) The oracle: Ancient Delphi and the science behind its lost secrets. Penguin, New York

Burke E (1775) The speech of Edmund Burke, Esquire, on moving his resolutions for conciliation with the colonies. James Rivington, New York

Cam H (ed) (1957) Selected historical essays of F.W. Maitland. Cambridge University Press, Cambridge
Carter J (1890) The ideal and the actual in the law. American Law Review 24:752–778
Carter J (1907) Law: Its origin, growth and function: Being a course of lectures prepared for delivery before the law school of Harvard University. G. P. Putnam's Sons, New York
Clark J (2021) The dissolution of the monasteries: A new history. Yale University Press, New Haven
Corbin A (1952) Corbin on contracts: One-volume edition. West, St. Paul
Corbin A (1962a) Corbin on contracts: A comprehensive treatise on the working rules of contract law, vol 6. West, St. Paul
Donald D (1995) Lincoln. Simon & Schuster, New York
Finley K (2011) Daniel J. Boorstin, historian. In: Medoff R (ed) Jewish Americans. Salem Press, Pasadena, pp 150–151
Fuller L (1978) The forms and limits of adjudication. Harvard Law Review 92:353–409
Gilmore G (1974a) The death of contract. Ohio State University Press, Columbus
Gordley J (1981) Equality in exchange. California Law Review 69:1587–1656
Gordley J (2023) Foundations of American contract law. Oxford University Press, New York
Grossman L (2002) James Coolidge Carter and Mugwump jurisprudence. Law and History Review 20:577–629
Güterbock C (1866) Bracton and his relation to the Roman law. J. B. Lippincott, Philadelphia
Holdsworth W (1932) Some aspects of Blackstone and his Commentaries. Cambridge Law Journal 4:261–285
Holdsworth W (1938) Some makers of English law. Cambridge University Press, Cambridge
Hyland R (2012) Gifts: A study in comparative law, [rev edn]. Oxford University Press, Oxford
Johnson J (2022) Workers' compensation laws by state (2023 guide). https://www.forbes.com/advisor/legal/workers-comp/workers-compensation-laws/
LaBrecque R (1987) Lost Undercover: An FBI agent's true story. Dell, New York
Lewis W (ed) (1909) Great American lawyers, vol. 8. John C. Winston, Philadelphia
Llewellyn K (1923) Relation of current economic and social problems to the Restatement of the Law, II. From the point of view of the economist and business man. Proceedings of the Academy of Political Science 3(10):25–34
Llewellyn K (1939) Review of Prausnitz, The standardization of commercial contracts in English and Continental law. Harvard Law Review 542:700–705
Llewellyn K (1941a) Common-law reform of consideration: Are there measures? Columbia Law Review 41:863–876
Llewellyn K (2008) The bramble bush: The classic lectures on the law and law school. Oxford University Press, New York
Llewellyn K, Hoebel E (1941) The Cheyenne way: Conflict and case law in primitive jurisprudence. University of Oklahoma Press, Norman
Lockmiller D (1938) Sir William Blackstone. University of North Carolina Press, Chapel Hill
Macneil I (1980) The new social contract: An inquiry into modern contractual relations. Yale University Press, New Haven
Maitland F (1901a) English law and the Renaissance. University Press, Cambridge
Maitland F (1902) History of English law. In: Cam H (1957), pp 97–121
Mechem P (1926–1927) The requirement of delivery in gifts of chattels and of choses in action evidenced by commercial instruments. Illinois Law Review 21: 341–374, 457–487, 568–609
Miller G (1909) James Coolidge Carter. In: Lewis W (ed) (1909), pp 1–41
Orth J (2020) 'Catch a falling star': The Bluebook and citing Blackstone's Commentaries. University of Illinois Law Review Online 2020:125–128
Pocock J (1975) The Machiavellian moment: Florentine political thought and the Atlantic republican tradition. Princeton University Press, Princeton
Pollock F, Maitland F (1968) The history of English law before the time of Edward I, 2nd edn, Milsom S (ed), 2 vols. Cambridge University Press, Cambridge
Prest W (2008) William Blackstone: Law and letters in the eighteenth century. Oxford University Press, Oxford

Rabban D (2013) Law's history: American legal thought and the transatlantic turn to history. Cambridge University Press, New York
Schwenzer I (2014) Divergent interpretations: Reasons and solutions. In: DiMatteo L (ed) International sales law: A global challenge. Cambridge University Press, Cambridge, pp 102–119
Snyder F (2003) The pernicious effect of employment relationships on the law of contracts. Texas Wesleyan Law Review 10:33–64
Tubbs J (2000) The common law mind: medieval and early modern conceptions. Johns Hopkins University Press, Baltimore
Weinrib E (2012) The idea of private law, rev edn. Oxford University Press, Oxford
Whitman J (1991) Why did the revolutionary lawyers confuse custom and reason? University of Chicago Law Review 58:1321–1368
Wickersham G (1924) Presentation address. ABA Journal 10:571–579
Witt J (2004) The accidental republic: Crippled workingmen, destitute widows, and the remaking of American law. Harvard University Press, Cambridge
Wooding L (2015) Henry VIII, 2nd edn. Routledge, London
Zamir E (2007) The missing interest: Restoration of the contractual equivalence. Virginia Law Review 59–138

Chapter 6
Judicial Restraint (Holmes)

Kessler called him '*ze g'date Xcholmes*,' the great Holmes. I remember asking the student sitting next to me how to spell that. As far as I know, Kessler favored no one else with that label. Holmes's is, like Homer's, a rare, unquestioned greatness. The image of the aged Holmes hovers in the mind: the snowy hair neatly parted, the sparkling eyes, the manly mien half-hidden behind a formidable military mustache. No one since has been able to pull on his boots. We are free to disagree with him, as many do today, but he stands in the middle of the road. Those who write inventively about American law often tip their hats as they pass by.

Boston

Oliver Wendell Holmes, Jr. (1841–1935)[235] was born into a distinguished Bostonian family. When the Civil War broke out, he immediately enlisted in the Union Army. After his service ended, he attended the Harvard Law School and participated in philosophical discussions with the Metaphysical Club,[236] whose members included the founders of philosophical pragmatism. Holmes published his lectures entitled *The Common Law* in 1881 and was appointed two years later to the Supreme Judicial Court of Massachusetts, where he was eventually to serve as chief justice. Among the speeches that he gave while on the Massachusetts court was 'The Path of the Law,' one of the most inspired texts in the law review literature.[237] Theodore Roosevelt appointed Holmes to the U.S. Supreme Court when he was 61, and he served as an

[235] For the biographical sketch, see Hyland (1999). For Holmes generally, see Budiansky (2019), White (1993), Holmes (1992), Howe (1963), Howe (1957).

[236] For the Metaphysical Club, see Menand (2001), pp. 201–232.

[237] See Holmes (1897).

R. Hyland, *Common Law Judging and the Great Tradition*, Ius Gentium: Comparative Perspectives on Law and Justice 100,
https://doi.org/10.1007/978-3-032-02307-0_6

associate justice until he was in his nineties. When he died in 1935, he left a portion of his estate to the federal government, which, as the Oliver Wendell Holmes Devise, has provided funding for a history of the Supreme Court.[238]

The Common Law

Holmes is the most renowned figure in the history of American law—'he flashed forth truth too dazzle-bright to hold'[239]—and of course we will not be able to do justice to his remarkable contribution. We will instead focus on his book, *The Common Law,* which is 'widely considered the best book on law ever written by an American.'[240] One reason for the book's reputation is that Holmes 'was the first lawyer, English or American, to subject the common law to the analysis of a philosopher and the explanation of a historian.'[241] However, his several perspectives point in different directions, and 'the facets of his thought were imperfectly integrated.'[242] Holmes wrote this one book, the grandest in American law, and then wrote no other. When I began teaching, my dean recommended Holmes's example as a career strategy.

The books we are reading do not describe the common law's manifest features. They aim at its essence and leave to others the task of depicting the observable. That is especially true of *The Common Law*, which remains 'the strangest of books.'[243] Holmes framed it as a work of legal history, a discussion of the origins of the common law. And yet the book is not a history. It does not accurately portray the common law either in its beginnings or as it was at the moment Holmes was writing, and it certainly does not describe the common law as we know it now.[244] It seems instead to be a meaningless assemblage of detail—'obscure and inaccessible, in addition to being rarely read.'[245] 'The lectures have long since become unreadable unless the reader is prepared to put forward an almost superhuman effort of will to keep his attention from flagging and his interest from wandering.'[246] Yet it remains the great book of our tradition.

---

[238] Goebel et al. (1971–); see White (1993), pp. 472–473.

[239] Llewellyn (1931a).

[240] Posner (1990a), p. 20.

[241] Howe (1963), p. 137.

[242] Posner (1990a), p. 61.

[243] Gilmore (1999), p. 385.

[244] See Rabban (2009), p. 423; Rabban (2003), pp. 1190–1193.

[245] Horwitz (1992), p. 110.

[246] Gilmore (1977), p. 52.

Logic and Experience

We find already on its first page the most famous sentence that Holmes wrote, one of the most quoted sentences in the common law: 'The life of the law has not been logic; it has been experience.'[247] Like many of Holmes's sentences, it was not meant to explain anything. It was instead a warning of what was to come. The sentence begins by pointing to the ideas that the book was about to refute, namely legal theories that suggest that consistency is essential to law. Logic occupied for Holmes the station that abstract reason held for Blackstone—a shorthand for a vision that absolutizes the virtues of simplicity, coherence, and predictability. Like Blackstone, Holmes wanted to convince his audience that cases cannot be decided simply by applying the rules. And experience played for him the role custom performed in Blackstone. As Blackstone preferred custom to reason, Holmes promoted experience over logic.[248]

Though the concepts of custom and experience point in a similar direction, their historical perspectives differ. Because Blackstone believed that English law was hatched fully feathered among the Britons and the Germans, Holmes thought that Blackstone lacked a sense of history. As Holmes read the *Commentaries*, he was troubled by its sense of inertia and stagnation, and he experienced 'the passionate demand that what sounded so arbitrary in Blackstone... should give some reasonable meaning.'[249]

Change

England was industrializing in Blackstone's day, and the common law was then developing a 'distinctly modern character,' including the principles that govern stock companies, partnerships, negotiable instruments, bankruptcy, and master and servant.[250] And yet those dramatic developments seemed to leave the surface of the common law so unruffled that, as Blackstone wrote, we can no more chart its growth 'than we can discern the changes of the bed of a river, which varies its shores by continual decreases and alluvions.'[251] While judges were making law 'with a sort of joyous frenzy,'[252] Blackstone, Maitland explained, 'wrote in a season of perfect calm.'[253]

For Holmes, in contrast, the common law was in perpetual motion, ceaselessly reinventing itself to accommodate social transformation. Though Holmes studded

---

247 Holmes (2009), p. 3.

248 For Holmes's understanding of experience, see Menand (2001), pp. 341–345.

249 Holmes and Laski (1953), vol. 1, pp. 429–430.

250 Plucknett (1956), p. 68.

251 Blackstone (2016), vol. 4, p. ☆402.

252 Gilmore (1977), p. 7.

253 Maitland (1966), p. 67.

his lectures with detailed descriptions of obscure institutions from the distant past, the essence of the Holmesian common law was change. While Blackstone sought wisdom from precedent, Holmes asked judges to look to the present and beyond it to the future. 'Precedents drawn from the days of travel by stage coach,' Justice Cardozo would later explain, 'do not fit the conditions of travel to-day.'[254]

Continuity

Despite their differences, when the time came to defend the common law against the challenge of deductive reason, Holmes fought shoulder to shoulder with Blackstone. Law is not a mathematical structure of axioms and corollaries that can decide cases with the logic of a syllogism. It is instead 'the story of a nation's development,' and judges properly resolve cases by reference to 'the felt necessities of the time, the prevalent moral and political theories, intuitions of public policy, avowed or unconscious, and the prejudices which judges share with their fellow-men.'[255] The common law is always racing to keep up with the times, and in the words of Grant Gilmore, whom we will soon meet, 'we are always outwitted and surprised by what actually happens.'[256] But if we live in such exciting times, why does the common law always seem so unflappable? That was the conundrum Holmes addressed in the first chapter of his book.

Before we explore his solution, it is worth noting the scale of the problem. American life constantly generates new ideas and produces novel contrivances and contraptions. How then can a legal system made to measure for a feudal kingdom a thousand years ago continue to govern post-industrial America? No, really. How has this unstructured legal system subsisted through the linguistic turn, the civil rights movement, the Sixties, deconstruction, four waves of feminism, the digital revolution, and gender fluidity, and survived into the age of artificial intelligence so hale and hearty that it has been fitted out with online search engines?

This was the mystery that Holmes solved, but his answer is so deeply embedded in his erudite case studies that it is difficult to locate. And yet all the sentences in his first chapter, including their references to long-vanished legal institutions, unite to relate a single exquisite thought.

---

[254] *MacPherson v. Buick Motor Co.*, 111 N.E. 1050, 1053 (N.Y. 1916) (Cardozo, J.).

[255] Holmes (2009), p. 3.

[256] Gilmore (1967), p. 471.

Form and Substance

Holmes solved the puzzle by distinguishing between the law's form and its substance.[257] Its *form* embraces everything we would be tempted to include in a definition of law, the sources we look to when we do legal research—codes, statutes, regulations, precedent. The law's *substance*, in contrast, corresponds to our evaluation of social needs, 'considerations of what is expedient for the community concerned.'[258] Holmesian substance therefore includes differing views of public policy, instinctive preferences, and even unarticulated convictions. 'No one will ever have a truly philosophic mastery over the law who does not habitually consider the forces outside of it which have made it what it is.'[259] Perceptions of social convenience are 'the secret root from which the law draws all of the juices of life.'[260] While the law's form seeks stability, its substance grapples with the confounding complexity of our march toward the future, and Gilmore believed that the task of the common law judge is to reconcile the two. 'The process by which a society accommodates to change without abandoning its fundamental structure is what we mean by law.'[261]

If they are to be more than just competent legal artisans, lawyers and judges must grasp something of the law's substance, and that means that they must become conversant with history, philosophy, and modern social science, and 'beyond these [have] a sense of the yearnings of the human spirit,' which is perhaps 'more than [a jurist] can ever hope to have.'[262] Few other fields of human endeavor demand such universality, and Holmes took the responsibility seriously. The great justice read the equivalent of a book a week for seventy years.[263] In addition to law, he followed philosophy, sociology, literature, religion, history, and economics. He read murder mysteries, poetry, and science, spent time with the classics and enjoyed the latest triumphs. Holmes understood what was needed to keep pace with the vast enterprise described by the common law.

When I think of the contrast between the law's form and its substance, my mind returns to two experiences I have had of Greece. I was asked to absorb the tenets of classical Greek culture as an undergraduate. I did my best to make sense of the epics, choral plays, philosophic dialogues, anecdotal histories, Archaic sculpture, temple colonnades, and the astonishing friezes, but the severe and unapproachable Greek ethos made me shiver. The term *classic* has always meant to me the chiseled marble that even on a summer's day chills the touch. Only later did I have a chance

---

[257] Holmes (2009), pp. 4, 7, 34–35.

[258] Id., p. 34.

[259] [Holmes] (1880), p. 234.

[260] Holmes (2009), p. 34.

[261] Gilmore (1977), p. 14.

[262] Sacks (1959), p. 218.

[263] Budiansky (2019), pp. 7–8. For Holmes on reading, see Holmes (1989).

to experience Hellas on my own, and nothing has surprised me more. What I had not imagined was the actual feel of the place, a mode of life that probably has not changed much since Plato. It involves warm evenings sipping resin-flavored wine on a terrace by the sea, long chats with friends amid swirls of laughter and dancing, and the incessant surprise of riotous colors, intense tastes, unrecognizable aromas, and spritely melodies nimbly plucked on unfamiliar stringed instruments. Greece is both austere and exuberant, and I have yet to reconcile the two visions.

Thesis

Holmes had better luck squaring the parallel processes of the common law, for he eventually grasped their relationship, and we will follow him through his intricate demonstration. These are some of the most challenging pages written about law. It is helpful to keep his goal in mind, which was to show how the law is able to maintain the appearance of consistency even as it adapts to change. It is also useful to know the trick in advance—the adaptation takes place largely out of sight.

We inherit rules and legal formulae that express the customs, beliefs, and needs of an earlier day.[264] With society perpetually at work, the terms of the problems evolve, and a rule may eventually lose its rationale. Inquiring minds then ask how such a rule ever came to be. Upon reflection, the precedent reveals itself to be somewhat appropriate for a fresh purpose, and the rule is launched on a new career. But because its form is not ideally suited to its new mission, it must be refashioned to embody its newly acquired substance. This is how the common law maintains its 'surface appearance of stability' and convinces lawyers and judges that the rule, though now somewhat refined and clarified, has governed for all eternity[265]—'The new which suits appears a[s] if it *had* always been.'[266]

Holmes analogized legal evolution to the cat clavicle.[267] The analogy is evocative but not exact, since the cat has not developed a new function for its collarbone. A better parallel may be the buttons on a jacket sleeve. In the late nineteenth century, at least by legend, buttons allowed surgeons to roll up their sleeves without removing their coats.[268] Sleeves with buttons eventually indicated social rank, and today's suit jackets still have those buttons. And yet, because working buttons make alterations difficult, off-the-rack coats have buttons but no buttonholes, and that has given the functional buttons on custom-made jackets a new purpose. Their proud owners may signal good fortune by nonchalantly leaving a button unbuttoned.

---

[264] Holmes (2009), p. 7.

[265] Gilmore (1982), p. 4.

[266] Llewellyn (1931b), p. 88.

[267] Holmes (2009), p. 34.

[268] Bucco (2016).

Historical Examples

With this running start, let us try to make sense of the odd array of historical examples that Holmes collected to prove his point. Since some of his interpretations are open to question, we will focus on the vision rather than the detail.[269]

Holmes believed that early legal liability was rooted in vengeance. Since retaliation implicated the entire clan, retribution was saved for intentional harm—murder or wounding—and there was no liability for negligence. As Holmes explained in a charming aside, even a dog distinguishes between being stumbled over and being kicked.[270]

English law also knew the institution of the *deodand* (owed to God), an animal or inanimate object responsible for killing a human being.[271] Deodands included falling stones and irons as well as killer pigs and kicking horses. By common law rule, the deodand was subject to forfeiture, even when the killing was by accident.

If the point of vengeance was to remediate intentional harm, how could there be liability for an accident? The answer was that the object was thought to have committed the crime intentionally. The owner had no personal liability—once the goring ox was stoned, its owner was quit.[272] As Holmes pointed out, we still kick a door when it pinches our finger.[273] Holmes did not bother to explain where he was going with this, but since he was shining his lamp into cobwebbed corners, the stakes must have been high.

When a sailor accidentally fell to his death from a ship, admiralty law forfeited the ship for having caused the death.[274] And when one ship caused damage to another, the offending ship was sold to cover the loss, even if its owner was not in control and could not have prevented the harm. The rule was there to make sure the victim was compensated. When the ship's owner is beyond reach, seizing the offending vessel may be the only realistic source for a remedy.[275] 'No *jus ad rem*/ Will comfort them/Whose *jus in re*/Has gone away.'[276] The law prefers the victim because the owner put the ship in motion and stood to profit from the voyage.

How clever. Holmes noticed the similarity between the deodand and the shipowner's liability in modern admiralty law—in both cases, the object that caused the

---

[269] In a law review article he published a few years earlier, Holmes advanced the same argument—both more explicitly and more tentatively. See H[olmes] (1876), pp. 424–434. 'It is only fair to admit at the outset that the opinions to be expressed are partly conjectural; and, as such, they are submitted to the judgment of the reader.' Id. p. 432.

[270] Holmes (2009), p. 5.

[271] Id., p. 8. For the deodand, see Pervukhin (2005), p. 237; Blackstone (2016), vol. 1, pp. ☆290–292.

[272] Exodus 21:28.

[273] Holmes (2009), p. 12.

[274] Id., pp. 25–26.

[275] Id., pp. 27–28; see also Lind (2009), p. 90.

[276] Gilmore and Black (1975), p. 589 note 1b.

harm was forfeited. But just pointing to a similarity does not prove a connection. Holmes would have had to show that the forfeiture remedy was justified not merely by its modern utility, but also by the continuing belief that an inanimate object might intentionally cause harm.

Holmes invited these doubts so he might celebrate a greater triumph. To prove his point, he quoted two of the U.S. Supreme Court's most distinguished judges, Justices Marshall and Story.[277] A ship's master and crew committed piracy, and the ship was seized, even though the owner was unaware of their criminal activity.[278] In his opinion, Story quoted a decision by Marshall: 'This is not a proceeding against the owner, it is a proceeding against the vessel for an offense committed by the vessel.'[279] Justice Story might also have quoted one of his own opinions: 'The thing is here primarily considered as the offender, or rather the offense is attached primarily to the thing.'[280]

With that striking bit of detective work, Holmes managed to trace the language of object personification into judicial opinions written by eminent American jurists. Holmes was grandstanding. Though a common law example would easily have done the job, this was a public lecture, and continuity across continents and millennia was more entertaining.

Holmes's demonstration pulled the rug out from under the argument that judges should just apply the law. The rule that is tranquilly waiting on the shelf until its number is called does not exist. When an old norm is applied as the world turns, its function must be reimagined. In other words, courts are not really applying the old rule at all.

Risk Allocation

In one of 'his astonishing series of lectures on Contracts,'[281] Holmes came up with an intriguing way to introduce another of the common law's central ideas. This is my slightly altered version of the hypothetical Holmes asked us to consider: one party promises the other that, for a fee, it will not rain tomorrow. If the promise is accepted, would a court make the promisor pay damages if it rains?[282] The example is so unexpected that it takes a moment to figure out what Holmes was driving at. If I breach a promise to deliver widgets, the court will doubtlessly make me remedy

---

[277] For Story, see Newmyer (1985); Dunne (1970).

[278] *The Malek Adhel*, 43 U.S. (2 How.) 210 (1844) (Story, J.) (cited in Holmes (2009), p. 29 note 82).

[279] *The Malek Adhel*, p. 234 (quoting *The Little Charles*, 26 F. Cas. 979 (C. Ct. D. Va. 1818) (No. 15,162) (Marshall, J.)).

[280] *The Palmyra*, 25 U.S. (12 Wheat.) 1, 14 (1827) (Story, J.) (quoted in Holmes (2009), p. 29). For a history of the doctrine of vessel personification, see Lind (2009), especially pp. 84–92. For a non-metaphorical reading of these cases, see Gilmore and Black (1975) §§ 9-3 to 9-4, pp. 589–594.

[281] Gilmore (1974a), p. 6.

[282] See Holmes (2009), pp. 269–270.

the harm—I have agreed to do something, I have not done it, and I can be said to be at fault for failing to perform. But what if I promise that it will not rain? I cannot possibly be responsible for a downpour. Will a court still grant a remedy for breach?

Why would anyone promise that it will not rain tomorrow? The hypothetical was standard in the case law,[283] but let me reformulate it for our purposes as the contract known today as *event weather insurance*.[284] The policy insures against financial loss when it proves necessary to cancel events that are particularly vulnerable to weather disruption—fairs, golf tournaments, film productions, and outdoor concerts. Let us think of the policy as a contract to pay damages for breach of the promise that it will not rain.

This is a standard type of insurance, and there is no doubt that the policy is enforceable.[285] But since the insurance carrier is not at fault, how would we describe the basis of liability? Holmes wanted to demonstrate that a contract can be held to have been breached without a finding of a moral failing. 'The law, he said, must not be confused with morals.'[286] A contract is simply an agreement to allocate risk.[287]

Holmes concluded this discussion with one of the most famous sentences in this book of famous sentences: 'The only universal consequence of a legally binding promise is that the law makes the promisor pay damages if the promised event does not come to pass.'[288] Holmes's statement has sometimes been misinterpreted to imply that a contract is a simple bet about the future. But no, a contract is not like an outside bet at roulette. It is a complex interaction, and the decision whether to enforce a contractual duty rests on a multiplicity of factors. Holmes's point was simply that moral culpability is not one of them. That is what Kessler meant by one of his favorite sayings: 'A breach of contract is not a tort.' By freeing the courts from the task of adjudicating moral responsibility, Holmes was hoping that judges might then more easily focus on social policy choices.

Law and Morals

Holmes had yet another reason for asking courts to leave behind the business of deciding moral culpability, a reason both more urgent and more controversial—and also harder to explain. It is with this idea that Holmes justified the consideration doctrine, though he did not take the time to explain. Here is the central thought:

[283] See id., p. 269 note 20 (citing *Canham v Berry*, (1855) 15 CB 597, 619, 139 Eng Rep 558 (Maule J); *Jones v How*, (1850) 9 CB 1, 9 (*in fine*), 137 Eng Rep 790, 794 (Maule J)).

[284] See Farley (2024), Gorki (2014).

[285] See *Casablanca Concerts, Inc. v. Am. Nat'l Gen. Agencies, Inc.*, 407 N.W.2d 440 (Minn. App. 1987). See also Restatement (Second) of Contracts § 2 comment d (1981).

[286] O'Brien (1988), p. 24 (quoting the recollections of Arthur Sutherland, Holmes's former legal secretary, who was in turn quoting Holmes).

[287] Holmes (2009), p. 272.

[288] Id.

though law and morality are separate fields, they sometimes prohibit the same wrongs, and when they do, the existence of a legal sanction tends to crowd out moral reasoning. Faced with a legal prohibition, most of us will not take the time to examine whether our course of action is also morally improper. And—here is the point—when moral reflection is preempted, we lose the opportunity to decide our duties for ourselves.

My students resist this idea because they believe that the law's real job is to punish moral wrongs. It is hard for them to see that an act like murder, though condemned by both law and morality, is condemned by each for its own reasons. To see what Holmes was getting at, it may be useful to drop farther down the spectrum of moral flaws and choose a breach that, because its social consequences are less severe, the law does not punish.

I will use one of my own shortcomings as an example. I do not like to wait my turn. When I have to wait, I usually cut in line. I am good at it, so most of the time no one notices. And yet since I am aware that my habit is a moral lapse, I am constantly at war with myself. The struggle is so unpleasant that I sometimes wish cutting in line were illegal. Since I usually obey the law, that would end my moral quandary.

At the same time, penalizing me would also make society worse off, and that is because an aspect of my temptation to cut in line is, curiously, a social good, for it gives me the chance to practice resolving moral dilemmas in difficult circumstances. 'To achieve maturity the opportunity of choice and therefore of making mistakes and of assuming responsibility for their consequences is indispensable.'[289] Henry Hart, whose work we will soon discuss, thought it essential for society to enlarge the space for individual decision-making. We learn 'wisdom in choosing by being confronted with choices and by being made aware that [we] must abide the consequences of [our] choice.'[290]

Combat

When Holmes stood behind a podium later in life, he often spoke about what military service had taught him about *duty*.[291] Still today, his thoughts offer insight into a judge's role.

Holmes was wounded three times during the Civil War, and each time he returned to the front. When he recovered from the wound he received at Ball's Bluff, he wrote to his mother to assure her that he stood coolly before his men, encouraged them, 'and did my duty I am sure.'[292]

---

[289] Kessler (1957b), p. 3.

[290] Hart Henry (1958), p. 410.

[291] See, e.g., Holmes (1895), pp. 89, 92.

[292] Letter from O[liver] W[endell] Holmes Jr. to his mother [Amelia Lee Jackson Holmes] (Oct. 23, 1861), in Holmes (1946), p. 13.

The meaning of *duty* evolved for Holmes with the years,[293] but as a young man, he was simply looking for personal autonomy:[294] 'I have laboriously and with much suffering of mind and body *earned* the right... to decide for myself how I can best do my duty to myself to the country and, if you choose, to God—.'[295]

That Holmesian understanding—that the moral life involves deciding one's duties for oneself—has become an element of common law judging. That is because individuals have the freedom to choose only if the law stays its hand. Courts should intercede to protect the foundations of important social institutions, but otherwise it is often best to allow the parties to work it out for themselves. The machinery of judicial process 'ought not to be set in motion unless some clear benefit is to be derived from disturbing the *status quo*. State interference is an evil, where it cannot be shown to be a good.'[296]

Why Enforce Contracts

Courts enforce some promises and not others, and the Holmesian notion of duty may help us understand when it is helpful for judges to get involved. This aspect of Holmes's thinking is essential for our discussion, but before we can approach it, we must first ask a question that we probably should have asked earlier: why do courts enforce contracts? Why is the breach of a contractual promise such a momentous event that society must maintain an extensive (and expensive) judicial apparatus to resolve contractual disputes?

Though contract law governs many types of promises, let us continue to assume that its central mission is to resolve commercial disputes. Before we can reason from this central concern, we will need to know what the market contributes to society.

Society aims to produce today what it will need to continue producing tomorrow. Since the goal is to avoid both shortages and surpluses, it might seem best to set up a central authority, equip it with fancy software and the latest artificial intelligence, and ask it to determine in real time the optimal inputs and outputs for each branch. But at least for the moment, it appears that no single entity is able to program the entire economy in advance: 'The knowledge of the circumstances of which we must make use never exists in concentrated or integrated form, but solely as the dispersed bits of incomplete and frequently contradictory knowledge which all the separate individuals possess.'[297] Moreover, it is challenging to predict trends, and even

293 White (1993), p. 72.

294 Letter from O[liver] W[endell] H[olmes] Jr. to his parents (May 16, 1864), in Holmes (1946), p. 122.

295 Letter from O[liver] W[endell] Holmes, Jr. to his mother (June 7, 1864), in Holmes (1946), p. 143.

296 Holmes (2009), p. 88.

297 Hayek (1945), p. 519.

sophisticated software cannot always know when something new is worth the gamble. We therefore leave much of the economy's planning function to the market, and that means to a vast number of individual bargains. 'Bargain is then the social and legal machinery appropriate to arranging affairs in any specialized economy which relies on exchange rather than tradition... or authority... for apportionment of productive energy and of product.'[298]

Commercial bargains can allocate resources properly only if those bargains are performed.[299] Contract law is there in the end to increase the reliability of commercial promises—'one of the main functions of our law of contracts is to keep this flow running smoothly.'[300] Of course, mechanisms exist outside the law for ensuring performance of contractual obligations,[301] and most contractual difficulties are resolved without the law's intervention.[302] But as the market increases in complexity, the role of judicial enforcement becomes more important. In the end, markets could not fully perform their planning function if the legal system did not enforce contracts.

Duty Again

Though the market depends on the judicial enforcement of contractual promises, society also gains when courts step back and allow individuals the freedom to discover and perform their obligations for themselves. Since these two goals conflict, courts need a principle to help them decide when to grant a remedy or when instead it might be better not to intervene. Holmes suggested judicial restraint—courts should step in only when their action is needed to protect important social institutions like the market. For promises that are not related to market exchange, like informal gift promises, the law often decides that it is best to allow promisors to decide for themselves whether to perform. By marking the boundary between the two fields, the consideration doctrine protects both the viability of the market and the critical realm of individual autonomy.

Webb v. McGowin

How might Holmes have decided our principal case? If the purpose of contract law is to protect the market, *Webb* is an easy case. The foundations of the market are not in play, and the courts should leave the decision to the promisor. When he was on

298 Llewellyn (1931f), p. 717.
299 Kessler (1952a), p. 69.
300 Kessler et al. (1986), p. 4.
301 Llewellyn (1931f), p. 720.
302 Id., p. 738.

the Massachusetts bench, Holmes decided a gratuitous promise case in just this way. 'What was done as a mere favor' cannot be turned into consideration, even if requested, unless the prior request 'implies an undertaking to pay.'[303]

It has perhaps by now become clear that conceptions of freedom are at the heart of the books we are reading—'"Freedom" is an underlying drumbeat and slogan that informs not merely life but law.'[304] Because freedom for Holmes meant allowing individuals to decide for themselves, he 'shows a continued interest in developments which will pay regard to the importance of human choice.'[305] As Grant Gilmore put the same thought, 'we may judge of the excellence of our society not by how much law we have but by how little we can make do with.'[306]

This Holmesian conception of freedom is to me the most thrilling insight in the history of the common law. And yet I do not think it can clinch the decision here. To me the case is about Webb. He exercised his freedom by risking his life to save a fellow human being and thereby became unable to work. We are now asking whether the law has the doctrinal resources to respect Webb's choice by allowing him to live out his life in dignity. How would Holmes respond if we put the question this way?

Holmes would have understood that this dispute is not about abstract freedom. McGowin made his choice and lived by it. In the curious posture of the case, the consideration doctrine is all that prevents the performance of McGowin's promise. Though the law should not compel McGowin to compensate Webb, it seems strange for it to serve as the main obstacle to the fulfillment of his wishes. Holmes promoted the consideration doctrine because he believed that it would ensure a realm for individual autonomy. He would not have let it stand in the way of a promisor who was seeking to perform his duty.

References

Blackstone W (2016) Commentaries on the laws of England, Prest W (ed), 4 vols. Oxford University Press, Oxford

Bucco C (2016) Surgeon sleeves—functional buttons: The history and what it means today! https://www.linkedin.com/pulse/surgeon-sleeves-functional-buttons-history-what-means-carmen-bucco.

Budiansky S (2019) Oliver Wendell Holmes: A life in war, law, and ideas. Norton, New York

Dunne G (1970) Justice Joseph Story and the rise of the Supreme Court. Simon and Schuster, New York

Farley M (2024) Weather insurance. https://www.usnews.com/insurance/glossary/weather-insurance

Gilmore G (1966) Law, anarchy and history. University of Chicago Law School Record 14(2):1, 5-7

Gilmore G (1967) On statutory obsolescence. University of Colorado Law Review 39:461–477

Gilmore G (1974a) The death of contract. Ohio State University Press, Columbus

[303] *Moore v. Elmer*, 61 N.E. 259, 259–260 (Mass. 1901) (Holmes, C.J.).

[304] Llewellyn (1960), p. 20.

[305] Sharp (1964), p. 268.

[306] Gilmore (1966), p. 7.

Gilmore G (1977) The ages of American law. Yale University Press, New Haven
Gilmore G (1982) What is a law school? Connecticut Law Review 15:1–6
Gilmore G (1999) Some reflections on Oliver Wendell Holmes, Jr. Green Bag 2d 2:379–394
Gilmore G, Black C (1975) The law of admiralty, 2d edn. Foundation, Mineola
Goebel J et al (1971–) The Oliver Wendell Holmes Devise history of the United States Supreme Court, Marcus M (ed), 13 vols (different publication dates). Cambridge University Press, New York
Gorki D (2014) When the show can't go on. Best's Review 114:45–46
Hart Henry (1958) The aims of the criminal law. Law & Contemporary Problems 23:401–441
Hayek F (1945) The use of knowledge in society. American Economic Review 35:519–530
H[olmes] O (1876) Primitive notions in modern law. American Law Review 10:422–439
[Holmes O] (1880) Review of Langdell, A selection of cases on the law of contracts, and Anson, Principles of the English law of contract. American Law Review 14:233–235
Holmes O (1895) The soldier's faith. In: Posner R (ed) (1992), pp 87–93
Holmes O (1897) The path of the law. Harvard Law Review 10:457–478
Holmes O (1946) Touched with fire: Civil War letters and diary of Oliver Wendell Holmes, Jr., 1861-1864, Howe M (ed). Harvard University Press, Cambridge
Holmes O (1989) Books. In: Hoffheimer M (ed) The early critical and philosophical writings of Justice Holmes, pp 1250–1253. Boston College Law Review 30:1221–1282
Holmes O (1992) The essential Holmes: Selections from the letters, speeches, judicial opinions, and other writings, Posner R (ed). University of Chicago Press, Chicago
Holmes O (2009) The common law. Harvard University Press, Cambridge
Holmes O, Laski H (1953) The correspondence of Mr. Justice Holmes and Harold J. Laski, 1916–1935, Howe M (ed), 2 vols. Harvard University Press, Cambridge
Horwitz M (1992) The transformation of American law, 1870-1960: The crisis of legal orthodoxy. Oxford University Press, New York
Howe M (1957) Justice Oliver Wendell Holmes, vol. 1: The shaping years, 1841–1870. Harvard University Press, Cambridge
Howe M (1963) Justice Oliver Wendell Holmes, vol. 2: The proving years 1870-1882. Harvard University Press, Cambridge
Hyland R (1999) Holmes, Oliver Wendell, Jr. (1841–1935). In: Gray C (ed) The philosophy of law: An encyclopedia, vol. 1. Garland, New York, pp 377–378
Kessler F (1952a) Freiheit und Zwang im nordamerikanischen Vertragsrecht. In: von Caemmerer E et al (eds) Festschrift für Martin Wolff: Beiträge zum Zivilrecht und internationalen Privatrecht. Mohr Siebeck, Tübingen, pp 67–78
Kessler F (1957b) In memoriam: Jerome N. Frank (1889–1957). Natural Law Forum 2:1–3
Kessler F et al (1986) Contracts: Cases and materials, 3d edn. Little, Brown, Boston
Lind D (2009) Pragmatism and anthropomorphism: Reconceiving the doctrine of the personality of the ship. University of San Francisco Maritime Law Journal 22:39–122
Llewellyn K (1929) Ueber den Rechtsunterricht in den Vereinigten Staaten: Ein Vortrag. Jherings Jahrbücher für die Dogmatik des bürgerlichen Rechts 79:233–266
Llewellyn K (1931a) Holmes. In: Llewellyn K (1931c), p. 108
Llewellyn K (1931b) Law and the modern mind: A symposium, I: Legal illusion, review of Frank, Law and the modern mind. Columbia Law Review 31:82–90
Llewellyn K (1931c) Put in his thumb. Century Co., New York
Llewellyn K (1931f) What price contract?—an essay in perspective. Yale Law Journal 40:704–751
Llewellyn K (1960) The common law tradition: Deciding appeals. Little, Brown, Boston
Maitland F (1966) Two lectures delivered by F.W. Maitland: Downing Professor of the Laws of England in the Easter term, 1889. Cambridge Law Journal 24:54–74
Menand L (2001) The metaphysical club. Farrar, Strauss and Giroux, New York
Newmyer R (1985) Supreme Court Justice Joseph Story: Statesman of the Old Republic. University of North Carolina Press, Chapel Hill

O'Brien D (1988) Sutherland's recollections of Justice Holmes. Supreme Court Historical Society Yearbook, pp 18–25
Pervukhin A (2005) Deodands: A study in the creation of common law rules. American Journal of Legal History 47:237–256
Plucknett T (1956) A concise history of the common law, 5th edn. Little, Brown, Boston
Posner R (1990a) Cardozo: A study in reputation. University of Chicago Press, Chicago
Rabban D (2003) The historiography of The common law. Law & Social Inquiry 28:1161–1201
Rabban D (2009) From Maine to Maitland via America. Cambridge Law Journal 68:410–435
Sacks A (1959) Mr. Justice Frankfurter. University of Chicago Law Review 26:217–221
Sharp M (1964) Mr. Justice Holmes: Some modern views—contracts. University of Chicago Law Review 31:268–278
White G (1993) Justice Oliver Wendell Holmes: Law and the inner self. Oxford University Press, New York

Chapter 7
History (Maitland)

The majority of the world's legal systems get on nicely without the consideration doctrine. Kessler thought that we should abolish it. Could we? And if we decide to keep it, would we recognize moral obligation as an exception?

Frederic Maitland

Let us consult Frederic Maitland (1850–1906),[307] Downing Professor of the Laws of England at the University of Cambridge. In his short life, Maitland established English legal history as a field of study and, at a frenetic pace, searched for, found, copied, edited, translated, introduced, proofread, and published a good number of its early records. He had something of Holmes's gift for aphorism and the rare 'power of making dry bones live.'[308]

Maitland's masterpiece, a history of English law in the early medieval period that he co-authored with Frederick Pollock,[309] chronicles what was 'among the half dozen most important events of the Middle Ages,' namely the rise of English law in the twelfth and thirteenth centuries as the principal alternative to Roman law in Western culture.[310] We will soon examine the formulary system that the English lawyers were then developing, but before we do, we can get a sense of the great book from the way that Maitland introduced the forms of action to his readers. 'Each of them lives its own life, has its own adventures, enjoys a longer or shorter day of vigour, usefulness and

[307] For Maitland, see Cantor (1991), pp. 48–78; Elton (1985); Fifoot (1971); Bell (1965).

[308] Cantor (1991), p. 50; Chaytor and Whittaker (1909), p. v.

[309] See Pollock and Maitland (1968).

[310] Cantor (1991), p. 59.

R. Hyland, *Common Law Judging and the Great Tradition*, Ius Gentium: Comparative Perspectives on Law and Justice 100,
https://doi.org/10.1007/978-3-032-02307-0_7

popularity, and then sinks perhaps into a decrepit and friendless old age.'[311] Maitland thought of legal institutions as living beings that are born, reach maturity, and expire in senescence.[312] Here he is again, describing the forms of action: 'A few are still-born, some are sterile, others live to see their children and children's children in high places. The struggle for life is keen among them and only the fittest survive.'[313]

Origins of Consideration

As we think about whether to keep the consideration doctrine, it may seem best to start by figuring out how we got ourselves into this fix. Unfortunately, the search for the doctrine's historical origins leads nowhere, and that is because historians have not been able to discover how we ended up with it. Or at least they tell a number of different stories. 'No other doctrine in English law can compete with "consideration" for the greatest diversity and complexity of historical explanations.'[314] As the historian John Baker explained, it is unclear whether consideration was a wholly English development or whether it was borrowed from the canon or civil laws.[315] It does not help that the older cases are sparse, badly reported, and spread over so many years that it is difficult to construct a reliable timeline.

Forms of Action

Even though we cannot locate the precise origin of the consideration doctrine, certain aspects of the story are generally accepted. It begins with the formulary procedure that we today call the *forms of action*. Those were the writs that governed common law procedure in the royal courts into the nineteenth century.[316] When the case fit one of the formulae, the plaintiff brought suit by purchasing a writ from the Court of Chancery. By the reign of Edward I (1239–1307),[317] there were about five hundred writs on the Chancery Register.[318] The writ instructed the local sheriff how to begin the process of resolving the dispute. There is no better introduction to the

[311] Pollock and Maitland (1968), vol. 2, p. 561.

[312] See Hyland (1995), pp. 204–206.

[313] Pollock and Maitland (1968), vol. 2, p. 561.

[314] Baker (2013), p. 1176. For works about the origin of the consideration doctrine, see Baker (2013), p. 1176 note 1; Laske (2020), p. 59 note 1.

[315] Baker (1971), p. 213.

[316] For a recent description of the forms of action, see Baker (2019), pp. 60–77; see also Van Caenegem (1988), pp. 29–61. For the early history, see Pollock and Maitland (1968), vol. 2, pp. 558–573.

[317] For Edward I, see Morris (2009).

[318] Bell (1965), p. 82.

intricate procedural world of the writ system than Maitland's posthumously published lectures, *The Forms of Action at Common Law*.[319] Maitland's lectures are slender, 'too slight for their theme,' as Fifoot wrote, and 'they dwindle at times into notes.'[320] And yet these lectures are some of the most affecting readings in the common law tradition, and they lose nothing of their brilliance when we concede that some of his contentions have been questioned.[321]

Early modern English law focused so thoroughly on finding the right form of action that 'substantive law has at first the look of being gradually secreted in the interstices of procedure.'[322] The procedural focus created a major gap in contract law: before the end of the 16th century, no writ authorized courts to enforce an oral exchange of promises not yet performed by either party.

Covenant, Debt, Assumpsit

If we imagine the writ system about 1600, three forms of action—Covenant, Debt, and Assumpsit—each had the potential to develop into a general cause of action for breach of contract, though they were all as yet quite far from the elements of the claim as we know it today.[323]

Two limitations prevented the writ of Covenant, the oldest of the three, from evolving into a general contractual action. From the mid-fourteenth century, it was available only if the defendant had executed a deed—a writing under seal. It also did not lie to recover a fixed sum of money (which, as we will see, was the province of Debt).

The second writ, Debt, was not designed to enforce promises. It provided a remedy for the breach of a preexisting legal obligation.[324] If there was no deed, the plaintiff had to plead the existence of a quid pro quo. Debt was also not well suited to enforcing an executory promise, and that is because the action could be maintained only for a liquidated (specific) sum. Another difficulty was that trial was usually by *wager of law* (compurgation): defendants prevailed if they swore by sacred oath that the alleged sum was not owed and simultaneously presented a designated number of oath-helpers (local citizens willing to swear that the defendant

---

319 Maitland (1963).

320 Fifoot (1971), pp. 97–98.

321 For the critique, see Elton (1985), pp. 44–48; Milsom (1958, 1968).

322 Maine (1891), p. 389.

323 The names of the forms of action are capitalized, following Maitland. For the three writs, see Maitland (1963), pp. 63–70; Barbour (1914), pp. 17–58. For the early history of Debt and Covenant, see Pollock and Maitland (1968), vol. 2, pp. 184–239.

324 For Debt, see Baker (2019), pp. 342–347; Maitland (1963), pp. 38, 48, 63; Ames (1913), pp. 88–96.

was telling the truth).[325] A defendant who swore the oath always prevailed, even if it was demonstrably false, for the oath-taker was not subject to cross-examination.

The writ of Assumpsit, the third of the actions, is the one history anointed to pave the way for the modern cause of action for breach of contract.[326] The writ was used when one party had undertaken a task (*assumpsit* in Latin) and performed it negligently. Before 1500, however, Assumpsit was generally not available for nonfeasance—when the defendant failed to perform at all. But Assumpsit also had benefits. Unlike Covenant it did not require a sealed writing, and unlike Debt it did not permit defendants to wage their law. As an offshoot of Trespass, 'that fertile mother of actions,'[327] Assumpsit was tried before a jury. At the time, juries were asked to investigate and discover the facts for themselves. That was an attractive procedural feature in smaller localities, and plaintiffs often preferred writs that involved juries as factfinders. Maitland believed that the writ of Assumpsit eventually triumphed because it offered trial by jury.[328]

Negligence dropped away as an element of Assumpsit at the end of the fifteenth century, and as the writ evolved from a tort claim to an action to enforce promises, courts had to decide which promises to enforce. Consideration became the test, but the old common lawyers kept the concept fluid.

Late in the sixteenth century, consideration increasingly came to mean reciprocity.[329] Perhaps the concept was being modeled on the quid pro quo required in Debt. Eventually, three elements were needed for a suit in Assumpsit: promise, consideration, and breach of promise. As the writ system was abolished over the course of the nineteenth century, the modern cause of action for breach of contract absorbed features from Assumpsit.[330] One of those features was the consideration doctrine.

Slade's Case

Though historians cannot explain the precise origins of the consideration doctrine, we may have better luck appreciating the historical circumstances that made it seem like a good idea. A brief look at *Slade's Case* (1602), one of the common law's great cases, may help us with the context.[331]

[325] For wager of law, see Thayer (1898), pp. 24–34.

[326] For the evolution from Trespass to Assumpsit, see Baker (2019), pp. 427–450; Maitland (1963), pp. 48–50, 65–72; Plucknett (1956), pp. 627–670; Ames (1888).

[327] Maitland (1963), p. 48.

[328] Maitland (1963), pp. 49–50.

[329] Ibbetson (1990), pp. 67–68, 99, 101, 103–104.

[330] For the abolition of the forms of action, see Baker (2019), pp. 74–76.

[331] *Slade's Case* (1602) 4 Co Rep 91a, 92b, 76 Eng Rep 1072, 1074 (KB). For a transcription of the manuscript reports, which include arguments of counsel, see Baker (ed.) (2010), pp. 460–479. The facts, the issue, and the procedure have been simplified. For a more detailed account, see Boyer (2003), pp. 125–134.

In 1595, Humphrey Morley agreed to pay £16 for all the ears of wheat and rye growing on John Slade's close. When Morley refused to complete the purchase, Slade sued in Assumpsit, even though he was suing for a specific sum and actions on a liquidated amount were the province of Debt. Of course, Slade had chosen Assumpsit because he was hoping to prevent Morley from waging his law. The underlying issue was therefore whether Morley should be allowed to escape liability by swearing an oath or whether he should instead have to risk his fate before a jury. The case was argued a number of times over several years. The courts eventually held that Slade could sue in Assumpsit.

The great English jurist Edward Coke (1552–1634),[332] then Attorney General, represented Slade and also drafted one of the surviving case reports. His opponent in this battle of titans, Francis Bacon (1561–1626),[333] the philosopher, politician, and later both Attorney General and Lord Chancellor, represented Morley. Bacon successfully distinguished Coke's precedents,[334] and since each side had good authority, it seems that the case law did not determine the outcome.[335] For our purposes, *Slade's Case* offers a nice example of how the common law can respond to a challenge with 'an astonishing act of judicial legislation.'[336]

Price Revolution

Why did the English courts feel a sudden need around 1600 to create a convenient remedy for breach of contract? It may have had something to do with a striking aspect of the Tudor economy now known as the *price revolution*.[337] Prices rose steeply in England between about 1510 and 1640, with the most dramatic climb taking place in the 1590s,[338] the decade in which *Slade's Case* was argued and Assumpsit triumphed. The price swings led to shortages, famine, and volatile price fluctuations in the grain market, problems aggravated by occasional bad harvests, which were particularly disastrous in the 1580s and 1590s.[339] Several factors drove the unprecedented inflation: population growth pressured food supplies; the currency was debased to facilitate military disbursements; interest rates fell; and the influx of New World silver expanded the money supply.[340]

---

332 For Coke, see Boyer (2003).

333 For Bacon, see Zagorin (1998).

334 Baker (1971), p. 227.

335 Ibbetson (1984), pp. 308–310.

336 Simpson (1958), p. 392.

337 See generally Mayhew (2013); Palliser (1992), pp. 152–186, 219–224; Ramsey (1963), pp. 113–146.

338 Palliser (1992), p. 153, fig. 6.

339 Id., pp. 219–221, fig. 13.

340 Ramsey (1963), p. 145.

Several of the cases that paved the way for the triumph of Assumpsit involved grain sales, and *Slade's Case* illustrates the underlying economic strain. Slade sowed his crop in November 1594. He sold it the following May to Morley, who promised payment in late June.[341] Though prices rose spectacularly in 1595, Morley refused delivery. While buyers usually do not breach in a rising market, the extreme volatility would have made anyone hesitate. With frequent breaches, losses soared and famines became catastrophic. These disastrous social consequences may have led the courts to wonder whether they should provide a remedy for the breach of unexecuted, oral agreements.

Common law courts were able to award lost profits for breach of contract.[342] But as prices oscillated, damages became disproportionate to the value of the transaction, and perjury may have become even more tempting. Courts likely wanted to enforce only those contracts that had actually been made. With written documentation usually unavailable and the parties incompetent to testify, judges would have sought an objective factor, especially if the deal was still unperformed. A quid pro quo would have provided some assurance—and may eventually have suggested the need for something like the consideration doctrine.

This hypothesis, though not implausible, must remain speculative, for I have found nothing in the case law to support it. For our purposes, it is enough to note that, since the original justification for the consideration doctrine remains obscure, we will not have to take it into account as we work to resolve *Webb v. McGowin*.

Uses of the Past

Maitland believed that a rule gets no points for a storied past. We should enforce only those rules that we would enact today: 'Every age should be the mistress of its own law.'[343] When we ask why we have a rule, our concern should be with its current benefits rather than its pedigree. As Corbin explained, 'It lies within the will of the court whether such previously created rule shall or shall not be applied. Even though there be a well-settled rule that has been applied for centuries, still the court may limit or disregard it.'[344]

Here lies a central paradox of the common law. Though we carefully analyze precedent, a rule's respected lineage does not mean that we have to follow it. The past supplies our vocabulary and structures our imagination, but it is often not our friend, and we owe it nothing. 'It ought always to be remembered that historic continuity with the past is not a duty, it is only a necessity.'[345] But if the past has no right

---

[341] For the dating, see Ibbetson (1984), p. 300.

[342] See *Robinson v. Harman* (1848) 1 Ex 850, 855–856, 154 Eng Rep 363, 365.

[343] Maitland (1906), pp. 489–487.

[344] Corbin (1914), p. 238.

[345] Holmes (1920), p. 139.

to determine our present, why do we usually begin our research by looking for precedent? Holmes resolved the paradox by suggesting that we must honor the past—until we reject it.

Maitland was in awe of Holmes—'I am among his worshippers'[346]—and he took the Holmesian paradox seriously. He refined Holmes's solution by proposing a different understanding of what it means to follow precedent: judges respect case law when they engage it in conversation. They pay tribute to earlier cases by exploring the problems our predecessors confronted and their reasons for resolving them as they did. If today's judges feel bound, it is because they agree. But they need not accept yesterday's answers—they are free to decide that a new day has dawned. A judge can honor a precedent by rejecting it.

Role of History

We search for a rule's original justification to help us decide whether it is worth keeping around. It is 'revolting,' Holmes thought, when we enforce a rule even though 'the grounds upon which it was laid down have vanished long since.'[347]

Legal history teaches us when to hold and when to fold. 'To-day we study the day before yesterday, in order that yesterday may not paralyse to-day, and to-day may not paralyse to-morrow.'[348] Legal history is there to 'clear away the rubbish that collects round every body of law.'[349] Maitland was led to this insight by his veneration for the common law, for which he 'came to have an admiration that was akin to love.'[350] Waste management may seem an indecorous role for a legal historian, and yet the task is a constant preoccupation of the great tradition. Posner too recommended that judges remain 'alert to the possibility that a current legal doctrine may be a mere vestige of historical circumstances and should be discarded.'[351]

Dracula

In his lectures on the forms of action, Maitland showed how the past can impose its will if we are unable to find the resolve to resist it, and he announced his insight in one of the common law's most striking sentences: 'The forms of action we have

346 Maitland (1965), pp. 72, 73 (letter no. 74).

347 Holmes (1897), p. 469.

348 Maitland (1901b), p. 439.

349 Maitland (1901a), p. 34.

350 Bell (1965), p. 9.

351 Posner (2008), p. 248.

buried, but they still rule us from their graves.'[352] Let us pause for a moment to enjoy Maitland's surprising Gothic image. I see Bela Lugosi dressed in white tie. He is standing on the landing of a stone staircase in a ruined castle, a lit taper in hand: 'I am... *Dra*-cula.' Both Maitland and Professor Van Helsing, the film's gumshoe, were vampire hunters.[353] They dedicated their lives to discovering hidden lairs, severing heads, and pounding stakes into monster hearts. History was a nightmare from which Maitland was trying to awake.

Alternative

If we were to ditch the consideration doctrine, what would we put in its place? Maitland himself did not pursue the question, but we have learned from him how to approach it. Let us now consider the suggestions of some of those who followed his counsel.

Sir William Holdsworth

We begin with the English legal historian William Holdsworth (1871–1944),[354] who was named Vinerian Professor at Oxford a century and a half after the author of the *Commentaries*. Holdsworth published the seventeen volumes of his *History of English Law* over the course of half a century.[355] His research convinced him that the consideration doctrine was an untenable artifact of archaic law.[356] More interestingly, he briefly laid aside the mantle of historian and interrupted his multi-volume treatise to argue for an alternative, one that he believed would simplify the consideration doctrine and make it easier to administer.[357] In addition to promises supported by consideration, courts should enforce all promises intentionally made—even when unsupported by consideration—as long as they have been recorded in writing and signed by the parties.

Is this the consideration doctrine we need today? Holdsworth's solution leaves the august rule in place but would also allow a writing to satisfy the requirement. As appealing as the proposal may seem, I believe that Holdsworth lost sight of the goal. The task he set for himself was to find a better alternative to the consideration

---

[352] Maitland (1963), p. 2.

[353] The film is Tod Browning's *Dracula* (1931). For the novel, see Stoker (2003). For Stoker, see Belford (1996).

[354] For Holdsworth, see Hanbury (2004); Baker (1984).

[355] Holdsworth (1922–72).

[356] See Holdsworth (1937), pp. 1–48.

[357] See id., pp. 47–48.

doctrine. But at the last minute, he took his eye off the ball and decided instead to simplify the rule and make it easier to administer. His solution ignores the lessons of the legal history he so brilliantly chronicled, particularly the fact that the common law is singularly uninterested in clear rules that can be applied without deliberation.

In fact, Holdsworth's proposal demonstrates why the common law dislikes abstract propositions. It ignores the consideration doctrine's main vocation, which is to distinguish promises made in the market—and therefore properly governed by contract law—from those that emerge from the gift economy and that are often best considered elements of social relationships. If courts were to enforce all serious promises reduced to writing, some gift promises would be swept up into the mix, even when the relationship has changed and the gift no longer makes sense.

In the end, Holdsworth adds arbitrary distinctions to those we have inherited and still does not solve the problem. 'The real question for the courts is what promises shall be enforced, not what is a sufficient consideration.'[358]

Lord Mansfield

Let us now seek advice from Blackstone's contemporary, William Murray, 1st Earl of Mansfield and Lord Chief Justice of King's Bench (1705–1793),[359] one of England's great judges.[360] Lord Mansfield agreed with Maitland: when a rule is no longer appropriate, a court can and should disregard it.[361] As for the consideration doctrine, Lord Mansfield preferred the civilian theory of *causa*, which he believed was a better fit for a modern economy. When deciding whether to enforce a promise, common law judges should take all relevant circumstances into account, and while a quid pro quo usually provides grounds for enforcement, it should not be an absolute requirement.

Lord Mansfield approved of the doctrine of moral consideration. 'Where [someone] is under a moral obligation, which no Court of Law or Equity can inforce, and promises, the honesty and rectitude of the thing is a consideration.'[362] Lord Mansfield's colleague, Justice Francis Buller (1746–1800),[363] stated the principle more broadly: 'Wherever a defendant is under a moral obligation, or is liable in conscience and equity to pay, that is a sufficient consideration.'[364]

---

[358] Corbin (1937), p. 453.

[359] For Lord Mansfield, see Poser (2013); Fifoot (1936).

[360] Holdsworth (1938), p. 161.

[361] Id., p. 167.

[362] *Hawkes v Saunders* (1782), 1 Cowp 289, 290, 98 Eng Rep 1091, 1091 (KB) (Mansfield J).

[363] For Buller, see Oldham (2004).

[364] *Hawkes v Saunders*, p. 1093. These sentences are dictum, for in the case before the court, there was sufficient consideration. See Swain (2005), p. 64; see *Hawkes v Saunders*, pp. 1093–1094 (Buller J) ('for here is both a loss to the plaintiff, and a benefit to the defendant').

Bosanquet and Puller

Shortly after Lord Mansfield died in 1793, two young English barristers, John Bosanquet (1773–1847)[365] and Christopher Puller (1774–1824),[366] decided to investigate whether there was authority for the proposition that moral obligation may serve as consideration. The two had been together at Eton, at Christ Church in Oxford, and again at Lincoln's Inn, and were at the time publishing influential reports of cases decided in Common Pleas. Both later became distinguished jurists—Bosanquet as a judge of Common Pleas, Puller briefly as Chief Justice of Bengal.

Their research convinced them that there was no case law support for the idea. The older cases did not mention moral obligation, and in those few recent cases that did, the doctrine added nothing. When a court enforced a subsequent promise to reciprocate, there was always more to the facts than a moral duty. Often a legally enforceable agreement had been suspended by the statute of limitations or by discharge in bankruptcy. In such cases, the subsequent promise was thought to revive the earlier legal obligation and waive the barrier to enforcement. In other cases, the beneficiary had requested the services before they were rendered, and the subsequent promise confirmed that a promise to pay was implicit in the initial request. When necessaries were supplied to an infant, a prior request was implied.[367] No English court had ever held that a simple moral obligation satisfied the consideration doctrine. The two barristers were proud of their discovery and published it in a detailed note to their report of *Wennall v. Adney*, a case from 1802.[368]

Wennall v. Adney

In *Wennall*, a servant broke his arm while he was driving a team of horses that belonged to his mistress. A bystander called in the lady's usual surgeon, but nothing was said of the fee. The surgeon sent his bill to the lady, she refused to pay, and the surgeon sued. The mistress had not promised to reimburse the surgeon, and the court rejected the surgeon's claim. In fact, the lady made no promise at all, and the doctrine of consideration had nothing to do with the case. Why then did the two young lawyers choose to append their learned note—which examined whether a moral obligation might serve as consideration—to precisely this case?

---

[365] For Bosanquet, see Barker (2004).

[366] For Puller, see Rigg (2004).

[367] See *Cooper v. Martin* (1803) 4 East 76, 102 Eng Rep 759, 761 (Ellenborough CJ).

[368] *Wennall v. Adney*, (1802) 3 Bos & Pul 247, 249 note (a), 127 Eng Rep 137, 138 note (a). For the argument that the note inaccurately reported the state of the case law, see Stoljar (1990). For a summary of this area of American law at the time, see E.L.P. (1854).

I can imagine the scene. The two lawyers were taking notes for their reports when Serjeant-at-Law John Williams (1757–1810),[369] the English barrister and well-known editor of Blackstone's *Commentaries,* rose for the surgeon. In the case at bar, Williams argued, the fact that the mistress had not subsequently promised to pay for the surgeon's services was irrelevant. A promise made after services have been rendered is always gratuitous and never enforceable. The notion of moral obligation, he explained, concerns a different question: did the surgeon's actions yield such a benefit to the mistress that, if she retained the benefit, she would be morally obligated to pay for it? 'It is not necessary that the mistress in this case should have made an express promise, for if she were liable there was no need of a promise to bind her; and if she were not liable, the promise would be nudum pactum [unenforceable].'[370]

The two young jurists stopped writing and looked at each other. The real question was hiding behind the one that everyone had been debating. Without more, a promise of recompense made after services are rendered is gratuitous and cannot be enforced. The actual question has nothing to do with the promise; it is whether a beneficiary (the lady, McGowin) has a legal duty to pay for services rendered without request. Serjeant Williams was arguing that the mistress owed compensation to the surgeon for the simple reason that he had provided services to her servant. As the good serjeant knew, the law was against him. Lord Mansfield himself had earlier held that a mistress was not deemed to have benefited from care rendered to her servant.[371] The overseers of the local parish were responsible for accidents occurring in their jurisdiction, and since they had received the benefit, perhaps payment could be requested of them.

Negotiorum Gestio

A house catches fire while the owner is away, and a passerby rushes in with an extinguisher. As a rampaging river threatens to engulf a car, a tow truck driver swims out to the vehicle, hooks a line to it, and pulls it to higher ground. A hurricane threatens, and a benevolent neighbor braves the wind to move the animals to shelter and close the storm shutters. Should the beneficiary have to pay compensation for these marvelous actions? And what if, as a result of the good deed, harm has come to the hero or the hero's possessions? The world's two major legal systems answer these questions differently.

Civil law jurisdictions support virtuous behavior, such as the emergency rescue of another's life or property. Provided that the rescue corresponds to the

---

[369] For Williams, see Carlyle (2004).

[370] *Wennall v. Adney*, 127 Eng Rep, p. 138 (reporting the argument of Serjeant Williams).

[371] *Newby v. Wiltshire*, (1784) 2 Esp 739, 170 Eng Rep 515, 516 (1785) 4 Dougl 284, 99 Eng Rep 883, 884 (Mansfield CJ). See also *Wennall v. Adney*, 127 Eng Rep, p. 137 (Lord Alvanley ChJ).

beneficiary's actual or probable wishes, the benefactor can recover expenses. The legal institution that governs the case is derived from the Roman law concept of *negotiorum gestio*—taking charge for another's benefit.[372] The common law of restitution, in contrast, does not generally allow recovery for benefits conferred without request. 'The law will never permit a friendly act, or such as was intended to be an act of kindness or benevolence, to be afterwards converted into a pecuniary demand.'[373] The common law rule respects the Holmesian view that individuals—here the beneficiaries of unrequested emergency services—should be allowed to determine for themselves what they owe their benefactors.

Human Life

'And so,' John Dawson (1902–1985)[374] wrote in a masterly article, 'we come to the ultimate, painful question:'[375] when a rescuer saves a human life, should we prefer the civil or the common law? If the rescuer is injured during the rescue, should we require the beneficiary to pay for the rescuer's medical care and loss of income? And if the rescuer perishes, should the rescuer's family be awarded an indemnity? 'In attempting to answer such a question, anyone must hesitate, for it provides a crucial test of our moral values and of the obligations of individuals to the community under the mounting perils of modern life.'[376]

Some civilian systems award recovery in these situations.[377] German law, for example, would favor the rescuer in our three rescue cases (*Mills*, *Harrington*, and *Webb*), even without the subsequent promise.[378] 'Whoever acts to assist an injured person or anyone in danger... thereby manages the affairs of the injured or threatened person.'[379] The idea is that rescue should be encouraged—it has high ethical value and benefits all members of society.[380]

---

[372] See Kortmann (2005), pp. 99–102; Dawson (1961a), pp. 817–823.

[373] *Glenn v. Savage*, 13 P. 442, 448 (Or. 1887). Despite the expansive language in the black letter, the Restatement approves the limitations suggested in *Glenn*. Compare Restatement (Third) of Restitution and Unjust Enrichment § 21 with that section's comment c, illus. 8 and Reporter's Note c (2011).

[374] For Dawson, see Harvey et al. (1986).

[375] Dawson (1961b), p. 156.

[376] Id., p. 154.

[377] See Stoljar (1984), secs. 242–257, pp. 141–152; Dawson (1961a), pp. 1095–1129.

[378] For a German case in some respects similar to *Harrington v. Taylor*, see BGH 7 Nov. 1960 – VII ZR 82/59, BGHZ 33, 251.

[379] Bergmann (2020), Vorbemerkung zu §§ 677ff, Rn. 150, p. 102 (translation).

[380] Koch (2011), pp. 207–208. For relevant cases in the law of Germany and other European countries, see id., pp. 203–217. Recent German case law generally limits the rescuer's recovery to expenses not covered by Germany's extensive social services laws. Id., pp. 210–211. For model principles, see von Bar (2006), art. 1:101, pp. 101–172.

In today's common law, in contrast, there is one rule when health care professionals provide services and a different rule for pretty much everyone else. A physician who provides emergency medical care may generally recover in restitution.[381] The usual justification is that a healthcare professional intends to charge for the services. For everyone else, the common law sticks to its principles: victims are not required to pay a rescuer's out-of-pocket expenses, and there seems to be no support for compensating the rescuer for injury or loss of life.[382] 'Surely for many acts of neighborly help, though inconvenience and risk may be involved, one must be prepared to say that reimbursement by the person in peril is neither needed nor deserved.'[383]

Promise of Recompense

Does it change the calculus if the beneficiary later promises to compensate the rescuer? The Restatement (Second) of Contracts suggests that it should. As the Restatement sees it, the subsequent promise confirms that the claim was not fabricated and also that the victim experienced the rescue as a benefit.[384] Unfortunately, the Restatement's reasoning seems beside the point, for establishing these two facts does not make the case any easier. The risk of fraud and the uncertainty about whether the rescue was beneficial do not arise in most rescue cases, and in any case they are not the hard questions that we have been working on.

One challenging issue is whether the beneficiary intended to make a binding commitment. If the answer is yes, an equally difficult question is whether the courts should enforce it. If the case comes up after the promisor has had a change of heart, enforcing the promise does not differ much from requiring compensation in the first place, which the common law has decided not to do. In such cases, providing a remedy probably does not fit the common law's mission statement:[385] 'If a man does a heroic act and is a mere volunteer, he cannot recover; nor can a subsequent promise to pay him be the basis of a recovery.'[386]

[381] See *Greenspan v. Slate*, 97 A.2d 390 (N.J. 1953); *Cotnam v. Wisdom*, 104 S.W. 164 (Ark. 1907).

[382] McInness (1994), p. 42.

[383] Dawson (1961a), p. 1125.

[384] Restatement (Second) of Contracts § 86 comment d (1981).

[385] For the argument that these promises should be enforced, see Henderson (1971), pp. 1154–1184; Note (1939), pp. 124–130.

[386] *State ex rel. Morgan v. Rusk*, 174 N.E. 142, 143 (Ohio App. 1930).

Baron Denman

In 1840, as the writ system was being dismantled and the foundations laid for the modern law of contract, English courts expressly refused to expand the doctrine of consideration. Baron Denman (1779–1854),[387] then Lord Chief Justice, relied on the perceptive note by Bosanquet and Puller to resolve the issue once and for all. He held that a promise of recompense will not be enforced if the sole consideration is moral obligation.[388]

Denman recognized that all promises intentionally and voluntarily made are 'commonly understood to have binding moral force.'[389] Allowing moral obligation to serve as consideration, therefore, 'would annihilate the necessity for any consideration at all, inasmuch as the mere fact of giving a promise creates a moral obligation to perform it.'[390]

Kessler's View

But what about the consideration doctrine itself? If we were writing on a clean slate, would we keep it? It is certainly a troublemaker. And if we decide to get rid of it, what would we put in its place—how would we figure out which promises to enforce?

As we conclude this discussion, let us turn to Kessler for advice. He would not have hesitated: he would have advised us to flip the script and abolish the consideration doctrine. Courts should enforce all promises that are intended to be legally binding. Attention would then shift to the important issue of making sure that the promises before the court are not seriously unfair or induced by improper conduct.

Kessler believed deeply in *freedom of contract*:[391] we should be free to make whatever promises we wish to make—and, if we choose, to make those promises legally binding. His co-author, Malcolm Sharp (1897–1980),[392] suggested that the burden of proof should be on those who oppose enforcement. 'Promises should be enforced unless some intelligible and controlling practical reason for not enforcing them is made to appear.'[393]

Kessler also thought that the consideration doctrine fails at the one thing it is asked to do—decide which promises courts should enforce. The preexisting duty rule is a great example. The rule can protect a party who, in a vulnerable moment,

---

[387] For Baron Denman, see Arnould (1873).

[388] *Eastwood v. Kenyon*, (1840) 11 Ad & E 438, 450, 113 Eng Rep 482, 486.

[389] Sacks (2001), p. 28.

[390] *Eastwood v. Kenyon*, 113 Eng Rep, p. 486.

[391] Kessler (1982), pp. 6–8.

[392] For Sharp, see Casper (1981); Kalven (1966).

[393] Sharp (1941), p. 785.

agrees to a one-sided modification, but it embarrasses itself when it gets in the way of modifications that make eminent commercial sense. The question of whether a contract was imposed by a stronger party on a weaker one should be discussed in terms of the defense of duress.

Once again we are arguing about different conceptions of freedom. As we remember, Holmes defended the consideration doctrine as a way to shelter a realm of private decision-making from judicial control. Kessler was also committed to freedom, but he had a different priority. He wanted to ensure that we can decide for ourselves which of our commitments should have legal force. Both Holmes and Kessler saw in the consideration doctrine a principle able to advance human freedom. They disagreed only about which freedom mattered more.

Webb v. McGowin

If we adopt Kessler's approach, how would we decide *Webb v. McGowin*? We would enforce every promise that was intended to be binding unless we find a good reason not to. As I write that sentence, the clouds part and light floods the plain. McGowin's promise was meant to be taken seriously. We have every reason to enforce it and no reason not to—except for the black-letter of the consideration doctrine itself. For Malcolm Sharp, *Webb* was not difficult: 'There is a promise, and it is not made under such circumstances that any intelligible policy would be served by denying its enforceability.'[394] It delights me when I think of the two of them. Kessler and Sharp had found their way to the land of milk and honey where the consideration doctrine has been put out to pasture and *Webb* is an easy case.

Seamless Web

The past is always trying to impose itself on the future. That thought of Maitland's is one of the great tradition's most compelling achievements. But if the idea is misconstrued, we lose the common law's essential connection to history. Though we want neither the rules nor our elders to order us around, we do best when we take advantage of their insights. Maturity, I was once reminded, is the ability to follow our parents' advice, even when it is right.

When the time comes to innovate in the law, we do not simply discard what we do not like. We ask instead how to get from where we are to where we want to be. We find the same insight in the volumes that Pollock and Maitland devoted to the history of early English law and that they summarized in one of the most memorable opening sentences in the record of historical writing: 'Such is the unity of all history

[394] Sharp (1941), p. 789 (discussing *Webb v. McGowin*).

that any one who endeavours to tell a piece of it must feel that his first sentence tears a seamless web.'[395]

If we abolish the consideration doctrine, we would have no trouble deciding *Webb*. Our task, however, is to figure out how to get *Webb* right while continuing to respect that pillar of the common law. We are getting there, but it will take a bit more work. 'The past is never dead. It's not even past.'[396] Those sentences in Faulkner's novel were spoken—and not by chance—by a lawyer.

References

Ames J (1888) The history of assumpsit. Harvard Law Review 2:1–18, 53–69
Ames J (1913) Lectures on legal history and miscellaneous legal essays, with a memoir. Harvard University Press, Cambridge
Arnould J (1873) Memoir of Thomas, First Lord Denman, formerly Lord Chief Justice of England, 2 vols. Longmans, Green, London
Baker J (1971) New light on *Slade's Case*. Cambridge Law Journal 29:51–67, 213–236
Baker J (1984) Holdsworth, Sir William Searle. In: Simpson A (ed) Biographical dictionary of the common law. Butterworths, London, pp 247–249
Baker J (ed) (2010) Baker and Milsom, Sources of English legal history: Private law to 1750, 2d edn. Oxford University Press, Oxford
Baker J (2013) Origins of the 'doctrine' of consideration 1535–1585. In: Baker J (ed) Collected papers on English legal history, vol. 3. Cambridge University Press, Cambridge, pp 1176–1201
Baker J (2019) An introduction to English legal history, 5th edn. Oxford University Press, Oxford
von Bar C (2006) Principles of European law on benevolent intervention in another's affairs (PEL Ben. Int.), Swann S, McGuire M (trans). Sellier, Munich
Barbour W (1914) The history of contract in early English equity. Clarendon Press, Oxford
Barker G (2004) Bosanquet, Sir John Bernard. Matthew H, Harrison B (eds) Oxford dictionary of national biography, vol 6. Oxford University Press, Oxford, p 695
Belford B (1996) Bram Stoker: A biography of the author of Dracula. Knopf, New York
Bell H (1965) Maitland: A critical examination and assessment. Harvard University Press, Cambridge
Bergmann A (2020) J. von Staudingers Kommentar zum Bürgerlichen Gesetzbuch, Buch 2: Recht der Schuldverhältnisse §§ 677-704. Otto Schmidt/De Gruyter, Frankfurt am Main
Boyer A (2003) Sir Edward Coke and the Elizabethan age. Stanford University Press, Stanford
Cantor N (1991) Inventing the Middle Ages: The lives, works, and ideas of the great medievalists of the twentieth century. William Morrow, New York
Carlyle E (2004) Williams, John. In: Matthew H, Harrison B (eds) Oxford dictionary of national biography, Brown R (rev), vol. 59. Oxford University Press, Oxford, p. 241
Casper G (1981) In memoriam: Malcolm P. Sharp. University of Chicago Law Review 48:1–5
Chaytor A, Whittaker W (1909) Preface to the first edition. In: Maitland (1936), pp v–vi
Corbin A (1914) The law and the judges. Yale Review 3:234–250
Corbin A (1937) Recent developments in the law of contracts. Harvard Law Review 50:449–475
Dawson J (1961a) Negotiorum gestio: The altruistic intermeddler. Harvard Law Review 74: 817–865, 1073–1129

[395] Pollock and Maitland (1968), vol. 1, p. 1.

[396] Faulkner (1951), p. 92.

Dawson J (1961b) Rewards for the rescue of human life? In: Nadelmann K et al (eds) XXth century comparative and conflicts law: Legal essays in honor of Hessel E. Yntema. A. W. Sythoff, Leyden, pp 142–159
E.L.P. (1854) The consideration of a contract. American Law Register 2:449–459
Elton G (1985) F.W. Maitland. Weidenfeld and Nicolson, London
Faulkner W (1951) Requiem for a nun. Random House, New York
Fifoot C (1936) Lord Mansfield. Clarendon Press, Oxford
Fifoot C (1971) Frederic William Maitland: A life. Harvard University Press, Cambridge
Hanbury H (2004) Holdsworth, Sir William Searle. Matthew H, Harrison B (eds) Oxford dictionary of national biography, Ibbetson D (rev), vol. 27. Oxford University Press, Oxford, pp 630–632
Harvey W et al (1986) In memoriam: John Philip Dawson. Harvard Law Review 99:1113–1125
Henderson S (1971) Promises grounded in the past: The idea of unjust enrichment and the law of contracts. Virginia Law Review 57:1115–1184
Holdsworth W (1922–72) A history of English law, different edns. Little, Brown, Boston
Holdsworth W (1937) A history of English law, vol. 8, 2d edn. Metheun, London
Holdsworth W (1938) Some makers of English law. Cambridge University Press, Cambridge
Holmes O (1897) The path of the law. Harvard Law Review 10:457–478
Holmes O (1920) Learning and science. In: Collected legal papers, [Laski H (ed)]. Harcourt, Brace, New York, pp 138–140
Hyland R (1995) Life, death, and contract. Northwestern University Law Review 90:204–218
Ibbetson D (1984) Sixteenth century contract law: *Slade's Case* in context. Oxford Journal of Legal Studies 4:295–317
Ibbetson D (1990) Consideration and the theory of contract in sixteenth century common law. In: Barton J (ed) Towards a general law of contract. Duncker & Humblot, Berlin, pp 67–123
Kalven H (1966) For M.P.S. University of Chicago Law Review 33:193–95
Kessler F (1982) Grant Gilmore as I remember him. Yale Law Journal 92:4–5
Koch S (2011) Unaufgeforderte Hilfeleistung in Notsituationen: Eine rechtshistorische und rechtsvergleichende Studie zu den zivilrechtlichen Aspekten der Nothilfe mit besonderer Berücksichtigung des Rechts der Geschäftsführung ohne Auftrag. Peter Lang, Frankfurt am Main
Kortmann J (2005) Altruism in private law: Liability for nonfeasance and negotiorum gestio. Oxford University Press, Oxford
Laske C (2020) Law, language and change: A diachronic semantic analysis of *consideration* in the common law. Brill Nijhoff, Leiden
Llewellyn K (1931f) What price contract?—an essay in perspective. Yale Law Journal 40:704–751
Maine H (1891) Dissertations on early law and custom, new edn. John Murray, London
Maitland F (1901a) English law and the Renaissance. University Press, Cambridge
Maitland F (1901b) A survey of the century. In: Maitland F (1911) 3:432–439
Maitland F (1906) The making of the German Civil Code. In: Maitland F (1911) 3:476–488
Maitland F (1911) The collected papers of Frederic William Maitland, Fisher H (ed), 3 vols. Cambridge University Press, Cambridge
Maitland F (1936) Equity: A course of lectures, Chaytor A, Whittaker W (eds), Brunyate J (rev), 2d edn. Cambridge University Press, Cambridge
Maitland F (1963) The forms of action at common law: A course of lectures. Cambridge University Press, Cambridge
Maitland F (1965) The letters of Frederic William Maitland, Fifoot C (ed), vol. 1. Selden Society, London
Mayhew N (2013) Prices in England, 1170–1750. Past & Present 219:3–39
McInness M (1994) Restitution and the rescue of life. Alberta Law Review 32:37–70
Milsom S (1958) Trespass from Henry III to Edward III, parts 1–3. Law Quarterly Review 74: 195–224, 407–436, 561–590
Milsom S (1968) Introduction. In: Pollock & Maitland (1968), vol. 1, pp xxiii–lxxiii
Morris M (2009) A great and terrible king: Edward I and the forging of Britain. Pegasus, New York
Note (1939) Promissory obligations based on past benefits or other moral consideration. University of Chicago Law Review 7:124–136

Oldham J (2004) Buller, Sir Francis, first baronet. In: Matthew H, Harrison B (eds) Oxford dictionary of national biography, vol. 8. Oxford University Press, Oxford, pp 617–619
Palliser D (1992) The age of Elizabeth: England under the later Tudors 1547–1603, 2d edn. Longman, London
Plucknett T (1956) A concise history of the common law, 5th edn. Little, Brown, Boston
Pollock F, Maitland F (1968) The history of English law before the time of Edward I, Milsom S (ed), 2d edn, 2 vols. Cambridge University Press, Cambridge
Poser N (2013) Lord Mansfield: Justice in the age of reason. McGill-Queen's University Press, Montreal
Posner R (2008) How judges think. Harvard University Press, Cambridge
Ramsey P (1963) Tudor economic problems. Victor Gollancz, London
Rigg J (2004) Puller, Sir Christopher. Matthew H, Harrison B (eds) Oxford dictionary of national biography, Potier J (rev), vol. 45. Oxford University Press, Oxford, p 539
Sacks D (2001) The promise and the contract in early modern England: *Slade's Case* in perspective. In: Kahn V, Hutson L (eds) Rhetoric and law in early modern Europe. Yale University Press, New Haven, pp 28–53
Sharp M (1941) Pacta sunt servanda. Columbia Law Review 41:783–798
Simpson A (1958) The place of *Slade's Case* in the history of contract. Law Quarterly Review 74:381–396
Stoker B (2003) Dracula [1897], Hindle M (ed), rev edn. Penguin, London
Stoljar S (1984) Negotiorum gestio. In: von Caemmerer E, Schlechtriem P (eds) International encyclopedia of comparative law, vol. 10, chap. 17
Stoljar S (1990) No obituary for *Wennall v Adney*. Journal of Legal History 11:250–269
Swain W (2005) The changing nature of the doctrine of consideration, 1750-1850. Journal of Legal History 26:55–72
Thayer J (1898) A preliminary treatise on evidence at the common law. Little, Brown, Boston
Van Caenegem R (1988) The birth of the English common law, 2d edn. Cambridge University Press, Cambridge
Zagorin P (1998) Francis Bacon. Princeton University Press, Princeton

Chapter 8
Imagination (Cardozo)

'And today at last Cardozo (my successor) came to luncheon—with his beautiful face and nature.'[397] Holmes was writing to his friend Harold Laski shortly after Cardozo's appointment to the U. S. Supreme Court. Laski was sorry that he could not join them. The newly appointed justice 'is a beautiful nature in every sense of the word.'[398] *Beautiful* is not often used to describe a man in correspondence, especially not when writing about a lawyer. Yet the word regularly surfaces when Cardozo's name is mentioned, sometimes in the pen of those who may have written the term only a handful of times. Justice Stone, for example: 'The recollection of a life so useful, so complete, so beautiful....'[399] Or Chief Justice Hughes: 'With us who had the privilege of daily association there will ever abide the precious memory not only of the work of a great jurist but of companionship with a beautiful spirit.'[400]

A Gentler Voice

Benjamin Cardozo (1870–1938)[401] enrolled in the Columbia Law School but left without a degree, staying only the two years necessary to allow him to sit for the bar exam. After practicing for more than twenty years as an appellate advocate, he was

397 Letter from Oliver Wendell Holmes to Harold Laski (May 3, 1932), in Holmes and Laski (1953), vol. 2, p. 1382.

398 Letter from Harold Laski to Oliver Wendell Holmes (May 16, 1932), in Holmes and Laski (1953), vol. 2, p. 1385.

399 Stone (1939), vol. 39, p. 3, vol. 52, p. 355, vol. 48, p. 373.

400 Charles E. Hughes, C.J., 'Proceedings in Memory of Mr. Justice Cardozo' (Dec. 19, 1938), reprinted in 305 U.S. v, xxviii (1938).

401 For Cardozo, see Kaufman (1998); Polenberg (1997); Posner (1990a).

R. Hyland, *Common Law Judging and the Great Tradition*, Ius Gentium: Comparative Perspectives on Law and Justice 100,
https://doi.org/10.1007/978-3-032-02307-0_8

appointed to a temporary position on the New York Court of Appeals, the state's high court. He was later elected to a regular seat and eventually served as chief judge. President Herbert Hoover, a Republican, named Cardozo, a Democrat, to succeed Holmes on the U.S. Supreme Court.

A few months after Cardozo's death, the country's three leading law reviews—Harvard, Yale, and Columbia—published the same portfolio of tributes to the great justice on identical pages.[402] That was a first, and it has not been repeated. The esteem was owed partly to Cardozo's personal qualities—'He is gone, and while the west is still lighted with his radiance, it is well for us to pause and take count of our own coarser selves'[403]—but also to the fact that Cardozo had almost single-handedly nudged American jurisprudence toward a new understanding of itself. Cardozo agreed with Holmes that rules alone cannot decide cases, but the two justices differed in their sense of craft.

Holmes was bold, direct, and aphoristic—'Three strokes, and he has said all that he sees, said most that there will be to see for half a century.'[404] During the Civil War, Confederate sharpshooters attacked Fort Stevens while Holmes was serving there. As bullets whizzed by—the story is perhaps apocryphal—Holmes noticed a civilian peering over the parapet. He yelled at the fellow, called him 'a damn fool,' and ordered him to get down before he got shot. President Lincoln, the civilian, got down and stayed down.[405] Whether Holmes was writing for the majority or in dissent, his thought was as clear as a trumpet blast and just as imposing. 'All is ready. Bugler, blow the charge.'[406]

Cardozo wrote in a gentler voice, different from anything else in the long history of the common law. As a lawyer's lawyer, he had learned to present legal argument with previously unknown subtlety—'with deft fingers and imaginative mind'[407]—but even as a judge, he could not still his inquiring intellect. While a Holmesian opinion seems to end the discussion, a Cardozian judgment presents the real question for the first time.

Over the years, law professors have subjected Cardozo's mysterious opinions to sentence-by-sentence *explications de texte*.[408] The articles are inevitably longer than the opinions they examine, and the secret remains unrevealed. Something in the facts triggered a thought in Cardozo's mind. He followed the trail until it petered out in a meadow, then wandered along whatever path or brook he found there, pursuing 'tentative gropings towards the inductive apprehension of a truth imperfectly discerned.'[409]

[402] Stone et al. (1939).

[403] Hand (1939), vol. 39, p. 11, vol. 52, p. 363, vol. 48, p. 381.

[404] Llewellyn (1931d), p. 902.

[405] White (1993), pp. 64–65; McPherson (1988), p. 757; see also Donald (1995), p. 519.

[406] Holmes (1962), p. 157.

[407] Douglas (1962), p. 612.

[408] For *Allegheny College*, see Bridgeman (2005); Townsend (1996); Konefsky (1987). For *MacPherson v. Buick Motor Co.*, see Zipursky and Goldberg (2016). For commentary to *De Cicco v. Schweizer*, see Corbin (1918).

[409] Cardozo (1931a), p. 342.

He saw a meaningful pattern in incomplete and incompatible ideas and miraculously conjured an aura to complete the composition, even when none of its individual elements would persuade on its own.[410]

Magician

I was once lucky enough to experience the performance of a renowned magician in an intimate setting. He took his place behind the narrow table in front of us and introduced himself. He was quiet, middle aged, and professional. He began by rolling up his shirt and jacket sleeves together. He would not be hiding anything there. Next he took a silver dollar from his jacket pocket, examined both sides briefly, and dropped it on the table. He immediately picked it up and held it out to us between his thumb and index finger. Unsmiling and unhurried, he moved his outstretched arm before us from left to right and back again. Once he had our attention, he closed his palm over the coin and immediately reopened it. The coin was gone. 'Wait!' someone called out. 'Could you please do that again? But... more slowly this time.' Now he smiled. He would be crazy to oblige us. We would be watching his every move. Amazingly, he agreed. He did it again, just like the first time, though perhaps even more slowly, teasing us, implicitly challenging us to find the trick. He reopened his hand. The coin was really gone.

Allegheny College

For those who have not read Cardozo's opinion in the *Allegheny College* case, the facts are straightforward.[411] Mary Yates Johnston pledged in writing that her estate would pay the college $5000 thirty days after her death. She asked that the fund bear her name and serve to educate students preparing for the ministry. Two years later, she made a down payment of $1000. The following year, for reasons best known to her, she revoked. Thirty days after her death, the college sued to recover the outstanding balance.

Johnston's pledge was a gift promise. Gift promises not made under seal are generally not enforceable at law.[412] 'The promise when first made was a promise of a gift for a specified purpose and was not then binding.'[413] It is hard to find a bargain on those facts, and yet if the college cannot prove either bargain or reliance, it cannot win the lawsuit. Cardozo nonetheless enforced her pledge. How he did so is still

[410] See, e.g., *Graf v. Hope Bldg. Corp.*, 171 N.E. 884, 886 (N.Y. 1930) (Cardozo, C.J., dissenting).

[411] *Allegheny Coll. v. Nat'l Chautauqua Cnty. Bank*, 159 N.E. 173 (N.Y. 1927) (Cardozo, C.J.).

[412] See Hyland (2012) para. 696-703, pp 340–343.

[413] Corbin (1939), vol. 39, p. 65, vol. 52, p. 417, vol. 48, p. 435 (discussing *Allegheny College*).

a mystery, though of course it is written down in black and white. He invoked a number of ideas, and when they are considered together, enforcing the promise seems to make sense.

Cardozo began by noting that New York courts were often willing to find consideration for charitable subscriptions (gift promises made to charitable institutions), and he then invoked the equitable doctrine of promissory estoppel, even though the college's reliance was minimal and equity would not have enforced the promise. He cast doubt on the usefulness of the consideration doctrine and mentioned other concepts and doctrines that suggest that promises lacking in consideration may sometimes be enforced. As he raced for the finish line, he announced that the promise was obviously supported by consideration: the college had accepted Johnston's down payment, established the fund that she requested, and named it in her honor.

In dissent, two of the court's seven judges pointed to the obvious fact that Mary Yates Johnston had not been looking for a bargain but had instead made a conditional gift promise. Since the condition had been fulfilled, the college could keep the down payment,[414] but it could not sue for the remainder.[415] Cardozo, however, interpreted the college's fulfilment of the condition as something akin to consideration and required Johnston's trustees to complete the promised gift. Cardozo's opinion is artful and I recommend it, especially 'for the characteristically Byzantine subtlety of the reasoning'[416]—and the opportunity to match wits with a great judge.

The Restatement (Second) of Contracts later concluded that charitable subscriptions may be enforceable.[417] The provision creates an exception not only to the consideration doctrine but also to the reliance requirement for promissory estoppel. The learned restaters justified the exception by noting that 'American courts have traditionally favored charitable subscriptions.'[418]

Storrs Lectures

In 1920, Cardozo was invited to give the Storrs Lectures at the Yale Law School, the most prestigious lecture series in American law. Cardozo responded with *The Nature of the Judicial Process*, one of the essential books of the American canon. The question Cardozo put to his distinguished audience seems to be precisely our question: 'What is it that I do when I decide a case?'[419]

---

[414] *Sipko v. Koger, Inc.*, 70 A.3d 512, 519 (N.J. 2013).

[415] 'If the promisor merely intends to make a gift to the promisee upon the performance of a condition, the promise is gratuitous and the satisfaction of the condition is not consideration for a contract.' *Stelmack v. Glen Alden Coal Co.*, 14 A.2d 127, 129 (Pa. 1940).

[416] Kessler and Gilmore (1972), p. 31 (discussing the *Allegheny College* case).

[417] See Restatement (Second) of Contract § 90(2) and illus. 17 (1981).

[418] Id. comment f.

[419] Cardozo (1921b), p. 10.

I have never felt as grateful for a sentence as I did the first time I came across that one. Kessler had recommended Cardozo's book, but as a first-year law student I did not yet feel the urgency. The pressure increased each year I taught contracts. I had figured out something to say about most of the cases in Kessler's casebook, but not *Allegheny College*. Not only could I not square it with the consideration doctrine, I could not even reconstruct Cardozo's argument. 'Professor, what exactly does the case stand for?' I had nothing meaningful to offer.

If I could put the method question to anyone who ever lived, I would choose to ask it of Cardozo. At the time he delivered those lectures, he was the acknowledged master of the modern form of the judicial opinion, a form that, for all practical purposes, he invented.

But Cardozo did not respond as I was expecting. That is because, when read as I was reading it, the question has no answer. Cardozo posed the question as he did not because he thought he could answer it but because he knew that many members of his audience thought they could. He was intimating that they had been thinking about the problem in the wrong way, but because he possessed a legendarily beautiful spirit, he would do nothing to deflate their self-confidence.

Instead of a method, Cardozo was modeling for his audience the thought process that took over when he was asked to decide a case. 'Show, don't tell,' the writing instructor urges. The reader who follows Cardozo step by step has not a technique to show for it but an experience. He recreated for his audience what happened as he turned his attention to a legal question and irreconcilable elements arose in his mind. The judge's basic task, Cardozo suggested, is to remain alive to the ideas about law and fact that flood the psyche—and Posner mentioned some of the factors: 'legal doctrine, institutional constraints, policy preferences, strategic considerations, and the equities of the case, all mixed together and all mediated by temperament, experience, ambition, and other personal factors.'[420] Everything, in other words, but the kitchen sink.

Whispers

The longer I think about Cardozo's approach, the more troubling it becomes. It is one thing for you and me to feel the pull of the facts and experience the thrill as a case decides itself inside us. Most of us are not charged with deciding cases. But we expect those who do this for a living to have precise tools. It is chilling when Cardozo, our great judge, admits that precision is not part of the equation and that the process is not guided by rules or methods. It is even more unsettling to note that, as Cardozo describes the process, no one is actually doing anything. The judge is simply present as the miracle of the imagination does its work. It is enjoyable to imagine a fiction writer hurrying to jot down what the characters are whispering, but

[420] Posner (2008), pp. 84–85.

it is disconcerting when a great judge implies that legal method can be reduced to logging the thoughts that emerge in the mind as the decision is drafted.

Rule and Exception

Applicable precedent is often the first factor to surface in a judge's mind.[421] Cardozo noted that judges look for the precedent that is nearest in tone and value to the case before the court.[422] That sounds reassuring, at least until Cardozo explains that judges do not need to follow case law. 'Little profit will come from a dissection of the precedents,' he would later write in a foundational opinion.[423] As Cardozo once explained, '*Stare decisis* is not in the constitution.'[424] There is often more than one relevant precedent, and the one that seems closest may be unjust, inappropriate, or plainly wrong. What it means to examine precedent is to reexamine it. As he took note of the relevant precedent, Cardozo seems to have begun by asking whether he should follow it: 'If the accepted rule which seems applicable yields a result which is felt to be unjust, the rule is reconsidered.'[425]

This is the central topic of the great tradition, the theme that unifies the books we are reading: when may a judge create an exception to a rule? As Benjamin Kaplan, a former associate justice on the Massachusetts Supreme Judicial Court, explained the problem, 'No matter how subtly a rule has been formulated to accommodate the factors that ought to bear on decision, there may always arise a case that, while falling nominally within the rule, presents some sympathetic element that tempts one to say, "On these very exceptional facts, the rule is obviated to such-and-such a degree."'[426] It is impossible to overestimate the importance of these inquiries, for it was 'the raising of such questions that made the common law.'[427]

Many factors arise once we begin to ask about exceptions, and Cardozo grouped them into the four methods that we will soon explore. Cardozo was not suggesting that judges must consider these factors, or that these are the only ones worthy of attention. He was instead focused on the precise topic of his lectures, *the nature of the judicial process*—what occurs in the mind of the common law judge as cases are decided.

---

[421] Cardozo (1921b), p. 19.

[422] Id., pp. 19–20.

[423] *Meinhard v. Salmon*, 164 N.E. 545, 547 (N.Y. 1928) (Cardozo, C.J.).

[424] Cardozo (1924), p. 132.

[425] Cardozo (1921b), p. 23.

[426] Kaplan (1983), p. 1850.

[427] Milsom (1968), p. lxix.

Personality of the Judge

One proof that Cardozo was not proposing a specific procedure is that some decisive factors flicker in and out of consciousness while others remain entirely unconscious. 'Deep below consciousness are other forces, the likes and dislikes, the predilections and the prejudices, the complex of instincts and emotions and habits and convictions, which make the [person], whether... litigant or judge.'[428] These are 'the forces that make law, but of which we know neither the sources nor their direction.'[429] They create 'an outlook on life, a conception of social needs' that, 'when reasons are nicely balanced, must determine where choice shall fall.'[430]

Cardozo was borrowing thoughts from the European free law movements.[431] Eugen Ehrlich (1862–1922),[432] one of the leading theorists, concluded that rules alone do not dictate decisions. 'The judge is never delivered up to the legal proposition, bound hand and foot, without any will of his own, and the more general the legal proposition, the greater the freedom of the judge.'[433] Cardozo endorsed Ehrlich's understanding and agreed that 'there is no guaranty of justice... except the personality of the judge.'[434]

Cardozo was rephrasing a Blackstonian intuition that echoes down the years, one quoted by both Weber and Cardozo—the vision of the common law judge as a 'living oracle.'[435] The judge, as Learned Hand noted, voices 'the dictates of a vague divinity' and works, as Cardozo suggested, in 'the land of mystery.'[436]

All that protects the legal process from injustice are the instincts, intuitions, and prejudices of the fallible human beings who occupy the comfortable swivel chairs at the front of American courtrooms. And it is actually worse than it seems—since, as we have just discussed, not all of the critical factors emerge into consciousness. As one of Cardozo's former law clerks described his process: 'Almost subconsciously he veers to the fair result and only extremely compelling reasons can turn him aside.'[437] The bulk of what protects our freedom is buried in the unconscious of

[428] Cardozo (1921b), p. 167.

[429] Frankfurter (1928), p. 438.

[430] Cardozo (1921b), p. 12.

[431] Id., p. 16.

[432] For Ehrlich, see Hertogh (ed) (2009); Rehbinder (1967).

[433] Ehrlich (2002), p. 174.

[434] Cardozo (1921b), pp. 16–17 (quoting Ehrlich (1917), p. 65). Cardozo placed the footnote reference after the sentence's first phrase, but the entire sentence is from Ehrlich. For the German original, see Ehrlich (1903), p. 21.

[435] See Cardozo (1921b), p. 19 (quoting Blackstone (2016), vol. 1, p. ☆69); Weber (1978), vol. 2, p. 767. For Blackstone, see above, p. 72.

[436] Hand (1939), vol. 39, p. 9, vol. 52, p. 361, vol. 48, p. 379; Cardozo, id., p. 18.

[437] Rauh et al. (1979), p. 7 (describing Cardozo's legal process) (quoting letter from Joseph L. Rauh, Jr., to Felix Frankfurter (Mar. 9, 1937)).

those wearing the black robes. 'In most cases the process is a subterranean one, and those who are its architects and artisans are unconscious of what they are doing.'[438]

No Vantage Point

We know something of what Cardozo's public took from his lectures. Those in attendance especially enjoyed Cardozo's portrait of 'the calm and impartial ideal judge,'[439] his clear delineation of four methods for deciding cases, and the comforting reassurance that the result in a majority of the cases was 'predestined.'[440]

If this was the message that Cardozo's audience took from his lectures, there can be no doubt at this remove that they misunderstood him. In fact, America's great common law judge used his moment at the podium to explain that there is no established method for resolving legal disputes. The point is so central to our work and will reappear so frequently in our discussion that it is worth sharpening the focus.

The great tradition's central insight is that there is no vantage point from which the judicial result can be judged. We can suggest factors for the judge to consider, and we can share our view about how a case should come out, but once the decision is announced, we can do little but try to understand the judge's thinking. The decision is highly personal and not at all the team sport we might expect. Provided the judge acts without impropriety and in the manner of the craft, we have no yardstick by which to determine whether a case has been decided correctly. 'Indeed, the notion of correctness, at least as we usually use the word in math or science or logic just isn't applicable.'[441] In fact, as Corbin explained, it is actually the other way around. Instead of enumerating criteria by which to evaluate the decisions, we should use those decisions to teach ourselves law: 'Generalizations must be tested and altered and restated and abandoned in accordance with their application (or rejection) by the courts to the ever-changing problems of life.'[442] That is why Corbin usually respected the court's ultimate ruling, even when its legal argument did not convince him.[443]

---

[438] Gilmore (1957), p. 27.

[439] Clark (1946), p. 267.

[440] Clark and Trubek (1961), p. 256.

[441] Kennedy (1986), p. 561.

[442] Corbin (1961), p. 201.

[443] 'In some matters of detail the reasoning of the court will be criticized herein; but this must not be regarded as in any way intimating unsoundness in the decision.' Corbin (1918), p. 363 (discussing *De Cicco v. Schweizer*, 117 N.E. 807 (N.Y. 1917) (Cardozo, J.)).

Worries

Some may reject this view out of hand. The assertion seems to justify any decision that a judge might reach, no matter how capricious, uninformed, or illogical. The worry gave even Llewellyn nightmares. 'We cannot leave our judges or officials wholly free, or let them utterly loose, without chaos; that is clear.'[444] Since we do not want judges to decide cases by flipping a coin, it may seem obvious that constraints have to be imposed—criteria independent of individual preferences—that can serve both to guide decisions and evaluate outcomes. This apparent need has led to a continuing effort to define the boundaries beyond which judges are not properly exercising their profession.

The problem with this concern is that it is entirely fabricated. How many common law judges have ever decided a legal question as a matter of whimsy? There are few published common law decisions that cannot make a reasonable case for themselves. The question is whether there is a serious risk that conscientious judges—the only ones who might heed our advice—would, without clear marching orders, disregard their understanding of the law and favor a party for which no good legal argument can be made. 'Most judges, like most serious artists, are trying to do a "good job"'[445] and take their calling seriously. 'In spite of occasional and notable aberrations, we can be thankful that the judicial office itself influences those who fill it to make wise choices.'[446]

Our task is to understand what judges do, not to tell them how to do it. And that is especially the case because there is no reason to think that we could do a better job than the judges. 'If the professors assume a position of critical superiority over the work of the judges, it is very often a false assumption.'[447]

What judges need is not a list of methods or constraints but rather greater self-awareness—'We are to set the judges free.'[448] Cardozo thought of the process as mysterious because our most meaningful access to it is through introspection. Most people, when they hear the facts of *Webb v. McGowin*, feel a tug. That common experience suggests that cases are not decided by applying rules to facts, not even by judges. Like us, judges do not look to books for illumination. They appeal instead to themselves. We may have expected judges to reach their decisions using a clearly defined process, but no, we now see, there is no method. Everyone is engaged in the same hazy activity, and there is no other.

---

[444] Llewellyn (1940a), p. 584.

[445] Posner (2008), p. 12.

[446] Corbin (1962b), p. 811.

[447] Corbin (2016), p. 175.

[448] Cardozo (1921a), p. 117.

Self-reflection

Because Cardozo had no method to propose, he turned to self-reflection to educate himself about his practice—something that no one had tried before. As he examined the factors that presented themselves to his consciousness, he was not worried about whether the process he was engaged in was normatively correct or even permissible. 'I am not concerned to inquire whether judges ought to be allowed to brew such a compound at all.'[449] When Corbin asked him to 'explain to our students the process by which he arrived at the decision of a case, with the sources to which he went for assistance,'[450] Cardozo responded by trying to understand how a decision arises in his mind with only minimal guidance from the legal sources. If there are limiting factors, they will be found in a judge's vision of 'the ideals and traditions of the crafts.'[451] These factors, as Cardozo was about to explain, are aesthetic in nature and have little to do with what we usually call *law*.

Four Methods

Cardozo's four methods are suggestive of the factors that spontaneously arise in the mind when a judge begins to consider the facts of a case. We will now examine these methods briefly to assure ourselves that they cannot be applied like a yardstick to a bolt of fabric. Instead, 'they bespeak the introspective gropings of an artist searching for his soul.'[452]

The *method of philosophy* focuses on logical consistency.[453] Cardozo did not want judges to overlook the virtue of uniformity—and yet he was not insisting. He recognized that a judge who absolutizes coherence may be indulging a personal preference.[454] The real purpose of the philosophical method is to demonstrate how to anchor a decision in the law. It is the device 'by which a result conceived of as right and just is made to square with principle and with the symmetry of the legal system.'[455]

And yet it is important not to pull too hard in the other direction. Cardozo was not saying that legal construction is irrelevant. If the proposed result does not fit the legal categories, there may be something amiss. 'If I cannot give a reason I should be willing to stand to, I must shrink from the very result which otherwise seems

[449] Cardozo (1921b), p. 10.

[450] Corbin (1964), p. 188 (quoting Corbin's suggestion for the topic of Cardozo's Storrs Lectures).

[451] Llewellyn (1940a), p. 589.

[452] Patterson (1939), p. 161 (discussing Cardozo's four methods).

[453] Cardozo (1921b), pp. 30–31.

[454] Id., p. 35.

[455] Id., pp. 42–43.

good.'[456] The Holmesian form of the law, like the eggshell, conceals the maturation process, but without it, the process could not take place. We spent time thinking about the facts of Webb's case precisely because we were looking at them through the lens of the consideration doctrine. We are not done until we find a way to anchor our result convincingly in the law.

Cardozo's second method was the *method of history.* Like Maitland, he wanted the law to avoid obsolete constraints. A precedent's historical pedigree justifies nothing. 'The decisions of the past contain wisdom, but they are not infallible. They were inspired by the genius of their time, but they are not revelation.'[457]

With his next method, *custom and social usage*, Cardozo was 'trying to make the law track lay understanding rather than force lay persons to conform their transactions to rigid legal categories.'[458] As we will see, Llewellyn found in this thought a way to rescue our system from incoherence.

The last of Cardozo's four methods, the *method of sociology*, examines social welfare, 'the needs of life in a developing civilization.'[459] Cardozo did not believe that a judge should always follow it. Because it is difficult to predict a decision's effects, judges should generally follow 'the customary morality of right-minded men and women,'[460] what 'every one of ordinary sense would, if he thought, recognize at once.'[461]

Not Discovery But Creation

When the methods suggest different results, which one should a judge prefer?[462] Cardozo provided no instruction manual: 'No recipe for the mingling of the ingredients has yet been formulated.'[463] Felix Frankfurter, who succeeded Cardozo on the U.S. Supreme Court, offered a standard response when asked how he would resolve a conflict among the Cardozian methods. 'Whenever Frankfurter was asked how he weighed the elements of history, precedent, custom, and social utility in reaching a decision, he was likely to reply, "When Velázquez was asked how he mixed his paints, he answered, With taste."'[464]

[456] Llewellyn (1960), p. 26.

[457] Corbin (1914), p. 246.

[458] Posner (1990a), p. 93.

[459] *MacPherson v. Buick Motor Co.*, 111 N.E. 1050, 1053 (N.Y. 1916) (Cardozo, J.).

[460] Cardozo (1921b), p. 106.

[461] *MacPherson v. Buick Motor Co.*, p. 1052 (quoting *Heaven v. Pender*, (1883) 11 QBD 503, 510 (Brett MR) (Eng.)).

[462] Cardozo (1921b), p. 113.

[463] Cardozo (1924), p. 64.

[464] Freund (1979), p. 4 (quoting Frankfurter in conversation).

Grant Gilmore, whom we will soon meet, conveyed the afterglow of Cardozo's lectures as he recounted the last class that Corbin taught at the Yale Law School.[465] After he retired, Corbin returned each year to teach one session of Gilmore's contracts course. He concluded the class by reading the passage from Cardozo's book in which the great judge explained that he had sought certainty during his early years on the bench but, unable to find the settled rules he was seeking, he became aware instead of 'how trackless was the ocean' on which we are embarked.[466] Cardozo's 'ultimate realization that certainty is not the goal... was evidently deeply meaningful to Professor Corbin.'[467] Holmes had had the same insight—'certainty generally is illusion'[468]—and as Corbin aged the thought pressed on him: 'Certainty is an illusion, and the illusion of certainty is the mother of injustice and turmoil.'[469]

Pervading Spirit

And yet Corbin may have been even more affected by a different aspect of Cardozo's book—his attempt, almost at the edge of language, to describe his experience of deciding cases. Once Cardozo accepted uncertainty as inevitable, he came to believe that it is best met with imagination. 'I have grown to see that the process in its highest reaches is not discovery but creation.'[470] The question that arises each time I read that sentence may also have intrigued Corbin—how does a judge engage in that creative process? Once Cardozo studied the facts of a case, and after many factors and concerns saturated his attention, what happened next? As Cardozo described it, 'a semi-intuitive apprehension of the pervading spirit of our law' comes 'to the rescue of the anxious judge.'[471]

Excuse me, but... *what?* Did Cardozo mean that he was not really working with law or facts or factors or the methods he had just described? He may have felt that he had achieved direct access to the law's 'pervading spirit,' what he elsewhere referred to as its 'animating principle,[472] its 'underlying motive, the indwelling creative energy.'[473] I reproduce Cardozo's words because it is important to hear them. Cardozo was attempting to describe an experience that, as far as I know, no other common lawyer has dared to put on paper.

[465] Gilmore (1964), p. 217.

[466] Cardozo (1921b), p. 166.

[467] Gilmore (1964), p. 217.

[468] Holmes (1897), p. 466.

[469] Corbin (1964), p. 188 (quoting his preface to the 1964 supplement to his contracts treatise).

[470] Cardozo (1921b), p. 166.

[471] Id., p. 43.

[472] *Meinhard v. Salmon*, 164 N.E. 545, 547 (N.Y. 1928) (Cardozo, C.J.).

[473] Cardozo (1921b), p. 43.

Cardozo later suggested that, as he resolved 'the sordid quarrels of one litigant and another,' he sought 'something that transcends... the petty and the ephemeral and the ignoble' and that he was able to grasp in those mundane disputes—the world in a grain of sand—'the workings of an eternal process of which these are but the shadows.'[474] Cardozo, it seems, had learned to assess earthly comings and goings from the perspective of a higher sphere. Because he was aware how disturbing his disclosure would be—for many reasons—he initially refused to allow his lecture series to appear in print. 'If it were published, I would be impeached.'[475]

Webb v. McGowin

How should we now approach *Webb v. McGowin*? I believe that Cardozo would advise against abandoning the consideration doctrine or creating a novel exception. Corbin, who knew Cardozo and ably channeled his thought, concluded that Cardozo was one who 'molds doctrine without repudiating it.'[476] Though Cardozo acknowledged that the consideration doctrine is a historical accident,[477] he also agreed with Holmes that a common law judge may not simply reject it as nonsense and refuse to enforce it.[478]

Cardozo would have heard in the facts of *Webb* the call of social welfare, for the great judge was 'sensitive to the immediate equities of the controversy to a degree rarely rivaled.'[479] The facts that pull at us would also have pulled at him—especially Webb's heroic act and his penury. And yet I do not think that he would want our compassion for Webb to decide the matter. He would instead have asked why the institution of contract was having such difficulty with the case, and he would have found it intriguing that the consideration doctrine was preventing the promisor from attaining his purpose.

Cardozo's opinions provide models for how he might next have proceeded. He may have looked for cases that resolve somewhat similar disputes using a variety of doctrines, and then he might have chosen a doctrinal solution that he believed would make few waves. He might for example have imagined the ways in which Webb could be said to have relied on McGowin's promise and then allowed himself to

[474] Cardozo (1931b), pp. 21–22. Cardozo was referring to the allegory of the cave in Plato's *Republic*, to be explored in the next chapter. See Plato (2004) 514a–520a, pp. 208–213. See below, p. 130.

[475] Corbin (1961), p. 198 (quoting Cardozo in conversation).

[476] Corbin (1939), vol. 39, p., 86, vol. 52, p. 438, vol. 48, p. 456.

[477] Cardozo (1921b), p. 56; *Allegheny Coll. v. Nat'l Chautauqua Cnty. Bank*, 159 N.E. 173, 175 (N.Y. 1927).

[478] Cardozo (1921b), p. 69 (quoting *S. Pac. Co. v. Jensen*, 244 U.S. 205, 221 (1917) (Holmes, J., dissenting)).

[479] Llewellyn (1960), p. 443.

enforce it as a matter of promissory estoppel. He would have had no point to make, and he would have left the surface of the common law largely unruffled.

I do not have within me creative resources sufficient to imagine how the great judge would have wound his inimitable way to his result, but I am confident that he would not have let the consideration doctrine stand in his way. 'A judge who could find "consideration"... in the *Allegheny College* case could, when he was so inclined, find consideration anywhere.'[480]

References

Blackstone W (2016) Commentaries on the laws of England, Prest W (ed), 4 vols. Oxford University Press, Oxford
Bridgeman C (2005) *Allegheny College* revisited: Cardozo, consideration, and formalism in context. UC Davis Law Review 39:149–186
Cardozo B (1921a) A Ministry of Justice. Harvard Law Review 35:113–126
Cardozo B (1921b) The nature of the judicial process. Yale University Press, New Haven
Cardozo B (1924) The growth of the law. Yale University Press, New Haven
Cardozo B (1931a) Law and literature and other essays and addresses. Harcourt, Brace, New York
Cardozo B (1931b) Law and the university. Law Quarterly Review 47:19-22
Cardozo B (1931c) Mr. Justice Holmes. Harvard Law Review 44:682–692
Clark C (1946) State law in the federal courts: The brooding omnipresence of *Erie v. Tompkins*. Yale Law Journal 55:267–296
Clark C, Trubek D (1961) The creative role of the judge: Restraint and freedom in the common law tradition. Yale Law Journal 71:255–276
Corbin A (1914) The law and the judges. Yale Review 3:234–250
Corbin A (1918) Does a pre-existing duty defeat consideration?—recent noteworthy decisions. Yale Law Journal 27:362–381
Corbin A (1939) Mr. Justice Cardozo and the law of contracts. Columbia Law Review 39:56–87, Harvard Law Review 52:408–439, Yale Law Journal 48:426–457
Corbin A (1961) The judicial process revisited: Introduction. Yale Law Journal 71:195–201
Corbin A (1962b) A tribute to Karl Llewellyn. Yale Law Journal 71:805-812
Corbin A (1964) Sixty-eight years at law. Kansas Law Review 13:183–196
Corbin A (2016) Farewell letter of Arthur Corbin to the Yale Law School Faculty. In: Calabresi G, The future of law and economics: Essays in reform and recollection. Yale University Press, New Haven, pp. 173–176
Donald D (1995) Lincoln. Simon & Schuster, New York
Douglas W (1962) Karl N. Llewellyn. University of Chicago Law Review 29:611–613
Ehrlich E (1903) Freie Rechtsfindung und freie Rechtswissenschaft. C. L. Hirschfeld, Leipzig
Ehrlich E (1917) Judicial freedom of decision: Its principles and objects, Bruncken E (trans). In: Drake J et al (eds) Science of legal method: Select essays by various authors (Modern Legal Philosophy Series, vol. IX). Boston Book Co., Boston, pp 47–84
Ehrlich E (2002) Fundamental principles of the sociology of law, Moll W (trans). Routledge, London
Frankfurter F (1928) Review of Cardozo, The paradoxes of legal science. University of Pennsylvania Law Review 77:436–438
Freund P (1979) Foreword: Homage to Mr. Justice Cardozo. Cardozo Law Review 1:1–4
Gilmore G (1957) Law, logic and experience. Howard Law Journal 3:26–41

[480] Gilmore (1974a), p. 62.

Gilmore G (1964) The assignee of contract rights and his precarious security. Yale Law Journal 74:217–261

Gilmore G (1974a) The death of contract. Ohio State University Press, Columbus

Hand L (1939) Mr. Justice Cardozo. Columbia Law Review 39:9–11, Harvard Law Review 52:361–363, Yale Law Journal 48:379–381

Hertogh M (ed) (2009) Living law: Reconsidering Eugen Ehrlich. Hart, Oxford

Holmes O (1897) The path of the law. Harvard Law Review 10:457–478

Holmes O (1962) Twenty years in retrospect. In: Holmes O The occasional speeches of Justice Oliver Wendell Holmes, Howe M (ed). Belknap Press, Cambridge, pp 154–157

Holmes O, Laski H (1953) The correspondence of Mr. Justice Holmes and Harold J. Laski, 1916–1935, Howe M (ed), 2 vols. Harvard University Press, Cambridge

Kaplan B (1983) Encounters with O.W. Holmes, Jr. Harvard Law Review 96:1828–1852

Kaufman A (1998) Cardozo. Harvard University Press, Cambridge

Kennedy D (1986) Freedom and constraint in adjudication: A critical phenomenology. Journal of Legal Education 36:518–562

Kessler F, Gilmore G (1972) Teacher's manual, Contracts: Cases and materials [mimeograph]. Little, Brown, Boston

Konefsky A (1987) How to read, or at least not misread, Cardozo in the *Allegheny College* Case. Buffalo Law Review 36:645–699

Llewellyn K (1931c) Put in his thumb. Century Co., New York

Llewellyn K (1931d) Review of Frankfurter, Mr. Justice Holmes. Columbia Law Review 31:902–905

Llewellyn K (1940a) On reading and using the newer jurisprudence. Columbia Law Review 40:581–614

Llewellyn K (1942a) The crafts of law re-valued. Rocky Mountain Law Review 15:1–7

Llewellyn K (1960) The common law tradition: Deciding appeals. Little, Brown, Boston

McPherson J (1988) Battle cry of freedom: The Civil War era. Oxford University Press, Oxford

Milsom S (1968) Introduction. In: Pollock & Maitland (1968), vol. 1, pp xxiii–lxxiii

Patterson E (1939) Cardozo's philosophy of law, part II. University of Pennsylvania Law Review 88:156–176

Plato (2004) Republic, Reeve C (trans). Hackett, Indianapolis

Polenberg R (1997) The world of Benjamin Cardozo: Personal values and the judicial process. Harvard University Press, Cambridge

Pollock F, Maitland F (1968) The history of English law before the time of Edward I, Milsom S (ed), 2d edn, 2 vols. Cambridge University Press, Cambridge

Posner R (1990a) Cardozo: A study in reputation. University of Chicago Press, Chicago

Posner R (2008) How judges think. Harvard University Press, Cambridge

Rauh J et al (1979) A personal view of Justice Benjamin N. Cardozo: Recollections of four Cardozo law clerks. Cardozo Law Review 1:5–22

Rehbinder M (1967) Die Begründung der Rechtssoziologie durch Eugen Ehrlich. Duncker & Humblot, Berlin

Stone H et al (1939) Mr. Justice Cardozo. Columbia Law Review 39:1–137, Harvard Law Review 52:353–489, Yale Law Journal 48:371–507

Townsend M (1996) Cardozo's *Allegheny College* opinion: A case study in law as an art. Houston Law Review 33:1103–1154

Weber M (1978) Economy and society: An outline of interpretive sociology, Roth G, Wittich C (eds), 2 vols. University of California Press, Berkeley

White G (1993) Justice Oliver Wendell Holmes: Law and the inner self. Oxford University Press, New York

Zipursky B, Goldberg J (2016) The myths of *MacPherson*. Journal of Tort Law 9:91–126

Chapter 9
Context (Llewellyn)

Karl Llewellyn (1893–1962)[481] chose a nursery rhyme as the epigraph for his first book. It tells of a wise man who jumped into a bramble bush and scratched out both his eyes. Once he saw he could not see, he jumped into another one and scratched them in again.[482]

The story long confused me. A bramble bush might scratch eyes out, but I could not see how it could scratch them in again. Then I noticed that, in Llewellyn's version, BRAMBLE BUSH is printed in all caps. The verse refers not to a forest thicket but to the book I was holding in my hands.

Breakthrough

The key to appreciating *The Bramble Bush* is understanding what it is not. Llewellyn was not trying to demonstrate that precedent does not tell us how to resolve disputes. That has been a central theme of the great tradition from the beginning. What he contributed was the explanation. Precedent does not because it cannot, and it cannot because it is not devised to decide cases. It is there instead to help judges decide them. Precedent is used when it fits and brushed aside when it does not. In the hands of an experienced judge, the case law rarely stands in the way of a reasonable result. But if decisions are not reached by applying precedent, we are back to our original question: how do judges decide cases?

The great tradition's opening movement concludes with Llewellyn's unnerving breakthrough. Once we review his demonstration, I think we will decide that much

[481] For Llewellyn, see Twining (2012), pp. 87–127, 535–543; Corbin (1962b); and in German, Rheinstein (1962).

[482] Llewellyn (2008), p. v.

R. Hyland, *Common Law Judging and the Great Tradition*, Ius Gentium: Comparative Perspectives on Law and Justice 100,
https://doi.org/10.1007/978-3-032-02307-0_9

that has long counted as learning about the common law proves to be excess baggage. In a Hollywood movie, this would be the end of Act I. The knowledge we were counting on has proved unreliable, and we will need a new approach. Hopefully our freshly opened eyes will allow us to discover within ourselves as yet untapped resources.

Karl Llewellyn

As a young man, Llewellyn spent his final three years of high school as a student in a classical *Gymnasium* in the German province of Mecklenburg (later a part of East Germany). He was back in Europe for his junior year abroad—in Paris this time—when the First World War broke out. He crossed the border, accompanied the 78th Prussian infantry to the Western Front, was wounded in battle, and received the Iron Cross, 2nd class. At the Yale Law School, he worked with Corbin and quickly adopted his mentor's 'impatience with doctrine and his almost obsessive concern with the operative facts of cases.'[483] Llewellyn joined the Columbia Law School faculty, and then, during the academic year 1928–1929, taught as Carnegie International Professor at the University of Leipzig in Germany. The following summer, he prepared lectures for his course on *Law and its Study*, an introduction to law taught in the week before term begin to entering Columbia law students. He published those lectures as *The Bramble Bush*, the book we are about to examine. Later in his distinguished career, Llewellyn revised some of the views that he expressed in his first book, but his early insights are the ones that contribute most directly to the great tradition.

Free Law Again

Free law was still flourishing in Germany as Llewellyn arrived, and Hermann Isay (1873–1938),[484] one of the movement's most insightful thinkers, was just then publishing a book about how German judges decide cases.[485] Isay argued that judges do not decide by applying a rule. 'It always still requires independent thought by the person charged with making the decision, and usually even a great deal of thought.'[486] Llewellyn already knew that—that was the understanding he had come to as he sat with Corbin and read Cardozo's opinions—but he had not been able to commit himself to it in print. It may have been Isay's talent for epigrammatic formulation that inspired Llewellyn to elaborate his vision, and *The Bramble Bush* was where he

483 Gilmore (1975), p. 680.

484 For Isay, see Rossmanith (1975), pp. 11–19.

485 See Isay (1929).

486 Isay (1929), p. 20 (translation).

previewed it for the first time. Those plucky thoughts from Free Law Weimar swirled together with what Llewellyn had learned from his teachers, travels, and readings and surprised him with an epiphany, which he excitedly decanted into sentences of sheer delight. During the following nine years, 'the formerly unproductive Llewellyn suddenly became enormously prolific.'[487]

What Officials Do

Shortly after Llewellyn returned from Germany, he summarized the lesson he learned from the free lawyers about how a judge approaches the decision process: 'He judges backward: Conclusion first. Rationalization to follow.'[488] Holmes had already announced the idea in the opening sentence of his first major piece of scholarship: 'It is the merit of the common law that it decides the case first and determines the principle afterwards.'[489] Llewellyn channeled the insight into an amusing tale about our two favorite Supreme Court justices: '"Judgment for the plaintiff," runs the old anecdote of Marshall; "Mr. Justice Story will furnish the authorities."'[490]

What matters most about a case is less the reasoning—which was added later—than the practical result. What we call *precedent* is best understood as a summary of the actual solution that a particular judge or panel of judges found appropriate for a particular dispute at a particular moment. Whether that decision is helpful for deciding a later case depends on whether future judges approve the likely consequences of that earlier decision. This discovery led Llewellyn to the most famous claim in his book: '*What these officials do about disputes is, to my mind, the law itself.*'[491] The sentence sparked controversy, as was intended, partly because it seems to reject the idea that the law is able to provide a standard for social conduct.[492] Behind Llewellyn's assertion glimmers a delightful portrait of the legal scholar as a young buck, but the sentence later embarrassed him, and he retracted it.[493]

And yet there is nothing wrong with the sentence. Holmes had already expressed a similar thought: 'The prophecies of what the courts will do in fact, and nothing more pretentious, are what I mean by the law.'[494] Since both sentences are generally misunderstood, it may be useful to restate the idea: all that we actually know about the common law is how judges allocate losses and benefits. 'The common law

---

487 Twining (2012), p. 109.

488 Llewellyn (1931b), p. 83.

489 [Holmes] (1870), p. 1.

490 Llewellyn (2008), p. 32.

491 Llewellyn (2008), p. 5.

492 See Twining (2012), pp. 147–151.

493 See Llewellyn (2008), p. 5 note 39; Llewellyn (1940a), p. 603 note 17.

494 Holmes (1897), p. 461.

begins and ends with the solution of a particular case.'[495] Everything else is speculative, including our theories about how judges decide cases. If we want to reconstruct the judicial process, we have no choice but to work backward from the case results.

A corollary of Llewellyn's controversial sentence is even more troubling. When it comes time to decide cases, judges care remarkably little about rules. I suspect I am not the first lawyer to discover how little weight judges give precedent during oral argument. Judges are chiefly interested in how to decide this case at this moment. 'Rather than beating appellate judges over the head with cases... appellate lawyers would be more effective if... they instead emphasized the practical stakes in the case and thus the consequences of the decision.'[496] The seemingly outrageous assertions that Llewellyn included in his book therefore strike me as essential practical advice for an advocate about to rise before an appellate panel: 'General propositions are empty'; they are 'baggage, impedimenta, stuff about the feet.' Those who learn nothing but the rules take away 'the shell and not the substance,' for 'rules alone, mere forms of words, are worthless.'[497] These formulations, some half remembered from his reading of Holmes and Ehrlich,[498] demonstrate that Llewellyn agreed with Isay that judges must think directly about who should win the case and why. Judges are therefore less interested in rules than in facts—the facts of this case and of many others. *Ex facto jus oritur*, as the old common lawyers liked to say, law arises from the facts.[499] The real discussion is in terms of the subtle differences between this case and the last one—and between both of those and the next one.

Shadow Puppets

Judges understand that legal concepts are illusions—mere 'shadows cast across the front stage by the movements of the courts unheeded in the rear.'[500] The fact that Llewellyn's book takes its title from a nursery rhyme suggests that anecdotes and metaphors do a lot of work in his thinking. We should therefore probably pay attention when he invokes the allegory of the cave from Plato's *Republic*.[501]

Llewellyn was suggesting that an exclusive focus on legal concepts masks the real decision process. The poet in Llewellyn felt the need for a metaphor to illuminate the thought, and what he found in his fingers was not exactly Plato's cave but

---

[495] [Holmes] (1871b), p. 716.

[496] Posner (2006), p. 1067.

[497] Llewellyn (2008), p. 4.

[498] 'General propositions do not decide concrete cases.' *Lochner v. New York*, 198 U.S. 45, 76 (1905) (Holmes, J., dissenting). 'As legal concepts, vague abstractions... are worthless.' Ehrlich (1918), p. 275 (trans.).

[499] *Adams v. Tanner*, 44 U.S. 590, 601 (1917) (Brandeis, J., dissenting).

[500] Llewellyn (2008), p. 6.

[501] See Plato (2004) 514a–520a, pp. 208–213.

instead a shadow puppet theater. On a white sheet, pulled taut across the front of the stage, shadows move to the rhythm of the gamelan. If someone were to lead us backstage, the reverie would vanish once we became aware of the elaborate mechanism needed to produce the illusion. The shadows that seem to glide spontaneously across the stage are not just dancing but danced.

Two Views of Precedent

How is it that we can usually find a precedent to justify any result? The question is a little like asking why eggs fit so nicely into egg cups. Because both egg cups and precedents are designed for their intended use, we have the egg cups—and the precedents—that we need. And since we want judges to reach wise decisions, it would make no sense to burden them with insuperable constraints. We idolize our great judges and marvel at how they ably shape recalcitrant case law into prudent results, but the truth is that pretty much any law school grad can do it. Judges can bend precedent because precedent is designed to be bent. Honestly, why would any legal system make life as hard for judges as we have always imagined it to be?

Llewellyn described several aspects of this useful plasticity, the most intriguing being its 'two-headed' or 'Janus-faced' nature.[502] 'For every question worth calling a problem, at least two contradictory solutions and propositions can be found in past decisions.'[503] Even if there is only one case on point, it can usually be read either broadly or narrowly, and one of the two readings may support the preferred decision.[504] Llewellyn did not come up with this on his own. Blackstone had noticed it, and Holmes and Cardozo blew up the balloon so big that it was ready to pop. But it was Llewellyn, 'one of the ablest, subtlest, most hard-working of Holmes' disciples,'[505] who described the situation with such precision that its devastating consequences could no longer be ignored.

The *loose or expansive view of precedent* allows a judge to take advantage of any helpful aspect of an earlier decision. A judge may rely on the earlier case even when its facts have little to do with the case to be decided. It is enough that one of its sentences seems to justify the court's desired result—even if the precedent involves a different area of the law and the issue presented is unrelated to the question the judge is now asked to decide.

I know. This seems absurd. And yet, we have already seen precedent used in exactly this way, and when we had the chance, we did not object. I am thinking of *Hoffman v. Porter*.[506] In 1800, the Porters conveyed land to 'Peter Hoffman & Son,'

---

[502] Llewellyn (2008), p. 69.

[503] Kessler (1969), p. 521.

[504] Llewellyn (2008), pp. 68–71.

[505] Frank (1931), p. 1125.

[506] *Hoffman v. Porter*, 12 F. Cas. 304 (C.C.D. Va. 1824) (No. 6577). See above, p. 32.

and because they did not have good title, the owners reentered and took possession. After Peter's death, his son John sued for breach of the covenant of good title, but since the conveyance did not run specifically to John, precedent was clear that the conveyance was void and the covenant therefore never arose.[507]

And yet if John could not sue, no one could hold the Porters liable. The judge had no trouble with the case: 'Justice … is clearly with the plaintiff, is clearly in favour of giving validity to the conveyance, and, I do not think that law ought to be separated from justice, where it is at most doubtful.[508]

Those bold words are John Marshall's, sitting as circuit judge. You may remember that Judge Samford cited Marshall's conclusion in his concurrence in *Webb v. McGowin*. If *Hoffman* can serve as precedent for *Webb*, though the two cases share no similarity of law or fact, the system is every bit as flexible as Llewellyn suggested.

The *strict view of precedent*, in contrast, is a time-honored technique for disregarding unwelcome case law. When a court treats a prior decision in this way, it implies that the earlier holding will control only those new cases that happen to have precisely the same facts. As Llewellyn put the idea for our amusement, 'This rule holds only of redheaded Walpoles in pale magenta Buick cars.'

Cardozo confirmed Llewellyn's view of the dual nature of precedent. 'Every lawyer knows... that a prior case may, at the will of the court, "stand" either for the narrowest point to which its holding may be reduced, or for the widest formulation that its *ratio decidendi* [legal rationale] will allow.'[509] In fact, the malleability of a precedent is nearly endless. Llewellyn eventually cataloged over sixty interpretive techniques, from suggesting that a rule is 'too firmly established to disturb' to explicitly overruling it.[510]

Llewellyn's demonstration is breathtaking—and more devastating than it seems. Precedent is usually available to justify any reasonable holding. This fluidity is one of the mechanisms by which the Holmesian form of the law gives the appearance of stability as social convenience charges ahead. While we can be grateful for such an astonishingly flexible system of precedent, we have to admit that it decides nothing.

No Vehicles in the Park

After listening to Blackstone's lectures, his student Jeremy Bentham decided that the common law should be replaced by a code.[511] Unfortunately, however, even a code cannot solve the problem. Every rule is flexible, whether it is found in precedent, code, regulation, or contract.

[507] Sheppard (1808), p. 236 (*237).

[508] *Hoffman v. Porter*, p. 305 (Marshall, Circuit Justice).

[509] Cardozo (1932), p. 20 (quoting Llewellyn (1930a), p. x).

[510] Llewellyn (1960), pp. 77–91.

[511] See Alfange (1969).

Let us turn for a moment to what may be 'the most famous hypothetical in the common law world:'[512] a sign at a park entrance announces 'No Vehicles in the Park,' and in smaller type cites to a municipal ordinance. Say that you have been stationed there and asked to enforce the prohibition. As your shift begins, a late model BMW pulls onto the sidewalk. You are surprised but do not hesitate. You kindly ask the driver to move the vehicle back into the street.

A father then appears with a daughter pedaling a tricycle. Does the tricycle come in? Is a tricycle a vehicle? You do not want to keep them waiting, and there is no one to ask. The two of them are obviously looking forward to spending time together on the grass. You figure that the prohibition is probably limited to motorized vehicles, so you wave them through.

A few minutes later, you stop a rider on a sleek messenger bike. As you block the entrance, the cyclist points to the tricycle you just let in. You sigh. It is true, the bike has no motor, but with small children toddling around, you cannot allow a cyclist to ride through the park at full tilt. The rider asks whether the bike might come in if it is walked. It is the same bike, whether ridden or walked, so if it is a vehicle, it is still a vehicle, and vehicles are not allowed in the park. But a cyclist walking a bike does not seem much different from a pedestrian out for a stroll. You let the cyclist walk on.

A veteran with a disability is now approaching in a wheelchair. A wheelchair is like a bike, but there is no way for the vet to dismount, and the vet is not going to run anyone over. A few minutes later, another wheelchair approaches, this one motorized. If *vehicle* means *motorized* vehicle, you will have to turn this visitor away. And yet this is pretty much like a standard wheelchair. Besides, those with disabilities should be allowed to visit the park like everyone else. You are a little uncertain, but the motorized wheelchair comes in.

As you turn back to the entrance, an eager visitor is smiling at you over the handlebars of a motorized scooter. Here you draw the line. The rider saw you wave through the motorized wheelchair and politely asks how the scooter is different. 'Because you can walk,' you say. 'The park is not a bike path. Park your vehicle over there and pick it up when you leave.' At that point, a big truck rumbles over the curb, loaded with chairs, tables, and a large folding tent. The crew has been instructed to set up for the Ball on the Square, the park's annual fundraiser. It would make no sense for them to lug the furniture to the center of the park. You let the truck in.

You have been interpreting the legal concept of *vehicle.* What that word means depends on the purpose we ascribe to the rule, for there is a 'never failing insertion of an implicit preamble of purpose into the construction of any statute.'[513]

And yet the rule's purpose is not written down anywhere. Is it to maintain a haven from noise and pollution in the midst of a busy urban environment or rather to create a site for elegant evening gatherings for those who contribute to the park's upkeep? Each of these purposes may play a role, together with others that may not

---

512 Schauer (2008), p. 1109. For the debate in which the hypothetical had a leading role, see Hart HLA (1958), pp. 607–11; Fuller (1958), pp. 662–664. For an overview of the discussion, see Schlag (1999).

513 Llewellyn (1941b), p. 194.

occur to us until the situation arises. What we call the ordinance's *purpose* is our collective understanding of how we want to use the park. A sign with the same wording located at the entrance to a different park may have a different purpose, and we would interpret it differently.

Predictability

Let us acknowledge that rules are by nature indeterminate and that courts take many factors into account when they decide cases. That means that we cannot reliably guess the next decision by reading the previous ones. And yet we also know that those without legal training are able to keep out of trouble and that lawyers can give helpful legal advice. How can that be?

It is due, counter-intuitively, to the fact that we usually do not pay much attention to the law. 'People generally don't know or don't care much about the rules of contract law and generally carry out their affairs with little regard for them.'[514] For most legal questions in most areas of the law, most of us would not know how to find the relevant legal rules, and that includes me. Llewellyn summarized our situation in what may be the most important sentence ever written about the common law:

> If most people shaped their conduct really with reference to the law and to their legal rights, for any serious fraction of their time, rather than with reference to the patterns of action, the patterns of thought, the standards of judgment which they inhale as the social atmosphere they breathe, then life in our society would become unlivable.[515]

Most of us do what we think is reasonable. How do we figure that out? We rely on Blackstonian custom—on criteria that are 'indwelling in the very circumstances of life.'[516] And a healthy judicial system allows itself to be guided by these reasonable expectations. 'If laws are not made thus to correspond with the wishes of educated public opinion, they lose half their effectiveness.'[517] The objective is to reduce what Kessler and Fine called 'the tension between the living law... and case law.'[518]

When judges follow common expectation, their decisions are predictable. If courts wish 'to make future decisions predictable, [they have] to go, whenever possible, to the facts of general business experience and understanding.'[519] And yet, social expectation is far from the only factor in the judicial calculus. The common law brings its own policies to the table, and as we are about to see, individual judges have their particular concerns as well. Nonetheless, even when a variety of factors come together to produce a decision, the goal is for the final result to accord as much as possible with what the rest of us would expect.

---

[514] Feinman (1983), pp. 844–845.

[515] Llewellyn (2008), p. 17.

[516] Llewellyn (1960), p. 122. For Blackstonian custom, see above, p. 70.

[517] Holdsworth (1928), p. 152.

[518] Kessler and Fine (1964), p. 436.

[519] Kessler (1952b), p. 1099.

Common Understanding

We have been talking about common expectation, so it is worth asking whether we can find the necessary commonality in today's diverse society. Research suggests that those with differing cultural backgrounds and commitments perceive the world differently and draw different lessons from their experiences.[520] Do these differences now prevent us from understanding reasonable expectation in the same way?

The common understanding we are seeking is far removed from the standard that each of us sets for ourselves—that vision of the smiling, relaxed, and exceptionally generous human being that we aspire to become. We are not even talking about the standards of daily behavior that we have come to expect from ourselves, our family, and our officemates. The social expectation the law is looking for involves instead a minimum standard of comportment, a benchmark below which social interaction becomes exceedingly difficult. And even here we do not need to agree on specific behavior. There will be a spectrum of approaches, a range of minimally acceptable actions. Even if it is something that I would never do, I may be able to accept that someone else might find it proper. I am thinking that we still have a general consensus about this minimum standard.

If we clarify the notion of reasonable expectation in this way, does it become precise enough to allow us to predict which actions will be acceptable? We can perhaps again allow ourselves to be guided by the experience of the common law jury. Juries are often asked to determine reasonableness. Though jurors come together from many walks of life, they are generally able to reach a verdict. The fact that the common law has long relied on community standards suggests not only that those standards exist but also that they are precise enough to do the job.

We may now be able to understand a bit better how judges use facts to decide cases. In a lecture that he delivered a few days before he died, Llewellyn argued that, in the hands of an able advocate, a statement of facts can convince a court—'The statement of facts, be it in the brief or be it oral, is the complete guts of your case.'[521] But just a minute. How can a recitation of facts convince anyone of anything?[522] The facts create conviction not by themselves but rather due to the common understanding they invoke. This also explains the *pull of the facts*. It is not the facts that are doing the pulling but rather a sense of what most of us expect in the situation the facts describe. This common understanding is probably as close as a legal system can get to the predictability that Weber thought essential for human freedom.[523]

[520] Kahan et al. (2012).

[521] Llewellyn (1962), p. 637.

[522] For the relation of fact to value in Llewellyn's work, see Casebeer (1977), pp. 676-684.

[523] See also Llewellyn (1931b), p. 83.

Webb v. McGowin

If case outcomes should follow reasonable expectation, *Webb* is not difficult. Both McGowin and Webb expected that the payments would continue, and those who have written about the case over the years have been sympathetic. 'We can agree that compensating [Webb] for an on-the-job injury was the right result.'[524]

Summing Up

The task we set for ourselves was to discover what the great tradition has to say about how common law judges decide cases. How have we done?

We have learned that rules alone do not decide cases, and that they do not because they cannot. We also now know that common law judges do what they can to attune their decisions to social expectation. We have seen that intuitions that arise as the judge thinks about the facts of the case, even those that remain unconscious, may contribute to the result. We know that additional factors also play a role, and we began to explore two of them. We looked first at Holmes's suggestion that the courts should exercise judicial restraint to allow individuals to make decisions for themselves. And we also began thinking about Maitland's recommendation that we should only adopt from the past the rules that we would enact today.

So far we have not mentioned the many other concerns that influence the decisions, and we have no plan at all for what judges are to do when the relevant factors conflict. To be honest, we have so far done little more than distance ourselves from what we now recognize as familiar but faulty thoughts about the judicial process—an experience that leaves us even more aware of our ignorance. 'To date, we have left much more of [the judge's task] to mere untutored and unguided experience than a system of Law has any business to.'[525] So now would be a great time to explore a few of the relevant factors and to think about how to accommodate them when they point in different directions.

References

Alfange D (1969) Jeremy Bentham and the codification of law. Cornell Law Review 55:58–77

Cardozo B (1932) Jurisprudence. In: Cardozo B (1947), pp 7–46

Cardozo B (1947) Selected writings of Benjamin Nathan Cardozo: The choice of Tycho Brahe, Hall M (ed). Fallon, New York

---

[524] Snyder (2003), p. 50 (discussing *Webb v. McGowin*).

[525] Llewellyn (1940a), p. 595.

Casebeer K (1977) Escape from liberalism: Fact and value in Karl Llewellyn. Duke Law Journal 1977:671–703
Corbin A (1962b) A tribute to Karl Llewellyn. Yale Law Journal 71:805–812
Ehrlich E (1918) Die juristische Logik. Mohr (Siebeck), Tübingen
Feinman J (1983) Critical approaches to contract law. UCLA Law Review 30:829–860
Frank J (1931) Review of Llewellyn, The bramble bush. Yale Law Journal 40:1120–1125
Fuller L (1958) Positivism and fidelity to law: A reply to Professor [HLA] Hart. Harvard Law Review 71:630–672
Gilmore G (1975) Friedrich Kessler. Yale Law Journal 84:672–682
Hart HLA (1958) Positivism and the separation of law and morals. Harvard Law Review 71:593–629
Holdsworth W (1928) The historians of Anglo-American law. Columbia University Press, New York
[Holmes O] (1870) Codes, and the arrangement of the law. American Law Review 5:1–13
[Holmes O] (1871b) Review of Bryce, The academical study of the civil law. American Law Review 5:715–716
Holmes O (1897) The path of the law. Harvard Law Review 10:457–478
Isay H (1929) Rechtsnorm und Entscheidung. Franz Vahlen, Berlin
Kahan D et al (2012) 'They saw a protest': Cognitive illiberalism and the speech-conduct distinction. Stanford Law Review 64:851–906
Kent J (1897) An unpublished letter of Chancellor James Kent [1828]. Green Bag 9:206–211
Kessler F (1952b) Review of Corbin on contracts, volume one. Yale Law Journal 61:1093–1104
Kessler F (1969) Arthur Linton Corbin. Yale Law Journal 78:517–524
Kessler F, Fine E (1964) Culpa in contrahendo, bargaining in good faith, and freedom of contract: a comparative study. Harvard Law Review 77:401–449
Llewellyn K (1926) Review of Campbell, Cases on mortgages of real property. Harvard Law Review 40:142–146
Llewellyn K (1929) Ueber den Rechtsunterricht in den Vereinigten Staaten: Ein Vortrag. Jherings Jahrbücher für die Dogmatik des bürgerlichen Rechts 79:233–266
Llewellyn K (1930a) Cases and materials on the law of sales. Callaghan, Chicago
Llewellyn K (1931a) Holmes. In: Llewellyn K (1931c), p. 108
Llewellyn K (1931b) Law and the modern mind: A symposium, I: Legal illusion, review of Frank, Law and the modern mind. Columbia Law Review 31:82–90
Llewellyn K (1931c) Put in his thumb. Century Co., New York
Llewellyn K (1940a) On reading and using the newer jurisprudence. Columbia Law Review 40:581–614
Llewellyn K (1941b) My philosophy of law. In: Julius Rosenthal Foundation (1941) My philosophy of law: credos of sixteen American scholars. Boston Law Book, Boston, pp 183–197
Llewellyn K (1960) The common law tradition: Deciding appeals. Little, Brown, Boston
Llewellyn K (1962) A lecture on appellate advocacy. University of Chicago Law Review 29:627–639
Llewellyn K (2008) The bramble bush: The classic lectures on the law and law school. Oxford University Press, New York
Plato (2004) Republic, Reeve C (trans). Hackett, Indianapolis
Posner R (2006) The role of the judge in the twenty-first century. Boston University Law Review 86:1049–1068
Rheinstein M (1962) Karl Nickerson Llewellyn, 1893–1962. Rabels Zeitschrift für ausländisches und internationales Privatrecht 27:601–605
Rossmanith G (1975) Rechtsgefühl und Entscheidungsfindung: Hermann Isay (1873–1938). Duncker & Humblot, Berlin
Schauer F (2008) A critical guide to vehicles in the park. New York University Law Review 83:1109–1134

Schlag P (1999) No vehicles in the park. Seattle University Law Review 23:381–389
Sheppard W (1808) The touchstone of common assurances, Hilliard E (ed), vol. 1 (first American edn). Isaac Riley, New York
Snyder F (2003) The pernicious effect of employment relationships on the law of contracts. Texas Wesleyan Law Review 10:33–64
Twining W (2012) Karl Llewellyn and the realist movement, 2d edn. Cambridge University Press, New York

Part III
Reintegration

Chapter 10
Institutional Settlement (Hart and Sacks)

The stock market collapsed in October 1929, a month after Llewellyn first delivered his *Bramble Bush* lectures at Columbia. By the time FDR came on board a little more than three years further along, thousands of banks had closed, production had come to a halt, and the world had entered the Great Depression.[526] Society dissolved into dramatic political conflict, and in response Congress provided for retirees, guaranteed workers the right to organize, and created agencies and commissions to get the economy back on track.

Those bitter arguments were largely put on hold while the country fought World War II, but the year following the Allied victory was the most cantankerous in the history of the struggle between workers and their employers.[527] In addition, spurred by the modern Civil Rights movement, racial segregation was held to violate the Constitution,[528] but the triumph was spoiled by mob violence, cross burnings, and lynchings. The country became more polarized than at any time since the Civil War, and the global confrontation between capitalism and communism made things even worse.[529] Many wanted nothing more than to get back to normal, but society was falling apart. The courts were to some extent still above the fray. Were they going to be able to fabricate a new common ground of reasonable expectation?[530]

---

[526] For a history of the Great Depression and the First and Second New Deals, see Kennedy (1999), pp. 34–315.

[527] Patterson (1996), p. 43.

[528] For a summary of post-war developments in civil rights, see id., pp. 149–151, 380–406.

[529] Id., pp. 395–396, 415.

[530] Id., p. 273.

R. Hyland, *Common Law Judging and the Great Tradition*, Ius Gentium: Comparative Perspectives on Law and Justice 100,
https://doi.org/10.1007/978-3-032-02307-0_10

The Legal Process

Beginning in the 1950s, Henry Hart and Albert Sacks taught a seminar at the Harvard Law School they called *The Legal Process*.[531] Many of their students soon became law professors, and a good number of them were so persuaded by the legal process approach that it set the terms for law school debate for the next two decades—and it continues to resonate today. 'In a deep sense,' Judge Calabresi wrote, 'we are all followers of Henry Hart and know the moves almost by instinct.'[532]

As a law student at Harvard, Henry Hart Jr. (1904–1969)[533] studied with Felix Frankfurter and was elected president of the law review. His clerkship with Justice Brandeis convinced him that a properly organized legal process is the law's defining characteristic.[534] Hart worked for federal agencies in Washington before returning to teach at Harvard.

Albert Sacks (1920–1991)[535] also studied law at Harvard, where he too was elected president of the law review and, as Hart's research assistant, assembled the materials for the legal process seminar. Sacks clerked for Justice Frankfurter and practiced law in Washington before joining the Harvard law faculty, where he ultimately became its dean.

Institutional Settlement

We will focus on a single idea from the legal process materials, perhaps its most inspired theme: the *principle of institutional settlement*. Hart and Sacks wanted to solve a problem that will seem hopelessly abstract: how to resolve jurisdictional conflict among the different branches and agencies of the expanded federal government. But their solution is a watershed. They elaborated it in the first chapter of their teaching materials and illustrated it with the most memorable of their celebrated problems—'The Case of the Spoiled Cantaloupes.'[536]

The principle of institutional settlement may seem far removed from our concerns. And yet it takes only a moment to see the connection. Though common law courts generally have the final say in common law matters, Congress, administrative agencies, and state legislatures occasionally intervene, often to tip the scales in favor of the weaker party. But when the time comes for common law judges to apply these protective statutes and regulations, they do not switch gears and prefer them to their

[531] For the history, see Eskridge and Frickey (1994).

[532] Calabresi (1982), p. 87.

[533] For Hart, see Purcell (2009).

[534] Freund (1969), p. 1596.

[535] For Sacks, see Byse (2009); Raiffa et al. (1991).

[536] Hart and Sacks (1994), pp. 1–68.

usual approach. Instead, they continue to take all the facts and circumstances into account, tossing statutory and regulatory provisions into the pot with everything else: 'Common law courts have the power to treat statutes in precisely the same way that they treat the common law.'[537] Hart and Sacks were going to suggest that common law judges would need to rethink their method.

Who Decides

Is a common law court always the right body to resolve a market dispute? Common law judges are always looking for the decision that reasonable parties would expect. But legislatures and agencies have a competing claim: they have to sew the country back together after the opposing sides have finally fashioned a political compromise. They commission scientific studies and draft legislation. When common law method disagrees with their solutions, which set of rules should we follow—and should the courts or the agencies make that decision?

Hart and Sacks knew that judges were often no longer able to grasp the remote consequences of their decisions. And yet the common law was not about to surrender its Blackstonian vocation as the master science that legislators fail to understand at their peril.

A donnybrook was brewing, and Hart and Sacks thought they knew how to head it off. Judges should decide only those cases that fall within their *institutional competence*.[538] Even if we admire common law courts, we have to acknowledge their limitations: they have no special expertise, no ability to investigate what is going on in the wider world, and they see the world entirely through the lens of their case method.[539] That is why, Hart and Sacks came to believe, a modern system of law and regulation works best when courts stay in their lane and do not second-guess government bodies with the necessary expertise—even in fields of the private law. The two scholars also knew that common law judges were not about to surrender their authority. To convince them, they decided to go back to basics and base their approach on the first principles of human existence. That is why one of the law's most remarkable books—a thousand-page exploration of the proper allocation of power among competing actors in the federal system—begins, like Blackstone's *Commentaries*, with a myth about the origins of human society.

---

[537] Calabresi (1982), p. 82.

[538] The notion of *institutional competence* appears only rarely in the Hart and Sacks materials, and yet it is a central element of legal process thinking. See Rudd (2006), pp. 1051–1059; Eskridge and Frickey (1994), pp. lx–lxii, xciii.

[539] See Landis (1938), pp. 30–39.

Nature of Society

Because getting society fed and clothed requires a division of labor, cooperation has become a primary social virtue.[540] Disputes impede productive cooperation, and to resolve them, society needs both a working consensus and institutions and procedures to embody it.[541] To Hart and Sacks, these necessary truths led inevitably to the principle of institutional settlement:

> Decisions which are the duly arrived at result of duly established procedures of this kind ought to be accepted as binding upon the whole society unless and until they are duly changed.[542]

That beautiful sentence summarizes the lesson that Hart and Sacks learned during their stints as Washington lawyers: the times were conflictual; difficult times require impeccable procedures; and the different governmental branches must cooperate.

This is the kind of grand vision that we expect when two former presidents of the *Harvard Law Review* put their heads together. And yet we miss the point if we ignore the drama—for a worried pulse beats beneath their genteel prose. The world had just survived the darkest days of the twentieth century, some of the bleakest moments in the history of humanity. Without level-headed restraint, chaos, anarchy, revolution, and dictatorship might be our future if we were again to allow our differences to divide us.

A society that disregards procedural principles soon falls victim to a 'disintegrating resort to violence.'[543] To Hart and Sacks, the principle of institutional settlement was therefore not just a useful theoretical construct—it was a matter of deadly earnest. Common law courts could no longer be allowed to pursue their quixotic quest for justice when it led them to trespass on the jurisdiction of other governmental agents.

Return Policy

Hart and Sacks patiently constructed their argument by combining the facts of a few decided cases with detailed context and commentary. With this running start, I think we are ready to take a look at the case they used as the door opener, a dispute about a railcar filled with spoiled cantaloupes. It may be easier to get a handle on the facts if we start by thinking about shopping, and particularly about one of shopping's great pleasures—the right to return wares that do not measure up.

---

[540] Hart and Sacks (1994), p. 1.

[541] Id., p. 3.

[542] Id., p. 4.

[543] Id., p. 10.

We can usually return any standard purchase. We have to make our decision before the end of the return period, but there is always enough time to kick the tires and decide whether the goods will do the job. This indulgence has a business purpose: a generous return policy takes the risk out of the decision—and also encourages brand loyalty and repeat business.[544] It would not have become standard policy if it did not benefit everyone involved. Of course, environmentalists have their doubts: the return, like much else in American life, is a guilty pleasure.[545]

Because this custom is so much a part of our lives, it may come as a surprise to learn that the law that governs the sale of goods, Article 2 of the Uniform Commercial Code, does not include anything like the generous customary return policy. According to the statute, only defective goods can be returned, and there is not much time to decide whether to keep or return them.[546] And once the return period has passed, the buyer's only recourse is to sue for money damages.[547] Our traditional practice is an aspect of consumer culture, while the Code's less forgiving provisions often apply to disputes among merchants.

Spoiled Cantaloupes

Our case, *Gillarde v. Martinelli*,[548] involved a carload of Jo Jo brand cantaloupes. They were grown in Yuma, Arizona, and shipped in crates bearing a clown face on their instantly recognizable label. In June 1943, Seller (our plaintiff), a Chicago distributor, purchased the melons from the grower and resold them to Buyer (our defendant), a wholesaler in Massachusetts, while the fruit was in a railcar rolling east.[549]

The lopes were inspected before shipment and rated U.S. Grade No. 1, as required by the contract, and yet they arrived in Massachusetts overripe and with telltale moldy stems. The expert found them to be infected with rot and later testified that the fruit must have been defective when shipped. Let us accept the expert's conclusion and assume, as the courts did, that the melons did not conform to the contract.

When Buyer opened the railcar and saw the rotting fruit, it let Seller know it was rejecting the melons and would leave them with the carrier. The railroad resold the

---

[544] Robertson et al. (2020), p. 172.

[545] See Paul (2024).

[546] See UCC §§ 2-601, 2-602 comment 3, 2-602(1).

[547] See id. §§ 2-606(1)(b), 2-607(2), 2-714(1).

[548] *L. Gillarde Co. v. Joseph Martinelli & Co.*, 168 F.2d 276 (1st Cir.), amended by 169 F.2d 60 (1st Cir. 1948) (reproduced in Hart and Sacks (1994), pp. 53–58). For the federal trial court decision, see *Joseph Martinelli & Co. v. L. Gillarde Co.*, 73 F. Supp. 293 (D. Mass. 1947) (in Hart and Sacks (1994), pp. 50–53).

[549] The facts, the legal issues, the procedure, and the court holdings have been simplified. The Hart and Sacks materials offer an extensive portfolio of relevant statutory and regulatory texts, a detailed discussion of the evidence, and the text of most of the decisions.

fruit several days later and reimbursed Seller for half the value of the delivery. The question then was who would bear the remaining loss.

Let us also assume, as the courts did, that because the goods did not conform to the contract, sales law gave Buyer the right to reject.[550]

The sale of goods is traditionally governed by state law, but in the 1930s, Congress decided that the commerce in fresh fruits and vegetables was a matter of national importance and asked the agencies to regulate it. And it was also clear that, by contracting subject to the regs, Buyer had agreed not to reject. Since Buyer rejected anyway, Seller sued Buyer for breach. And since Seller delivered defective cantaloupes, Buyer counterclaimed for the difference between the contract price and the value of the spoiled fruit.

Decisions

A number of judges heard the case. Before we talk about their decisions, let us see whether we can sort this out on our own. Seller promised U.S. Grade No. 1 cantaloupes and breached by delivering spoiled fruit. Buyer also breached by violating its promise not to reject. Seller would like Buyer to pay full price. Buyer does not want to pay anything for rotting fruit. Who should win? And why?

How to begin? It seems obvious that Seller should not get top dollar for spoiled fruit, but it should also not be responsible for what happened when Buyer left the melons to rot in the railcar. To make things easier, assume the fruit was discarded as worthless. If we ask Buyer to pay the reduced value of the spoiled fruit as it arrived in the railcar, Seller would recover the value of the fruit that it actually supplied. We would hold Seller for supplying defective goods and Buyer for the loss brought about by its wrongful rejection. Each party would pay for the damage it caused. That is an answer we might expect.

The case eventually reached the First Circuit, the federal appeals court that sits in Boston, one of the country's great courts. The First Circuit balanced the equities and came to a solution like ours—it required Buyer to pay only the reduced value of the defective cantaloupes. Contracts cases like *Gillarde* rarely reach the U.S. Supreme Court, so a circuit court decision on these questions would normally end the matter. But we are not yet finished with the case, and that is because, as Hart and Sacks were eager to explain, more was at stake than a fair result.

Let us take a moment to celebrate our achievement. We now know that we can think our way through a complex case. We focused on finding a result that made sense. And a panel of judges from one of the country's most distinguished courts reached the same conclusion we did. I conclude that we are well on our way to understanding the teachings of the great tradition.

[550] See *Joseph Martinelli & Co. v. L. Gillarde Co.*, 73 F. Supp. 293, 296 (D. Mass. 1947).

Reconsideration

We now are ready to think about the earlier stages of the lawsuit. Seller first filed a complaint with the administrative tribunal that had been established to hear cases involving the violation of federal agriculture regulations. The administrative law judges had decided that the regs were designed to eliminate the *rejection evil*—the devastating consequences to sellers when buyers rejected in breach of their contracts. To convince buyers not to reject, they imposed a Draconian penalty: buyers who rejected in breach of contract would have to pay full price for the goods and—here is the penalty—they would not be allowed to counterclaim if they received defective goods.[551]

The administrative judge in *Gillarde* followed regulatory precedent and awarded Seller full price for the cantaloupes. Buyer appealed to the federal trial court, which reversed and ruled for Buyer. As we have seen, the First Circuit affirmed the trial court's decision and ordered Buyer to pay only the reduced value of the defective fruit.

Our disappointed Seller asked the First Circuit to reconsider. Though such petitions are rarely granted, the First Circuit agreed to rehear the case, probably because the Department of Agriculture, the U.S. Attorney for Boston, and the Attorney General of the United States all filed briefs arguing for rehearing.

We now come to the conflict of jurisdictions that convinced Hart and Sacks to begin their materials with this case. The administrative judge followed agency precedent designed to advance national policy goals. The First Circuit rejected the agency's decision and resolved the dispute as if it were a typical sales case. The First Circuit was now being respectfully requested to rethink its approach. Which should prevail: the agency's data-driven policy decision or common law notions of fairness? Even more importantly, should the court or the administrative agency have the final say?

Reversal

The First Circuit changed its mind and instructed the trial court to decide for Seller. The court did not ask whether the rejection penalty was needed to fulfill the legislative purpose, nor did it balance fairness to the parties against the need for national uniformity. It simply decided to let the agency have the last word.

---

[551] Hart and Sacks suggested that the administrative courts uniformly imposed this penalty on buyers who rejected in breach of contract. See Hart and Sacks (1994), p. 43. And yet, an Agriculture Decision cited by the First Circuit allowed just such a breaching buyer's counterclaim. See *D. B. Bruno & Co. v. S. Goldsamt, Inc.*, 1 A.D. 605 (1942) (cited in *L. Gillarde Co. v. Joseph Martinelli & Co.*, 168 F.2d 276, 281 (1st Cir. 1948) (reproduced in Hart and Sacks (1994), p. 55). For present purposes, it will be assumed that the administrative decisions were uniform.

Let us refocus. We have been asking how common law judges decide cases. *Gillarde* is a contracts dispute, and once we heard the story about rotting cantaloupes, we discovered that we are pretty good at finding a reasonable remedy. But on rehearing, the First Circuit rejected our decision and left the question to the administrative agency. What does this decision mean for our work? Are common law judges no longer allowed to concoct their own brew?

Farmers and Distributors

When the produce market declined, wholesalers in big eastern cities tended to reject perfectly good wares so they might repurchase at the new lower price. The produce they rejected was then lost. Farmers complained to their representatives, and in 1930, Congress passed the Perishable Agricultural Commodities Act (PACA),[552] a historic political compromise designed to resolve a simmering dispute about an essential element of national commerce.

By the time *Gillarde* reached the courts shortly after the war, many feared that prices would collapse in a global depression,[553] and the federal government continued to stabilize the market. In that world of a volatile produce market and extensive federal price support, common law method was no match for government economic strategy. When a court's preferred outcome conflicts with important governmental policies—Hart and Sacks were politely suggesting—the court should stand down.

Webb v. McGowin

What can we learn from the cantaloupe case? To begin, I think we should acknowledge the heroic conception of legislation that shines through the first chapter of the materials. But we will also want to recognize that not every statute courageously forges a historic compromise between competing national interests. Some statutes, Posner suggests, may disadvantage those we might most want to help and instead transfer wealth from unorganized consumers to powerful interest groups.[554] Judges with a nuanced understanding of legislation may want to think twice before signing on as the legislature's agent.

When national disputes and grand bargains are not in play, common law courts may continue their search for an appropriate solution. But the notion of institutional settlement does not leave things as they were, for it destroys the illusion that common law courts rule an autonomous fief. They play a role in a complex governmental structure, and that role will at times constrain their discretion.

[552] Pub. L. No. 71-325, 46 Stat. 531 (1930) (codified as amended at 7 U.S.C. §§ 499a–499t (2018)).
[553] Sumner (2007), p. 4; Benedict (1966), pp. 465–469.
[554] Posner (1990b), pp. 276–278, 353–356.

References

Benedict M (1966) Farm policies of the United States, 1790–1950: A study of their origins and development. Octagon, New York
Byse C (2009) Sacks, Albert M. In: Newman R (ed) pp 476–477
Calabresi G (1982) A common law for the age of statutes. Harvard University Press, Cambridge
Eskridge W, Frickey P (1994) An historical and critical introduction to The Legal Process. In: Hart H, Sacks A (1994), pp li-cxxxvi
Freund P (1969) Henry M. Hart, Jr.: In memoriam. Harvard Law Review 82:1595–1597
Hart H, Sacks A (1994) The legal process: Basic problems in the making and application of law, Eskridge W, Frickey P (eds). Foundation, Westbury
Kennedy D (1999) Freedom from fear: The American people in Depression and war, 1929–1945. Oxford University Press, New York
Landis J (1938) The administrative process. Yale University Press, New Haven
Newman R (ed) (2009) Yale biographical dictionary of American law. Yale University Press, New Haven
Patterson J (1996) Grand expectations: The United States, 1945-1974. Oxford University Press, New York
Paul P (2024) When you return those pants, the planet pays. New York Times (Jan. 12), p A23
Posner R (1990a) Cardozo: A study in reputation. University of Chicago Press, Chicago
Posner R (1990b) The problems of jurisprudence. Harvard University Press, Cambridge
Purcell E (2009) Hart, Henry Melvin, Jr. In: Newman R (ed), pp 255–256
Raiffa H et al (1991) In memoriam: Albert M. Sacks. Harvard Law Review 105:1–22
Robertson T et al (2020) Many (un)happy returns? The changing nature of retail product returns and future research directions. Journal of Retailing 96:172–177
Rudd J (2006) The evolution of the legal process school's 'institutional competence' theme: Unintended consequences for environmental law. Ecology Law Quarterly 33:1045–1090
Sumner D (2007) Farm subsidy tradition and modern agricultural realities. American Enterprise Institute. https://cail.ucdavis.edu/research/farmbill07/aeibriefs/20070515_sumnerRationales-final.pdf

Chapter 11
Hypothetical Negotiation (Posner)

Richard Posner (1939-)[555] may be 'the most important legal thinker of our time.'[556] He co-founded the legal method that we know as *law and economics* and applied it to many fields, both within the law and beyond. And he is by far the most frequently cited contemporary American legal scholar.[557]

We will focus here on Posner's book, *The Economic Analysis of Law*.[558] After nine editions, it remains the leading text about how economics can help resolve legal disputes.[559] Posner argues that economic theory can explain legal rules in all fields of the law and that it can also suggest worthwhile reforms.

Not everyone has been convinced. Reviewing the book's first edition, Arthur Leff (1935–1981)[560] explained his ambivalence: the book is of 'high intellectual quality,' and the mind behind it 'supple, strong and even (in a sense) sensitive,' and yet it presents 'four hundred pages of tunnel vision' in a 'peculiarly relentless tone.'[561] Even so, some of Posner's insights will prove indispensable.

---

555 For Posner, see Domnarski (2016).

556 Kagan (2007), p. 1121; see also Sunstein (2017).

557 Domnarski (2016), p. 1; Shapiro (2021), p. 1602.

558 Posner (2007).

559 Domnarski (2016), p. 73.

560 For Leff, see Peters (1981).

561 Leff (1974), pp. 462, 452.

R. Hyland, *Common Law Judging and the Great Tradition*, Ius Gentium: Comparative Perspectives on Law and Justice 100,
https://doi.org/10.1007/978-3-032-02307-0_11

Richard Posner

At Harvard Law School, Posner was elected president of the law review and graduated first in his class. He clerked for Justice Brennan and then joined the University of Chicago Law School, where he founded the *Journal of Legal Studies*, the principal publication in the field of law and economics. Posner was later appointed judge on the Seventh Circuit. He began writing about jurisprudence in the 1990s and has been especially forthcoming about how he decides cases.[562]

I have not met Judge Posner, and yet I have long been a fan. When my comparative study of the law of gifts was in production a number of years ago, my editor suggested that I ask for blurbs for the back of the book. Since Posner was the country's leading legal intellectual, I sent him the manuscript and hoped that he would favor it with a sentence or two. He did not respond, and I thought I knew why. Early in the book, I argue that the law-and-economics approach to gift giving is incoherent.[563] And yet I was still eager to know what he thought about my work. On the Friday afternoon before the deadline, I called his chambers and asked his secretary whether he had had a chance to review it. She put me on hold, then came back to say that he had not received my manuscript but would be happy to take a look at it. It was, I explained, too late. The typescript was over nine hundred pages long, and the jacket copy would be finalized on Monday. She thought it was worth a try. On Monday morning I had mail from him. He apologized for not having been able to read to the end but hoped that the attached paragraph would do the job.

Productive Loss

What if resolving a case as society would expect is not in society's best interest? When social expectation points in one direction and social welfare in another, is it better to follow custom or to move society forward? The great tradition long assumed that judges can do both at the same time, but as we studied the Hart and Sacks materials, we learned that the decision we might expect may not always offer a public benefit. Which of the two goals should a judge prefer?

Posner argues that judges should not worry about doing equity between the parties.[564] When a court investigates who was at fault, it is looking backward.[565] Judges should instead make the loss productive by announcing a rule designed to prevent similar losses in the future. For example, the judge might incentivize proper safety

---

[562] See, e.g., Posner (2013), Posner (2008).

[563] See Hyland (2012) para. 50–75, pp. 38–49.

[564] Posner (2007) § 2.2, pp. 25–26.

[565] Radin (1940), p. 68.

precautions by imposing liability on the party that most economically could have avoided the loss.[566]

The great tradition has already convinced us that judges should consider all the facts and circumstances of the case. Posner is now asking us to include the potential consequences to third parties as well—what we might call the *second-order considerations*. Moreover, Posner believes that the common law has long reached its decisions by taking these consequences into account: 'The common law is best (not perfectly) explained as a system for maximizing the wealth of society.'[567] Holmes had predicted that the rational study of the law would eventually require the mastery of statistics and economics,[568] and Llewellyn agreed that 'economic theory offers in many respects amazing light.'[569] What Posner contributed was a series of clever ideas about how economics might be put to work to decide cases.

But wait a minute. Did we take a wrong turn somewhere? Maybe we should have objected earlier when we learned that judges are expected to evaluate the social consequences of their decisions. Can a judge really assess whether a proposed safety precaution will be efficient? Most judges have no more expertise in making these judgments than the rest of us, and as social needs become more complex, it will likely get even more challenging to 'gauge their direction, their extent, or their significance.'[570] It seems that we are now asking judges 'to solve a controversy they cannot understand, by a rule whose import they cannot guess.'[571] And if we pursue this path, how would the law differ from social science engineering? Posner re-opens his hand. The law has disappeared.

Mature Discipline

The great tradition has an answer. The law's job description is to decide disputes in a meaningful way. To pursue its mission, it has now begun to borrow from other fields, and no one is seriously worried that the law will be absorbed by them. It learns efficiency from economics, adopts interpretive method from literary criticism, and draws on social science research to gauge the potential consequences of its rulings. Since the common law is now approaching its thousandth birthday, maybe it has earned the right to consider itself a mature discipline.

---

[566] A safety precaution is proper when it costs no more than the loss it is intended to prevent. See Posner (2007) § 6.1, pp. 167–171 (elaborating the *Hand Formula*, as suggested in *United States v. Carroll Towing Co.*, 159 F.2d 169, 173 (2d Cir. 1947) (Hand, J.)).

[567] Posner (2007) § 2.2, p. 25. For the principle of wealth maximization, see id. § 1.2, pp. 10–15.

[568] Holmes (1897), p. 469.

[569] Llewellyn (1925), p. 682.

[570] Llewellyn (1989), p. 66.

[571] Llewellyn (1925), p. 670.

True Grounds

Precedent does not play a major role in Posner's approach to judging. Instead, when asked to decide a case, his approach 'is first to ask [him]self what would be a reasonable, sensible result, as a lay person would understand it.'[572] Since judicial rhetoric conceals rather than illuminates, he believes that law schools should teach students to dig beneath doctrinal argument and locate 'the true grounds' of the decisions.[573]

This is a classic statement of great tradition wisdom. Doctrine is form. It provides the concepts and images judges use to explain a judgment that rests on concerns of social expectation and expediency. The project reminds me of a well-known writing prompt: 'Describe a building as seen by a man whose son has just been killed in a war. Do not mention the son, war, death, or the old man doing the seeing.'[574] The fiction writer's job is to present observable detail in a way that causes a sense of significance to arise in the reader. The judge's task is to use the law's conceptual vocabulary to resolve disputes in a way that we will conclude is socially meaningful.

Efficient Breach

The notion of *efficient breach* is one of the most intriguing ideas to emerge from law and economics, and Judge Posner has been an enthusiastic proponent.[575] The basic idea is that a party should be permitted to breach a contract when the breach would improve that party's position and would not harm anyone else.[576]

We have learned that the work of the judge is to integrate legal doctrine and social expectation into a convincing whole. What would happen if we were also to require the decision to maximize social wealth?

Let me put a case.[577] Manufacturer sells Distributor 100 window air conditioners for a total price of $30,000. A heat wave threatens as the delivery date approaches, units fly off retail shelves, and the wholesale price for the hundred rises to $40,000. A second distributor, Overbidder, sells chiefly to luxury retail stores that are willing to pay a premium.[578] The only units available for sale are those that Manufacturer

[572] Farnsworth (2006), p. 1095 (quoting Posner and Heymann (2006) (Posner, Day 1)).

[573] Posner (2007) § 2.2, p. 25.

[574] Gardner (1985), p. 203 (exercise 4d).

[575] See Posner (1972) § 3.8, p. 57.

[576] Birmingham (1970), p. 284.

[577] Economists have developed sophisticated models of efficient breach and no longer work with simplified scenarios like the one used here. Klass (2014), p. 370.

[578] The term *Overbidder* has been borrowed from Eisenberg (2005), pp. 998–1006.

has earmarked for Distributor. Overbidder offers Manufacturer $45,000 for immediate delivery. What should Manufacturer do?

Posner suggests that Manufacturer should breach the contract with Distributor and deliver the units to Overbidder. Manufacturer will pay $10,000 in damages—the additional funds that Distributor will need to buy those units when they become available. Manufacturer still earns a tidy extra profit. And because the air conditioners will have found their way to the place where they are most highly valued, society is better off and no one is worse off.[579] When resources are being used where their value is highest, 'we say they are being employed efficiently.'[580]

At this point in his demonstration, Posner may have sensed that his readers would wonder whether judges are permitted to encourage a breach of contract. To shore up his argument, Posner cited a single source, a thought from Holmes that we know well: 'The duty to keep a contract at common law means a prediction that you must pay damages if you do not keep it—and nothing else.'[581] The idea is clear—a breach of contract represents an economic decision rather than a civil wrong.

Contract Law

Let us now try to integrate the perspective of wealth maximization with the two other factors that we have been discussing—legal precedent and social expectation. To understand the challenge, we will need to ask a question that Posner did not. Overbidder paid Manufacturer an urgency premium of $5,000. Who has the better claim to it, Manufacturer or Distributor?[582]

We will begin with precedent. By delivering to Overbidder, Manufacturer breached its contract with Distributor. Should Distributor's damages include the urgency premium? The principal purpose of contract remedies is to place injured parties in the position they would have been in had the contract been performed.[583] Distributor will recover $10,000 in expectation damages—the difference between the contract price and the current market price. Once those damages are paid, Distributor is in the same position as if Manufacturer had performed.

In other words, Manufacturer keeps the extra profit. As the Restatement notes, the notion of efficient breach therefore 'accords well with the assumption of

[579] Economists focus on *effective demand*—demand backed by ability to pay. Efficiency therefore need not coincide with social welfare. Posner acknowledges that the term *efficiency* 'has limitations as an ethical criterion of social decisionmaking.' Posner (2007) § 1.2, p. 11; see also Posner (2007), p. 141 (Problem 1); Kaplow and Shavell (1994).

[580] Posner (2007) § 1.1, p. 9.

[581] Id. § 4.10 note 1, p. 119 (quoting Holmes (1897), p. 462). For the similar sentence found in Holmes (2009), p. 272, see above, p. 85.

[582] The question was suggested by Detlef Leenen.

[583] Restatement (Second) of Contracts, Reporter's Note to chap. 16, pp. 101–102 (1981).

contract law.'[584] The scant case law suggests that Distributor will recover standard expectation damages and nothing more.[585]

Restitution

The law of restitution offers a different take. We began to explore restitution earlier when we asked whether recovery is available for benefits conferred without request.[586] A different aspect of restitution requires parties to disgorge (surrender) all profits wrongfully obtained, particularly when the wrong was deliberate: 'The unjust enrichment of a conscious wrongdoer... is the net profit attributable to the underlying wrong.'[587] Since the profit in our hypothetical results from conscious wrongdoing, the drafters of the Restatement (Third) of Restitution concluded that the requirement to disgorge profits 'is inherently at odds with the idea of efficient breach.'[588] A party who breaches a contract to gain additional profit 'engages in precisely the conduct that the law of restitution normally condemns.'[589]

But is a breach of contract the type of legal wrong that should require the breaching party to disgorge all gain? It is contract law, not the law of restitution, that answers that question, and as we have just seen, a breach of contract, even when intentional, is not usually treated as a tort.[590] As a result, the law of restitution, though reluctantly, agrees with contract law: the extra profit remains with Manufacturer.[591]

Social Expectation

Let us now consult our third factor, social expectation. The drafters of the Restatement (Second) of Contracts sensed that readers would feel uncomfortable with efficient breach: 'The traditional response is not without its shortcomings.'[592]

The problem is that we would not expect the law to reward Manufacturer for intentionally breaching the contract, especially since sales contracts allocate the risk of a rising market to the seller and the corresponding benefit to the buyer. My

584 Id., pp. 100–101.

585 See *Acme Mills & Elevator Co. v. Johnson*, 133 S.W. 784 (Ky. 1911); Restatement (Third) of Restitution and Unjust Enrichment § 39 comment h, illus. 15 (2011).

586 See above, pp. 103–104.

587 Restatement (Third) of Restitution and Unjust Enrichment § 51(4).

588 Id. § 39 comment h (2011).

589 Id.

590 Id. § 39 comment a (2011).

591 Id. § 39(1)–(2).

592 Restatement (Second) of Contracts, Reporter's Note to chap. 16, p. 100.

intuition tells me that the law should reward Distributor's foresight. Efficiency concerns cannot help us here, since wealth maximization requires only that the units end up with Overbidder. Since the efficient result is achieved in either case, the judge's task is to find a way to accommodate the legal precedent that favors efficient breach with the social expectation that finds it suspect.

Though judges should consider efficiency, they cannot stop there. They will strive for a comprehensive solution that integrates efficiency concerns with both legal precedent and the socially-expected result. The challenge begins where Posner's efficiency calculus leaves off.

Gift Promises

Posner addressed *Webb v. McGowin* directly and explained how he would decide it. When thinking about *Webb*, how should we combine our three perspectives—efficiency, legal precedent, and social expectation?

Posner thinks of McGowin's commitment to Webb as a gift promise.[593] Gift promises are most valuable if donees can rely on them, and donees can best rely if courts enforce them. Donors too gain, since rational donors would like their donees to receive the maximum benefit. Posner therefore finds it efficient to enforce gift promises. What about social expectation? Those of us who feel the tug for Webb would expect the court to enforce McGowin's promise. As for legal precedent, it goes the other way: courts often do not enforce gift promises.[594] In other words, the three factors line up differently in Webb's case—efficiency and social expectation support Webb, while precedent points in the other direction.

The simplicity that is so impressive in Posner's approach is also the reason it disappoints. Once Posner settles on the efficient result, he puts down his pencil. Life in the fast lane. Must be nice. But as far as our work is concerned, he has only made it more difficult. We already had a lot to worry about. Now he has added another factor.

Hypothetical Negotiation

Is there an easy way to accommodate the three factors?

We may have what we need in the Posnerian notion of a 'hypothetical voluntary transaction,'[595] which I will call *hypothetical negotiation*. The method uses market wisdom to resolve disputes—even those disputes that have nothing to do with a market transaction. The method is fun and easy to use. We have only to imagine a

[593] Posner (2007) § 4.2, p. 99.

[594] See Hyland (2012) para. 693–709, pp 338–347.

[595] Posner (1985), p. 100.

film of the real-world events that led to the lawsuit. We freeze the frame at the critical juncture and imagine what happens as the parties step out of the film and negotiate. The deal that rational negotiators would come up with at that moment may offer a useful legal solution.[596]

Eckert v. Long Island Railroad

Let us watch as Posner analyzes the well-known case of *Eckert v. Long Island Railroad*.[597] A speeding locomotive was running in reverse and without a cowcatcher. As it approached a populated area, the locomotive's engineer negligently failed to reduce speed and also failed to blow the whistle. Henry Eckert saw the train appear out of nowhere and immediately thought of the child playing near the tracks. In a frantic dash, he tossed the child free, but the engine clipped Eckert's leg, and he died that night from his injuries. Eckert's personal representative sued the railroad in tort. Everyone agreed that the railroad was negligent. In defense, the railroad responded that Eckert caused his own death by knowingly running in front of an onrushing train. The New York high court ruled that Eckert was not at fault and held the railroad liable. Was the court's decision efficient?

Posner is not concerned with fault. He is interested instead in incentivizing proper safety precautions, and a hypothetical negotiation may point us in the right direction. If, as the train rounded the bend, a rational railroad would have hired Eckert to save the child, then the railroad should now pay Eckert's family the fee that it would then have agreed to.[598]

Before we can recreate the negotiations, we will have to make a few assumptions. We must assume at the outset that Eckert was not negligent for attempting the rescue. This is a curious assumption, since Eckert's negligence was the legal question before the court, but negotiation is only possible if we assume that Eckert's recovery was not barred by his own negligence—we will rely on the negotiation, not precedent, to decide the case. We will also assume that the railroad was aware that its engineer was negligent and that it had potential exposure to two wrongful death claims—one from the child for simple negligence, the other from Eckert if he attempted the rescue. And let us in addition assume that the child would have been killed by the speeding locomotive, that the lives of Eckert and the child were of equal value, and that Eckert would attempt the rescue for the right fee.

[596] The version of the hypothetical bargain addressed here has been called the 'naive conception.' See Charny (1991), p. 1878.

[597] Posner (2007) § 8.1, p. 250 (discussing *Eckert v. Long Island R.R. Co.*, 43 N.Y. 502 (1871)). For a more complete statement of the facts, see *Eckert v. Long Island R.R. Co.*, 57 Barb. 555 (N.Y. Sup. Ct. 1870).

[598] Posner (2007) § 8.1, p. 250.

If we also accept, as it seems Eckert did, that it was more likely than not that both Eckert and the child would survive the rescue, then the railroad should have paid Eckert to give the rescue a try. Hypothetical negotiation turns a legal decision into a question of probabilities, and much of the difficulty vanishes.

Webb v. McGowin

Now that we have completed our brief Posnerian apprenticeship, let us imagine a hypothetical negotiation in the *Webb* case. We begin by visualizing the events as a film running in slow motion. We are inside lumber mill No. 2 (wide angle shot). Webb is standing on the upper floor (low angle shot). He pushes the pine block to the edge of the deck (knee angle shot). As gravity lays claim to the block, Webb sees McGowin standing below (high angle shot). Webb has only an instant to decide (eye level closeup). Will he let go of the block, or will he hold on and fall with it (oblique angle shot)? The frame freezes. We are now to envision what rational parties in that situation would agree to.

McGowin is aware that he will be seriously injured or killed. He asks Webb to fall with the block and divert its path. If Webb is incapacitated, McGowin promises to pay him $15 every two weeks for the rest of Webb's life. A rational person with sufficient funds in McGowin's position would certainly make that offer.

A rational person in Webb's shoes, however, would likely not be persuaded. A very substantial pension might tempt him, but it would have to be one that would dramatically raise his family's living standard and perhaps also leave something for his children. McGowin's promise does not come close. In fact, the amount McGowin promised may have been something like Webb's usual wage. I do not see how rational parties could get to Yes here.

Implied Contract

Let us turn for a moment from our rational actors to our two protagonists. Given the promise that McGowin made after the event, it seems likely that he would have made the same promise at the moment of danger. As for Webb, he chose to fall with the block without any guarantees. If we give him a moment to reflect as he begins to fall, he will realize that this will not go well. If he had been asked at that moment, would our actual Webb have accepted the guarantee of a small pension? We have every reason to think so.

The kaleidoscope clicks again. We leave law and economics behind, and we find ourselves before a strange new constellation. Our two actors would have made this deal. If we imply a contract, the consideration problem vanishes. So then why not simply enforce this implied agreement? We would be binding parties to promises that exist merely because we have imagined them, and those encountering the common law for the first time may find this troubling. But it is not as worrisome as it might appear, for when the need arises, 'entire promises [can] be found by reading between the lines.'[599] Contract negotiations rarely address all the important issues, and a court often has to fill gaps before it can enforce a contract.

If I were convinced that it would be a helpful legal construction, I would happily embrace this solution. Of course, I still have doubts about whether it makes sense to construe Webb's heroic act and McGowin's generosity as a contractual exchange. But this problem does not delay me for long. I am not trying to find a legal description that flawlessly fits our facts. My main goal is to decide the case in Webb's favor. To do that, I am going to have to find a contract, and that means I will have to find some way to dodge the consideration doctrine. For my narrow purpose, an implied contract may be less of a stretch than the rarely used doctrine of moral obligation.[600]

I find the issue oddly perplexing. I will start with what I think I know. I want to decide the case for Webb. All that stands in the way is the consideration doctrine. I cannot abolish it, so I will have to finesse it. I am looking for a solution that does not call attention to itself. From this point of view, implying a contract offers an attractive solution.

And yet I am not happy with the construction. When I ask why, I hear myself say that I am pushing the doctrine of offer and acceptance too far. But why does that worry me? I am doing everything I can to circumvent the clear mandate of the consideration doctrine. Why should I care more about one doctrine than another? Besides, common law doctrine is meant to be reshaped. Why do I place such weight on getting the definition of offer and acceptance right?

I barely have access to these thoughts. They are there chiefly as a feeling of discomfort. The oracle is uttering strange sounds, and I am doing what I can to decipher them.

If I had to guess, I would say that I am worried that this solution may have consequences that I cannot predict and may later regret. Contract law serves several purposes, but I prefer to reason from what I believe to be its central mandate: ensuring that parties can rely on promises made in the marketplace. If we want to use the market to distribute resources, it usually makes sense, before enforcing a contract, to assure ourselves that the parties have come to terms. Though judges often imply promises to round out a deal, I cannot predict what might happen if they were to start finding promises when there was no deal at all, when the parties did not negotiate—or could not possibly have done so. 'The fact that they never spoke or in any real sense ever met and the fact that the transaction they are said to have entered into is

---

[599] Corbin (1939), vol. 39, p. 59, vol. 52, p. 411, vol. 48, p. 429.

[600] It may seem that a contract concluded while the block hangs like a Sword of Damocles over McGowin would be voidable under the doctrine of *duress*, but in fact the doctrine does not apply. A contract may be avoided when the compulsion emanates from the other party but not when it is due to an external source. See Restatement (Second) of Contracts § 175(1); *Chouinard v. Chouinard*, 568 F.2d 430, 433–434 (5th Cir. 1978).

bizarre... might give one pause.'[601] Contract law would be appropriating a vast authority to reshape society—an authority that I do not think fits its mission and that I am not convinced it would use wisely.

Each of the factors and approaches we are considering is useful, but none can decide the cases properly until it is integrated with the others. We will take the Posnerian notions of efficiency and hypothetical negotiation on board, but they will be only two factors among many.

References

Birmingham R (1970) Breach of contract, damage measures, and economic efficiency. Rutgers Law Review 24:273–292

Charny D (1991) Hypothetical bargains: The normative structure of contract interpretation. Michigan Law Review 89:1815–1879

Corbin A (1939) Mr. Justice Cardozo and the law of contracts. Columbia Law Review 39:56–87, Harvard Law Review 52:408–439. Yale Law Journal 48:426–457

Domnarski W (2016) Richard Posner. Oxford University Press, New York

Eisenberg M (2005) Actual and virtual specific performance, the theory of efficient breach, and the indifference principle in contract law. California Law Review 93:975–1050

Farnsworth W (2006) The role of law in close cases: Some evidence from the federal courts of appeals. Boston University Law Review 86:1083–1096

Fish S (1994) There's no such thing as free speech... and it's a good thing, too. Oxford University Press, Oxford

Gardner J (1985) The art of fiction: Notes on craft for young writers. Vintage, New York

Holmes O (1897) The path of the law. Harvard Law Review 10:457–478

Holmes O (2009) The common law. Harvard University Press, Cambridge

Hyland R (2012) Gifts: A study in comparative law, [rev edn]. Oxford University Press, Oxford

Kagan E (2007) Richard Posner, the judge. Harvard Law Review 120:1121–1122

Kaplow L, Shavell S (1994) Why the legal system is less efficient than the income tax in redistributing income. Journal of Legal Studies 23:667–681

Klass G (2014) Efficient breach. In: Klass G et al (eds) The philosophical foundations of contract law. Oxford University Press, Oxford, pp 362–387

Leff A (1974) Economic analysis of law: Some realism about nominalism. Virginia Law Review 60:451–482

Llewellyn K (1925) The effect of legal institutions upon economics. American Economic Review 15:665–683

Llewellyn K (1989) The case law system in America, Gewirtz P (ed), Ansaldi M (trans). University of Chicago Press, Chicago

Newman R (ed) (2009) Yale biographical dictionary of American law. Yale University Press, New Haven

Peters E (1981) Arthur Leff as a scholar of commercial and contract law. Yale Law Journal 91:230–234

Posner R (1972) Economic analysis of law. Little, Brown, Boston

Posner R (1985) Wealth maximization revisited. Notre Dame Journal of Law, Ethics & Public Policy 2:85–106

[601] Fish (1994), p. 167 (discussing *Webb v. McGowin*).

Posner R (2007) Economic analysis of law, 7th edn. Aspen, New York
Posner R (2008) How judges think. Harvard University Press, Cambridge
Posner R (2013) Reflections on judging. Harvard University Press, Cambridge
Posner R, Heymann P (2006) Tap dancing: a TNR online debate. New Republic Online, Jan 31, 2006
Radin M (1940) Law as logic and experience. Yale University Press, New Haven
Shapiro F (2021) The most-cited legal scholars revisited. University of Chicago Law Review 88:1595–1618
Sunstein C (2017) Richard Posner, leader of a legal revolution. Bloomberg (Sept. 3, 2017)

Chapter 12
Doubt (Gilmore)

No one better understood the devastating consequences of Llewellyn's discoveries than Grant Gilmore (1910–1982).[602] He reviewed *The Bramble Bush* at its first commercial publication and concluded that Llewellyn had been right about everything.[603] Llewellyn charted a path around the rigidity of classical jurisprudence and showed us how to think creatively in the law. Though little more than twenty years had passed since Llewellyn first gave those lectures, Gilmore noted that Llewellyn's ideas had already become as obvious as the roundness of the Earth and the circulation of blood. Llewellyn's only mistake was to have believed that he had meaningfully reconstructed jurisprudence. In fact, he left it a colossal wreck.

Contract Is Dead

By the time another twenty years had passed, Gilmore had made peace with the challenges and presented his reflections in the lectures he delivered in 1970 at the Ohio State Law School and called *The Death of Contract*. The book's message is summed up in its cryptic opening, one of the common law's most enigmatic passages: 'We are told that Contract, like God, is dead. And so it is.'[604] And the thought returns for a cameo in the book's concluding sentence: 'Contract is dead—but who knows what unlikely resurrection the Easter-tide may bring.'[605] Gilmore recognized the value of repetition in a literary text: he taught for several years in the Yale French department

[602] For Gilmore, see Peters (2009).

[603] Gilmore (1951), p. 1252.

[604] Gilmore (1974a), p. 3.

[605] Id., p. 103.

R. Hyland, *Common Law Judging and the Great Tradition*, Ius Gentium: Comparative Perspectives on Law and Justice 100,
https://doi.org/10.1007/978-3-032-02307-0_12

before enrolling in the Yale Law School. Those two mysterious sentences about the death of contract perfectly encapsulate his vision, but before we can make sense of them we will first have to learn a little more about his book.

Gilmore's provocative title was not meant to suggest that common law courts no longer decide contracts cases. The title refers instead to the demise of *classical contract doctrine*. Already in 1920, Samuel Williston, Corbin's Harvard counterpart, admitted how hard it was to unify the unruly principles of contract law. 'The law of contracts... after starting with some degree of unity now tends from its very size to fall apart.'[606]

Llewellyn understood the disintegration of contract doctrine as tragedy: 'Life struggling against form, or through form to its will—"pity and terror—."'[607] Gilmore saw it instead as tragicomedy—and welcomed its decline with a smile. The scale of the decay was for him vaster than it was for others, so sweeping that it is difficult to appreciate. Gilmore did not just mean that contract law could use some rethinking. He meant that its entire conceptual structure, and especially all that is taught in the first-year contracts course, is nonsense. No part of that doctrine has ever had the least impact on the judicial mind.

Angels and Demons

In Gilmore's telling, contract doctrine arose in the middle of the nineteenth century and died a slow death at the beginning of the twentieth. At that critical moment, one conception of common law adjudication—the belief that rules decide cases—was replaced by another—the understanding that decisions are fact-sensitive rulings intended to reach meaningful results. Gilmore's book pretends to recount the history of the conflict and its eventual resolution, but what he actually produced is a morality play in which angels do battle with demons. Corbin and Llewellyn, wearing the blue jerseys of Yale and Columbia, joined Cardozo alongside the heavenly host, while Langdell and Williston suited up in Harvard crimson and followed Holmes into battle for the evil spirits. Gilmore's loyalty was not in question. Cardozo, Gilmore told his students, 'I admire with a reverence just this side of awe.'[608]

We recognize the names, but the characters Gilmore described do not resemble the historical figures whose work we have come to admire. This should not worry us. In the great tradition, historical accuracy is a subsidiary virtue. 'I often say,' Cardozo wrote, 'that one must permit oneself, and that quite advisedly and deliberately, a certain margin of misstatement.'[609] What counts is vision, and Gilmore's little book

[606] Williston (1920), vol. 1, p. iii.

[607] Llewellyn (1931f), p. 751 (quoting Aristotle's definition of tragedy).

[608] Hutchinson (2002), p. 70 (quoting Gilmore in the classroom).

[609] Cardozo (1931a), p. 341.

presents such an affecting view of the modern common law that few who read it escape its hold.

Christopher Columbus Langdell (1826–1906),[610] one of the villains in Gilmore's drama, was a more influential legal educator than anyone teaching in America today. He served as dean of the Harvard Law School for twenty-five years, and the school's flagship building still bears his name. Langdell invented the case method and also created the first casebook. Harvard's President Eliot, that institution's great innovator, thought Langdell 'a man of genius' and believed that appointing him as dean of the law school was, along with two of his other successes, 'the best piece of work I did for Harvard University.'[611] And yet thanks to Gilmore, Langdell's accomplishments do not matter. They will never matter. Whenever Langdell's name is mentioned, for all eternity, what will immediately come to mind is Gilmore's savage epithet: 'Langdell seems to have been an essentially stupid man who, early in life, hit on one great idea to which, thereafter, he clung with all the tenacity of genius.'[612]

Samuel Williston (1861–1963)[613] too was worthy of Gilmore's steel. He taught at Harvard for half a century, and served both as reporter for the first Restatement of Contracts and as the 'superb draftsman' who drew up the Uniform Sales Act.[614] The American Bar Association awarded him its first Gold Medal, and toward the end of his long teaching career, he received honorary degrees from both Harvard and Yale. Llewellyn co-dedicated his Sales casebook to Williston, and Corbin acknowledged Williston to be 'my chief teacher in the law of Contracts.'[615] And yet to Gilmore, Williston was always the slowest student in the class.

Parallel Structures

The facts did not matter to Gilmore. He was on a mission to demonstrate the fatuity of the consideration doctrine, the 'balance-wheel of the great machine' of classical contract thinking.[616] He argued that Holmes dreamed up the consideration doctrine to restrict the promises courts might enforce. Holmes's goal, Gilmore argued, was to free business from liability. With that goal in mind, Holmes decided that no one should ever be liable to anyone for anything.[617] Williston dutifully incorporated this reductivist understanding into the first Restatement of Contracts.

---

[610] For Langdell, see Kimball (2009), Ames (1909).

[611] Eliot (1887), p. 97 (genius); Letter from Charles Eliot to Henry S. Pritchett (Apr. 13, 1915), pp. 1–2 (Small Manuscript Collection, Harvard Law School Library, quoted in Kimball (1999), p. 66 note 37) (best piece of work).

[612] Gilmore (1977), p. 42.

[613] For Williston, see Rakoff (2022), Farnsworth (2009), Williston (1940).

[614] Scott (1963), p. 1331.

[615] Corbin (1963b), p. 1327.

[616] Gilmore (1974a), p. 18.

[617] Id., p. 14.

The francs-tireurs from Yale and Columbia shot back, arguing that consideration 'is not in any meaningful sense *a* topic,' and that the case law offers no 'simple and uniform' consideration doctrine to determine when promises would be enforced.[618] Cardozo was constantly adding and expanding exceptions to the consideration doctrine, while Corbin amassed a portfolio of cases in which courts had enforced promises that were lacking in Holmesian consideration.[619] The courts did not follow the consideration doctrine, and as Llewellyn was soon to explain, 'where doctrine does not square with case-results, that doctrine *is not law*, in a case-law field.'[620]

In 1932, the drafters of the first Restatement of Contracts accepted both the (so-called) Holmesian and Cardozian positions and restated rules for each. In principle, no contract can be concluded without consideration.[621] However, many exceptions allow promises to be enforced in its absence.[622] The two parallel structures were each able to resolve most of the cases, and yet, though they would often produce conflicting results, the drafters made no attempt to reconcile them. The surrender to incoherence was exhilarating.

Good Story

Here too it is useful to note how creatively Gilmore deployed his sources. He portrayed Holmes as the unfeeling scholar who insisted on doctrinal rigor and had no use for social justice. And yet Holmes had early on criticized Langdell's obsession with logical consistency, calling him 'the greatest living legal theologian,'[623] and because Langdell refused any reference to the outside world, Holmes decided that he 'represents the powers of darkness.'[624] As for Cardozo, he was a monk of the Holmesian order. He quoted frequently from *The Common Law* and always with approval. 'Here is the text to be unfolded,' he wrote of it. 'All that is to come will be development and commentary.'[625] And as we know, Holmes welcomed Cardozo to the Court as his worthy successor. Among 'a few masters,' Holmes wrote to Cardozo, 'you hold a conspicuous place.'[626]

Gilmore knew all of this, but he also knew better than to let it stand in the way of a good story. 'History, let us conclude, is a systematic distortion of the past, designed

---

[618] Llewellyn (1941c), p. 778; Corbin (1963a) § 109, vol. 1, p. 487. See above, p. 106.

[619] Gilmore (1974a), p. 63.

[620] Llewellyn (1938), p. 1269.

[621] Restatement of Contracts § 19(c) (1932).

[622] Id. §§ 85, 86–94.

[623] [Holmes] (1880), p. 234.

[624] Letter from O.W. Holmes Jr. to Frederick Pollock (Apr. 10, 1881), in Holmes and Pollock (1942), pp. 16, 17.

[625] Cardozo (1931b), p. 683.

[626] Letter from Oliver Wendell Holmes to Benjamin N. Cardozo (Dec. 15, 1928), quoted in Rauh et al. (1979), p. 10.

to tell us something meaningful about the present.'[627] Yalies were the creative jurists who ably adjusted the law to the facts, while the impassive scholars at Harvard clung to their rigid rules. The story ended, as of course it had to, with the death of the heartless Holmesian construction. As we finish Gilmore's book, we are convinced that contract doctrine sprang full blown from the mischievous imaginations at Harvard Law, led its brief, cloistered existence in the classrooms of Langdell Hall, perished in obscurity, and now lies by the side of an untraveled road in an unmarked grave.

Why Doctrine

Deep in the scholarly mind sits a hieroglyph. It is the unanswerable question that motivates a lifetime of research but that rarely appears in print. While Gilmore was having all this fun penning his parable, his mind was working on a different challenge. He had learned from a career teaching contracts that doctrine is unable to provide a roadmap for decision. But if we are not using doctrine to decide cases, why do we spend so much time adjusting and readjusting precedent?

This is the real topic of Gilmore's little book. He was aware of the usual answers. He recognized that doctrinal constructions provide a useful framework for anchoring decisions in the law. But if doctrine provides a number of answers to every case, how can it anchor anything?

Stilk v. Myrick

Early in the ninteenth century, two sailors jumped ship as their British merchant vessel was lying at anchor in Cronstadt, an island harbor off the coast of St. Petersburg. When it proved impossible to recruit replacements, the ship's captain asked the crew to work the ship home short-handed and, as compensation, promised to divvy up the deserters' wages among them. When the vessel reached London, the master refused to pay the additional recompense, and a sailor's suit for the bonus reached the Court of King's Bench. In *Stilk v. Myrick,* Lord Chief Justice Ellenborough refused to enforce the captain's promise.[628] Maritime law required sailors to continue to perform their duties even with a depleted crew, so the sailors were already obligated to work the ship home. Since a promise to perform a

---

[627] Gilmore (1966), p. 6.

[628] See *Stilk v. Myrick*, (1809) 2 Camp 317, 170 Eng Rep 1168 (KB) (reported by John Campbell (1779–1861)); 6 Esp 129, 170 Eng Rep 851 (KB) (reported by Isaac Espinasse (1758–1834), junior counsel for the sailor). For a discussion of the reporters and their reports, see Luther (1999), pp. 527–537.

pre-existing duty does not create a bargain, Lord Ellenborough seems to have held that the captain's promise lacked consideration.

In his contracts treatise, Williston took up the question of whether a promise to perform a preexisting duty may serve as consideration.[629] When a contract is to be modified, as was the case in *Stilk*, a fresh bargain is needed—some adjustment on both sides.[630] One party's promise to do what is already owed generally cannot support a modification. The logic is inescapable and needs no elaboration. But Williston lost focus, veered off course, and claimed that the preexisting duty rule was designed to prevent one party from taking advantage of the other in exigent circumstances: 'Especially common is the situation where a... contractor... finding the contract unprofitable, refuses to fulfil his agreement but is induced to fulfil it by the promise of added compensation.' There—for the only time in his multi-volume treatise—Williston cited *Stilk*.[631]

Gilmore took one look at Williston's paragraph, noticed the disconnect, and immediately pounced.[632] *Stilk* was not a case in which the consideration doctrine saved a captain from a promise he made under duress. The offer to distribute the deserters' wages came not from the crew but from the captain, who was doing his best to bring his ship home. Gilmore conveniently ignored the fact that Corbin himself had linked *Stilk*, the preexisting duty rule, and the possibility of duress.[633] He called out the Holmesian consideration doctrine as a cheap scam.

Merchant Seamen

Gilmore was right about the disconnect, and yet Williston may have been onto something. We do not know the exact date of the captain's promise, but it must have been within a few years of the Battle of Trafalgar (1805). Britain was then engaged in a life-or-death struggle against Napoleon, and the Royal Navy was Britain's main line of defense. The members of the *Stilk* crew were merchant seamen and not tars in the Royal Navy, but seamen too were often pressed into duty.[634] A sailor's objection 'would have been as idle as the protest of a goldfinch popped into a cage.'[635] By statute, seafarers' articles were to specify the compensation and had to be concluded in writing before the ship sailed.[636] Special rules discouraged unscrupulous captains

[629] Williston (1920), vol. 1, § 130, pp. 275–276.

[630] Restatement (Second) of Contracts § 71 (1)–(2) and comment b (1981); *Goncalves v. Regent Int'l Hotels, Ltd.*, 447 N.E.2d 693, 700 (N.Y. 1983).

[631] Williston (1920), vol. 1, § 130, p. 276 note 12.

[632] Gilmore (1974a), pp. 22–28.

[633] See Corbin (1918), p. 373 and note 20.

[634] Dancy (2015), p. 125.

[635] Melville (2017), chap. 1, p. 4.

[636] Luther (1999), pp. 542–545.

and owners from refusing to pay wages, while deserters were penalized and their wages forfeited.[637] In that highly-regulated field, a captain's oral promise, made far from home port, was not going to carry much legal weight.

On crossings to the West Indies, death and desertion took a constant toll. If sailors were allowed to insist on additional wages when the ship was understaffed, as Lord Kenyon observed, a captain might have to accept extravagant demands just to bring the ship home.[638] Lord Ellenborough was of course aware that the crew in *Stilk* had not tried to coerce a raise. But if the captain's promise was enforceable, any sailor could get a jury trial by claiming to have been promised a bonus. To check those lawsuits, Lord Ellenborough decided that, as a matter of law, a captain's mid-voyage promise was not supported by consideration.

Once again, Gilmore was working creatively with the facts. He was right to suggest that *Stilk* was a policy decision based on maritime law, but he overshot the mark when he claimed that the case had nothing to do with the consideration doctrine.[639] Moreover, Gilmore's prediction of the doctrine's demise was exaggerated. The English Court of Appeal, one of the high courts in England and Wales, expressly reaffirmed the holding in *Stilk* in 1979[640] and again in 1990.[641] A court in our day might feel a tug for the sailors, and the case 'might... have been decided differently if... tried today.'[642] But that makes it especially noteworthy that the Lord Justices of Appeal nonetheless reaffirmed the principle that a promise to perform a preexisting obligation is not consideration for a promise to modify a contract.

Gilmore's View

What did Gilmore think of Lord Ellenborough's decision in *Stilk*? In his Ohio State lectures, Gilmore devoted more pages to the case than to any other decision. He also included it in the contracts casebook he edited with Kessler and discussed with his students for decades. For Kessler, as I remember, the case was easy. If the seamen had coerced the raise, the promise could have been avoided for duress. Lack of consideration alone was never a good reason to refuse to enforce a promise. What did Gilmore think? He did not say.

Gilmore also mentioned *Mills v. Wyman* and *Webb v. McGowin*. Were they rightly decided? Gilmore was amused by the fact that the Restatement approved both *Webb*, which enforced the promise, and *Mills,* which did not, even though the drafters were

---

[637] Id.

[638] *Harris v. Watson*, [1791] Peake 102, 170 Eng Rep 94 (KB) (Lord Kenyon).

[639] Gilmore (1974a), p. 26.

[640] See *North Ocean Shipping Co. Ltd. v. Hyundai Construction Co. Ltd.* [1979] 3 WLR 419, 426–427, [1979] QB 705.

[641] See *Williams v. Roffey Bros. & Nicholls (Contractors) Ltd*, [1990] 2 WLR 1153, 1170 (CA), [1991] 1 QB 1, 21.

[642] Id. (Purchas L J).

unable to distinguish the two cases.[643] As the two opinions lay open on his desk, he might have explained how they should be decided. He did not take the bait.

Gilmore enjoyed watching judges bushwhack their way through the underbrush to avoid inconvenient doctrine and reach the desired result, but it was rare for him to take a position on whether the court got the case right. We might therefore conclude that his lectures cannot help us further in our quest. But that would be a mistake. This is one of the most profound books ever written about the questions we are working on.

Death of God

The traditional notion of God no longer provides an undisputed foundation for theology, just as the doctrinal concept of contract no longer dictates decisions in the common law. And yet congregants continue to attend religious services and judges still search for the right result. Why do worshipers persevere once they are overwhelmed with doubt? And if there is a good legal argument on both sides of the case, how do we explain 'the effort, and the importance of the effort, of each individual deciding officer to reach what *he* thinks is *the* right answer'?[644]

Gilmore had been at Yale for several years when in 1950 Paul Tillich, existentialist and Death-of-God theologian, delivered the Terry lectures,[645] and Gilmore, as I imagine him, was there. As Tillich concluded the final lecture, he summarized his thought in what may be the best sentence he ever wrote: 'The courage to be is rooted in the God who appears when God has disappeared in the anxiety of doubt.'[646]

Certainty is available neither in theology nor in law. So then why do religion and law not lose their authority? Perhaps the answer is that we still need something to hold onto. Judges come to appreciate that judicial decision-making engages them in the awesome project of creating meaning—for themselves, for the litigants, for society. Their understanding of what is proper—so deeply felt because conscientiously constructed from all that matters most—is the law that appears once we recognize that nothing will relieve us of the task of deciding for ourselves. This is law beyond law, law without law, law after law.[647]

---

[643] See Gilmore (1974a), pp. 74–75; Restatement (Second) of Contracts § 86 illus. 1, 7 (1981). See above, pp. 25–26, 33–34.

[644] Hart and Sacks (1994), pp. 149–150.

[645] See Tillich (2014).

[646] Id., p. 175.

[647] See Wheeler (1983).

Anxiety

Gilmore's lectures are great fun, but each time I reread them, I feel more intensely the unnerving anxiety that lingers just below their surface. 'We are like spies in an alien land,' Gilmore had written a few years earlier, 'cut off from any contact with headquarters, with no way of ever finding out whether the intelligence which we diligently collect and relay is what is required of us or is even relevant to our vague and ambiguously stated mission.'[648]

Doubt remains Gilmore's legacy to us, the most important factor we discuss. The answer is always receding: 'The path of law leads not to the revelation of truth but to the progressive discovery of infinite complexity.'[649] Gilmore summarized this thought in the commencement address he delivered a few days before he died. 'What makes law, its study and practice, qualitatively unlike most other things that human beings do is that we can never be sure of anything.'[650]

References

Ames J (1909) Christopher Columbus Langdell. In: Lewis W (ed), pp 465–489
Cardozo B (1931a) Law and literature and other essays and addresses. Harcourt, Brace, New York
Cardozo B (1931b) Law and the university. Law Quarterly Review 47:19–22
C[orbin] A (1908) Part payment of a debt as consideration for a promise. Yale Law Journal 17:470–473
Corbin A (1918) Does a pre-existing duty defeat consideration?—recent noteworthy decisions. Yale Law Journal 27:362–381
Corbin A (1961) The judicial process revisited: Introduction. Yale Law Journal 71:195–201
Corbin A (1963a) Corbin on contracts: A comprehensive treatise on the working rules of contract law, vol 1. West, St. Paul
Corbin A (1963b) Samuel Williston. Harvard Law Review 76:1327–1329
Dancy J (2015) The myth of the press gang: Volunteers, impressment and the naval manpower problem in the late eighteenth century. Boydell Press, Woodbridge
Eliot C (1887) President Eliot's Address. In: Winsor J (ed) A record of the commemoration, November Fifth to Eighth, 1886, on the Two Hundred and Fiftieth Anniversary of the founding of Harvard College. John Wilson, Cambridge, pp 96–99
Farnsworth E (2009) Williston, Samuel. In: Newman R (ed) pp 593–594
Gilmore G (1951) Review of Llewellyn, The bramble bush. Yale Law Journal 60:1251–1253
Gilmore G (1966) Law, anarchy and history. University of Chicago Law School Record 14(2):1, 5–7
Gilmore G (1968) Response to Coif award. University of Chicago Law School Record 16(1):30–31
Gilmore G (1974a) The death of contract. Ohio State University Press, Columbus
Gilmore G (1977) The ages of American law. Yale University Press, New Haven
Gilmore G (1981) For Arthur Leff. Yale Law Journal 91:217–218
Gilmore G (1982) What is a law school? Connecticut Law Review 15:1–6

[648] Gilmore (1968), p. 30.
[649] Gilmore (1981), p. 218.
[650] Gilmore (1982), p. 3.

Hart H, Sacks A (1994) The legal process: Basic problems in the making and application of law, Eskridge W, Frickey P (eds). Foundation, Westbury
[Holmes O] (1880) Review of Langdell, A selection of cases on the law of contracts and Anson, Principles of the English law of contract. American Law Review 14:233–235
Holmes O, Pollock F (1942) Holmes-Pollock letters, Howe M (ed), vol 1. Harvard University Press, Cambridge
Hutchinson D (2002) Remembering Grant Gilmore. Green Bag 2d 6:67–72
Kimball B (1999) 'Warn students that I entertain heretical opinions, which they are not to take as law': The inception of case method teaching in the classrooms of the early C. C. Langdell, 1870–1883. Law and History Review 17:57–140
Kimball B (2009) The inception of modern professional education: C. C. Langdell, 1826–1906. University of North Carolina Press, Chapel Hill
Lewis W (1909) Great American lawyers, vol. 8. John C. Winston, Philadelphia
Llewellyn K (1931f) What price contract?—an essay in perspective. Yale Law Journal 40:704–751
Llewellyn K (1938) The rule of law in our case-law of contract. Yale Law Journal 47:1243–1271
Llewellyn K (1941c) On the complexity of consideration: A foreword. Columbia Law Review 41:777–782
Luther P (1999) Campbell, Espinasse and the sailors: Text and context in the common law. Journal of Legal Studies 19:526–551
Melville H (2017) Billy Budd, sailor (an inside narrative). In: Hayford H et al (eds) Billy Budd, sailor and other uncompleted writings. Newberry Library, Northwestern University Press, Evanston, pp 1–72
Newman R (ed) (2009) Yale biographical dictionary of American law. Yale University Press, New Haven
Peters E (2009) Gilmore, Grant. In: Newman R (ed) (2009), p 221
Rakoff T (2022) Professor Samuel Williston (1861–1963). In: Goudkamp J, Nolan D (eds) Scholars of Contract Law. Hart, Oxford, pp 175–200
Rauh J et al (1979) A personal view of Justice Benjamin N. Cardozo: Recollections of four Cardozo law clerks. Cardozo Law Review 1:5–22
Scott A (1963) Samuel Williston. Harvard Law Review 76:1330–1332
Tillich P (2014) The courage to be, 3d edn. Yale University Press, New Haven
Wheeler J (1983) On recognizing 'law without law,' Oersted Medal response at the joint APS-AAPT meeting, New York, 25 January 1983. American Journal of Physics 51:398–404
Williston S (1920) The law of contracts, 4 vols. Baker, Voorhis, New York
Williston S (1940) Life and law: An autobiography. Little, Brown, Boston

Chapter 13
Altruism (Kennedy, Unger)

In his book *In Praise of the Laws of England*, Sir John Fortescue (c. 1394–1479),[651] Chief Justice of King's Bench, tried to convince an imaginary prince to study English law.[652] The prince eventually agreed that the common law is 'exceptional among all other laws of the earth, among which I see it shine like Venus among the stars.'[653] Though there have always been naysayers, centuries of common lawyers have held this 'traditional reverence for the common law.'[654] 'So venerable, so majestic, is this living temple of justice, this immemorial and yet freshly growing fabric of the Common Law, that the least of us is happy who hereafter may point to so much as one stone thereof and say, The work of my hands is there.'[655]

That widespread acclaim ended abruptly in the 1970s. Critical legal studies (CLS) then assumed the mantle of the great tradition and provoked the most profound rethinking of the common law since the end of the writ system. The Crits (as they were fondly known) condemned many of the scholars who preceded them and argued that the common law, far from embodying justice, contributes to a system that empowers the powerful and disadvantages the disadvantaged. 'The system by which the rich and powerful, white and male, stay rich and powerful, generation after generation, has a very strong legal component.'[656] CLS occupied the center of American legal thought for about a decade. Though its suggestions were radical,

---

651 For Fortescue, see Barnes (2008), pp. 46–60; Wood (1994), pp. 44–69; Holdsworth (1938), pp. 59–65.

652 See Fortescue (1997), pp. 1–80.

653 Id., pp. 79–80.

654 Holdsworth (1938), p. 163.

655 Pollock (1886), p. 111.

656 Clark et al. (1985), p. 10 (remarks of Duncan Kennedy).

R. Hyland, *Common Law Judging and the Great Tradition*, Ius Gentium: Comparative Perspectives on Law and Justice 100,
https://doi.org/10.1007/978-3-032-02307-0_13

nothing about it was as shocking as its tone. Its thinkers conveyed a sense of oracular certainty that, as Patricia Williams put it, made it seem that '*they had reached a place which was Beyond the Power of Words... and experienced godhood.*'[657] Roberto Unger, one of the most creative CLS thinkers, expressed the Crits' contempt for their predecessors in words that find little precedent in centuries of writing about the common law:

> When we came, they were like a priesthood that had lost their faith and kept their jobs. They stood in tedious embarrassment before cold altars. But we turned away from those altars and found the mind's opportunity in the heart's revenge.[658]

That attitude convinced Posner that critical legal scholars were 'unassimilable and irritating foreign substances in the body of the law school.'[659] And Kessler was also not impressed: 'Regrettably, this school's contribution to contract law has so far not been especially impressive.'[660] We might regret the disenchantment, but more was gained than lost. CLS located the genius of the common law and has helped it achieve more of its promise.

Constructive Criticism

The next three chapters explore recent transformations of the great tradition. The texts are difficult, particularly because they share the additional complication that their authors are attempting a radical reorientation of the common law. Blackstone, as we know, was convinced that the common law does not adjust well to quick fixes. The Crits disagreed, and it may at first seem that their impatience would make them a poor fit for the great tradition. But in fact they have given the common law greater self-awareness. The common law remains the system we know, different only in that it has become mindful of its defeats—and of the traces they have left behind. The great tradition is still there, despite CLS's self-confident assertions of originality, and beneath it remains the tradition's signature humility. Unger concluded what is probably still his best book with an admission every bit as forlorn as the darkest of Gilmore's avowals: 'But our days pass, and still we do not know you fully. Why then do you remain silent? Speak, God.'[661]

---

[657] Williams (1987a), p. 402.

[658] Unger (1986), p. 119.

[659] Posner (1981), p. 1128.

[660] Kessler (1988), p. 114 (translation) (discussing critical legal studies).

[661] Unger (1975), p. 295.

Everything Is Political

Duncan Kennedy, a CLS founder whose work we are about to discuss, described critical legal scholars as 'a rag-tag band of leftover '60s people and young people with nostalgia for the great events 15 years ago.'[662] To understand their mindset, we will have to 'imagine someone who first started thinking seriously about law as a student in law school in the late 1960s.'[663] That decade's central insight was that everything is political, and if everything is political, the law cannot be otherwise. A judge who owns rental property is likely to sympathize with landlords, while those who pay their bills on time may not understand those who fall behind. As Posner suggested, 'The law is shot through with politics.'[664]

Baked In

And yet the claim that the law is political does not square with experience. Given the vast number of people involved in the judicial process, it is hard to see how case outcomes can express political commitments. Juries are drawn from a cross-section of the population with a rainbow of political views. Skilled advocates cross-examine witnesses, object to hearsay, and insist on the production of original documents. Experienced appellate judges, each with law clerks who excelled in law school, scrutinize the trial courts' rulings. All of the many individuals involved in the process have political views, but they certainly do not all have the same one. Of course there is still prejudice and miscarriage of justice, but it is hard to see in the common law a systematic privileging of a single viewpoint—unless, as is often the case, it is when the system tips the scales in favor of the disadvantaged. In big city courtrooms across the country, judges regularly extend deadlines for those without a lawyer, offer unsolicited advice, berate opposing counsel, and when all else fails, subvert the meaning of statutes and precedent to protect the underprivileged.

CLS acknowledged all of this. Its critique begins here. We are about to encounter the CLS argument that will carry us into the heart of the common law, but before we do, it is important to recognize what it is not. When they were writing at the top of their game, CLSers were not focused on the now obvious fact that, because legal rules are inherently indeterminate, the individual judge's political views play a role in the outcome. The more telling argument was instead the very different claim that political bias is baked into the law. Judges further the interests of the powerful unawares—and even when they try not to.

---

[662] Clark et al. (1985), pp. 8–9 (remarks of Duncan Kennedy).

[663] Gordon (1982), p. 282.

[664] Posner (2008), p. 9.

Legal Liberalism

We begin with the approach that critical legal studies defined itself against. As Robert Gordon explained, the Crits shared a 'common disenchantment with legal liberalism.'[665] It is not easy to define this target precisely, both because there is 'no single, unambiguous thing called liberalism'[666] and because the Crits tended to apply the tag *liberal* to many of the very different ideas with which they disagreed.[667] But they all believed that an essential first step was to cast off liberal thinking: 'One must start by knowing what is going on, by freeing oneself from the mystified delusions embedded in our consciousness by the liberal legal worldview.'[668]

Dualities

Both *liberty* and *liberalism* come from the Latin word *liber*, which is in turn related to *libet* (it is pleasing or agreeable) and also to *libido*, with its connotations of pleasure and desire.[669] *Liber* describes individuals who follow their will or pleasure, who are unrestrained, uninhibited, independent, those who are their own masters, and—importantly for our purposes—who are in that sense free. In the early modern period, moral and political theories developed this individualist perspective into a critique of the autocratic *ancien régime*. Though liberalism can take a variety of forms, liberals tend to defend six values —'freedom, human rights, pluralism, security, the rule of law, and democracy.'[670]

What the Crits correctly challenged about liberalism was its tendency to neglect the social nature of human existence. Its various versions fail in different ways to grasp that both individuals and their wishes are social constructs—and that they could not exist without society. As a result, liberalism does not provide meaningful criteria for choice among conflicting yearnings[671]—whether to surrender to convenience and drive to work or instead to act virtuously and take the train, whether to stay late at the office or instead spend time with the family. For liberalism, the human condition is constantly wracked by 'insoluble contradictions or "antinomies."'[672]

These contradictions reappear in the law as conflicting answers to legal questions. The law is thus perpetually torn between the 'spheres of reason and of desire, of fact and of subjective values, of freedom and of necessity, of the development of

---

665 Gordon (1982), p. 282.

666 Freeden (2015), p. 1.

667 Hutchinson and Monahan (1984a), p. 209 note 43.

668 Freeman (1981), p. 1231.

669 See Lewis and Short (1966), pp. 1056–1060.

670 See Sunstein (2025), p. 1.

671 Hutchinson and Monahan (1984b), p. 1496.

672 Id., p. 1493.

the self and of the need for communal relationships, of the free interaction of civil society and of the demands of the state, of the controlling importance of empirical fact and the controlling importance of ideas.'[673] The contradictions cannot be resolved from the point of view of the isolated individual—and that is because each of the competing positions can muster good reasons in its favor.

Competing Justifications

These opposing arguments come together in the law as matched pairs of competing justifications, each providing a powerful rejoinder to the other. This helps explain why a good argument can usually be constructed on both sides of every serious case. Mark Kelman summarized the idea in technical terms: 'The legal system is invariably simultaneously *philosophically committed* to mirror-image contradictory norms, each of which dictates the opposite result in any case (no matter how "easy" the case first appears).'[674] This idea has surfaced so often in our readings that it no longer seems troubling. And yet, CLS will soon take advantage of it to surprise us.

If a legal system is constantly repeating the same arguments and countering them with the same pre-programmed responses, why does anyone take legal argument seriously? Because the competing positions are not makeweights. They point to the factors that judges in fact have to reconcile before almost any case can be resolved. In pages of exquisite lucidity, James Boyle imagined such a dialogue.[675] Plaintiff's lawyer asks the court to adopt a clear rule—norms with well-defined boundaries are easy to administer. Defense counsel responds that a rigid rule would tie the court's hands and constrain business enterprises—a flexible rule allows commerce to adjust to changing conditions. Plaintiff's lawyer replies that the norm must not be so uncertain as to inhibit business planning.... Those trained in legal metaphysics can continue the argument indefinitely, producing subtle variations on society's need for both stability and flexibility. 'Each argument conjures up a believable picture of "the good life"' and yet 'for each argument or technique there is a counterargument.'[676]

These initial insights are uncomfortable, but they are not new. Kessler himself had explained that 'rule and counter-rule often express different value systems struggling for recognition,'[677] and then concluded: 'Our living law of contracts is not a closed system of harmonious rules but an open system of social action rich in dynamic complexity and full of contradictions.'[678]

[673] Frug G (1980), pp. 1074–1075.

[674] Kelman (1987), p. 13.

[675] See Boyle (1985), pp. 1056–1059. For further illustrations, see Fischl (2001), pp. 790–791; Llewellyn (1950), pp. 401–406.

[676] Boyle (1985), pp. 1048, 1051–1052.

[677] Kessler (1952a), p. 68 (translation); see also Kessler (1952b), p. 1093.

[678] Kessler (1952b), p. 1094.

Individualism and Altruism

Duncan Kennedy (1942-),[679] now an emeritus professor at the Harvard Law School, pointed the way to the next step.[680] Kennedy clerked for Justice Stewart and was named Harvard's Carter Professor of General Jurisprudence in 1996.[681]

In a seminal article, Kennedy argued that the pairs of competing contentions form a single, overarching dichotomy, one that opposes two 'distinct visions of human nature and human fulfillment'[682]—*individualism* and *altruism*.[683] All of the law's competing justifications channel one or the other of these 'two opposed rhetorical modes,'[684] and when each set is rethought as a meaningful whole, the result is a pair of 'irreconcilable visions of humanity and society, and... radically different aspirations for our common future.' [685] The fierce competition between the two positions turns the law into a field of 'irreducible, irremediable, irresolvable conflict.'[686]

Those who support individualism argue that individuals have the right to pursue their goals without social interference as long as they do not violate the rights of others. Altruism, the competing rhetorical mode, provides the theoretical foundation for a more communal organization of society. It is allied with notions of sharing, sacrifice, and solidarity,[687] and, as critical legal thinker Jay Feinman explained, it fosters attitudes of concern and caring and encourages meaningful connection with others.[688] CLSers believed that the common law has long been skewed toward the individual, and they recommended a radical reorientation. Since individuals can achieve their goals only when society provides the opportunities, the conditions for a productive life should be widely shared.

Kennedy translated the two categories from political theory into our legal vocabulary—individualism expresses itself in law as the respect for individual rights, while law operates altruistically when it places limits on the exercise of those liberties.[689] In the vocabulary of the great tradition, we might say that courts act altruistically when they work from their understanding of social welfare, while they favor individualism when they stand back and allow the parties to exercise their legal rights freely.

---

[679] For Kennedy, see Kennedy (2021); Goodrich (2001).

[680] See Kennedy (1976).

[681] Doctorat honoris causa (2011).

[682] Kelman (1987), p. 3.

[683] Kennedy (1976), p. 1685.

[684] Id.

[685] Id.

[686] Kelman (1987), p. 3.

[687] Kennedy (1976), p. 1718.

[688] Feinman (1983), p. 843.

[689] Kennedy (1976), p. 1721.

Practical Consequences

When a court adopts the individualist argument, it often favors a party with resources. A court that evicts a tenant for nonpayment of rent prefers the landlord's individual right to possession to the altruist concern that everyone should have a home. As judges evict tenants day after day, they offer the powerless up to the profit-oriented decisions of the wealthy. Though these decisions follow precedent, they are not politically neutral, for they favor one social group over another.

Whenever I reach this point in the CLS argument, I feel dissent rising within me. No, I hear myself say, the Crits are making a category error: it is not the law that is unfair to the tenant, it is the social structure. The housing market would collapse if courts were to stop enforcing lease agreements. The real problem is that so many tenants are without resources.

I have been here many times before. And it always comes as a shock when I eventually recall the CLS argument that we discussed as we began this chapter. We had no reason to object when CLS borrowed from the great tradition the claim that there is generally a good legal argument on both sides of every case. The idea seemed innocent then, but now not so much. If that premise is correct, then all of these eviction proceedings could come out the other way. A judge who wants to keep the tenant in the premises will always be able to find a defense. 'No case *has to* be decided one way rather than another.'[690]

Rule and Exception

If the law has the resources to decide cases either way, why do judges not rule more often for the disadvantaged? As Kennedy explained in a brilliant aperçu, it is because the opposing legal arguments do not compete as equals. One of the two contentions is considered the general rule, the other the exception—and the exception is available only in case of demonstrated need. We are familiar with this structure from our study of the consideration doctrine: 'Even today, despite widespread judicial and scholarly acceptance of promissory estoppel, the rhetorical dominance of consideration still relegates promissory estoppel to a secondary role.'[691] Kennedy noticed that the general rule usually incorporates the individualist position while the altruist standpoint is relegated to the exception. That means that the party seeking to relax the rigor of a rule is the one who has the burden of persuading the court.[692]

Kennedy has proved his point. The cards are often stacked against the weaker party, and that is even true—or especially true—when judges follow precedent and impartially apply the rules.

[690] Baron (2001), p. 800.

[691] Feinman (1984), p. 680.

[692] Kennedy (1976), p. 1738.

Law and Equity

Roberto Unger (1947-)[693] picked up where Kennedy left off. Unger was born in Brazil and worked to oppose the Brazilian military dictatorship in the 1970s and 1980s, then completed a doctorate in law at Harvard before joining the Harvard faculty. Unger has advised two Brazilian presidential candidates and served as Brazil's Minister of Strategic Affairs.

Unger's theoretical work has been called 'the most powerful social theory of the second half of the [twentieth] century.'[694] We will not try to do justice to his vast oeuvre. Instead, we will discuss only a single aspect of one lecture—'one of the longest and most indigestible after-dinner speeches on record.'[695]

In this lecture, *The Critical Legal Studies Movement,*[696] Unger borrowed from Kennedy the dichotomy between individualist rules and altruist exceptions and mapped it onto the common law's two opposing currents, law and equity. The rules at law are often imbued with an individualist spirit, while equity is often 'more ethical than law.'[697] We have seen this dichotomy at work. The consideration doctrine holds individuals only to those promises that are part of a bargain, while the equitable notion of promissory estoppel can grant a remedy, even without a bargain, as long as the promisee has reasonably relied.

Unger believes that the border between the two subfields is uncertain because it is contested—it is political rather than legal. This boundary traces the temporary truce between the *dominant* (legal) position—which favors those with resources—and the countervailing, *deviationist* (equitable) principles—which may sometimes assist the impoverished.[698]

Unconscionability

CLS aimed not only to understand the world but also to disrupt and change it. To restructure the common law, progressive lawyers should urge judges to limit the reach of general rules and apply instead the defenses embodied in both equity and a handful of compassionate legal doctrines. The *unconscionability doctrine*, a deviationist legal defense, is designed to assist parties stuck in unfair contracts. Might it become a tool for social change?

An English case from Blackstone's day defined unconscionable promises as those that no one not under delusion would make and that no honest and fair person

[693] For Unger, see Press (1999).
[694] Hawthorn (1987), p. 766.
[695] Collins (1987), p. 388.
[696] Unger (1986).
[697] Ames (1908), p. 106.
[698] See Unger (1986), pp. 15–22.

would accept.[699] Unconscionability offers protection to those with few resources, and therefore represents a hard-won proletarian position on conflicted terrain. In a case that has found its way into the casebooks, a door-to-door sales rep convinced the Joneses, at the time welfare recipients, to purchase a home freezer for three times its maximum retail value.[700] The court held that the price term was unconscionable, and the buyers, who had already paid much of the purchase price, were allowed to keep the freezer. If courts were to restructure consumer bargains more often, it might greatly improve the lot of the disadvantaged. 'Every contracts case has the potential for revolutionary creative activity.'[701]

Might Unger's strategy succeed? Unconscionability is what lawyers call an *affirmative defense*.[702] We might restate the doctrine like this: 'All otherwise valid contractual promises are enforceable, *except* those that are unconscionable.' When formulated as an exception, buyers like the Joneses can avoid their contract only by convincing the judge that the contract is seriously unfair.[703] To make the unconscionability defense more widely available, we could instead make *conscionability* the exception: 'No contractual promise is enforceable, *unless* it is conscionable.' The burden of persuasion and proof would then shift from the disadvantaged to those who control the bargain. To recover the price, a seller would have to demonstrate that the bargain is not unfair. Creditors would have to work harder to collect a debt. Legalese would vanish. If we were to follow this Ungerian strategy, doctrine by doctrine from one end of the common law to the other, individualism would give way to social solidarity, and barriers to social equality would fall. This is an inspired idea.

Form and Substance Again

But there is a rub. If the great tradition is right, Unger's idea cannot succeed. Unconscionability is doctrine, an aspect of the Holmesian form of the law, and it tends to remain relatively stable over time. Of course, common law judges constantly tweak the system to fit both their policy choices and our evolving expectations—so if a political movement were to compel businesses to change their practices, the courts might recognize the shift and reformulate the unconscionability doctrine accordingly.

But that is not how Unger understands the mechanism. He proposes that we start by asking courts to reformulate legal doctrine. Perhaps he is hoping that a shift in

[699] *Earl of Chesterfield v. Janssen*, (1751) 2 Ves Sen 125, 155, 28 Eng Rep 82, 100.

[700] *Jones v. Star Credit Corp.*, 298 N.Y.S.2d 264 (Sup. Ct. 1969).

[701] Feinman (1983), p. 858.

[702] *Strausberg v. Laurel Healthcare Providers, LLC*, 304 P.3d 409, 418-19 (N.M. 2013).

[703] Unconscionability is a question of law, and the argument is to the judge rather than the jury. See UCC § 2-302(1); Restatement (Second) of Contracts § 208 (1981).

the law's form will alter its substance. Anything is possible, but that is not how the great tradition has understood the dynamic. Trying to convince judges to reconfigure the law without an active social movement would mean rowing upstream.

Webb v. McGowin

Both Kennedy and Unger would favor Webb, an injured employee. And yet a victory in the case would not satisfy Unger. He would want the courts to enlarge the reach of moral consideration as a countervailing principle and use it to nudge contract law in the direction of social solidarity. But the holding in *Webb* has not attracted a following, and in the nine decades since the case was decided, the courts have not tried to expand its reach.

Better Outcomes

For purposes of argument, let us agree that capitalism exploits the working classes and that the law is biased in favor of the powerful. Let us also take the CLS challenge seriously and ask what the courts can do to help solve the problem.

Poverty Litigation

Forty years ago, the law firm in Washington DC where I was working as an associate assigned me for six months to the nearby office of Neighborhood Legal Services. The program's income guidelines were so strict that our clients were usually single moms living on welfare, and in that time I represented between fifty and sixty tenants. My assignment was to keep my clients in their apartments.

Lawyers for the landlords typically started the eviction process by choosing a single return date for a dozen or more cases. The clerk in Landlord and Tenant Court read the docket at nine in the morning, and as the cases were called, lawyers rose and demanded judgment. Most of the time, no one rose for the tenant. The clerk stamped the file and called the next case: 'Judgment!'... Stamp... 'Judgment!'... Stamp... 'Judgment!'... Stamp... 'Judgment!' Often more than a hundred cases were called in a single morning.

Landlords were usually suing to evict tenants who were not paying rent. My clients' landlords were slumlords, and defending them required no special legal talent. Every apartment violated the housing code, the violations were not just technical, and the landlord lawyers always agreed to a repair and a rent reduction. Few tenants had lawyers, and those without counsel negotiated on their own behalf.

When they were unable to reach an understanding, they waited for the clerk to call the matter a second time, and the judge heard the case.

Sometimes the landlord wanted to evict the tenant for other reasons—either to sell or renovate the property or because the tenant was mistreating the apartment or using it for illegal activity. For these cases, the D.C. Code required the landlord to serve a *notice to quit*.[704] The judges interpreted the statute to require the landlord to include the applicable code provision in the notice. As it turned out, the code's housing chapter had recently been revised and renumbered, and many landlord lawyers had not updated their forms.

As soon as I noticed an outdated citation, I insisted on a hearing. The judge took one look at the flawed reference and dismissed the case. The technical requirements for the notice to quit were so complex that there was almost always something wrong with the way it was drafted or served, and no matter how trivial the flaw, the judge dismissed the case.

One morning, a lawyer with a gold Rolex joined me on the front bench—a seasoned trial attorney who had taken a tenant's case pro bono. He did not settle with the landlord's lawyer, and when the case was called, he invited his client, her baby in her arms, to join him in the well of the court. The client had lost her job but was actively looking for work. Although she had missed a couple of rent payments, she believed she would soon be able to get current and was asking for a short grace period. The lawyer argued that a short delay would be sensible and humane: evicting the young family would produce suffering out of proportion to the loss of a few weeks' rent.

That kind of argument often works in the eight-figure commercial matters the lawyer handled in federal court just down the street, but it carried no weight in Landlord and Tenant Court. The judge listened with growing irritation and did not bother to ask opposing counsel to respond. 'Judgment!' he called out, banging his gavel. And then to the clerk, 'Next!'

The trial attorney was offering a compelling reason why the mother and her child should be allowed to stay in the apartment, while my argument was the kind of inconsequential quibble that makes people dislike lawyers. And yet my objection was an automatic winner, while the trial lawyer's social policy argument earned him only the thump of a gavel.

Annual Percentage Rate

Our legal services office was located around the corner from the Walker-Thomas Furniture Company, the defendant in the case that defined the modern unconscionability doctrine,[705] and one of its customers soon came to me for advice. My client

---

[704] See Loewinger (1986), pp. 67–68, 83–86, 147–154.

[705] See *Williams v. Walker-Thomas Furniture Co.*, 350 F.2d 445 (D.C. Cir. 1965).

bought a sofa from the company for $900, payments to be made monthly. He made half the payments, was furloughed from his job, and for the moment could pay nothing more. Walker-Thomas threatened to repossess the sofa. My client and I went over the contract but could find no defense.

As I slowly reread the agreement, I noticed the APR, the statement of the consumer loan's annual percentage rate required by the Truth in Lending Act.[706] I tried several times to calculate the rate according to the instructions provided in the regulations, but I came up with a different number each time, and it was never the APR stated on the loan document.[707] I called the store, reached the credit manager, gave him my client's loan number, and asked how he had calculated the APR. He asked why I was calling. I told him I had calculated the rate myself and come up with a different result. There was a pause. 'Wha'd'ya want, kid?' He was angry. I told him I wanted to make sure that the contract was in order before I allowed my client to make another payment. 'I mean. *What. Do. You. Want?* Do you want me to forgive the loan?' It took me a moment to understand. 'OK,' I said. 'Fine,' he said, 'he can keep the sofa.' He slammed down the phone. In other words, I thought to myself, the fact that I am not very good at math constitutes a defense in a consumer credit transaction.

The defenses that worked were always technical, and that was the experience at other legal services offices as well. 'For many experienced tenant attorneys defects on the face of the petition, which are frequent because of the complexity of the law and the incompetence of both landlords and their attorneys, constitute the first line of defense in a summary proceeding.'[708] I never asked a judge to expand countervailing doctrine. The real difficulty was that I was doing nothing to fix the underlying social crisis. Large numbers of Washingtonians did not earn enough to afford decent living quarters. My clients did not need creative legal theories. They needed a steady job.

Consent Decrees

Tenants ended up in court because they found themselves at the beginning of the month with a hole in their budgets, often for reasons beyond their control. If they did not appear on their court date, they were evicted. Those who answered when their cases were called adjourned with the landlord lawyers to the metal tables in the anteroom. The landlord lawyers worked with the tenants to come up with a payment

---

[706] For the rules currently in force, see 15 U.S.C. § 1606; 12 C.F.R. §§ 226.18(e), 226.22(b) (2023).

[707] Tables now aid calculation. See Appendix J to Part 1026—Annual Percentage Rate Computations for Closed-End Credit Transactions, 58 Fed. Reg. 16535 (Mar. 20, 2023) (to be codified at 12 C.F.R. pt. 1026).

[708] Lazerson (1982), p. 124 (discussing the experience of lawyers for the South Bronx Legal Services Corporation).

plan, they put it in writing, and both parties signed. A month or two of back rent was excused, and the tenant agreed to make payments going forward.

I knew something the tenants did not. Those settlement agreements were structured as consent judgments. Judges never excused tenants who violated those decrees. Given their exigent circumstances, most of those tenants would eventually breach, the landlords would be entitled to immediate possession, and the tenants would be out on the street. Those settlement agreements were just another step in the eviction process.

What to Do

Would it help if I put together a team of lawyers to represent the tenants summoned every morning to the Landlord and Tenant Division? The judge would dismiss most of those cases, and we would achieve two things: landlords would have to abide by the housing code, and they would be required to respect the procedural rights that make eviction more difficult. Posner claims that our efforts would be both futile and counter-productive.[709] If slumlords are no longer able to rent substandard apartments to tenants with few resources, those apartments will be torn down and redeveloped. My clients would have to move, and moving would destroy their community without improving their situation.

I agree with Unger. It is tragic that human beings, including so many children, live in degrading conditions. But I cannot see how litigating one case at a time can change that. It can protect the rights of a few tenants, but our social structure limits what the law can accomplish. 'No law can provide adequate wages and working conditions and decent and affordable housing to those without means.'[710]

Law Is Political

The common law is systematically biased in favor of individualism. Actually, we already knew that. At its birth, American contract law adopted the Holmesian view that individual reflection is essential to the moral life. But like all general principles, this one too has to be interpreted with compassion. With every judicial decision, one social group is preferred to another, and an unyielding focus on individual rights can devastate those without resources. The common law has cobbled together a few rules to add altruism to the mix, but since it is the common law we are talking about, the measures are not systematic, they are hampered by their historical origins, and the finished job looks patched rather than new.

---

709 Posner (2007) § 16.6, pp. 504–507.

710 Isay (1902), p. 33 (translation).

We now see another reason why judges do not decide cases by simply applying a rule—and that is because every meaningful decision requires reflection about whether to prefer the individualist general rule or the altruist exception. I think we can now better understand why, as Kessler put it, the 'technical doctrines of the law of contracts cannot possibly provide the courts with the right answers.'[711]

References

Ames J (1908) Law and morals. Harvard Law Review 22:97–113

Barnes T (2008) Shaping the common law: From Glanvill to Hale, 1188–1688, Boyer A (ed). Stanford Law Books, Stanford

Baron J (2001) The undersell: An essay on Duncan Kennedy's A critique of adjudication. Cardozo Law Review 22:797–816

Boyle J (1985) The anatomy of a torts class. American University Law Review 34:1003–1064

Clark R et al (1985) A discussion on critical legal studies at the Harvard Law School. Harvard Society for Law & Public Policy, Cambridge; Federalist Society for Law & Public Policy Studies, Washington

Collins H (1987) Roberto Unger and the critical legal studies movement. Journal of Law and Society 14:387–410

Doctorat honoris causa: l'UQAM rend homage à six personnalités lors des collations des grades de juin. UQAM Salle de presse. https://salledepresse.uqam.ca/communiques-de-presse/doctorat-honoris-causa-printemps-2011/

Feinman J (1983) Critical approaches to contract law. UCLA Law Review 30:829–860

Feinman J (1984) Promissory estoppel and judicial method. Harvard Law Review 97:678–718

Fischl M (2001) It's conflict all the way down. Cardozo Law Review 22:773–796

Fortescue J (1997) On the laws and governance of England, Lockwood S (ed). Cambridge University Press, Cambridge

Freeden M (2015) Liberalism: A very short introduction. Oxford University Press, Oxford

Freeman A (1981) Truth and mystification in legal scholarship. Yale Law Journal 90:1229–1237

Frug G (1980) The city as a legal concept. Harvard Law Review 93:1057–1154

Goodrich P (2001) Duncan Kennedy as I imagine him: The man, the work, his scholarship, and the polity. Cardozo Law Review 22:971–990

Gordon R (1982) New developments in legal theory. In: Kairys D (ed) (1982a), pp 281–293

Hawthorn G (1987) Practical reason and social democracy: Reflections on Unger's Passion and politics. Northwestern University Law Review 81:766–790

Holdsworth W (1938) Some makers of English law. Cambridge University Press, Cambridge

Hutchinson A, Monahan P (1984a) Law, politics, and the critical legal scholars: The unfolding drama of American legal thought. Stanford Law Review 36:199–245

Hutchinson A, Monahan P (1984b) The 'rights' stuff: Roberto Unger and beyond. Texas Law Review 62:1477–1540

Isay H (1902) Rechtsgeschäft und wirtschaftliche Machtverschiedenheit. Franz Vahlen, Berlin

Kairys D (ed) (1982a) The politics of law: A progressive critique. Pantheon, New York

Kelman M (1987) A guide to critical legal studies. Harvard University Press, Cambridge

Kennedy D (1976) Form and substance in private law adjudication. Harvard Law Review 89:1685–1778

Kennedy D (2021) My path to law and modernization at Yale, 1968–70: A memoir of radicalization. Journal of Institutional Studies 7:753–767

[711] Kessler (1943), p. 639.

Kessler F (1943) Contracts of adhesion—some thoughts about freedom of contract. Columbia Law Review 43:629–642
Kessler F (1952a) Freiheit und Zwang im nordamerikanischen Vertragsrecht. In: von Caemmerer E et al (eds) Festschrift für Martin Wolff: Beiträge zum Zivilrecht und internationalen Privatrecht. Mohr Siebeck, Tübingen, pp 67–78
Kessler F (1952b) Review of Corbin on Contracts, volume one. Yale Law Journal 61:1093–1104
Kessler F (1988) Metamorphosen im Amerikanischen Vertragsrecht. Juristenzeitung 43:109–116
Lazerson M (1982) In the halls of justice, the only justice is in the halls. In: Abel R (ed) The politics of informal justice, vol. 1: The American experience. Academic Press, New York, pp 119–163
Lewis C, Short C (1966) A Latin dictionary. Clarendon Press, Oxford
Llewellyn K (1950) Remarks on the theory of appellate decision and the rules or canons about how statutes are to be construed. Vanderbilt Law Review 3:395–406
Loewinger K (1986) Loewinger on D.C. landlord-tenant law. Michie, Charlottesville
Pollock F (1886) Oxford law studies. In: Pollock F (1890) Oxford lectures and other discourses. Macmillan, London, pp 91–111
Posner R (1981) The present situation in legal scholarship. Yale Law Journal 90:1113–1130
Posner R (2007) Economic analysis of law, 7th edn. Aspen, New York
Posner R (2008) How judges think. Harvard University Press, Cambridge
Press E (1999) The passion of Roberto Unger: A Harvard law professor jettisons his past and sets out to destabilize Latin America. Lingua Franca 9(3):44–53
Sunstein C (2025) On liberalism: In defense of freedom. MIT Press, Cambridge
Unger R (1975) Knowledge & politics. Free Press, New York
Unger R (1986) The critical legal studies movement. Harvard University Press, Cambridge
Williams P (1987a) Alchemical notes: Reconstructing ideals from deconstructed rights. Harvard Civil Rights-Civil Liberties Law Review 22:401–434
Wood N (1994) Foundations of political economy: Some early Tudor views on state and society. University of California Press, Berkeley

Chapter 14
Empathy (Frug)

Mary Joe Frug (1941–1991)[712] was captivated by people. In her book *Postmodern Legal Feminism*,[713] she turned the spotlight away from the law and shined it on those of us who read cases and on the parties we read about. This will seem strange and new, and yet Frug was pulling together different strands of the great tradition.

Feminist Jurisprudence

Frug taught on several law faculties before joining the New England Law School. She was an active participant in the debates about feminist jurisprudence—a movement that aims to reform the law to so that it respects all genders.

In 1991, while a fellow at Radcliffe's Bunting Institute, she was murdered on a quiet street not far from her home in Cambridge. She was about fifty years old. Her book was published after her death. It is rare for a law professor to die as a victim of violence. Let Frug's death stand here for how hard it has been for women to attain the positions necessary to publish on the questions we have been examining.

---

712 For Frug, see In Memoriam: Mary Joe Frug 1941–1991 (1990).

713 Frug (1992).

R. Hyland, *Common Law Judging and the Great Tradition*, Ius Gentium: Comparative Perspectives on Law and Justice 100,
https://doi.org/10.1007/978-3-032-02307-0_14

Individuals

Before I began to read Frug's work, I paid little attention to the people in the cases. They disappeared behind legal labels—promisors and promisees, buyers and sellers, debtors and creditors. Once I noted who was plaintiff and who defendant, I referred to them all with a lawyerly wave of the hand as the *parties*.

To decide disputes dispassionately, it seemed to me, judges must ignore the messiness of the actual quarrel and compare the parties' actions to what we would expect from reasonable people. That is how I explained to myself why judges reduce the individuals who appear in court to something like markers in a boardgame. 'It is not John and Richard personally whom they considered, but John and Richard as members of a group, a fungible John and Richard.'[714] Before Frug, no theorist in the great tradition had figured out how a focus on personal experience might help judges decide cases.

Mary Joe Frug found that path. The tradition's interest in facts and circumstances led her naturally to an empathetic embrace of those who come before the court. Everyone knows that individuals are involved in the disputes before the courts. Without them and their stories, many of us would not be doing law. But the law has never cared as much for those in distress as we do. Frug insisted that the law allow itself to feel their pain.

With her 'voracious appetite for people,'[715] Frug was the right person for the job. She had a 'particular, special way of connecting with other people,' always 'leaning towards that other person, eagerly, curiously, with her wonderful kind of spun sugar delight.'[716] When she described someone, it was 'a whole rich story, full of attention to details,' always 'wrapped in the cozy, embracing sympathy' of a novelist and hoping to enlist sympathy and understanding for the person whose story it was.[717] 'She would bend over to people eating next to us and ask what they had had for dinner and if they liked it.'[718]

Why did individuals so intrigue her? Partly because she authentically loved people. But it was also conceptual. Her distinctive focus revealed a truth that the law usually seeks to disguise: *each of us is unique*. And yet Llewellyn too recognized the idea and even considered its consequences: we decide 'based on individual experience,' and can thus never gain 'objective knowledge of the facts as they really are.'[719]

I come together with my students a couple of times a week, but they are not in any meaningful sense a class. Each of them is involved in a personal quest, all are running their own races, and the hurdles they find in their way are their own.

---

[714] Radin (1935), p. 56.

[715] Memorial Service for Mary Joe Frug (1992), p. 640 (remarks of Cynthia Wardell).

[716] Id., p. 643 (remarks of Mopsy Strange Kennedy).

[717] Id., p. 644.

[718] Id., p. 657 (remarks of Stephen Frug).

[719] Llewellyn (1989), p. 53.

Teaching means being fascinated with, and moved by, their experiences and difficulties. Though I have had some success attending to their individual challenges, I have long reduced my students to a single common denominator: they are minds, individual intelligences. Thanks to Frug, I now see that students stumble over different things because they have led different lives and have drawn different lessons from their experiences.

Frug has convinced me to add their details back into the mix. And yet I still find a willed disremembering essential for a university educator. I do not want my teaching to vary according to the group characteristics of my students—whether race, gender, college affiliation, or anything of the kind.

As I have paid more attention to my students as individuals, the human beings in the cases have come alive for me. Statements of facts now only whet my appetite, and I always want to know more. The parties have become for me the people they are everywhere but in the law.

Portraits

Frug began to people the law by identifying different types of casebook readers and portraying them in a marvelous series of miniatures.[720] Many will recognize something of themselves in one or the other of these portraits.

Feminists, as Frug described them, have gender on their minds and are always on the lookout for bias. I read Frug's portraits broadly. Others share some of the feminist's traits, particularly those working for racial and ethnic equality. Though each commitment is personal, and different types of discrimination speak to different communities and create stereotypes that are painful in different ways, each shapes what we take from our reading. Political engagement quickly uncovers a judicial opinion's lack of compassion—and that is true whether the cause is progressive or conservative.

Woman-centered readers notice when a court fails to give working women their due. This portrait also captures something of the perspective of single parents, of law students supporting a family, of people living with disabilities, and of those for whom English is a second language. *Readers with a chip on their shoulders* have been hurt in the past and read the holdings through the lens of their ordeals.

Our relationship with the law often flows not from our typicality but from our uniqueness. Because each of us has a different take on the law, legal concepts separate as much as they unify, and judicial opinions miseducate some as they educate others. As for the individuals before the court, since legal concepts are designed to capture only a narrow aspect of their lives, those categories can get in the way of the common law's mission, which is to consider all the facts and circumstances of the

[720] Frug (1992), pp. 56–59.

case. That is why Frug asked judges to move past the expectations of a reasonable person and pay attention to the actual needs and wants of the specific individuals before the court.

Can the common law continue along its traditional path once we acknowledge human uniqueness? If we shift our standpoint slightly, this intricate web of perspectives shows how to solve the problem it seems to create: a flood of new ideas will emerge from 'this happily cacophonous universe' and, 'this multivalent way of seeing,'[721]—and these insights may offer useful solutions.

Allied Van Lines v. Bratton

In a couple of chapters in her book, Frug let us look over her shoulder as she worked her way through a well-known contracts casebook.[722] The record has survived for one of the cases she singled out for attention, and I think the additional facts make it easier to see what it would mean for the law to take individuals seriously.

Two women separately contracted with Allied Van Lines to transport their household effects, and in both moves, the women's belongings were lost. Neither woman declared a value for her shipment, and a default provision in their moving contracts limited the amount they could recover.[723]

Neither woman read the contract before signing it. Roberta McKnab told the carrier that she wanted all available insurance and was incorrectly informed that no additional insurance was available. The Florida Supreme Court relieved her of the liability limitation: she had not had 'a reasonable and fair opportunity to value her goods.'[724] Ila Bratton, in contrast, was not misinformed, and no one prevented her from reading the contract. In her case, the court enforced the limitation and reduced her recovery to about half the value of her loss.

The movers, Frug thought, put Ms. Bratton in an impossible situation. 'The house was really cold,' Ms. Bratton testified, 'and the men were tired. They were in a hurry to get out.'[725] Ms. Bratton did what Frug believed many women would do—she empathized with the moving crew, neglected her own interests, and signed the contract without reading it. 'Women are socialized to consider and value others' feelings above their own, and Mrs. Bratton simply acted like a woman in this

---

[721] Williams (1989), pp. 2143, 2151.

[722] Frug (1992), pp. 53–107 (examining Dawson et al. (1982)).

[723] *Allied Van Lines, Inc. v. Bratton*, 351 So.2d 344 (Fla. 1977) (discussed in Frug (1992), pp. 95–102, and in Dawson et al. (1982), pp. 448–452).

[724] *Allied Van Lines, Inc.*, p. 348.

[725] Frug (1992), p. 99 (quoting Dawson et al. (1982), p. 449 note 2, which was quoting *Allied Van Lines, Inc.*, p. 346 note 3). Ms. Bratton's statement is recorded in Trial Transcript, vol. 2, p. 154 (testimony of Ila Bratton), *Allied* File.

situation.'[726] By enforcing the liability clause against her, Frug argued, the court punished Ms. Bratton for being a woman.

Duty to Read

Under the contract's liability limitation, a customer received full compensation for loss only by entering the shipment's dollar value in the blank provided.[727] With a declared a value, the price of the move increased somewhat. If no value was declared, the carrier's liability was limited to $1.25 per pound.

Ms. Bratton signed without declaring a value, and the Florida Supreme Court held that her recovery was limited to poundage. The court was not moved by the fact that she was unaware of the liability limitation. 'No party to a written contract in this state can defend against its enforcement on the sole ground that he signed it without reading it.'[728] This principle, sometimes called the *duty to read*, is a standard feature of the common law of contract. 'Generally, one who assents to a writing is presumed to know its contents and cannot escape being bound by its terms merely by contending that he did not read them.'[729] The reason is clear: if the terms of a written agreement were to bind only those with knowledge of them, no one with decent legal advice would ever read a contract.

Standard Form Contracts

The contract of carriage for an interstate move is a type of *standard form contract*.[730] The party with greater bargaining power usually drafts the terms and offers the contract to the weaker party on a take-it-or-leave-it basis.[731] Contract law governs these contracts, now staples of daily life,[732] even though traditional contract doctrine lacks the tools to protect the reasonable expectations of the weaker party.[733] As the German free lawyers asked long ago, 'Can and should we calmly look on as, with the help

[726] Frug (1992), p. 100.

[727] See Form Household Goods Carrier Bill of Lading & Straight Bill, p. [1], *Allied* Record [pp. 138–39].

[728] *Allied Van Lines, Inc. v. Bratton*, 351 So. 2d 344, 348 (Fla. 1977).

[729] Restatement (Second) of Contracts § 157 comment b (1981).

[730] See Slawson (1971).

[731] Rakoff (1983), p. 1177; Llewellyn (1960), id. For consumer contracts, see Restatement of Consumer Contracts, Introduction (2024).

[732] Slawson (1971), p. 529.

[733] Llewellyn (1939), pp. 700–701; Kessler (1957a), pp. 1174–1175.

of the legal system itself, the weak are ruthlessly oppressed and exploited by the strong?'[734]

Customers generally do not read the fine print, and they often would not understand it if they did.[735] Since consumers are usually unaware of the terms, those who draft the forms have every incentive to shift burdens our way.[736] Frug believed that the courts should acknowledge the asymmetry and protect weaker parties.[737] The social expectation is that courts will not enforce contracts lacking in meaningful reciprocity.[738]

And yet judicial attempts to reduce the imbalance have had only moderate success[739]—'the consumer-purchase transaction is still stumbling about, a diagnosed disease seeking a nostrum.'[740] Some courts find it irrational to insist on the duty to read when in fact no one reads, and they refuse to enforce terms that most consumers would find objectionable.[741] 'Courts in construing and applying a standardized contract seek to effectuate the reasonable expectations of the average member of the public who accepts it.'[742] Some courts enforce liability limitations like the one in Ms. Bratton's contract only if the customer's choice was 'absolute, deliberate and well informed.'[743]

Justice Hatchett

The *Bratton* decision was unanimous. Justice Joseph Hatchett (1932–2021),[744] who drafted the opinion, was the first African American appointed to the Florida Supreme Court. Hatchett grew up in a poor, segregated neighborhood, his father a fruit picker, his mother a housekeeper. After serving on the Florida Supreme Court, he was the first Black judge appointed to the Fifth Circuit—the court that hears appeals from the Deep South—and later served as Chief Judge of the Eleventh Circuit. Hatchett 'demonstrated deep compassion for people, especially the less fortunate and

---

734 Isay (1902), p. 6 (translation).

735 Bakos et al. (2014), p. 1.

736 See Rakoff (1983), p. 1227.

737 Frug (1992), p. 101.

738 See above, pp. 70–71.

739 Warkentine (2008), p. 471.

740 Leff (1970), p. 142.

741 See *James B. Nutter & Co. v. Estate of Murphy*, 88 N.E.3d 1133, 1139 (Mass. 2018); *Berkson v. Gogo LLC*, 97 F.Supp.3d 359, 389–390 (E.D.N.Y. 2015); *Woodruff v. Bretz, Inc.*, 218 P.3d 486, 491 (Mont. 2009); *Lauvetz v. Alaska Sales and Service*, 828 P.2d 162, 164–165 (Alaska 1991).

742 Restatement (Second) of Contracts § 211(3). comment e.

743 *Trans-American Van Serv., Inc. v. Shirzad*, 596 S.W.2d 587, 590–591 (Tex. App. 1980) (quoting *Anton v. Greyhound Van Lines, Inc.*, 591 F.2d 103, 108 (1st Cir. 1978)).

744 For Hatchett, see Green (2018).

oppressed.'[745] The justice must have thought long and hard before deciding against Ms. Bratton. What might have convinced him?

Perhaps he did not want to throw a wrench into a uniform federal regulatory scheme. The limitation of liability clause is mandated by federal law[746] and represents the kind of grand national bargain that Hart and Sacks encouraged courts to respect.[747] Hatchett applied the limitation without asking whether it was fair on the facts before him: 'It is not essential to the validity of such a limitation that it be shown that the shipper was aware of it, or that he had read it, or that it had been explained to him, or his attention called to it... every shipper is conclusively presumed, in such a case, to have read and assented to the provisions... whether he in fact assented or not.'[748]

Alternative Criterion

The common law is committed to the principle of full compensation, and 'arrangements limiting liability contravene a strong public policy.'[749] To prevent what amounts to forfeiture, a customer's assent should be considered 'effective only if given after "a fair opportunity to choose."'[750]

We are back on familiar terrain. The common law's principle of full compensation points in one direction, the principle of institutional settlement in another. Can we find a solution that both respects the principle of institutional settlement and also accommodates the particular circumstances of Ms. Bratton's move?

Moving Day

Our events took place in October 1973 when Ms. Bratton, 62 years old at the time, was moving from her home in Canton, Ohio.[751] She left school after her junior year in high school and worked until she got married. Her two children were grown and

---

745 Florida courthouse named for influential judge (June 29, 2023) (quoting Judge Charles R. Wilson).

746 See 49 C.F.R. § 1307.201(c)–(d) (1968).

747 See above, pp. 143–144.

748 *Allied Van Lines, Inc. v. Bratton*, 351 So.2d 344, 348 (Fla. 1977) (quoting *Atl. Coast Line R.R. Co v. Dexter,* 39 So. 634, 635–636 (Fla. 1905)).

749 *Chandler v. Aero Mayflower Transit Co., Inc.*, 374 F.2d 129, 135 (4th Cir. 1967).

750 *Chandler*, p. 135 (quoting *N.Y., New Haven & Hartford R. R. Co. v. Nothnagle*, 346 U.S. 128, 135 (1953)).

751 For Bratton, see Trial Transcript, vol. 1, p. 86 (testimony of Ila Bratton), *Allied* File; Deposition of Ila M. Bratton, pp. 3–6, *Allied* File. Ms. Bratton was white, as were the lawyers and the others who testified at trial. The race of Allied's drivers is not mentioned in the documents. They did not

out of the house. Her husband handled the family's finances.[752] When he died four years earlier,[753] Ms. Bratton felt the need for a fresh start and decided to relocate to Orlando, Florida.

Allied's agent left her with the conviction that Allied would provide full coverage if anything happened to her belongings. 'I figured it would cover full loss, you know, the price of my whole shipment. That is what I thought; or I would have taken out more insurance, sure, because I lost - - You lose everything you have.'[754] No one explained the liability limitation to her.

On the day of the move, Ms. Bratton pre-paid the tariff in cash. The helper told Ms. Bratton that he had a drinking problem, and she made him the cup of coffee he asked for. He told her that this was his first trip with Allied and mentioned that it would also be his last.

It was late when the crew finished loading. 'Well, they had all the doors open. The house was froze from 4:30 until 10:30. The furniture was all gone, and all there was left was a stove.'[755] As the last order of business, the movers asked her to sign the documents. The driver held them up to the small light over the stove[756] and pointed to the signature lines. Ms. Bratton signed as directed. 'The light wasn't very bright, but the driver said, "sign here and sign here." He wanted to get out. He was turning the pages so fast that I don't think he wanted me to read them.'[757]

Loss

Ms. Bratton's belongings never arrived. The judicial opinions suggest that her household effects were destroyed in transit,[758] but that is not what happened. Two weeks after the agreed delivery date, Ms. Bratton called Allied and 'learned her shipment had been hijacked by the Allied helper on the van.'[759] Because Allied admitted liability and contested only the amount of damage, there was no testimony as to the circumstances of the loss, but the events can be reconstructed.[760] The movers left Ms. Bratton's home, had the load weighed, and took a room in a motel. After

---

testify, and their race was not revealed at trial. Information provided by Ren Werrenrath, counsel for Allied Van Lines.

[752] Deposition of Ila M. Bratton, pp. 46–47.

[753] Id., p. 46.

[754] Trial Transcript, vol. 1, p. 93 (testimony of Ila Bratton), *Allied* File.

[755] Id., p. 98.

[756] Id., pp. 100, 99, 102 (testimony of Ila Bratton).

[757] Id., p. 99.

[758] See *Allied Van Lines, Inc. v. Bratton*, 330 So.2d 521, 522 (Fla. Ct. App. 1976), *quashed*, 351 So.2d 344, 346 (Fla. 1977).

[759] Brief of Respondent Ila M. Bratton (March 10, 1977), p. 2, *Allied* Record.

[760] Information provided by Ren Werrenrath, counsel for Allied Van Lines.

the driver fell asleep, the helper stole the truck and drove through the night to Detroit, where he sold what he could from the back of the van. Allied eventually delivered to Ms. Bratton what was left—broken dishes, one shoe, one glove, one coat.[761]

The jury awarded Ms. Bratton full compensation, $10,630,[762] and found that 'her failure to read the bill of lading and ascertain its true nature [was] excusable under all of the circumstances.'[763] The jury also concluded that Bratton acted 'as a person of ordinary prudence would have acted under the circumstances.' The trial court entered judgment on the verdict, and the Florida appellate court affirmed. As we know, the Florida Supreme Court reversed and, by enforcing the liability limitation, it reduced Ms. Bratton's recovery to somewhat less than half of the jury's award.

Fair Opportunity to Choose

As we have seen, some courts enforce the liability limitation only if the customer has been given 'a fair opportunity to choose.' Did Ms. Bratton have that opportunity? Federal regulations require the limitation to appear on the face of the bill of lading in bold letters and a distinctive color.[764] The block letters on Ms. Bratton's contract were printed in red,[765] but the provision was less conspicuous than it might seem. It had no heading, and there was nothing to suggest its importance. And the liability clause was do or die—if the shipper failed to declare a value, compensation would be greatly reduced.

The case is not about the duty to read—it is not about Ms. Bratton at all. The problem was with the limitation clause. To say that it is badly drafted is a ridiculous understatement. It is technical, compressed, and seriously convoluted. I have taught commercial bills of lading for forty years, but I had not previously encountered this clause. I first examined it in the quiet of my office and had to read it twice before I was convinced that I understood it. Ms. Bratton had not finished high school, and her husband had managed the family finances. If unsophisticated consumers are unable to understand a term in their contract, it may be procedurally unconscionable.[766] But since the clause in this contract was mandated by federal regulation, it would be a heavy lift to convince a court that it is incomprehensible as a matter of law.

---

[761] Deposition of Ila M. Bratton, p. 42, *Allied* File.

[762] Trial Transcript, vol. 3, p. 396 (Jury Verdict), *Allied* File; Verdict, Question (4), *Allied* Record [pp. 130–131].

[763] Verdict, Question (2), id.

[764] See 49 C.F.R. § 1307.201(c)–(d) (1968).

[765] Trial Transcript, vol. 3, p. 358 (closing argument of Ren Werrenrath), *Allied* File.

[766] See *Burch v. Second Judicial Dist. Court of State ex rel. County of Washoe*, 49 P.3d 647, 650 (Nev. 2002).

Detroit

I am now thinking about what Ms. Bratton lost. 'Mrs. Bratton had her accumulations of a lifetime in that van.... She had 27 years of a very happy marriage to her husband; but because of this loss, she doesn't have anything to commemorate that....'[767] She lost the flag from her husband's military funeral. She lost photos from her wedding, boxes of pictures of her children growing up, of her grandchildren, and of her mother and father. She lost engraved sterling from her twenty-fifth wedding anniversary, and the family Bible.[768] She had wanted to take those things with her in her car, but the appraiser told her not to. 'He said, if I stopped at a motel, somebody could break in the car and take them. He would put them in the truck and pack them in barrels and guarantee they would get down there all right. So, he talked me out of it.'[769]

My thoughts now turn to the helper. Neither he nor the driver testified at trial, and yet I see the sequence as in a movie. The helper needed a drink but had no cash. Once he was sure the driver was asleep, he slipped the keys out of the pocket of his colleague's overalls. He drove through the night and got to Detroit around dawn on a cold Monday morning. He parked the van, opened the back doors of the cargo bay, and began to sell off Ms. Bratton's possessions. Once he had enough for a few drinks, he got back in the truck and drove off.

I cannot get the scene out of my mind. May I consider it? The thrust of the tradition since Blackstone tells me to take account of all the facts and circumstances of the case, together with the factors that come to mind as I think about them. And yet Allied's lawyer warned the members of the jury that they were to disregard these facts: 'She has a sad case. We don't deny that. It is a regrettable situation where she did lose her goods; but we don't think - - and the Judge will instruct you that as a matter of law you shall not let sympathy sway your decision in this case.'[770] Really? Why not? Why is the empathy I feel for Ms. Bratton irrelevant?

Question of Law

As these scenes flicker in my mind, I have to remind myself that we are working on a question of law. There is nothing in the liability limitation or the regulations to require the customer to be informed of the choices. As a result, those with a traditional view of the law would simply enforce the limitation clause. Nonetheless, as

[767] Trial transcript vol. 1, p. 80 (opening statement of Joseph Williams, plaintiff's lawyer), in *Allied* File.

[768] Id., pp. 120–125 (testimony of Ila Bratton).

[769] Id., vol. 2, p. 178.

[770] Trial Transcript, vol. 3, pp. 361 (closing argument of Ren Werrenrath), in *Allied* File.

Ms. Bratton's trial counsel explained to the jury, 'the crux of this case is whether Mrs. Bratton was given an adequate opportunity to fairly choose between higher and lower rates of coverage for her furniture.'[771] I agree that this is the relevant question, but since the law establishes no such requirement, why does it seem so obvious?

Empathy

Why do I feel the tug for Ms. Bratton? Since I actually want to know, let me track it as far as I can. On one side is Ms. Bratton. When she was preparing to leave the home she shared for a couple of decades with her husband and to set out for a new life, she signed a contract without reading it. It was late at night and she was doing what she could to help the movers. No one explained the operative provision to her, the liability limitation, which was so convoluted that she would not have understood it without help. On the other side we have the moving crew. The crew's helper stole her belongings and sold them on the streets of Detroit. If I weigh the equities, Ms. Bratton wins. How could anyone decide differently?

Once I admit to myself how I want the case to come out, I find in my mind a legal argument that points me to a question I had not thought of. What was the scope of the liability limitation? The federal bureaucrats who drafted it must have had in mind a scenario in which the truck tips over and belongings spill out. The purpose of the poundage rate is to allocate some of that risk to the consumer. But what about the very different risk that a member of the moving crew might hijack the van, auction off the goods, and keep the proceeds? The liability limitation cannot possibly transfer that risk to the customer.

I check the case law and discover that it is against me. The courts enforce the liability limitation even when the moving crew steals the goods. The company is liable only for its own theft.[772] I understand the argument: since Allied does not hire the drivers and helpers, it would not reduce theft to make Allied pay for these losses—it would not be an efficient Posnerian safety precaution. But the argument does not convince me. If Allied were held liable, it would have an action over against the local moving company, and that might encourage local movers to do a better job running background checks.

Between Ms. Bratton and Allied, who should suffer this loss? Allied may have had little ability to prevent the theft, but Ms. Bratton had none. And if someone had explained the liability limitation to her, she would not have had to file this lawsuit. The jury, the trial court, and the appellate court all agreed that the loss should fall on Allied. The Florida Supreme Court disagreed. Its decision may have seemed wise

[771] Trial Transcript, vol. 3, p. 370 (Williams), *Allied* File.

[772] See *Glickfeld v. Howard Van Lines*, 213 F.2d 723, 727 (9th Cir. 1954).

given the facts included in the court record,[773] but it is less convincing in the context of the story as we know it now.

When I think about Ms. Bratton as an individual rather than as the party who has been designated the *shipper*, I am outraged at the extreme imbalance of fault. This is empathy—a disciplined attentiveness to context rather than a surrender to raw emotion—and I now think that it is essential to feel it. Empathy is what leads beyond a bloodless reading of the documents and convinces me to search for a way to right a wrong.[774]

Processes of Life

As we learned from Hart and Sacks, the great tradition urges courts to accept institutional settlements—like the one that produced this liability clause. The *Bratton* court was surely trying to avoid the chaos that would result if a party could escape a liability limitation by proving that the signature was made late on an icy evening, that there was nowhere to sit down, and that the documents were unreadable in the dim light of the stove.

I will now calm down and take a step back. It is not our job to decide this case. Our work is only to understand why it is difficult. With a federal regulation directly on point, the case should be easy. But curiously it is not. If we examine Ms. Bratton's situation as Frug suggested, legal arguments pop up out of nowhere. Law is today 'more and more related to the organic processes of life outside of the law.'[775] As I read our contemporary mindset, I believe that we now care more about people than we do about legal concepts. We also prefer the result we reach after we wrestle with the facts to a solution dictated by the legal sources. These insights give some sense of what it means to do law now that Mary Joe Frug has passed through here.

Webb v. McGowin

As we turn back to *Webb v. McGowin*, I find myself posing different questions. To begin, I notice the thoughts and feelings that are rising within me.

I also want to know more about the facts. Who is McGowin, and why did he offer Webb a pension? That is a curious thing for someone to do. And how did Webb support himself after the payments stopped? Did he have a spouse and a family to take care of—or to take care of him?

Every decision allocates resources among many individuals, including those with only a tenuous connection to the litigation—families, relatives, friends, and

---

[773] See *Allied* Record.

[774] For the distinction between empathy and sympathy, see West (2013), pp 248–249, 251, 266–270.

[775] Frankfurter (1928), p. 438.

employees—some of whom are united in bonds of mutual dependency. The law has generally thought of these bonds as irrelevant, but if the common law's mission is to take all the facts and circumstances into account, should it not consider the consequences to everyone within the circle of concern? Mary Joe's method of empathetic interest now joins hands with the great tradition's insistence on contextualization. As Cardozo once put it, 'The law does not stand upon punctilios if there is a starving wife at home.'[776]

References

Bakos Y et al (2014) Does anyone read the fine print? Consumer attention to standard-form contracts. Journal of Legal Studies 43:1–35

Dawson J et al (1982) Cases and comment on contracts, 4th edn. Foundation, Mineola

Florida courthouse named for influential judge (June 29, 2023), United States Courts, www.uscourts.gov/news/2023/06/29/florida-courthouse-named-influential-judge

Frankfurter F (1928) Review of Cardozo, The paradoxes of legal science. University of Pennsylvania Law Review 77:436–438

Frug M (1992) Postmodern legal feminism. Routledge, New York

Green R (2018) Judge Joseph Woodrow Hatchett: A Florida legend in the fight for equality and justice. 11th Circuit Historical News 15(2):1, 20–28

In memoriam: Mary Joe Frug 1941–1991 (1990). Yale Journal of Law & Feminism 3: [ix]-[xii]

Isay H (1902) Rechtsgeschäft und wirtschaftliche Machtverschiedenheit. Franz Vahlen, Berlin

Kessler F (1943) Contracts of adhesion—some thoughts about freedom of contract. Columbia Law Review 43:629–642

Kessler F (1957a) Automobile dealer franchises: Vertical integration by contract. Yale Law Journal 66:1135–1190

Leff A (1970) Contract as thing. American University Law Review 19:131–157

Llewellyn K (1939) Review of Prausnitz, The standardization of commercial contracts in English and continental law. Harvard Law Review 52:700–705

Llewellyn K (1960) The common law tradition: Deciding appeals. Little, Brown, Boston

Llewellyn K (1989) The case law system in America, Gewirtz P (ed), Ansaldi M (trans). University of Chicago Press, Chicago

Memorial Service for Mary Joe Frug (1992) New England Law Review 26:639–658

Radin M (1935) The chancellor's foot. Harvard Law Review 49:44–67

Rakoff T (1983) Contracts of adhesion: An essay in reconstruction. Harvard Law Review 96:1173–1284

Slawson W (1971) Standard form contracts and democratic control of lawmaking power. Harvard Law Review 84:529–566

Warkentine E (2008) Beyond unconscionability: The case for using 'knowing assent' as the basis for analyzing unbargained-for terms in standard form contracts. Seattle University Law Review 31:469–548

West R (2013) The anti-empathic turn. Nomos 53:243–288

Williams P (1989) The obliging shell: An informal essay on formal equal opportunity. Michigan Law Review 87:2128–2151

---

[776] *Coler v. Corn Exchange Bank*, 164 N.E. 882, 885 (N.Y. 1928) (Cardozo, C.J.), *aff'd*, 280 U.S. 218 (1930).

Chapter 15
Community (Williams, Macneil)

We conclude our survey with Patricia Williams's book, *The Alchemy of Race and Rights*,[777] a text in which she shared a few of her difficult moments in the law. *Alchemy* was written in so many different genres that it reads 'a bit like a scrapbook':[778] 'Entries from Williams's diary, scenes from her encounters with diverse people, memos to colleagues, dreams, fantasies, excerpts from papers she has delivered at academic conferences, closing arguments from her favorite trial, and even the occasional legal polemic come together in a disorderly collage that eschews any linear argument.'[779] To all of that she adds a dose of raw emotion. 'Rejecting conventional standards of academic detachment, she discloses her most intimate feelings and doubts, and even her own emotional instability.'[780]

Williams (1951-)[781] practiced law in the offices of the Los Angeles City Attorney and the Western Center on Law and Poverty, then was awarded a MacArthur Fellowship. She spent much of her career on the faculty of the Columbia Law School and now holds a distinguished chair at Northeastern University. Williams is a central participant in the discussions about critical race theory, which, in addition to pursuing an activist political agenda, encourages 'the development of counter-accounts of social reality by subversive and subaltern elements of the reigning

[777] Williams (1991).

[778] The Stories of Law (1992), p. 779.

[779] Id.

[780] Bartlett (1992), p. 393.

[781] For Williams, see The HistoryMakers (2019).

R. Hyland, *Common Law Judging and the Great Tradition*, Ius Gentium: Comparative Perspectives on Law and Justice 100,
https://doi.org/10.1007/978-3-032-02307-0_15

order.'[782] Critical storytelling has now become a source of legal understanding,[783] and Williams's book is arguably the masterpiece of the genre.

Bad Morning

On the day her journal begins, Williams has not been able to change out of her bathrobe. She had noticed the similarity between a report on the morning news and a case that she had been reading, a decision from the 1830s about an enslaved person named Kate.[784] Kate was sold, then escaped, but was soon recaptured and returned. Her new owner decided that Kate was defective and asked to rescind the sale. The seller conceded that Kate was stupid, but stupidity in a slave did not allow the buyer to return the merchandise. The buyer responded that Kate was not stupid but crazy, and craziness permitted the sale to be canceled. The Louisiana Supreme Court, in its wisdom, decided that it mattered little whether Kate was crazy or stupid. She was in any case useless, and the buyer could get her money back.

Henry Adams Bullard (1788–1851),[785] the judge who drafted the opinion, was not a native Southerner. He was born in Massachusetts, graduated from Harvard College, studied law in Boston and Philadelphia, and then moved to Louisiana, where, before he was appointed to the state supreme court, he was elected to Congress and became a slaveholder. Bullard's background creates another bridge to the second event that ruined Williams's morning—a comment by a Harvard Law School dean that after an extensive search, the Harvard law faculty had not found a Black woman sufficiently qualified to join its ranks.

Part of our task will be to figure out what a text about bathrobes and bad moods has to do with the great tradition. Let us begin with form. Williams was writing about the present moment in the first person, a voice that 'has always been troublesome in the language of the law.'[786] A first-person narrative asks the reader to respond emotionally. But sentiment and passion seem incompatible with legal objectivity, and Max Weber argued that legal analysis can be rational only if it leaves emotion at the door.[787] 'We are taught that heartfelt instincts subvert the law and defeat the security of a well ordered civilization, whereas faithful adherence... to stare decisis and clearly stated authority, would as a matter of course lead to a

[782] Crenshaw et al. (1995), p. xiii (Introduction).

[783] See Delgado and Stefancic (2017), pp. 44–57; Farber and Sherry (1993); Abrams (1991); Scheppele et al. (1989). Velleman cautioned against the *projective error*—confusing the subjective feeling of satisfaction that a compelling ending can offer with an objective understanding of the underlying problem. See Velleman (2003), pp. 19–22.

[784] See Williams (1991), pp. 3–4 (quoting *Icar v. Suares*, 7 La. 517 (1835)).

[785] For Bullard, see Karachuk (1998); Bonquois (1940).

[786] Gates (1991), p. 768.

[787] See above, p. 56.

bright, clear world.'[788] Williams would like to move us past these limits: 'We must be ruled by our complete selves, by the intellectual and emotional content of our words.'[789]

Benetton

For those who have not personally experienced the dehumanizing effect of racial discrimination, there may be no better introduction than Williams's account of a holiday shopping trip in Manhattan.[790] Williams was examining a Benetton shop window in New York's Soho district when she saw a sweater that she thought might make a great gift for her mother. She pressed the door buzzer so she might slip inside to take a closer look, but she soon realized that she was not going to be buzzed through. When she squeezed her face against the window to look inside, she noticed the sales clerk, a gum-chewing white teenager. He looked at her quizzically for a moment, mouthed 'We're closed,' and blew a pink bubble. It was early on a Saturday afternoon on one of the last weekends before the holidays, and several white shoppers were examining the merchandise inside.

Rationalized Irrationality

Both of Williams's contributions to the great tradition emerge from a rereading of her Benetton story. The first flows from the observation that our daily manners are permeated with racism. Within our daily conventions 'myriad images of racial cliches perpetuate their unspoken subtexts of devaluation' and operate 'as a hidden scripting of rationalized irrationality.'[791] The common law will now have to rethink the Blackstonian bond between custom and freedom.

This is the shadow side of the common law's fearless disregard for rules. The same flexibility that encourages judges to decide cases as they think best also allows unexamined prejudice to influence the outcomes. Bias can find many entry points. Before judges hear testimony, Posner explained, they tend to give each witness a *prior*—a grade based on the witness's appearance together with 'a general sense of the honesty of the class of persons to which the witness belongs.'[792] The judge 'will often have formed before the witness begins to testify an estimate of the likelihood

[788] Williams (1987b), p. 134.

[789] Id.

[790] Williams (1991), pp. 44–51.

[791] Williams (1997), p. 55.

[792] Posner (2008), p. 66.

that the testimony will be truthful.'[793] Prejudice easily plays a role in these assessments, and Williams drew the lesson: 'As long as they are not unlearned... laws become described and enforced in the spirit of our prejudices.'[794]

Antidotes

Mary Joe Frug recommended that judges empathize with the parties and acknowledge the emotions that arise within them as they think about the facts. But since a judge's emotions may channel prejudice, Williams suggested that the common law correct for this bias by paying attention to the emotions—and the emotional needs—of the parties who come before the court. This presents a bend in the road as dramatic as any in the history of the common law. Judges are now to take into account both how they feel about the facts of the case as well as how victims of prejudice experience the legal process.

If judges follow this path, the common law will likely find itself creating more exceptions. But exceptions are not unproblematic, since they have often served to discriminate. To counter the risk, Williams has another suggestion: 'In the words of an old Cherokee proverb, [it is] as simple as trying to walk a mile in another's moccasins.'[795] Judges will want to appreciate the world from points of view that they might otherwise never experience. 'It really is possible to see things—even the most concrete things—simultaneously yet differently.'[796]

This too is already in the great tradition. 'The best that a judge can do is to put himself so far as possible in the position of that person or persons, knowing their history and experience and their relations with other [people] and things, and then to determine what his own meaning and intention would have been.'[797] If the judge would feel honored as the subject of the exception, it is probably beneficial. If instead the judge experiences a loss of dignity, the exception is likely discriminatory.

Group Affiliation

Williams's second contribution to the great tradition is a highly productive paradox. We are about to examine the first of its elements—Williams's recommendation that judges explore the group affiliations of those who appear before them. We then turn

[793] Id., p. 65.

[794] Williams (1991), p. 67.

[795] Williams (1997), p. 69.

[796] Williams (1987a), pp. 410–411.

[797] Corbin (1960) § 536, p. 34.

to the second aspect of the paradox, her view that judges must nonetheless decide cases predictably and in a way that affirms individual rights. Social welfare versus individual rights, context versus legal norms. Though in some ways this is uncharted territory, it is also strangely familiar.

If we return for a moment to Williams's experience at the Benetton store, we can see why she believes that the law must take account of group affiliation. A white sales clerk hears the door buzzer, looks up, and notices that the shopper seeking admission is a Black woman. He reflects for a moment, then denies her request. I feel a punch in the gut. This is a teaching moment for the great tradition. Black people face many of their problems as members of a group—the group of human beings who happen to have dark skin. 'The simple matter of the color of one's skin... profoundly affects the way one is treated [and] radically shapes what one is allowed to think and feel about this society.'[798]

We are, all of us, affiliated with social groups—groups defined not only by race, ethnicity, and gender, but also by many other conditions. Group affiliations frame how we react to the world and how others react to us. Williams is now asking judges to explore how the lives of those who appear before them have been shaped by the context of their experiences. The common law will now have to expand its perspective. The common law seeks to hold individuals responsible for their actions, but making them accountable for characteristics they did not choose and cannot change may not deliver equal treatment.

Critique of Rights

Some CLSers questioned whether adding or expanding individual rights is a helpful goal for a progressive political movement.[799] Though it takes years of struggle to anchor an individual right in the law, it was argued, the right sheds its quality as a social good as soon as it is legally recognized. Instead, it then becomes an individual possession.[800] Some Crits therefore suggested shifting the focus away from abstract rights and toward concrete goals—'a seat in the front of the bus, repatriation of treaty-guaranteed sacred lands, or a union card to carry into the grape vineyards.'[801]

Williams disagreed. The CLS critique did not appreciate the symbolic importance that rights have for the disenfranchised:[802] 'The experience of rights-assertion has been one of... empowerment of the *in*ternal and very personal sort.... For blacks, then, the attainment of rights signifies the due, the respectful behavior, the collective

[798] Williams (1987a), p. 404 note 4.

[799] For the CLS critique of rights, see Tushnet (1993); Tushnet (1989); Tushnet (1984).

[800] Ivison (2008), p. 5.

[801] Williams R (1987), p. 120.

[802] See Williams (1987a), pp. 404–406; see also Klare (2015), pp. 3–13; Fischl (1992), p. 786 note 26; Delgado (1987), pp. 303–307.

responsibility properly owed by a society to one of its own.'[803] Black people feel secure in their rights when courts apply the law straightforwardly and do not engage in the manipulations that Blacks have come to associate with discrimination. The Weberian notion that predictable rules yield freedom now re-echoes in the great tradition.

This view may have left a mark in the *Bratton* case.[804] As we discussed, Justice Hatchett enforced the liability limitation in a household moving contract, even though the equities seemed to be with Ms. Bratton, the consumer whose goods were lost in the move. Since Hatchett was known for his compassion for the less fortunate, I wondered why he might have ruled as he did. One of the justice's former law partners suggested an explanation. 'I think he had an engrained sense of the importance of the law being predictable. Perhaps that grew out of life experience of the unfairness inherent when the law is flexible according to the color of one's skin. Certainty and predictability give freedom.'[805]

Williamsian Paradox

Williams is asking judges to perform two incompatible tasks at the same time: They are to take account of the particular needs of a multitude of different social groups while still deciding cases predictably. Let us call this dilemma the *Williamsian paradox.*

This puzzle is yet another version of the conundrum that has occupied us from the beginning: if judges take account of the prodigious variety of conditions in which individuals lead their lives, will their decisions still make sense as law?

The New Social Contract

We can work with a paradox once we grasp how its conflicting branches represent parts of a functional whole. Does the great tradition offer a standpoint from which the two tasks that Williams has set for the courts reveal themselves to be aspects of a single process?

This would be the moment to present another of the tradition's great books, *The New Social Contract*, lectures that Ian Macneil delivered at Northwestern University in 1979.[806] If I were not writing on borrowed pages, I would open a new chapter, but

---

[803] Williams (1987a), pp. 414, 416.

[804] *Allied Van Lines, Inc. v. Bratton*, 351 So.2d 344 (Fla. 1977). For Justice Hatchett's opinion in the case, see above, pp. 196–197.

[805] Email from Michael McMahon.

[806] Macneil (1980).

instead I will have to limit myself to essentials. I believe that Macneil's *relational theory of contracts* provides the perspective we are looking for.

Macneil (1929–2010)[807] was one of America's leading contract theorists. He began his teaching career at the University of Dar es Salaam and later taught on the Cornell, Virginia, and Northwestern law faculties. For much of his adult life, Macneil also served as Chief of the Macneil Clan on the Scottish island of Barra.[808]

Macneil arranged contractual transactions along a spectrum. At one end are *discrete* transactions—interactions like the one-time purchase of gasoline at an interstate service station—while *relational* transactions take their place toward the other bound—contracts, like the turnkey sale of an oil refinery, a 'semi-joint-venture going relation'[809] that requires detailed planning and performance with a mindset of mutual trust and long-term cooperation. Macneil noticed that much of traditional contract law is constructed with the discrete transaction in mind.[810] As a result, it often lacks the concepts and the flexibility needed to resolve disputes involving long-term contractual relations.[811]

Macneil's writings are challenging: 'It is often difficult to discover the precise meaning beneath Macneil's cryptic examples and terse literary references.'[812] So instead of writing scholarly commentary, let us allow ourselves to be swept up by the spirit that animates Macneil's demanding body of work. I think it will surprise us with the understanding we need to address the Williamsian paradox.

Think Globally, Act Locally

Pretty much everyone who writes about the common law of contract begins with the bargain that some A enters into with some B. Macneil began instead with *society*. 'In the beginning was society.... This surely must be the most forgotten fact in the modern study of contracts.'[813] When I think of the social aspects of life, I imagine for some reason all those people waiting in Times Square for the ball to drop on New Year's Eve. Society represents for me a vast agglomeration of individual human beings. But that is not what the term meant to Macneil. He understood society instead as a functioning organism in which each of us plays a part.

To see what Macneil saw, we will have to imagine all of global society at once, all of the diverse activities that make up humanity's living and working on earth, and especially the entire world market as a single, all-embracing process. Is this even

807 For Macneil, see Morgan (2022).

808 Macneil (2013), p. xviii.

809 Llewellyn (1941a), p. 873.

810 Macneil (1980), p. 72; see also Eisenberg (2000), p. 805.

811 Macneil id., p. 10.

812 Mitchell (1982), p. 607. For Macneil's work, see Campbell et al. (eds.) (2013).

813 Macneil (1980), p. 1.

possible? We might take the high-speed elevator up to the top of the world's tallest building, step out onto the observation deck, drop a quarter into the telescope, and scan the horizon. But no building is tall enough for our purpose. So let us instead open Google Earth. After admiring the blue marble for a moment, I spin the globe and zoom back in. Suddenly I am several hundred klicks off the Chilean coast, hovering over lobster boats at anchor in the sunny harbor of San Juan Bautista. A couple of spins later, I see just below me Karakoksha, a grassy town in the Altai surrounded by virgin forests of Siberian pine. Sometime later, I am suspended above a grove of date palms on the outskirts of the Ksar of Ouargla in the Algerian Sahara. As Macneil is about to explain, all of these locales are tightly connected to each other—and to us.

We are joined together by *exchange*. 'Because Macneil sees exchange occurring almost everywhere, his theory becomes in effect a general theory of the social order.'[814] And we will be among his most appreciative readers, for we started in this direction a couple of chapters ago when we asked why courts enforce contracts.[815] To avoid shortages and surpluses, a society structured by a division of labor has to do some economic planning. A 'primal root of contract is specialization of labor and exchange,' for such a society 'requires some process of reciprocal distribution of product.'[816] 'The village pottery maker will soon either starve or take to working in the fields instead of making pottery if those who use the pottery fail to share the food from the fields.'[817] Macneil's theory of contract begins here, for when the planning process is outsourced to the market, contract law becomes its organizing mechanism.

The relatively simple trick that will eventually resolve the Williamsian paradox is to recognize that the global production process operates on both discrete and relational levels at the same time—and by means of the same transactions. The dual nature of these transactions is difficult to grasp, and that is because only one of the two processes is visible. When we zoom down from above, we see only individual bargains—countless marketgoers buying and selling the vast array of products that they find it worth their time and money to exchange. The other, invisible aspect of these transactions is their relational nature—their relationship to each other. These individual exchanges turn out to be but elements of a single collective process, an all-encompassing system of global exchange. The social relationship that binds us together with people we will never meet, with most everyone else on the planet, is our collective need to produce today everything that we will need when we again begin to produce tomorrow. This relationship can be imagined but not observed. And yet now that we have spun the globe a few times and spent time perched above some of the global economy's far-flung outposts, we may be able to visualize the

---

[814] Whitford (1985), p. 545.

[815] See above, pp. 87–88.

[816] Macneil (1980), pp. 2, 4.

[817] Macneil (1974), p. 698.

single, insanely elaborate network that trades every day in Pacific crayfish, Siberian pine nuts, and Saharan dates—and sends them speeding around the planet.

What genial intelligence could possibly organize these vast flows? How do we get the required inputs to the right place at the right time for the next stage in production? The surprise, as Adam Smith noted, is that it requires no organization at all. As we pursue our individual interests, the invisible hand of the market automatically moves productive resources to their proper locations. Each producer, 'by pursuing his own interest... frequently promotes that of the society more effectually than when he really intends to promote it.'[818]

When I take a walk to the bakery in the morning for fresh bread, I am sometimes granted a fleeting image of this extraordinary organism. If I get to the bake shop early enough, a loaf of sourdough rye is waiting for me on the shelf behind the counter. As I walk home with the crusty bread in its crinkly paper wrapper, my mind is suddenly flooded with a vision of those who produced the flour, the yeast, the salt, and the caraway seeds, the bakers who baked the loaf, and the web of transportation and retailing that placed it on that shelf, still warm, in time for breakfast. For an instant, that vast notional panorama appears before me and fills me with awe. Though my purchase is a single, voluntary exchange, my transaction is also a necessary link in an intricate social mechanism. If my students are to learn contract law later that morning, I have to be provided with funds to spend for breakfast and there has to be something there for me to purchase. My transaction is discrete and relational at the same time.

Ms. Britton

We are reading Macneil to see whether his approach can help judges render decisions that make sense as law while also taking group affiliation into account. To see how this might work, it may be useful to tackle another hypothetical, a variation on Ms. Bratton's case from the last chapter. Like Ms. Bratton, our new plaintiff—we will call her Ms. Britton—signed a moving contract without reading its terms. However, Ms. Britton's failure to read the bill of lading was not due to an icy kitchen and an impatient moving crew. The problem was rather that Ms. Britton cannot read. She is a member of the group of our fellows who are said to be *unlettered* or *functionally illiterate*—they are not able to read and write sufficiently to participate in social life as productively as they otherwise might.[819] The group includes one in five American adults—most of whom also have only limited financial resources.[820]

Ms. Britton left high school before graduation to get a job to pay the rent. She has now saved enough to move to a town in the next state, where she has accepted

[818] Smith (1976), p. 456.

[819] Egloff et al. (2011), p. 14.

[820] Onwuegbuzie (2004), p. 444.

steady employment and can afford a small apartment. The mover sent her a booklet about the move, but no one told her it was important or took the time to explain it. After the moving van was loaded, the helper spread the documents on the kitchen counter, pointed to the signature blanks, and Ms. Britton made her mark. No one mentioned the different insurance options. The move began on a wintry morning and was going well until the truck went into a skid, broke through the guardrail, and landed in the river with Ms. Britton's possessions. Will we enforce the liability limitation against her?

I have my conclusion before I can finish typing the hypothetical. Of course, I will relieve her of the limitation. What I am looking for is a way to explain the result and a legal construction I can use to anchor the solution in the law.

What does the global economy need from this transaction? In a world constantly upended by innovation, new businesses open, old ones close, and workers will need moving companies. Movers need a fair price and protection against uninsured liability. As for Ms. Britton, if she is to start strong in her new job, she will need cutlery and a bed. What does the perspective of social reproduction teach us about how best to allocate this loss?

The relational aspect of a transaction is largely invisible to the common law judge. When it is important, the feds sometimes intervene to make sure that transactions fulfill their role in the global economy. That is the deeper thought behind the Hart-and-Sacksian pitch about respecting national political compromises. What role does the liability limitation play in the global enterprise? The federal agency decided that the needs of social reproduction are satisfied when the consumer is allowed to select one of the enumerated options. The question of informed choice, which is not mentioned in the legal sources, pops up here at last, and we can see why. If the consumer does not have a meaningful opportunity to choose, the liability clause cannot serve its purpose, and it then makes no sense to apply its default provision.

To think about the contract as a discrete transaction, we turn to contract law. For once the rule is clear: illiteracy is not a defense.[821] The courts give two reasons for the rule.[822] First, Ms. Britton was at fault—those who cannot read act negligently if they sign a contract without understanding its terms.[823] The rule is also meant to protect the unlettered themselves. If they could avoid any written contract they cannot read, merchants might choose not to do business with them. Does the common law have the resources for a convincing reply?

---

[821] See *Green Tree Financial Corp. v. Lewis*, 813 So.2d 820 (Ala. 2001); *Merrill, Lynch, Pierce, Fenner & Smith, Inc. v. Benton*, 467 So.2d 311 (Fla. App. 1985) (citing *Allied Van Lines, Inc. v. Bratton*).

[822] See *Merrill, Lynch, Pierce, Fenner & Smith, Inc. v. Benton*, p. 313.

[823] Id. (quoting *Sutton v. Crane*, 101 So.2d 823, 825 (Fla. App. 1958), in turn quoting 12 Am. Jur., Contracts sec. 137, p. 630 (1938)).

Fault

The question of fault suggests a comparison: which of the parties was more negligent—Ms. Britton for signing without asking for an explanation, or the moving company for requiring her to sign without offering one? Should Ms. Britton have hired a lawyer or should the moving crew have explained the liability options?

Since the movers knew about the clause and also knew that she did not, my intuition is that they should have raised the issue—and the case law offers some support.[824] In fact, why not ask the movers to explain it to every consumer, literate or illiterate, except those who say they do not need to hear it?

Resolving the Paradox

Our preferred solution conflicts with both a federal regulation and the common law rule, but that should not worry us. We are trying to understand the lessons of the great tradition, and Williams and Macneil complete a thought that we have been working on since we first opened Blackstone. The courts are there to resolve disputes—which means to find a meaningful solution to the problem that brought the parties to court. When that difficulty is common to a group—we see this only from the relational perspective—that group's problems have to be solved if the rest of us are to achieve our own goals. We live in a community—which means we really all are in this together.

Webb v. McGowin

Does our new perspective help as we try to decide *Webb v. McGowin*? If we need sawmills, we also need sawmill workers. Courts should do what they can to assist injured workers and their families, as long as what they demand does not put the mills out of business. So before we can describe the relational perspective in our case, we will need to know something about McGowin's situation. We will revisit the question a little later.[825]

---

[824] See *Spitze v. Baltimore & Ohio RR Co.*, 23 A. 307, 309–310 (Md. App. Ct. 1892) (by implication).

[825] See below, pp. 277–278.

Kate's Case

What would the great tradition have to say about the decision in *Icar v. Suares*,[826] the lawsuit about the enslaved person named Kate that Williams was reading as we opened her journal? The decision is certainly a trainwreck, but what I am wondering is whether the common law as we now understand it has the resources for a more successful solution.

The events took place in the 1830s in New Orleans, and the court record survives.[827] Kate was about twenty years old and had just arrived from Charleston, South Carolina.[828] Rose Icar, the plaintiff buyer, was unmarried, 'a free woman of colour.'[829] Kate ran away six days after the sale. The police located her and kept her in the Jefferson Parish jail until Rose's representative arrived.

The lawsuit turned on whether Kate was affected with the 'habit of running away.'[830] Since Kate was new to the area, a witness suggested that she may have lost her way,[831] but the trial judge heard the evidence and found that Kate was subject to the vice of running away at the time of the sale. After personal inspection, he decided that Kate was either absolutely useless or very inconvenient, and he canceled the sale.[832]

Methodological Error

If we restrict our focus to questions of method, we can identify two difficulties with the decision. The first is a failure to identify with a victim of oppression. By running away, Kate made clear that she was neither crazy nor stupid but rather supremely aware of her lamentable situation.

The court also failed to examine the facts in a relational perspective. If the court had reflected on what those like Kate would have needed to make a meaningful contribution, it would have dismissed the buyer's action and set Kate free. Sixty years earlier, Lord Mansfield did just that.[833] The contract for the sale of the slave in that case was valid, but Lord Mansfield held that the condition of slavery was so

---

[826] *Icar v. Suares*, 7 La. 517 (1835) (discussed in Williams (1991), p. 3). See above, p. 206.

[827] See *Icar* Record.

[828] Petition, *Icar* Record, p. 812 (age); Testimony [of Witness for the Defendant] (Apr. 4, 1834), *Icar* Record, p. 821 (Kate had arrived from Charleston three weeks before she ran away).

[829] Document annexed to Petition, *Icar* Record, p. 813. The printed opinion refers to the plaintiff buyer as both male and female. The handwritten original makes clear that Rose Icar was a woman.

[830] La. Civ. Code art. 2505 (1825).

[831] Testimony [of Witness for the Defendant], *Icar* Record, p. 820 (witness name illegible).

[832] *Icar v. Suarez* (1st Dist. Ct., Apr. 1834) (Watts, J.), *Icar* Record, pp. 822–823.

[833] See *Somerset v. Stewart*, [1772] Lofft 1, 19, 198 Eng Rep 499, 510 (KB).

odious that nothing could support it but positive law. Since English law had no relevant statute at the time, he set the enslaved person free.

As a legal matter, the decision in Kate's case fails due to a technical obstacle—the codification of slavery and the implicit rejection of the factors from the great tradition that Lord Mansfield understood were essential. It is enough to note that it is not always possible to take full advantage of common law wisdom.

What is inspiring about the common law is that it continually opens itself to new concerns. Kate's case demonstrates that injustice may result when courts do not follow the common law's evolving approach—or are prohibited from doing so. If even this distressing decision confirms our thinking, perhaps we have understood something of the case that can be made for the common law.

Fragmented Unity

Things seem to be going well, but I am worried. We have now given up on pretty much everything that seemed reliable as we set out. Rules were the first to go. Then we lost precedent. Social expectation has been pretty good to us, but we just learned that it too has flaws. We were looking for rationality, but instead we ended up with altruism, empathy, and a sense of community. Impartiality would be nice, but it seems that courts will have to choose sides. I like the idea of personal responsibility, but I now see that it can easily be pushed too far. And even as we took efficiency and institutional settlement on board, we recognized their limits. Historical critique and the omnipresence of doubt speak to our present condition, but if we doubt and criticize everything, it is going to be tough to make decisions.

In our Hollywood movie, this is the end of Act Two. We have had a lot of fun, but we are now going to have to come up with a meaningful solution to *Webb v. McGowin*, and I am not sure how we are going to do that. Will we be able to pull together the conflicting approaches that we have explored and use them to produce a convincing result? The problem is not that we will have trouble finding answers. It is rather that we are going to have a lot of them, and they may point in different directions. Are these approaches so idiosyncratic that we will not be able to fit them together? Maybe we have been collecting markers from different board games. Maybe the law can no longer find convincing solutions to our differences. Maybe the common law's future is not that bright.

And yet, as we also know, that is not how Hollywood movies end.

References

Abrams K (1991) Hearing the call of stories. California Law Review 79:971–1052

Bartlett K (1992) Review of Williams, The alchemy of race and rights. Sydney Law Review 14:393–395

Bonquois D (1940) The career of Henry Adams Bullard, Louisiana jurist, legislator and educator. Louisiana Historical Quarterly 23:999–1106

Campbell D et al (eds) (2013) Changing concepts of contract: Essays in honour of Ian Macneil. Palgrave Macmillan, Basingstoke, Hampshire
Corbin A (1960) Corbin on contracts: A comprehensive treatise on the rules of contract law, vol 3. West, St. Paul
Crenshaw K et al (1995) Critical race theory: The key writings that formed the movement. New Press, New York
Delgado R (1987) The ethereal scholar: does critical legal studies have what minorities want? Harvard Civil Rights-Civil Liberties Law Review 22:301–322
Delgado R, Stefancic J (2017) Critical race theory: An introduction, 3d edn. New York University Press, New York
Egloff B et al (2011) Funktionaler Analphabetismus im Erwachsenenalter: Eine Definition. In: Zielgruppen in Alphabetisierung und Grundbildung Erwachsener: Bestimmung, Verortung, Ansprache. Bertelsmann, Bielefeld, pp 11–31
Eisenberg M (2000) Why there is no law of relational contracts. Northwestern University Law Review 94:805–822
Farber D, Sherry S (1993) Telling stories out of school: An essay on legal narratives. Stanford Law Review 45:807–855
Fischl M (1992) The question that killed critical legal studies, review of Kelman, A guide to critical legal studies. Law & Social Inquiry 17:779–820
Gates H (1991) Contract killer, review of Williams, The alchemy of race and rights. The Nation, June 10, pp 766–770
Ivison D (2008) Rights. McGill-Queen's University Press, Montreal
Karachuk R (1998) A workman's tools: The law library of Henry Adams Bullard. American Journal of Legal History 42:160–189
Klare K (2015) Critical perspectives on social and economic rights, democracy and separation of powers. In: Alviar García H et al (eds) Social and economic rights in theory and practice: Critical inquiries. Routledge, London
Llewellyn K (1941a) Common-law reform of consideration: Are there measures? Columbia Law Review 41:863–876
Macneil I (1974) The many futures of contracts. Southern California Law Review 47:691–816
Macneil I (1980) The new social contract: An inquiry into modern contractual relations. Yale University Press, New Haven
Macneil R (2013) Preface. In: Campbell D et al (eds) (2013), pp xv–xxi
Mitchell R (1982) Review of Fried, Contract as promise, and Macneil, The new social contract. McGill Law Journal 27:591–617
Morgan J (2022) Professor Ian Roderick Macneil (1929–2010). In: Goudkamp J, Nolan D (eds) Scholars of Contract Law. Hart, Oxford, pp 295–330
Onwuegbuzie A (2004) Reading comprehension among African American graduate students. Journal of Negro Education 73:443–457
Posner R (2008) How judges think. Harvard University Press, Cambridge
Scheppele K et al (1989) Symposium on legal storytelling. Michigan Law Review 87:2073–2494
Smith A (1976) An inquiry into the nature and causes of the wealth of nations, Campbell R, Skinner A (eds), vol. 1. Clarendon Press, Oxford
The HistoryMakers (2019) Patricia J. Williams. https://www.thehistorymakers.org/biography/patricia-j-williams
The Stories of Law (1992) Review of Williams, The alchemy of race and rights. Harvard Law Review 105:779–784
Tushnet M (1984) An essay on rights. Texas Law Review 62:1363–1404
Tushnet M (1989) Rights: An essay in informal political theory. Politics & Society 17:403–530
Tushnet M (1993) The critique of rights. SMU Law Review 47:23–36
Velleman J (2003) Narrative explanation. Philosophical Review 112:1–25
Williams P (1987a) Alchemical notes: Reconstructing ideals from deconstructed rights. Harvard Civil Rights-Civil Liberties Law Review 22:401–434

Williams P (1987b) Spirit-murdering the messenger: The discourse of fingerpointing as the law's response to racism. University of Miami Law Review 42:127–158
Williams P (1991) The alchemy of race and rights. Harvard University Press, Cambridge
Williams P (1997) Seeing a color-blind future: The paradox of race. Farrar, Straus and Giroux, New York
Williams R (1987) Taking rights aggressively: The perils and promise of critical legal theory for peoples of color. Law & Inequality 5:103–134

Part IV
Conclusion

Chapter 16
Reconsideration

The time has come to gather together the lessons we have learned from the great tradition and give our principal case another try.

Webb v. McGowin

Here once again are the facts that Webb's lawyer presented to the Alabama appellate court. In 1925, Joe Webb was working for the W.T. Smith Lumber Company in Chapman, Alabama, when he was asked to clear the upper floor of sawmill No. 2. Following usual practice, he pushed a pine block weighing about seventy-five pounds to the edge of the deck. He was just about to let it go when he saw J.G. McGowin standing on the floor directly below. Webb could have released the block and stayed safely on the upper deck, but if he had done so, the block would have struck McGowin with such force that it would have seriously injured or killed him. Webb tried to prevent harm to McGowin by the only means available, which was to fall with the block and divert its path in the air. Webb managed to save McGowin, but he was seriously injured in the fall. His right leg and arm were broken, the heel of his right foot torn off, and he was unable to work for the rest of his life. A month later, McGowin promised to take care of Webb for the remainder of Webb's life at the rate of $15 every two weeks, beginning on the date of Webb's injuries. The payments were made regularly for more than eight years but stopped a month after McGowin's death. Webb sued McGowin's estate for the unpaid installments.

The consideration doctrine was the main hurdle to enforcing the promise. Since Webb had fully performed before McGowin made his pledge, the trial court concluded that there was no bargain, no consideration, and no contract. McGowin's

R. Hyland, *Common Law Judging and the Great Tradition*, Ius Gentium: Comparative Perspectives on Law and Justice 100,
https://doi.org/10.1007/978-3-032-02307-0_16

executors would therefore not be allowed to continue making the payments. The Alabama appellate court reversed and remanded the case for trial.[834] The Alabama Supreme Court denied the petition for review but noted that the case raised a question that had not previously been decided in Alabama and indicated that it agreed with the appellate court's decision.[835] The case remains unique in American law. In *Mills* and *Harrington*, the two somewhat similar cases we have discussed, the courts refused to enforce promises made to compensate for damages or expenses related to rescue attempts.[836] Despite the lack of precedent, the Restatement (Second) of Contracts approved the appellate court's decision in *Webb* and created for it the exception generally known as *moral consideration*.[837]

What insights have we gained from the great tradition about how to resolve the case? A few of the approaches we explored seem now particularly relevant.

Mary Joe Frug

I start by stepping into Webb's shoes. For a split second, the block is balanced on the rim of the mill's upper deck. As it is about to escape my grasp, I look down and see McGowin. The block will crush him.

Each time I get this far, the scene goes blank, and I cannot see what happens next. The height would have intimidated me. The block would have landed on McGowin before I realized that there was a choice to be made.

What went through Webb's mind eight years later when the payments stopped? Just a minute. I need a moment. My mind is still back up there on the deck with Webb. He is doing his usual job on a typical day and looks down. With a jolt to the heart, he sees that a life is at risk. The case is a monument to his heroism. If McGowin's executors had not stopped the payments, we would never have heard of Webb or learned of his valiant act. The consideration doctrine has made him immortal—earning him his own section in the Restatement and a permanent place in the legal imagination. And yet as I stand in his shoes, I see that all I really want is an exception to the consideration doctrine.

I turn next to Webb's family. I know nothing of them, but I will take into account the possibility that Webb was married and that his wife worked in the home. Though Ms. Webb was surely proud of her husband's heroic deed, it was going to be difficult to put dinner on the table once the payments stopped. It is likely that the pension anchored their budget.

---

[834] *Webb v. McGowin*, 168 So. 196 (Ala. Ct. App. 1935).

[835] *Webb v. McGowin*, 168 So. 199 (Ala. 1936).

[836] *Mills v. Wyman*, 20 Mass. (3 Pick.) 207 (1825); *Harrington v. Taylor*, 36 S.E.2d 227 (N.C. 1945).

[837] Restatement (Second) of Contract § 86 (1981).

What about McGowin's heirs? We know nothing about them. Perhaps they were indigent and counting on the inheritance. On the other hand, Webb saved the life of their benefactor. A compassionate heir may have wanted to ensure that Webb had enough to live on.

I will now imagine the situation from the standpoint of McGowin's executors. If I were their lawyer, I would remind them that their fiduciary duty runs not to Webb but to the heirs. I would suggest that they withhold payment until Webb produces documentation. If he has none, they should deny Webb's claim and make him prove it. Without a contract, they have no right to continue the payments.

Just now, standing in the shoes of the estate's lawyer, I see something I had not seen before: the consideration doctrine is not the issue. The real question is who has the better claim to that portion of the inheritance, Webb or McGowin's heirs. That is going to be hard to resolve, and scratching our heads about the consideration doctrine is not going to help us settle it.

If we were to confront this question directly, how might we try to resolve it? What might McGowin have said? He probably never thought about it. By promising Webb a pension, McGowin decided to deprive his heirs of whatever amounts Webb would ultimately receive. The payments were made regularly for eight years, and as far as we can tell, they stopped only because of McGowin's untimely death. I think McGowin would have wanted Webb to get paid.

Duncan Kennedy, Roberto Unger

Kennedy and Unger would see in McGowin's promise an ode to compassion, and they would not want the consideration doctrine to defeat the altruistic impulse. And their political perspective would shine a new light on the events. There was an obvious need for better safety precautions. Employers should provide safe walkways and proper warnings, and a worker should not be asked to drop a heavy block onto a busy mill floor. Kennedy and Unger might even suggest revising the statute to allow suits against employers who fail to take elementary precautions.

Grant Gilmore

Gilmore's perpetually open mind reminds me of two of my favorite artworks, both early impressionist paintings, one by Monet, the other by Renoir, and both depicting La Grenouillère, an inlet along the Seine near Paris.[838] The two painters worked side by side on the same summer afternoon, but each was drawn to a different aspect of

[838] Monet, *La Grenouillère* (1869); Renoir, *La Grenouillère* (1869). For the cultural setting, see Siegel (2024), pp. 147–175.

the scene. Monet presented a timeless image of sky reflected in choppy water, while Renoir suggested the ephemerality of casual conversation. Both works are convincing. Neither is better than the other.

The jurists charged with deciding *Webb* accommodated the facts and the law as they thought best, and their outcome is convincing. And yet if they had decided the case the other way, no one would have objected—or even noticed.

Richard Posner

The pine block hovers as the parties negotiate. A rational McGowin would offer to pay Webb a small pension for the rest of his life if he is incapacitated in the fall. A rational Webb, however, would likely not accept. A reasonable mill worker would not risk death or lifelong disability in exchange for something like his usual wage.

What if we pose the question after the events? Webb risked his life with no promise of compensation. He needs help and would now gladly accept whatever he is offered. A hypothetical negotiation understood in this way would lead to a deal—and give the court another reason to enforce the promise.

Frederic Maitland

Of the norms we inherit, Maitland believed, we should enforce only those that we would enact today. The consideration doctrine would fail this test. It was born as an element of the writ system and designed to limit the jurisdiction of the royal courts. Scholars have long suggested that we abolish it.

The problem today is that the consideration doctrine misallocates the burden of proof. It limits enforcement to promises that are part of a bargain and relegates all others to an exception—like promissory estoppel. Kessler and Sharp suggested that all seriously intended promises should be binding unless there is a good reason not to enforce them. They would shift the discussion from whether there is a bargain to possible reasons for not enforcing the promise.

As for McGowin's promise, the heirs have a competing interest. Under the consideration doctrine, they would win unless the promise is contractual. If we were without the consideration doctrine, the court would turn to the relative merits of the claim of the heirs. And I think we know the answer. By promising a lifelong pension, it seems that McGowin wanted to favor Webb.

Oliver Wendell Holmes

The peculiar posture of the case would have amused the great justice. The consideration doctrine should favor party autonomy, but here the doctrine prevents McGowin from fulfilling his promise. McGowin, not the law, should have the last word about whether to reward Webb. Holmes would have found a way to get Webb paid.

William Blackstone

Blackstone taught that precedent is valuable because it expresses the court's understanding of what was needed at the moment to satisfy social mores.

I therefore think that Blackstone would have wondered why we are arguing about how the case should come out after a court has already decided the question. If common law decisions resulted from an abstract application of law, then we might try to second-guess them at a later time. But since they testify rather to an evaluation of contemporary sensibility, we are without the tools we would need to grasp the relevant social context—especially for a case decided nearly a century ago.

Max Weber

We conclude where we began—with Weber's conviction that predictability is the benchmark of a rational legal system. Would Weber have insisted on predictability, everywhere and always, or would he have agreed with Llewellyn that answers to legal questions do not all need to be predictable to the same extent? 'What law needs is a manageable degree of certainty and predictability—enough to get on with; more here and maybe less there.'[839]

Judicial predictability is rarely relevant when a human life is at stake. If we freeze the frame and give Webb a few minutes to think, his questions would likely be practical: 'Should I try to divert the block or instead shout to those below? What would happen if I can never work again?' Webb would settle on a course of action before anything he might know about the law would occur to him.

If McGowin had asked how to ensure that the payments to Webb could continue after his death, his lawyer might have advised him to put the promise in writing and state a quid pro quo. Or he might have suggested adding a codicil to his will. But at no point would McGowin or his lawyer have thought about moral consideration.

Max Weber was a scholar, not an ideologue. Once he understood that moral consideration did not need to be predictable, he might well have embraced the generative power of occasional exception.

---

[839] Llewellyn (1940a), p. 599.

Promissory Estoppel

If we decide for Webb, how would we anchor the result in the law?

The doctrine of moral consideration is a questionable choice. The court's decision was so unusual that we still read the case in the casebooks. Was there an alternative that might have called less attention to itself?

If the court had relied instead on the doctrine of *promissory estoppel*, the case would have disappeared into the reporters. The reach of this equitable institution has expanded over the years,[840] but even at the time *Webb* came up for review, it might have provided a respectable home for the decision. The first Restatement of Contracts, published a few years before the case was decided, illustrated promissory estoppel with a hypothetical that would have needed little adjustment to accommodate the facts of *Webb*:

> A promises to B to pay him an annuity during B's life. B thereupon resigns a profitable employment, as A expected that he might. B receives the annuity for some years, in the meantime becoming disqualified from again obtaining good employment. A's promise is binding.[841]

Did Webb rely on McGowin's promise? It is tempting to think that an Alabama court might have found reliance if Webb had decided not to look for a new job or make other long-term arrangements. We will return to promissory estoppel after we learn more about the facts of the case.

Summing Up

Let us take stock. The books of the great tradition seem to agree that McGowin's promise should be enforced—though Holmes and Weber may need some convincing.

But what is striking is the general lack of objection. Our authors wrote at different times, started from different premises, and suggested different approaches to case adjudication—in fact, they disagree with each other about nearly everything. And yet they do not seem far apart about how to decide *Webb*. If we find a decision that can earn a thumbs up both from a free marketeer like Richard Posner and a radical social theorist like Roberto Unger, if it might be affirmed both by Blackstone, for whom the common law was always striving to return to its original perfection, and by Maitland, who experienced the common law's past as a tragic burden, and if it might even sway both Holmes, who favored the consideration doctrine, and Gilmore, its most sardonic critic, that decision has a lot going for it. Now that I see there will be no thunder from Olympus, the result in *Webb* seems so appropriate that I can no longer remember why it once baffled me.

---

[840] See, e.g., Yorio and Thel (1991); Farber and Matheson (1985).

[841] Restatement of Contracts § 90 illus. 2 (1932).

This is great news. And yet it does not entirely solve our problem. The fact that we agree about *Webb* does not mean that other cases will be as easy. And with that thought we find ourselves before a piece of unfinished business. *Webb* is unique in the case law. In *Mills* and *Harrington,* the two cases that frequently follow *Webb* in string citations, the courts refused to enforce the promise. We have not solved anything if we now have to conclude that those two cases were wrongly decided.

Mills v. Wyman

In 1821, Seth Wyman's grown son Levi fell ill in Hartford, Connecticut, and Daniel Mills gave him shelter and comfort until he died. Seth learned that Mills was caring for his son and promised that he would reimburse Mills. But by the time Seth made his promise, Mills was no longer taking care of Levi. Seth did not pay, Mills sued, and though the court found the father's refusal disgraceful, it held that his promise was not supported by consideration and refused to enforce it.[842]

Of our three rescue cases, Mills's claim is the weakest. McGowin regularly performed his promise, while Seth Wyman made no payments to Mills. Moreover, the promise in *Mills* came not from Levi, the son who recuperated in Mills's inn, but from his father. That does not create a consideration problem, but it does alter the hypothetical negotiation. Let us imagine the scenario. Levi is ailing but without funds as he arrives in Hartford. Mills writes to Seth to say that he will care for his son if Seth guarantees payment. Would a rational parent accept? Maybe most would step up, but some might want their adult children to stand on their own two feet. I do not know how to work through the Posnerian calculus when it is rational to choose either alternative, but it certainly makes the case for enforcement less convincing. Holmes would not have enforced the promise, and as far as I can tell, none of our other authors would have felt compelled to do so either.

Harrington v. Taylor

Lee Taylor assaulted his wife and then assaulted her again when he found her the next day at the home of her friend, Lena Harrington. Lee's wife was about to chop off his head when Lena diverted the axe and saved his life, but at the sad cost to her of a mutilated hand. Though Lee promised to pay Lena's damages, he made only a small down payment. Lena sued, and the consideration doctrine again barred enforcement.[843]

---

[842] *Mills v. Wyman*, 20 Mass. (3 Pick.) 207 (1825).

[843] *Harrington v. Taylor*, 36 S.E.2d 227 (N.C. 1945).

This is a closer case. As a wife-beater, Lee loses his claim to our sympathy. Because he was the aggressor, Kennedy, Unger, Frug, and Williams would be tempted to enforce the promise. In a hypothetical negotiation, Lee almost surely would have asked Lena to save his life, though a rational Lena most likely would not have accepted. Holmes would oppose enforcement. As for me, I would like Lena to recover, but since Lee made only a small down payment and then backed away, I am not convinced that he was serious about the promise.

Reconciled

The uninterrupted history of payment we find in *Webb* distinguishes it from the other two cases. It is fair to conclude that McGowin intended to keep his word, while the facts of the other two cases are not as convincing. If we put the consideration doctrine aside for a moment and compare the real-world events that led to the decisions, *Webb* shares almost nothing with the other two cases, and it is curious that they have been yoked together for so long.

Since the three decisions can be reconciled, *Webb* now seems about as convincing as a decision can be.

Tightly knit Web

When judges assume their judicial personae, they are not taking a position on how we should lead our lives. They are instead trying to identify the minimum standard of comportment society requires of parties in a particular situation. To that narrow question, there is usually only a limited spectrum of appropriate answers. To choose among them, judges consider many factors, far more than those we have had the opportunity to explore here, and they are influenced unconsciously by many more. As these factors come together in the mind, an experienced jurist experiences a tightly knit web that focuses attention and constrains the result. And yet jurists do not all come to the same solution. They may find different factors relevant or find the same concerns more or less compelling. I admit it is deeply unsatisfying that we are still unable to describe the relative significance of the various factors—or even to name them all. Our understanding of the process remains intuitive.

Goal Posts

My lawyer friend Bill Brown was always telling me not to move the goal posts. Whatever I was hoping to accomplish when I set out has to count as success when I achieve it. Our goal was to find a meaningful explanation for the decision in *Webb v. McGowin*. It has taken some time, but I think we have found what we were looking for.

And yet we are not done. We have limited our discussion to the circumstances of the three moral consideration cases as we find them stated in the opinions. For the discussion we have wanted to have, it would have made no sense to worry about facts that the judges themselves did not consider. And yet as the great tradition assures us, cases are best decided by taking into account all their facts and circumstances. Would the three decisions still seem meaningful if we were to broaden the context to include facts that the judges chose not to discuss or could not have known?

References

Farber D, Matheson J (1985) Beyond promissory estoppel: Contract law and the 'invisible handshake.' University of Chicago Law Review 52:903–947

Llewellyn K (1940a) On reading and using the newer jurisprudence. Columbia Law Review 40:581–614

Siegel H (2024) Painting with Monet. Princeton University Press, Princeton

Yorio E, Thel S (1991) The promissory basis of Section 90. Yale Law Journal 101:111–167

Chapter 17
The Facts of Life

For each of our three cases, a rich and complicated record survives in case files, archives, and local lore.[844] I do not mention this expanded context to my students. Once we take the fuller picture into account, the legal questions change, the original answers become irrelevant, and we are left with the strange feeling that the real disputes are still out there waiting to be resolved.

Mills v. Wyman

Let us first reexamine *Mills v. Wyman*, beginning once again with the facts as Justice Parker stated them in his opinion for the Supreme Judicial Court of Massachusetts.[845] In 1821, Levi Wyman was returning from a sea journey to a foreign country when he fell ill in Hartford, Connecticut. Levi was in distress and without funds, and Daniel Mills took him in and cared for him. Upon learning that Mills was tending to his ailing son, Levi's father Seth wrote to Mills and promised to reimburse him. Unfortunately, Levi had already died from his illness. Seth did not pay, and Mills sued. Since Mills had incurred his expenses before Seth made his promise, the trial court held that Seth's promise lacked consideration and refused to enforce it. The state supreme court affirmed.

---

[844] For Watson's discussion of the three cases, see Danzig and Watson (2004), pp. 119–148, 149–184, 185–213; Watson (1997).

[845] *Mills v. Wyman*, 20 Mass. (3 Pick.) 207 (1825).

R. Hyland, *Common Law Judging and the Great Tradition*, Ius Gentium: Comparative Perspectives on Law and Justice 100,
https://doi.org/10.1007/978-3-032-02307-0_17

Parties

The court record describes plaintiff Mills as an innkeeper and yeoman (small farmer) and the defendant, Seth Wyman, as a colonel and a gentleman.[846] Seth owned a farm in Shrewsbury, located near Worcester, Massachusetts, and perhaps had been an officer in the militia.[847] Levi was the youngest of Seth's seven children.[848] Levi was then about 25 and 'had long ceased to be a member of his father's family.'[849]

The only mention in the record of Levi's sea voyage is in the trial court's opinion—perhaps a witness mentioned the fact at trial.[850] In his opinion for the supreme court, Justice Parker indicated further that Levi was 'on his return from a foreign country.'[851] There is no such evidence in the record. Justice Parker may have been misled by the trial judge's statement that Levi was a 'stranger' in Hartford.[852]

Levi arrived at Mills's inn in Hartford on February 5, 1821, and stayed about two weeks.[853] As an innkeeper, Mills was expecting compensation and asked for payment. Levi was without resources but was confident that his father would take care of the bill.[854] Since Levi was obviously unwell, Mills called in Dr. John Comstock (1787–1858),[855] a local physician, author, and veteran of the War of 1812, and purchased the medication that the good doctor prescribed.

From the record, I get the sense that Mills was an able and compassionate host and Levi a high-maintenance guest. As for Levi's illness, Dr. Comstock diagnosed Levi as being in 'a state of indisposition' and at times in 'a state of delirium' and recommended that Mills hire assistants to keep Levi from hurting himself.[856] Mills hired two men, but despite their best efforts, Levi managed to leap out of a chamber window—'to the imminent hazzard of his life, and to the very great alarm of the family and the boarders.'[857]

---

[846] See Record Book, p. 224, *Mills* CCP Record.

[847] See Watson (1997), pp. 1762–1765.

[848] Id., p. 1764 note 89.

[849] *Mills v. Wyman* (Ct. Com. Pl., Dec. 1824) (Howe, J.), *Mills* SJC Files.

[850] Id.

[851] *Mills v. Wyman*, p. 209.

[852] Judgment (Dec. 6, 1824), p. 1, *Mills* SJC Files.

[853] *Mills v. Wyman* (Ct. Com. Pl., Dec. 1824) (Howe, J.), *Mills* SJC Files.

[854] Deposition of Nathaniel Wales and Norman Pease, *Mills* SJC Files.

[855] For Comstock, see Drake (1879), p. 211; for one of his scientific textbooks, see Comstock (1836).

[856] Deposition of John L. Comstock (Nov. 29, 1824), Depositions copy, *Mills* SJC Files.

[857] Deposition of Nathaniel Wales and Norman Pease, *Mills* SJC Files (spelling as in original).

Promise

On February 5, as soon as Mills learned that Levi could not pay his bill, he wrote to Levi's father, Seth. We do not have Mills's first letter, but it seems from Seth's reply that Mills reported on Levi's condition and suggested that Seth come up for a visit. Seth responded on February 24 with a letter that Mills received four days later. Seth wrote that he was unable to make the trip, noting that 'the going is very bad'[858]—which likely referred to the conditions on the late-winter roads. It was in this letter that Seth made the promise that led to the dispute: 'I wish you to take all possible care of him and if you cannot have him at your house I wish you to remove him to some convenient place and if he cannot sattisfy you for it I will.' Seth also asked for more news of his son.

Mills understood Seth's promise as a guarantee of payment and wrote back on March 3.[859] He tallied up the expenses, asked Seth for the $16 he believed was due, and appended an accounting—two weeks' room and board ($6), fire and candles ($3), a gallon of spirits ($1), and meals and compensation for the two men who spent four days and nights trying to keep Levi safe ($6). Mills also attached the physician's bill ($6).[860]

Mills's letter allows us to correct another misimpression from Parker's opinion—that Levi died from his illness while at the inn. In fact, Levi survived, and by the time Mills received Seth's letter, Levi was already gone from the inn. He 'was tolerable smart when he left' and was thinking of heading home by way of Springfield.[861] It seems that Levi married a few months later, had at least one daughter, and lived on for years, maybe decades.[862]

Lawsuit

Mills filed his lawsuit three years later in the Court of Common Pleas in Worcester, the county of Seth's residence, alleging damages in the amount of $27.43.[863] The sheriff served the writ (complaint) and attached Seth's farm and buildings.[864] In his

---

858 Letter of Seth Wyman to Daniel Mills (Feb. 24, 1821), *Mills* SJC Files (spelling as in original).

859 Letter from Daniel Mills to Seth Wyman (Mar. 3, 1821), *Mills* SJC Files.

860 Id.

861 Id.

862 Watson (1997), p. 1757.

863 Writ of Attachment (May 20, 1824); *Mills* SJC Files.

864 Property was attached upon service of process. The purpose was initially to compel the property owner to appear in court. Attachment later became a means of ensuring satisfaction of judgment. See Howe (1834), pp. 155–156.

answer, Seth denied making any enforceable promise and put 'himself on the Country'[865]—leaving the decision to the jury.

The writ alleged several claims, but attention eventually focused on those sounding in Assumpsit. Mills's lawyer presented three separate theories of consideration—Seth's natural affection for his son, the expenses that Mills had already incurred in providing care to Levi, and finally, Mills' implicit promise to continue to provide Levi with medicines and attention.

The case was tried, and the jury decided for Mills: 'The Jury agree that the Plaintiff [Mills] has supported his action and have assessed damages to the amount of $26.95.'[866]

As the jury made clear in the verdict, Seth's promise was meant to cover the expenses that Mills had already incurred. Seth was unwilling to pay, and his lawyer asked the trial judge to set aside the verdict.

Judge Howe

Samuel Howe (1785–1828) presided at trial.[867] He was a conscientious Unitarian and distinguished judge whose judgments were seldom overturned on appeal.[868] Howe decided that there was no consideration to support Seth's promise and set the verdict aside. In his brief opinion, Howe addressed the three consideration arguments, but not all of them explicitly.

He first ruled that the family relationship between Levi Wyman and his father was insufficient to provide legal consideration. Regarding the care that Mills had already provided, Howe noted that Mills incurred his expenses before Seth made his promise. He did not find it necessary to complete the thought: care provided in the past—past consideration—could not support Seth's subsequent undertaking. Howe found no reason to mention the third theory—that Seth promised to pay for the care that Mills might provide in the future. Since Levi had already left the inn, no further expenses were incurred, no contract was concluded, and Mills had no damages. Finding 'no evidence of any consideration for this promise,' Howe set the verdict aside and directed the entry of a nonsuit. Mills appealed.

---

865 The clerk recorded Seth's answer on the back of the final page of the writ.

866 Verdict (n.d.), *Mills* SJC Files. Watson understood Seth's letter to promise compensation for care Mills might provide in the future. See Watson (1997), pp. 1761–1762. That interpretation conflicts with the jury's implicit conclusion that Seth promised to pay for the expenses that Mills had already incurred.

867 For Howe, see Watson (1997), pp. 1769–1770; Ellis (1850).

868 See Letter of Samuel Willard (Oct. 23, 1849), p. 53, in Ellis (1850), pp. 51–58; Williams (1828), pp. 7, 15; Parker (1828), pp. 13–14.

Appeal

John Davis and Charles Allen represented Mills on appeal. Davis (1787–1854)[869] would later represent Massachusetts in both houses of Congress and serve as the state's governor. Allen (1797–1869)[870] later served both in the state legislature and in Congress and received honorary degrees from both Harvard and Yale.

The two lawyers did not dispute that Mills had incurred his expenses before Seth made his promise. They argued instead that Seth was bound by a moral obligation to Mills. Seth was obligated to support his impoverished son, even though the son had come of age. He therefore owed Mills for offering the support that Seth should have provided to his son.[871]

They also argued from precedent. A decade or so earlier, the Massachusetts high court had enforced a promise made to express a debt of gratitude, though it was otherwise lacking in consideration. The court found it sufficient that the promise was made voluntarily and in writing.[872] Seth's promise too was deliberate and was also made in writing. The court was right, the advocates argued, to enforce such promises.

Justice Parker

Before he was named to the Supreme Judicial Court, Isaac Parker (1768–1830)[873] served in Congress and as U.S. Marshal for Maine (then a part of Massachusetts). As chief justice, he presided over the state's constitutional convention in 1820, and as the first Royall Professor of Law at Harvard, he drew up the plan that led to the founding of the Harvard Law School. In his eulogy at Parker's funeral, Justice Story praised Parker's sense of 'an original, intrinsic equity, a clear perception of abstract right and justice, and the best mode of adapting it to the exigencies of the case.'[874]

We now know that Parker misstated some of the facts in *Mills*. Why did he suggest that Levi died while in Mills's care? Though the record on appeal contains only nine brief documents, it is possible that Parker did not read them—or at least that he did not reread them. When speaking privately to his law students, Story mentioned that Parker 'was a good-natured, lazy boy when at college, became a good-natured,

[869] For Davis, see Fuess (1930); Kinnicutt (1854).

[870] For Allen, see Hoar (1902).

[871] *Mills v. Wyman*, 20 Mass. (3 Pick.) 207, 208 (1825) (Davis and Allen in support of the exceptions).

[872] See *Bowers v. Hurd*, 10 Mass. 427, 429 (1813) (Parker, J.). During oral argument in *Mills*, Justice Parker admitted that he had second thoughts about that earlier decision. The case was later overruled. See *Hill v. Buckminster*, 22 Mass. (5 Pick.) 391, 400 (1827) (Parker, C.J.).

[873] For Parker, see Sutherland (1967), pp. 49–59; Drake (1879), p. 688.

[874] Story (1852), p. 814.

lazy lawyer, and made afterward a good-natured, lazy judge.'[875] That might explain why, when the time came to draft the opinion, Parker could no longer remember the details.

But it may also have been because Justice Parker had something on his mind. He had come to agree with Judge Howe that moral obligation should not count as consideration, and he was eager to explain why. Another of Story's comments about Parker may also be relevant. Parker 'always decided right, but gave miserable reasons for his opinions.'[876] That was because for Parker, common sense meant 'steering by the light of the Ten Commandments.'

Innkeeper Mills, Parker wrote, 'acted the part of the good Samaritan.'[877] Parker was referring to the familiar Biblical parable in which a legal scholar asked Jesus how to achieve eternal life.[878] When Jesus asked what the scholar had found in Scripture, the scholar said that he knew he was to love God and love his neighbor as himself but wondered who he should consider to be his neighbor. Jesus responded with the story of a traveler who was robbed, wounded, and left half-dead by the side of a road. No one lent him a hand until a compassionate Samaritan bound the traveler's wounds and found him lodging. As the Samaritan paid for the wounded man's accommodation the next morning, he urged the innkeeper to take care of his guest and added 'whatsoever thou spendest more, when I come again, I will repay thee.' Jesus turned to the scholar. 'Go, and do thou likewise.'

Like Howe, Parker was a devout Unitarian. Neither of them was concerned with the principal characters in the allegory—the wounded traveler, the innkeeper, or even the good Samaritan. They were thinking instead of the passers-by—those who noticed the injured man by the side of the road and 'passed by on the other side.'[879]

Henry Giles

To reconstruct Parker's thought, it may be useful to consult the Unitarian divine, Henry Giles (1809–1882).[880] From the fact that Seth promised to reimburse the innkeeper, Giles would have concluded that Seth understood his obligation. Once recognized, duty should be obeyed. 'This inward power of conscience is the true distinction of spiritual life; and the righteous submission to it in our own hearts, we maintain, is the faith which justifies.'[881] Conscience is critical for a Unitarian, for

[875] Williams (1914), p. 36 (quoting the diary of Rutherford B. Hayes (Nov. 27, 1843), who was quoting Justice Story).

[876] Id.

[877] *Mills v. Wyman*, 20 Mass. (3 Pick.) 207, 209 (1825).

[878] Luke 10:25–37.

[879] Lord Mansfield relied on the same aspect of the parable when deciding a similar case. See *Newby v. Wiltshire*, 2 Esp 739, 742, 170 Eng Rep 515, 516 (KB 1784) (quoting Luke 10:31).

[880] For Giles, see Rich (1891).

[881] Giles (1839), p. 3.

there is no worldly penalty for breach of duty and also nothing like eternal damnation: 'There is no room in the same universe for a good God and an eternal hell.'[882] The only punishment that Seth would suffer would be the one that he might later inflict on himself: 'The worst, the most hardened, the most degraded of human creatures, those whom the world may think have bidden farewell to conscience, have moments in the dark silence of thought when the sword of remorse with all its poisoned tortures sinks into their wounded bosoms.'[883]

One of the *great interests of society* that counsels against enforcing moral obligation is the need to give the remorse that lives within individual conscience a chance to work improvement. This same concern speaks in favor of the consideration doctrine, and it is easy to appreciate where it will lead. Holmes was born into Parker's Boston just a decade and a half after the decision in *Mills v. Wyman*.

Homecoming

Seth promised to compensate Mills for his trouble. Why then did he not send payment? Perhaps something about Levi's homecoming changed Seth's mind.

Mills's invoice reached Seth after Levi began his trip home from Hartford, a trip of about eighty miles. It was the middle of a New England winter, and Levi was still recuperating. And yet even if he had traveled only ten miles a day, he would have made it home in the first days of March—about the time that Mills's letter arrived.

Young Levi had been away for some time. His father, a gentleman and a colonel, would surely have asked about his plans. If the old soldier did not like Levi's answer, the two could easily have butted heads—prompting Seth to decide that the best contribution he could make to his son's upbringing would be to let him take care of his debt to Mills on his own.

Whatever Seth's reasons for not sending payment, he felt strongly about it, for Mills kept trying to get paid, and Seth did not give in.[884] Mills did not rely on Seth's promise, so the law has little reason to enforce it—and it might have good reason not to. When a father is deciding how to raise his son, the law might well want to tiptoe backward and leave the two of them to work it out on their own.

Harrington v. Taylor

In our second rescue case, the husband, Lee Taylor, assaulted his wife and then assaulted her again the next day when he found her at the home of her friend, Lena Harrington. Lee's wife defended herself with an axe. She knocked Lee to the floor and

---

[882] Id., p. 50.

[883] Id., p. 13.

[884] Writ of Attachment (May 20, 1824), *Mills* SJC Files.

was swinging the axe toward his neck when Lena reached in to protect him. Lena diverted the axe and saved Lee's life, but the blade mutilated her hand. Lee promised to pay Lena's damages, but he made no more than a small down payment. Lena sued Lee in contract, but the trial court decided that Lee's promise lacked consideration and dismissed her claim.[885] The North Carolina Supreme Court affirmed.[886]

After the courts refused to enforce Lena's contract claim, she sued in tort, alleging that, by assaulting his wife, Lee proximately caused Lena's injuries. The judge allowed the case to go to trial, and Lena and her daughter testified.[887] The judge then dismissed Lena's tort claim as well, a decision that was again affirmed on appeal.[888]

The transcript of the testimony survives. Though the two witnesses offered somewhat different versions of the events, together they give some idea of what happened that afternoon.[889]

Hamlet

The events took place in 1945 in Hamlet, a small town in the Sandhills region of southcentral North Carolina, not far from the South Carolina line.[890] Hamlet, the 'Hub of the Seaboard,' became something of a boomtown after the Seaboard Air Line Railroad chose the town as its rail hub shortly before 1900.[891] At the time of the lawsuit, as many as thirty trains pulled into the Queen Anne-style Hamlet Depot every day. To accommodate the many passengers who changed trains there, the town of about five thousand had more than its share of hotels, boarding houses, and restaurants.

---

[885] *Harrington v. Taylor* (Sup. Ct., May 28, 1945) (Olive, J.), *Harrington* Trial Record (Contract).

[886] *Harrington v. Taylor*, 36 S.E.2d 227 (N.C. 1945).

[887] Lena had two daughters, Dorothy Strickland, who testified at trial, and Ruby Legrand, each of whom named a daughter after the other. To reduce confusion, I refer to Dorothy Strickland as *Lena's daughter Dorothy*, and to Dorothy Miller (1946–), Ruby's daughter, as *Lena's granddaughter Dorothy*.

[888] *Harrington v. Taylor* (Sup. Ct., May 27, 1946) (Stevens, J.), *Harrington* Trial Record (Tort), p. 16; *Harrington v. Taylor*, 40 S.E.2d 367 (N.C. 1946).

[889] For the testimony, see *Harrington* SC Record 593, pp. 5–15.

[890] For the town of Hamlet, see Simon (2017), pp. 17–43. For the town's founding, see Hutchinson (1998), pp. 191–196.

[891] For the Seaboard Railroad, see Johnson (1995).

Newtown

All of those involved in the events were people of color.[892] Charlotte E. 'Lena' Harrington (c. 1896–1967) was born in Virginia, one of eighteen children, and was between 45 and 49 years old at the time of her injury. Lena and her family moved into their house on East Main Street, 'south of the railroad tracks,' as she put it, in about 1932. Her husband moved out a couple of years later. At the time of the incident, Lena was living in the house with her two daughters, Dorothy and Ruby, then 21 and 17.

The house was located in Newtown, one of Hamlet's Black neighborhoods. Like other nearby homes, Lena's was a single-story, unpainted wood shotgun with a corrugated tin roof. It was built on an elevated wood foundation and had doors and porches front and back. The privy was in the backyard. The home's wooden walls were wallpapered on the inside, and though they were without insulation, the fireplace in the living room and the Warm Morning stove in the den kept the house warm through the winter.

Lena Harrington

To support herself after separating from her husband, Lena took in washing and ironing for white clients in Hamlet. She washed eighteen loads and earned about $27 a week. She did the washing in big tubs behind the house and wrung out the laundry with a hand wringer. Water was pumped from a well in the backyard next to the house. After her injury, Lena could no longer do the washing and had difficulty cooking for herself. At the time of trial, somewhat over a year after she was injured, Lena was still not earning.

Lena was of medium height, heavy and stocky, with a dark complexion. She was a churchgoer and known to be fun to be with. She raised her six grandchildren as their mother and gave them a loving home. All six graduated from high school.

Lena had a strong personality and kept her grandchildren in line. As Lena's granddaughter remembers it, Lena did not allow cutting up in school, sleeping in church, or sassing back. 'She was a tough lady when she was here. She didn't take no junk, didn't take no tea for the fever. She didn't let nobody run over her—Black, white, or nobody.' When Lena died, many came to pay their respects, both Black and white, including Hamlet's mayor. 'Everybody respected her, they respected Grandma.'

---

[892] Other than the court records, no formal archive relating to the case has been identified. Unless otherwise noted, the descriptions of the people and the town are drawn from trial testimony, communications with Lena Harrington's granddaughter, Dorothy Miller, and her husband Percy, conversations with other residents of Hamlet and neighboring Rockingham, and a range of publicly available sources, including census records, local directories, and contemporary newspapers.

Taylor Family

Lee Walter Taylor (c. 1903–1958) was between 40 and 44 years old at the time of our events. He worked full-time cleaning rail cars as a Seaboard carman.

Lee's altercation was with his second wife, Arnisea. Arnisea was 32 at the time of the events. In his brief, Fred Bynum, Lee's lawyer, called Arnisea 'this great big woman.'[893] Lee married Arnisea sometime before 1940, and at the time of the incident, they were living together with Della Mae, then age 19, Lee's daughter from his first marriage. Lee owned their house, a wooden structure, located about a block up the hill from Lena's place. At the time of the legal proceedings in 1946, Arnisea had returned to her home in South Carolina and did not testify at trial.

Robert Taylor was about twelve years older than his brother Lee. At the time of the dispute, Rob was living alone in one of the wooden shotgun houses a few doors down East Main Street from Lena.

Altercation

Lee and Arnisea got into a fight late at night on Sunday, January 7, 1945. It would be helpful to know more about their quarrel, but neither Lee nor Arnisea testified at trial. George Steele, Lena's lawyer, alleged that 'the defendant [Lee] assaulted and beat up his wife,' that Arnisea left home to report the assault to the police, that for Arnisea's protection the police brought her to Lena's house shortly after midnight, and that Arnisea spent the rest of the night with Lena.[894] Lee denied the allegations,[895] and Lee's lawyer surmised that, since Lee seemed to be 'a courteous negro,' it was more likely that it was for Lee's protection rather than to protect his wife that the police took Arnisea to Lena's home that night.[896] At the time, as Lena put it, 'both of them had the devil in them.'[897]

Lee stopped by Lena's house at noon the next day and spoke with Arnisea on the porch. He returned a couple of hours later to ask her to come home with him. Arnisea told him she would be home once Lee's older brother Rob was back from work.

Lee cycled back to Lena's place later in the afternoon, but Rob was not with him. Arnisea saw Lee outside without Rob and locked the windows and doors. Lee saw

---

[893] Brief for Defendant, Appellee (Nov. 14, 1946), p. 1, *Harrington* SC Record 593.

[894] Complaint (contract) para. 2, *Harrington* SC Record 594, p. 4; Complaint (tort) para. 2, *Harrington* SC Record 593, p. 2. Lena's allegations were made on information and belief. Nothing in the record suggests that Steele reviewed the police report or interviewed Arnisea. No police report of the incident has survived.

[895] Answer para. 2, *Harrington* SC Record 593, p. 4.

[896] Brief for Defendant, Appellee, p. 1, *Harrington* SC Record 593.

[897] Cross-examination of Lena Harrington, *Harrington* SC Record 593, p. 14.

Lena in the yard gathering firewood and asked about Arnisea. Lena told him he could go inside and talk to her. Lee tried to open the door, and Lena later testified that he 'was good and mad' when he saw it was locked. Lena scolded Arnisea from outside, and when she unlocked the door, Lena and Lee walked through the back door and into the kitchen.

It was January, and Lena continued into the den to start a fire in the stove. When Arnisea saw Lee, she tried to hide behind the bedroom door, but Lee saw her, and they started to tussle, Lee got angry. 'Come on,' he yelled. 'I thought I told you to come on home. I mean for you to come.' 'I was coming when Rob come,' she said. He grabbed her and began to pull. 'Well, he come to kill me,' Arnisea shouted. 'Turn me loose! Turn me loose!' Lee was pulling her toward the back of the house. Lena's daughter Dorothy testified that he was 'pulling her as rough as a man could pull a woman.'[898]

Lena kept a washstand with a basin next to the back door, and that is where she kept her axe. The boys in the neighborhood who cut wood for her did not like to use a dull blade, so Lena made sure this one was sharp.

As Lee was pulling on Arnisea, she suddenly broke free. Lena was in the den when she heard the commotion and did not see who first grabbed the axe, but when she looked up, Arnisea had it.[899] She lifted it, Lee stepped back, and she swung. The blunt end hit Lee in the head and he fell. 'I just stood there,' Lena testified, 'and I couldn't even move, just standing there with the wood in my hands.'[900] Lee got up and grabbed Arnisea again. Arnisea hit him on the side of the head, this time with the blade, and he fell again. Dorothy testified that Arnisea was 'treating him pretty badly.'[901] Lee tried to push himself up but lacked the strength and fell back down on his face, then rolled over onto his back. 'Let me kill him!' Arnisea yelled back. 'If I don't, he is going to kill me.'

Arnisea raised the axe to strike him one last time. 'Lord, don't kill him!' Lena yelled as she rushed toward them. Arnisea swung the axe toward Lee's head and neck. Lena grabbed for the handle but caught the blade. She managed to divert the blow, but the axe smashed her hand against the back door and almost severed two of her fingers. Lena then stepped over Lee, and she and Dorothy took the axe from Arnisea.

Everything stopped as they dealt with the blood from Lena's mangled right hand. They poured kerosene on the wound to stop the bleeding and took her to the nearby office of Dr. Joseph Robinson (1890–1950), an African American physician. Dr. Robinson stitched up the wound but was unable to repair Lena's hand. The stitches did not come out until March, and Lena's hand was so raw that she kept it wrapped until the weather warmed in April. Lee too was injured, with wounds to his head, neck, and back.

---

[898] Cross-examination of Dorothy Strickland, *Harrington* SC Record 593, p. 8.

[899] Cross-examination of Lena Harrington, id., p. 15.

[900] Id., p. 10.

[901] Cross-examination of Dorothy Strickland, id., p. 8.

Promise

Lena alleged that, at a later date, never specified, Lee promised to pay for her damages. No amount was mentioned, there was no writing, and the record contains no evidence of a promise. Lee gave Lena $20, and though his lawyer was 'quite confident the defendant hopes to help the plaintiff voluntarily,'[902] Lee paid nothing more.[903] Arnisea paid Lena $23, which allowed Lena to pay $22 to her doctor, less than half the bill for stitching up her hand. Lena never found the cash to pay the rest. According to the complaint, she spent considerable sums on treatment.[904] Lena's lawyer estimated that her total loss from the accident was about $12,500.[905]

Lawyers

Lee's attorney was Fred Bynum (1882–1963), a corporate lawyer in neighboring Rockingham, a town of about 3,600. Bynum, a dean of the local bar,[906] was about 64 at the time of the lawsuit and represented the Seaboard rail line. Lee worked for the railroad, and his supervisor may have referred him to Bynum.

George Steele Jr. (1914–1952) represented Lena. He also had his law office in Rockingham, was 32 years old, had been in practice for only five years, and was to die just six years later.[907] Steele was a scion of one of the town's leading manufacturing families.

The clerk of the Superior Court allowed Lena to file her pleadings without paying the usual filing fee,[908] and the same order designated Steele as Lena's counsel. The trial judge may have contacted Steele because the young lawyer had earlier argued a pro bono matter before the North Carolina Supreme Court.[909]

---

[902] Brief for Defendant, Appellee, p. 2, *Harrington* SC Record 593.

[903] Complaint para. 8, *Harrington* SC Record 594, p. 5.

[904] Complaint para. 6, *Harrington* SC Record 593, p. 5.

[905] Complaint para. 9, *Harrington* SC Record 594, p. 6.

[906] London (1963), p. 1.

[907] 'Funeral Rites Today for George S. Steele,' *Richmond County Journal,* June 4, 1952, p. 1.

[908] Order Granting Leave to Sue as a Pauper, *Harrington* SC Record 594, p. [19].

[909] See *Ex parte Steele*, 18 S.E.2d 132 (N.C. 1942). Steele was co-counsel.

Tort Claims

Steele proposed two main theories of liability in Lena's tort case. The North Carolina Supreme Court can be read to have rejected both of them in a single sentence: 'The injury is not one which the defendant [Lee] could have reasonably foreseen or anticipated.'[910] The sentence requires a little unpacking.

By pulling on Arnisea as he did, Steele argued, Lee committed the tort of assault.[911] Since the assault set in motion the events that led to Lena's injury, Lee should be liable for all the harm for which his acts were the proximate cause. The legal knot that Steele had to untie was how Lee could be liable for Lena's injury when Arnisea swung the axe.

Though North Carolina case law on the question is scarce, the principles were well established. If the blow from Arnisea's axe represented what is known as *an independent intervening or superseding cause*, Lee would not be liable for Lena's injuries.[912] To avoid the effect of this doctrine, Steele argued that Lee and Arnisea should be considered *joint tortfeasors*.[913]

However, even if Lee was a joint tortfeasor, he would be liable for Lena's injuries only if he could be said to have caused them—if a person of ordinary experience, standing in his shoes, would reasonably have anticipated that Arnisea's final axe stroke might naturally follow from his actions.[914]

The trial court heard the evidence and, without explanation, dismissed the action.[915] The North Carolina Supreme Court affirmed on the grounds stated in the single sentence that we read earlier. The court had previously held that, when the actions of the second actor (Arnisea, in our case) are themselves tortious, they insulate the first actor (Lee) from liability.[916] Implicit was the conclusion that Arnisea's final swing of the axe was not justified as self-defense. We will return to the question in just a moment.

Steele's second theory was based on the *doctrine of rescue*: a wrong that imperils the life of the victim is also a wrong to a potential rescuer.[917]

Lena's claim involved an interesting twist on the rescue doctrine. The immediate agent of the harm to Lena was not Lee, the defendant in the lawsuit, but rather a third party (in our case, Arnisea). This raised the same question of proximate cause that we have already discussed, namely whether Arnisea's intervention should

---

910 *Harrington v. Taylor*, 40 S.E.2d 367, 367 (N.C. 1946).

911 Plaintiff Appellant's Brief, pp. 2–6, *Harrington* SC Record 593.

912 See *Gen. Am. Life Ins. Co. v. Stadiem*, 25 S.E.2d 202, 205 (N.C. 1943).

913 See *West v. Collins Baking Co.*, 181 S.E. 551, 552–553 (N.C. 1935).

914 See *Harton v. Forest City Tel. Co.*, 54 S.E. 299, 302 (N.C. 1906).

915 *Harrington v. Taylor* (Sup. Ct., [June] 1946) (Stevens, J.), in *Harrington* SC Record 593, p. 16.

916 *Butner v. Spease*, 6 S.E.2d 808, 810–811 (N.C. 1940).

917 The doctrine was discussed earlier. See *Eckert v. Long Island R.R. Co.*, 43 N.Y. 502 (1871)), discussed above, pp. 158–159.

insulate Lee from liability. By deciding this question as it did, the court also rejected liability under the rescue doctrine.

Lee's Resources

Did Lee have the resources to pay Lena's claim? Arnisea told the census worker in 1940 that Lee owned his home and that his annual income was $700—only slightly higher than the federal minimum wage and half of what Lena was taking home from her laundry business. If Arnisea's figures are accurate, Lee would likely not have been able to provide Lena with regular support—let alone pay the $12,500 in damages that her lawyer alleged.

Does this additional information change our view of Lena's case? Let us consult our readings.

Mary Joe Frug

We begin by stepping into the shoes of the participants. I feel tremendous admiration for Lena and will now try to experience the events from her point of view. A man is lying immobile a few feet in front of me. A large woman raises an axe and is about to kill him. I hesitate. I might have yelled to distract her, but I would not have reached for the axe. If Arnisea had paused, I might have tackled her, axe and all. Or I hope that is what I would have done. Lena was fearless and rose mightily to the occasion.

I turn next to George Steele, Lena's lawyer. He had been admitted to the bar a few years earlier, and the judge may have assigned him the case. Since the consideration doctrine was going to be a hurdle, his complaint should have described Lee's promise. When was the promise made, and where? Was Lee staring at Lena's bloody hand, still in shock from being clubbed with an axe, or did he make the promise later, after Lena told him that she could not pay her doctor and would no longer be able to make a living doing laundry? Was Lee suggesting that he intended to take on a legally enforceable obligation or was he only expressing remorse and the hope that he might one day be able to make it up to her? Did he use the word *promise*, or was that Steele's creative pleading?

If Steele had demonstrated that Lee made the promise and meant it, the judge might have been willing to find an exception to the consideration doctrine. But Steele produced no evidence of a promise.[918]

---

[918] Because Lena's contract claim never went to trial, the record contains no testimony about a promise. Yet the fact that Steele could not include its amount in the complaint suggests that it was too indefinite to enforce.

Moreover, to make it plausible that Lee intended to commit himself to supporting Lena until her retirement, Steele could have described Lee's line of work and whatever he knew of Lee's financial resources, but Steele mentioned none of it. Since we have no details to suggest a serious promise and also no proof that Lee had access to sufficient funds to make it good, Lena's contract claim collapses long before I get to the consideration doctrine.

I will now try to step into Arnisea's situation. My attempt will not succeed. I can no more access the mind of a battered Black woman in the South in the 1940s than I can imagine what it is like to swim the Hellespont. And yet if I understand our method, I must work myself into the mindset of each of the participants. Here common law method may require patches that we have yet to come up with.

Steele alleged that Lee assaulted Arnisea the night before the altercation. She was so frightened when she noticed that he was outside in the yard that she locked the doors and windows. Because she was feeling threatened, it made sense for her to defend herself, and the axe was what she found within reach. The question has to do with her last blow. Lee was lying at her feet, bleeding, stunned, and unable to move. Was it reasonable for Arnisea to try to kill him? That is what Lena's tort suit comes down to.

North Carolina law does not recognize the *battered spouse syndrome*.[919] Arnisea would have been able to claim self-defense only if she reasonably believed that there was an imminent threat that Lee would kill her or cause her great bodily harm and that the threat could be averted only by the use of deadly force. We do not have enough information to decide whether Arnisea's actions were reasonable under this test.

Lee did not testify, and so I will leave his thoughts unexplored.

This is the best I can do to reconstruct events from the different perspectives. When I look more closely, Lena did not have a serious contract claim. Her only chance was her cause of action in tort—but since her tort claim is not relevant to our work on the consideration doctrine, we do not need to decide it.

Patricia Williams, Ian Macneil

Did Lena suffer discrimination—either because she was a woman or because she was Black?

Judge Hubert Olive (1895–1972)[920] heard Lena's contract claim. Olive had fought in World War I, served in the state house of representatives, and just barely lost the Democratic primary for Governor in 1952. He was considered one of the most scholarly laypersons of his day.

[919] See *State v. Norman*, 378 S.E.2d 8, 14–15 (N.C. 1989) (citing cases).

[920] For Olive, see Holland (1991); C[rosby] (1972).

Judge Henry L. Stevens, Jr. (1896–1971)[921] heard Lena's tort claim. As a decorated veteran of World War I, he was chosen to be the National Commander of the American Legion in 1931, and in the depths of the Great Depression joined with the American Federation of Labor to find a million jobs for unemployed veterans. Some considered Stevens to be the greatest public orator of his generation.[922]

Did Lena suffer prejudice because the judges who decided her case were Southern white men?

It does not seem so. Judge Olive's ruling on Lena's contract claim was unobjectionable, particularly because there was nothing in the complaint to suggest an enforceable promise. As for Lena's claim in tort, Judge Stevens allowed her to present her evidence, despite the causation difficulties, and the justices of the North Carolina Supreme Court agreed that he was right to dismiss the claim. That ruling too was legally unobjectionable, though it is also possible that the judges unconsciously favored Lee. As we have noted, Lee's lawyer described him as 'a courteous Negro,'[923] while Arnisea may have seemed to them a hysterical wife bent on revenge.[924]

Duncan Kennedy, Roberto Unger

Universal health care and a more ample safety net would have improved Lena's situation, but deviationist doctrine in the form of moral consideration would not have helped her. Enforcing Lee's promise would only have shifted the burden from one poor person to another.

Richard Posner

The frame freezes as Arnisea's axe reaches the top of its swing. 'If I rescue you,' Lena asks Lee, 'will you contribute to my support?' Lee wants to take the deal but has no resources. For an economist, 'a desire not backed by ability to pay has no standing,'[925] and for Lee any price would have been too steep.

[921] For Stevens, see Powell (2013); Ingram (1994).

[922] McGowen and McGowen (1971), p. 421.

[923] Brief for Defendant, Appellee, p. 1, *Harrington* SC Record 593, also in Danzig and Watson (2004), p. 208.

[924] It has been suggested that the white police officers did not respond properly the night before to Arnisea's claim of domestic violence. If they had arrested Lee for the assault, Arnisea might not have needed to defend herself, and Lena might not have been injured. See Penningroth (2022), pp. 1208–1209 and note 30.

[925] Posner (1990b), p. 357.

Oliver Wendell Holmes

Absent institutional concerns, Holmes would want Lee to decide for himself whether to perform his promise. Was the welfare of a brave citizen like Lena a matter of social importance? Though the question is a good one, Lena's welfare, as we have just discussed, was not at stake. No amount of judicial enforcement could have wrung what Lena needed from Lee's resources. But even if Lee had had the funds, Holmes might have responded that it is precisely when survival hangs in the balance that we want to leave the decision to the parties. It would be dreadful for the state to make the important decisions and leave only small change to the rest of us.

Max Weber

Our final challenge comes from Max Weber's focus on predictability. The results in our three cases are predictable only if they can be reconciled. We now understand why a court might refuse to enforce the promises in *Mills* and *Harrington*. Once we learn more about the accident in the sawmill, will it still make sense to decide *Webb* the other way?

Webb v. McGowin

'What law student does not remember... the falling block?'[926]

Joe Webb, the court tells us, was employed in a sawmill in Alabama in 1925 when he was asked to clear the mill's upper floor. As was the practice, he pushed a piece of unneeded scrap to the edge of the deck. Just as he was about to release it, he saw J.G. McGowin standing on the ground below. To save McGowin from injury or death, Webb fell with the block and diverted its path in the air. The block missed McGowin, but Webb himself was seriously injured in the fall and left with a permanent disability. McGowin promised Webb a small lifetime pension and paid it regularly for more than eight years.

A month after McGowin's death, his executors decided not to continue the payments, and Webb sued the estate for the unpaid installments. The estate demurred on a number of grounds, including that McGowin's promise was without consideration.[927] The trial court sustained the demurrers and refused to enforce the promise.[928] The appellate court reversed.[929] It invoked the doctrine of moral consid-

---

[926] Knapp (2013), p. 1359.

[927] See Demurrers to Complaint, *Webb* Record 768, pp. 2–4.

[928] *Webb v. McGowin* (Cir. Ct., Butler Cnty., Apr. 1935) (Gamble, J.), *Webb* Record 768, p. 7.

[929] *Webb v. McGowin*, 168 So. 196 (Ala. Ct. App. 1935).

eration and reinstated Webb's action. The Alabama Supreme Court refused to hear the case but noted that it approved the appellate decision.[930]

After Webb won his appeal, the trial court calendared the case for trial, but the parties settled the matter before a jury could be picked. No evidence was presented in the proceedings, so there was none to preserve in the court record.[931] And yet there is plenty of additional information to consider. I have reviewed the case file, examined the documents available in the archives, and spoken with those who know something about the case. From that material and those discussions, I have constructed a more detailed understanding of the events that led to the controversy. Though the added detail fills some gaps, the events remain opaque. Nonetheless, I believe that we now have what we need to decide the dispute.

Employer and Employee

Until now, we have been missing the central reality of the case—at the time of the accident, J.G. McGowin was the president of the W.T. Smith Lumber Company, Webb's employer. In other words, Webb was claiming that he saved his boss's life. Though the opinions do not mention the fact, two of the appellate judges, as we will see, were personally acquainted with McGowin and well aware of it.

W.T. Smith Lumber Company

The W.T. Smith Lumber Company was one of the oldest lumber processors in Alabama. It was headquartered in Chapman, a red-clay town located in the longleaf pine forest of south-central Alabama, about a third of the way from Montgomery to Mobile. The logging camp that opened there in the 1880s grew to a modest lumber business, and Chapman long led a frontier existence as a railside village. The company changed hands a couple of times before the McGowin family purchased it in 1905.

The McGowins transformed the sawmill into one of the most dynamic enterprises in Alabama. At the height of the mill's operations, a couple of decades after our events, a thousand workers operated three sawmills, a veneer mill (creating hardwood veneer for meat packing plants), a box factory (using scrap to make shipping crates for fruit and vegetables), two heading mills (producing barrel caps), and a tight barrel stave mill (making oak barrels for oil and whiskey).[932] The writer Carl Carmer described what came to mind as he toured the extensive facility in the

[930] *Webb v. McGowin*, 168 So. 199 (Ala. 1936).

[931] For Watson's findings about the case, see Danzig and Watson (2004), pp. 149–184.

[932] Maunder (1977), pp. 10 (recollections of Floyd McGowin), 38 (recollections of Earl McGowin).

1920s: '*Lettuce crates for Albion,/Lath for Tokio,/Barrel staves for Marion,/Piers for old Bordeaux!/Paving blocks for Omaha,/Roofs for Guayaquil,/Window-sash for Panama,/Girders for Mobile!*'[933]

Track was laid thirty miles or more into the forest, and the harvested logs were transported by narrow-gauge rail back to the town and unloaded into the log pond in front of the sawmill. The McGowins operated fourteen locomotives pulling 125 log cars over almost 200 miles of track and manufactured yearly about 73 million board feet of lumber.[934] Logging crews slept in box cars on rough-hewn bunks and took their meals in the dining cars. When singer-songwriter Hank Williams (1923–1953)[935] was a boy, his father worked as a log-train engineer for W.T. Smith, and Hank's first recollection was of living in a boxcar near Chapman.[936] One of the music legend's last songs, *The Log Train*, recorded in 1952, gives a sense of what it was like to live in the town and work on the trains.[937]

Webb's accident took place in sawmill No. 2. The mill specialized in processing large, high-grade timbers, up to 32 feet long, as many as 200 trunks a day. A couple of years after the accident, James Saxon Childers, an Alabama writer, had a chance to tour the mill. 'Then, once the high-pitched rasping momentarily has ended, the carriage upon which the exmonarch of the forest is riding is stopped. A man standing behind three levers pulls one of them and a great steel rod with spikes upon it shoots upward, catches the tree and flings it about as if it were a match; turning it into the position which is desired by the director, and making it possible for the whirling saws again to slash their unerring way through the heart of the giant pine.'[938]

Chapman

Chapman was a company town, and W.T. Smith owned everything in it.[939] Wages were low, most residents had little money—the average wage for unskilled labor was about two dollars a day—and not more than about a dozen employees owned their own homes.[940] The company employed between a thousand and twelve hun-

933 Carmer (1928).

934 Fickle (2014), p. 104; Anderson and Huber (1999), pp. 19–20.

935 For Williams, see Escott et al. (2004); Williams (1981).

936 Escott et al. (2004), p. 5.

937 Maunder (1977), pp. 33–35 (recollections of Earl McGowin). For the song and its background, see Anderson and Huber (1999).

938 Childers (1927), p. 8.

939 Appleyard (2000), p. [v]. Description of Chapman collated from McGowin (2015), pp. 3–9; Jones (2010), pp. 63–71; Jones (2005), pp. 36–37, 68, 76; Collier (1986), p. 12; Maunder (1977), pp. 43–49 (recollections of Earl McGowin), 72 (recollections of Nicholas McGowin).

940 Letter from J.G. McGowin to Southern Pine Association (July 27, 1933), WTS Presidential Files, b. 5, f. SPA (gray); Letter from J.G. McGowin to H. Stanley (Feb. 8, 1927), WTS Presidential Files, b. 5, f. Sta-Ste (wages); Williams (1981), p. 8 (quoting Taft Skipper) (home ownership).

dred workers, Black and white in nearly equal numbers, and it housed them in two to three hundred company-owned homes, arranged in separate neighborhoods and rented at minimal rates.[941] Most plots included a large yard with shade trees, a garden, a barn, a small pasture large enough for a milk cow, and sometimes a chicken coop. Indoor plumbing came later. Life followed the rhythm of the mill whistles, which blew six days a week—at four in the morning as reveille, at six as work began, and again at six in the evening when the mills shut down for the day.[942]

The company built separate schools, churches, lodge halls, playgrounds, and baseball diamonds for the Black and white communities, and sponsored a host of sporting and cultural events, including sports competitions, dances, Saturday night movies, and Chautauqua programs with speeches and music.[943] McGowin was especially proud of the school, which ran through the ninth grade.[944] In the section of homes rented by Black families, residents operated cafes and small juke joints.[945]

Two doctors and a nurse resided full-time in Chapman, and W.T. Smith provided the equipment needed to set up the town clinic. A small mandatory monthly salary deduction funded the medical staff and provided employees and their families with complete medical care, except for the price of prescription medicines, which were sold at cost.[946] The company also covered hospital care for accident victims.

The company store, which operated at a nominal profit, carried fresh meat, fruit and vegetables, hardware and farm tools, dry goods, school supplies, and a full line of clothing, and it also included a pharmacy. Because trains on the Louisville & Nashville Railroad arrived from the Gulf Coast daily, there was also fresh seafood. Workers paid at the store in cash, scrip, and company tokens called *clacker*,[947] and a mule-drawn dray provided home delivery along the town's unpaved streets.

Many of those who lived in Chapman loved the place. 'I was talking to a group of preachers and I told them I'd rather live in Chapman than in Heaven. They asked why. I said, Well, you have to die to go to Heaven but if you abide by the rules, you can live and stay in Chapman.'[948]

---

[941] See, 'Additional Notes,' McGowin Papers, b. 4707, f. [no label].

[942] 'Chapman as Seen in the Editions of *Lumbering Along*,' *The Butler County News*, Sept. 28, 1978, McGowin Papers, b. 4674, f. [Clippings, etc. – Folder 7] (quoting J.O. Dunn). See also 'J.O. Dunn came to Chapman 1908,' id., b. 4707, f. [no label]; Rev. J.W. Joyner, 'Joygrams,' id.

[943] For the music and dancing that the company sponsored in the Black community, see Jones (2010), pp. 68, 69.

[944] Letter from J.G. McGowin to Prof. Sam Morgan (July 28, 1924), WTS Presidential Files, b. 5, f. Mo (brown).

[945] Jones (2010), pp. 63, 66.

[946] For the company's medical plan, see Letter from J.G. McGowin to Mr. S.W. Pipes, Jr. (Aug. 6, 1928), WTS Presidential Files, b. 5, f. Pi-Q (brown).

[947] Maunder (1977), p. 44 (Earl McGowin) (clacker, scrip, and checks); Kelley (1956) (clacker). Examples of unused W.T. Smith scrip are preserved in WTS Files, b. 25 (undated, probably 1910s). An unused pay envelope, also undated, is in b. 14.

[948] 'Chapman as Seen in Editions of *Lumbering Along*,' *The Butler County News*, Sept. 28, 1978, McGowin Papers, b. 4674, f. [Clippings, etc. – Folder 7] (quoting Zell Peagler). For the handwritten notes of the interview with Peagler, see McGowin Papers, b. 4707, f. [no label].

The whistles have now fallen silent, and the company store and the other facilities are gone, along with the locomotives, the logging trains, and all but a couple of the workers' homes. The McGowin family compound is still there, 'the fine homes behind tall pines on cool, gently-sloping knolls,'[949] and the town is still involved in the lumber business. The property is under new ownership, and the old mills have been replaced by a state-of-the-art plywood factory.

J.G. McGowin

James Greeley McGowin (1871–1934) was the central figure in the Chapman landscape and the one who, we are told, was standing beneath the falling block. He was 54 at the time of Webb's accident. McGowin was born on a farm in a small village in south-central Alabama and named for Horace Greeley (1811–1872), the editor of the *New-York Tribune*. His father bought an interest in a sawmill in southern Alabama in the 1880s, and McGowin grew up in the lumber business.[950] After attending rural schools, he briefly enrolled in business school, but he was largely self-educated. 'I have never attended college and have had very little literary advantages.'[951]

At the time the McGowins acquired W.T. Smith in 1905, prevailing forestry practice was 'to cut out and get out': set up a temporary camp, clear cut the forest, and move on.[952] The business prospered, and soon the firm owned six sawmills and several logging camps in and around the small town.

McGowin managed the business from the moment his family purchased the company and was elected its president in January 1925, seven months before Webb was injured. McGowin had by then become the patriarch of a respected Alabama family.[953] He 'loved his work, and treated it almost like a religion' and held 'the status of patron saint and cult figure' in the close-knit sawmill town.[954] 'He had an interest in people, a real concern for them. He knew them, knew their families and kept up with their problems.'[955] When his employees were in the hospital, he wrote to the attending physician to ensure that they received the best care.[956] His employees named their children after him—today, decades later, their descendants are still naming their children after him—and they fondly recalled the moments they spent together. 'I remember that MR. J. G. McGowen would make his rounds in the

949 'The Empire Dissolves,' *The Montgomery Advertiser*, Sept. 25, 1965, p. 4.

950 Appleyard (2000), pp. 14–16; Fickle (2014), pp. 66–67.

951 Letter from J.G. McGowin to Earl M. McGowin (July 28, 1924), p. 1, WTS Files, b. 1, f. 9.

952 Collier (1965), p. 53.

953 'Early History,' [pp. 2–3], McGowin Papers, b. 4707, f. [no label].

954 Appleyard (2000), p. 35; McGowin (2015), p. vii (patron saint).

955 Maunder (1977), p. 70 (recollections of Nicholas McGowin).

956 See, e.g., Letter from J.G. McGowin to Dr. George Blue (Feb. 27, 1929), WTS Presidential Files, b. 2, f. Dr. John Blue.

afternoon about 2 P.M. & take my straw hat off me & wear it himself. I had a lot of fun with MR. J. G. McGowen.'[957]

McGowin was of medium height, 'a well-groomed man with a strong, handsome face.'[958] In the surviving photos, even in family gatherings, he is usually dressed in a suit, a dress shirt, and a tie.

He was devoted to the company and the lumber industry and had little time or inclination for cultural pursuits. And yet he kept himself informed. He read half a dozen daily papers from cities in the South as well as the *New York Times,* and he gifted subscriptions to *The New Yorker* and the Sunday *Times* for the holidays.[959]

McGowin was not impressed by fame or position. He once wrote to a sitting U.S. Senator, 'You are badly wrong in the attitude you are taking in many public questions. I want to get you down for the night with me and straighten you out.'[960] He despised both religious bigotry and the Klan, expressed those sentiments openly and repeatedly, and made sure that there was no Klan chapter in Chapman.[961] 'I do not think I ever knew of a more damnable organization that did more indecent things and got by with them than did the Ku Klux.'[962]

McGowin died unexpectedly from pneumonia on January 1, 1934, at the age of 63, a complication from a second appendix operation.[963] The local papers remembered him as one of Alabama's great citizens.[964] His death reverberated like 'the fall of the mightiest pine in all the forests of Alabama.'[965]

McGowin Family

At the time of Webb's accident, the McGowins were raising their family in a house located beside the tracks near the mill, and their children attended the town's elementary school. Two years later, McGowin built Edgefield, a colonnaded mansion

[957] Letter from Jaycee McCarty to Earl McGowan (spelling as in original) (Feb. 11, 1980), McGowin Papers, b. 4707, f. History File (1), reprinted in Appleyard (2000), p. 35.

[958] McGowin (2015), p. 9.

[959] Appleyard (2000), pp. 36–37 (reading); Ward (1934); Letter from J.G. McGowin to *The New Yorker* (Dec. 15, 1932), WTS Presidential Files, b. 5, f. N (brown); Letter from *The New York Times* to J.G. McGowin (Dec. 21, 1932), WTS Presidential Files, b. 5, f. N (brown).

[960] Letter from J.G. McGowin to Hon. J. Thomas Heflin (Oct. 12, 1927), WTS Presidential Files, b. 6, f. Ham-Har.

[961] Letter from J.G. McGowin to Hugo L. Black (June 5, 1926), WTS Files, b. 1, f. 1; Letter from J.G. McGowin to W.B. Cloe (May 18, 1926), id.; Appleyard (2000), p. 37; Letter from J. G. McGowin to P.G. Shook (Oct. 6, 1928), WTS Presidential Files, b. 5, f. Shi-Shy; Letter from J.G. McGowin to E. Wooten (Nov. 16, 1927), WTS Presidential Files, b. 5, f. W (brown).

[962] Letter from J.G. McGowin to Senator John H. Bankhead (Apr. 22, 1933), p. 1, WTS Presidential Files, b. 2, f. Senator John Bankhead (gray).

[963] McGowin (2015), p. vii.

[964] 'J. Greeley McGowin,' *The Greenville Advocate*, Jan. 5, 1934, p. 2.

[965] Graves (1934).

set among trees on the edge of town. Visitors often stayed at the McGowin home and dined with the family.[966]

McGowin wanted his children to travel abroad to obtain 'the finest possible education' and then return to Chapman to run the family business.[967] All four brothers—Floyd, Earl, Julian, and Nick—attended the University of Alabama and then studied in Oxford at Pembroke College, Earl as a Rhodes Scholar.[968] The family later made an important gift to allow Pembroke to construct a new library, which still bears the McGowin name.

McGowin chose Joe, an older brother, and Floyd, his oldest son, to execute his will. Joe (1867–1937) was one of the mills' owners and later chaired the board of the oldest daily newspaper in Alabama, the *Mobile Press Register*.[969]

Floyd, Earl, and Julian took over the lumber business at McGowin's death. The three brothers ran the company together but divided responsibilities.

Floyd (1900–1981), the oldest son, succeeded his father as president, and W.T. Smith prospered under his direction.[970] Tree farming was a new idea at the time, and Floyd earned national recognition when the company replaced the railroads with trucks and became a pioneer in selective harvesting and practical forestry.[971]

Earl (1901–1992),[972] the Rhodes scholar, was the company's vice-president in charge of sales. He also served for twenty years in the Alabama legislature, where he was said to represent 'the most liberal and progressive thought in Alabama politics.'[973]

Julian (1904–1973), the third brother, was an expert equestrian who pioneered and developed inventory techniques that became widely used in the industry.[974]

The brothers built W.T. Smith into one of the largest lumber processors east of the Mississippi, a timber products conglomerate that, by 1949, held more than 200,000 acres of forest land. In that year, the renowned photojournalist Margaret Bourke-White (1904–1971)[975] took a photo of the three brothers—dressed in business suits, wearing fedoras, and standing on a magnolia log in front of their mill. It ran as the lead image for an article on the New South in *Life* magazine.[976]

---

[966] Maunder (1977), p. 88 (recollections of Estelle McGowin Larson).

[967] Collier (1986), p. 14. See also Maunder (1977), pp. 19–20 (Floyd McGowin).

[968] Collier (1986), pp. 15–18.

[969] Appleyard (2000), p. 35.

[970] 'N. Floyd McGowin, President: National Lumber Manufacturers Association, 1957–1958,' wood-bound photo tribute presented by the NLMA, McGowin Papers, b. 4727; Smith (1959), p. 5.

[971] Collier (1965), pp. 57–58; Fickle (2014), p. 190.

[972] For Earl McGowin, see Collier (1986).

[973] 'Dixon and Graves to Take up Problems at Conference,' *The Birmingham News*, June 9, 1938, p. 1.

[974] Description of Julian McGowin from McGowin (2015), pp. 13–15, 248–251, 259–260, 318–319.

[975] For Bourke-White, see Goldberg (1986); Bourke-White (1963).

[976] The New South (1949), p. 79.

Joe Webb

Joseph Wilson Webb (1872–1943) was born in the hardscrabble world of Giles County, Tennessee, just north of the Alabama border. He was 53 at the time of the accident in mill No. 2.[977] He and his family were working class whites.

When the Panic of 1873 threw many out of work—this now from family lore—the Webbs left for Texas, which had largely been spared the destruction of the Civil War.[978] Joe was still a newborn, too young for a long wagon trip. His parents left him with an older sibling, who was instructed to find a family to care for him. Webb grew up in Giles County, finished fourth grade, and learned to read and write. There he met his future wife, Emma Lessie Graves (1878–1955), who was about six years his junior. They married in 1894 and eventually had eight or nine children.

A photo of Joe and Lessie survives. Joe's face is sunburnt, chiseled, and stern. He is sitting on the wooden seat of a buckboard wagon, loosely holding the horse's reins. He has on a wide-brimmed black felt hat and a long-sleeved shirt buttoned to the neck. Lessie is standing beside him with her hand resting lovingly on his shoulder. She is wearing long calico, her hair is pulled back, and she is smiling for the camera. Webb may have begun to work in the lumber industry twenty years before the accident, though he probably did not come to W.T. Smith until after 1920.

Carpenter

Sawmill No. 2 was built on wood stilts at the edge of—and partially extending over—the large pond into which logs were discharged from the railcars.[979] The logs were captured by the heavy chains that extended into the pond and then pulled up to the saw, probably by oxen. The trunks entered the mill with the bark still attached—debarkers were not introduced until the 1950s.[980] A saw blade sliced off the bark as the trunk was spun around, and side slabs with bark fell to the ground. Then the trunk was guided back and forth through the spinning steel to produce timber.

The accident that caused Webb's injuries took place in mill No. 2 on Monday morning, August 3, 1925. The original mill No. 2 had burnt down at the end of March, four months earlier.[981] 'It was a very spectacular fire, seemingly catching from one end to the other at the same time, and we didn't even get a chance to get a

---

[977] Little documentary material survives concerning Joe and Lessie Webb. The following account draws in part on information provided by his granddaughter, Janice Webb Hammond.

[978] Spratt (1955), p. 285.

[979] An engraved aerial view of W.T. Smith's Chapman facility was printed on the firm's stationery in the early 1920s. See, e.g., Letter from J.G. McGowin to Earl McGowin (April 12, 1921), in McGowin Papers, b. 4680, f. 9.

[980] Collier (1965), p. 141.

[981] Letter from J.G. McGowin to L. Sevier (April 1, 1925), WTS Files, b. 1, f. 10.

hose on it.'[982] When reconstructed, the new mill was built on solid terrain at the edge of the pond. The mill floor was about twelve feet above the ground, and the structure had an extensive catwalk system and an attic room for filing saws.[983] On the date of the accident, the new mill was not yet ready[984]—and would not begin operation until the following spring.[985] Webb was one of the company's carpenters,[986] and given the date of the accident, he was probably working to rebuild the facility.

Powell's Account

The documents offer two accounts about how Webb was injured.

The appellate court based its decision on the facts as Dempsey Powell (1863–1949),[987] Webb's lawyer, described them in his brief on appeal.[988] Webb was 'engaged in clearing the upper floor of mill No. 2.' Instructed to remove a seventy-five-pound block of pine, Webb pushed the wood to the edge of the upper deck and tipped it over. As he was about to let go, he looked down and saw McGowin 'on the ground below and directly under where the block would have fallen.' Webb could have remained safely where he was, but then the block would likely have struck McGowin with enough force to injure or kill him. Webb made an instant decision to keep hold of the wood and divert its fall. The block missed McGowin, thereby preventing him from suffering grievous bodily injury and perhaps saving his life. Webb, however, was seriously injured in the fall, which broke his right forearm and wrist and his lower right leg and heel.

As I try to imagine the event as Powell was describing it, I see Webb making a split-second decision to angle the block's trajectory hard to the right to protect those standing below. The effort pulled him off balance, and he followed the block down to the ground. His right heel hit first and absorbed the brunt of the impact while his right arm fractured as he reached out to break his fall.

This version of the story has a backstory. It is perhaps best to start with Powell. He had by then practiced law for nearly fifty years and, already in his seventies, was

---

982 Letter from J.G. McGowin to Julian McGowin (Apr. 1, 1925), WTS Files, b. 1, f. 8.

983 Appleyard (2000), p. 120. For a picture of mill No. 2 after it was reconstructed, see the color postcard in Ms. Julian Greeley [*recte* J.G.] McGowin Travelogue 1939, book 2, McGowin Papers, b. 4712, third folder.

984 Letter from J.G. McGowin to Taylor Brothers Lumber Company (September 29, 1925), WTS Presidential Files, b. 5, f. Ta-Te.

985 'William Curry Jones,' *Lumbering Along*, p. 4 (n.d.) (photocopy), McGowin Papers, b. 4707, f. [no label]. See also Appleyard (2000), p. 119.

986 Appleyard (2000), p. 243.

987 For Powell, see Owen (1921).

988 See *Webb v. McGowin*, 168 So. 196, 196–197 (Ala. Ct. App. 1935) (quoting [Brief for Plaintiff-Appellant] (May 8, 1935), pp. 1–3, *Webb* File, f. 10 (Appeal: Briefs), which essentially restated Webb's Amended Complaint para. 5 (April 8, 1935), in *Webb* Record 768, pp. 5–7.

one of the most prominent lawyers in Alabama. Powell had been a state senator and was once appointed to sit as special judge on the Alabama Supreme Court to avoid having the case decided by an equally divided court.[989] Powell ran for lieutenant governor in 1930 on the ticket of the Jeffersonian Democrats, a party backed by the Ku Klux Klan.[990]

As Webb described the events for the complaint, he was drawing on his recollection of an accident that had occurred nine years earlier. He had long been unable to work and still walked with a painful limp. Since Webb's benefactor was no longer alive, Powell likely explained, Webb's pension could continue only if there had been a quid pro quo for McGowin's promise. We will come back to their conversation shortly.

Earlier Version

There is an earlier account of the accident, one that may also have come from Webb but that was recorded while the events were fresh. Since Webb's condition was serious, he was taken to an infirmary in nearby Georgiana, where he was treated by Dr. James Watson (1875–1926). W.T. Smith sent only 'very bad cases' to Dr. Watson.[991]

To comply with the Alabama workers' compensation law, someone in the company office filled out the Employer's First Report. It was dated eight weeks after Webb's injury. We will examine the report in detail in just a moment. I think we will then conclude that its description of the events was copied from an earlier report that was completed shortly after the accident. In the space provided to 'Describe fully how injury occurred,' the company's representative wrote the following: 'In building saw mill when sawing a piece of timber off he was holding it up and he became over balanced and fell to the ground.'[992] It is hard to know whose voice this is. This might be what Webb told the company's representative—but it might also be the words of the supervisor who witnessed it, helped Webb up, and brought him to the infirmary.

Webb was engaged, it says, in '[re]building [the] saw mill.' It was the beginning of August, and by then the timber frame and roof of the great space would have been complete.[993] It is no longer possible to determine where in the mill the accident took

---

[989] See *City of Birmingham v. Birmingham Waterworks Co.*, 42 So. 10, 14 (Ala. 1906) (on rehearing).

[990] Feldman (2015), pp. 201, 203, 207.

[991] Letter from J.G. McGowin to Katie L. Autrey (Apr. 1, 1926), WTS Files, b. 1, f. 1.

[992] 'Employer's First Report of Injury for Which Compensation is Claimed or Paid, Under the Workmen's Compensation Law of Alabama,' sec. C, para. 3 (Sept. 26, 1925), *Webb* File, f. 1 (Workers' Comp Claim).

[993] The new mill was 'forty feet wide up to the saw, and fifty-six feet wide from there up. The total length of the mill is planned to be 232 feet.' Letter from J.G. McGowin to J.F. McGowin (Apr. 29, 1925), p. 1, WTS Files, b. 1, f. 8.

place. In Powell's account, Webb had been asked to clear 'the upper floor of mill No. 2.' If Webb had fallen from high up in the mill—from the attic or a catwalk—he would likely not have survived.

The workers' comp report says that Webb fell 'to the ground,' and in Powell's complaint the fall was 'to the ground below.' My guess is that Webb was working on what would become the main mill floor, about twelve feet above the dirt at ground level. Webb might have been standing at the edge of the finished part of the floor and holding one end of a heavy plank as his co-worker cut it to size. If Webb was momentarily distracted, the waste could have separated before he was ready, and he would have lost his balance. In his Surgeon's First Report, filed on the same day as the Employer's First Report, Dr. Watson labeled the heelbone fracture an os Calcis, which commonly results from a fall from a ladder, and indicated that the break in Webb's right forearm was a Colle's fracture—consistent with a fall on an outstretched arm.

This is the earliest account of the events that I have located. In this version, Webb's fall was unintended, a simple accident. There is no mention of an attempt to save McGowin's life or that there was anyone whose life needed to be saved, and there is no allusion to Webb's wrestling with the block as he fell. Of course, the company's representative might not have learned of Webb's motivation or might not have thought it relevant, though the two additional lines available were left blank.

This early report finds an echo ten years later in correspondence between two lawyers for McGowin's estate.[994] Calvin Poole (1893–1990) was the estate's trial counsel. In his early forties at the time, he was 'a wise man and extremely adept country lawyer.'[995] As pretrial discovery came back, Poole wrote to the estate's probate lawyer to summarize Webb's answers to interrogatories.[996] Poole was stating the 'real facts of the case' as he had come to understand them, presumably after reading Webb's answers and interviewing those who knew something about the events. 'On one occasion when Mr. McGowin was making one of his daily rounds at the mill, some workman was sawing off a timber in the overhead of one of the mills and the timber was about to fall just as Mr. McGowin was passing under it, and [Webb] intercepted the timber to keep it from falling and fell himself and was rather badly hurt.' This comes secondhand from Webb, a decade after the events. If we set aside for the moment the suggestion that McGowin was there at the time, here again Webb seems to have been involved in a typical accident on a construction project. As a length of board unexpectedly separated, Webb tried to keep control of it, lost his balance, and fell.

---

[994] Letter from [Calvin Poole] to T.M. Stevens (Jan. 11, 1935), *Webb* File, f. 19 (Correspondence: Lawyers).

[995] McGowin (2015), pp. 222, 225.

[996] Webb's written responses do not survive.

Daily Schedule

At this very late date, we will not be able to resolve the discrepancies between the two versions. And since I want to base my decision on the facts, I have to admit that I do not have clarity about one of the matter's central elements. I also want to mention other reasons why I will not rely on Webb's account of his heroic deed to reach my conclusion.

To begin, McGowin may not have been in the mill when the accident took place. When mill No. 2 was operating, McGowin's daily schedule was so regular you could set your watch by it.[997] He was at the mills by six when work began and made his rounds for about an hour. 'He would talk to the men, knew almost all of them by name, listened and advised, was concerned and generous.'[998] Then he walked the short distance back to his home, breakfasted shortly after seven, and was at his desk in the company office by eight.

The workers' comp report indicates that Webb was injured at eight in the morning and that he stopped work one minute later. If mill No. 2 had been in normal operation, McGowin would have been sitting at his desk and working on his correspondence. McGowin had a ferocious work ethic. He dictated many letters a day, and much of his voluminous correspondence survives. If some problem arose, his office was nearby, and he could have made it quickly to the mill. And yet from my impression of him, it is just as likely that he trusted his experienced supervisors to address production issues. His mind was focused elsewhere—on his customers, on the market, and on the industry.

But on the day of the accident the new mill was still under construction.[999] In the comprehensive archives of McGowin's correspondence, there is nothing to help us understand McGowin's daily schedule while they were rebuilding the mill. McGowin would have been in charge, and there was a lot to do. 'Everything is so disorganized, seemingly on account of our fire, and it is going to be such a big job to build back again.'[1000] As he supervised the construction, he might have passed below the spot where Webb was working. And yet it seems strange to think that someone as experienced as McGowin would have been standing where construction work was going on a few feet above. Perhaps he was distractedly making a point to a contractor. Accidents happen. We will never know.

---

[997] For McGowin's schedule, see Appleyard (2000), p. 35; Maunder (1977), pp. 10 (Floyd McGowin), 35 (Earl McGowin), 69 (Nick McGowin), p. 88 (Estelle McGowin Larson).

[998] Maunder (1977), p. 88 (Estelle McGowin Larson).

[999] See Maunder (1977), p. 46 (Earl McGowin).

[1000] Letter from J.G. McGowin to Earl M. McGowin (n.d., around May 1, 1925), p. 1, WTS Files, b. 1, f. 8.

Looking Down

Another doubt arises when I put myself in Webb's shoes as he looked down from above. As the block began to fall, he saw someone directly below. In the unlit mill, it would have been difficult, in the fraction of a second available, to identify who that was. And yet the amended complaint alleges that Webb knew he was saving his employer. 'He saw the said J. Greeley McGowin on the ground below.'[1001] How could he know that the person passing below was his boss? Perhaps the man below was wearing a business suit. Or perhaps Webb glimpsed a white boater—the stiff-brimmed straw hat that McGowin, like others of his social status, wore against the summer heat. Maybe Webb looked down and saw a straw hat, assumed it was his boss, and did what he could to save him. But others also wore suits and boaters. It could have been a prospective customer, an engineer, or a contractor. Perhaps Webb saw McGowin at his elbow when he came to and concluded that McGowin had been there all along. I know I am being ungenerous to our hero, but I also have to admit that there is not the least corroboration for Powell's version of the events.

No News Report, No Recollection

If Webb had saved McGowin's life, the incident would have attracted the attention of a newspaper reporter. Whatever McGowin did was news. 'The Butler County Sportsmen Club met at the court house here Saturday morning, with the president, J.G. McGowin, presiding.'[1002] The McGowin family also appeared frequently in the Society column. 'Mrs. J. Greely McGowin and Miss Estelle McGowin will sail on the "Vreendam," with Miss Margaret Booth, early in June, for a European tour. They will attend the graduation of Earl McGowin in June, from [Pembroke] college, Oxford.'[1003] If a mill worker had been seriously injured while saving the life of one of Alabama's leading entrepreneurs, that would have been news in every paper in the state. But as far as I can tell, there was no such reporting.

And McGowin would also have told someone. Floyd, McGowin's oldest son, was already working full-time for the company, and though he was often away soliciting business, he may have been in the office on the day of the accident, and also a month later when McGowin made his promise. Since McGowin was attached to his wife and his sons, and since they often talked things over, I have no doubt that, if Webb had indeed saved McGowin's life, McGowin would have mentioned it to them. And yet in none of their many journals, diaries, and personal letters did any of

[1001] Amended Complaint para. 5 (Apr. 8, 1935), *Webb* Record 768, p. 5.

[1002] 'Sportsmen Club Hears Distinguished Speakers.' *The Greenville Advocate*, Dec. 2, 1925, p. 1.

[1003] 'Personals.' *The Montgomery Advertiser*, May 17, 1925, p. 17.

them ever discuss it. And when the payments to Webb were reconsidered eight years later, no one had heard of him.

Correspondence

We are discussing a fleeting event that took place a hundred years ago in a poorly lit sawmill under construction in a small town deep in Lower Alabama's pine forests. Such events normally have a short half-life in collective memory. But these were not normal circumstances, and that is because the McGowins were not a traditional household. They were instead a family 'perseverant in recording their history and their thoughts in books and in letters.'[1004] They engaged enthusiastically in epistolary exchange, often writing weekly to one another about intriguing moments and shared recollections. Just as importantly, Earl, McGowin's second son, had a passion for preserving even the most ephemeral traces of his own and his family's lives. His archives contain a wealth of mementos and the great bulk of his correspondence for his entire adult life, including originals of the letters he received and copies of those he sent, the individual correspondence threads meticulously fastened together with straight pins.

This exceedingly comprehensive family scrapbook makes it possible to trace the lives and thoughts of family members year by year, and at times week by week, over the course of more than half a century. And yet in all this paper, Webb's heroic act is never mentioned. In fact as far as I can tell, Webb's name appears only on one occasion in the family archive, and that is when, during the litigation, the time came to estimate the amount that Webb was likely to recover.[1005]

Long Memories

The more one reads, the greater the doubts. Mill workers had long memories. When he retired in 1949, William Curry Jones, one of the company's supervisors, recounted some of the memorable incidents that he had experienced in the mills. He recalled what happened on one occasion when a snake, on another a possum, was found in timber as it was being processed. The mill once processed a big longleaf tree where

[1004] Letter from Mrs. Curtis Bush Hasty, III, to Earl McGowin (June 18, 1988), p. 1, McGowin Papers, b. 4700, f. [Miscellaneous] – LE [?].

[1005] See 'Estate of J.G. McGowin, Chapman, Alabama: Proposed Plan for Termination of Administration of Executors' (attached to Letter from J.H. Lehmann to N. Floyd McGowin (Oct. 27, 1936)), WTS Files, b. 7, f. 8.

wild bees had built a hive, and the 'boys really had a big time eating that honey.'[1006] Jones did not mention McGowin's close call.

Olive Spann, editor of *Lumbering Along*, interviewed other old-timers and took down their recollections.[1007] 'The engine rolled off sidewise.... Mr. Booker did not jump and went down with the engine. He was gravely injured.'[1008] A skunk, surprised as the saw cut into its log, let off such a stink that they shut down the mill and sent the workers home to change their clothes.[1009] Some of those who recorded their memories were working in the mill when Webb was injured. With their feeling of bonhomie and local pride, someone would have remembered Webb's selfless act. But as far as I can determine, it left no trace, and Webb's name appears in none of the many accounts I have read of local events.

Ballads

Lumber workers composed ballads that turned accidents and other misfortunes into heroic exploits.[1010] In *The Wreck of Number Five*, Joe Cook recounted a mishap that occurred on a logging train not far from Chapman. That was in September 1925, a month after Webb's accident.[1011] 'The engine turned over and killed Fletcher McCreary dead,/And between the boiler and a log it caught poor Jetty's leg.' Or *A Veteran of the Rails*: 'But out from under the engine the engineer sailed,/And saved his life but lost one leg,/And the rest of his life he wore a peg.'[1012] Or *The Saddle Horse Coon*: 'At last one night great sadness came to my buddy and me/When his hound got killed by a falling tree.'[1013] Had a millworker saved the life of J.G. McGowin, the town's folk culture would not have left the deed to languish in

---

1006 'William Curry Jones,' *Lumbering Along*, p. 4 (n.d.) (photocopy), McGowin Papers, b. 4707, f. [no label]. A similar interview is quoted in Appleyard (2000), pp. 118–119.

1007 For the handwritten notes, see McGowin Papers, b. 4707, f. [no label]. Other recollections are preserved in the 'Grass Roots Special Edition,' *The Butler County News*, Sept. 28, 1978, McGowin Papers, b. 4674, f. Clippings, etc. – Folder 7.

1008 'Chapman: As Seen in Editions of *Lumbering Along*,' *The Butler County News*, Sept. 28, 1978, McGowin Papers, b. 4674, f. [Clippings, etc. – Folder 7]; handwritten interview notes, G. D. Booker and #7 Spot, b. 4707, f. [no label].

1009 '#3 Mill' (handwritten note), McGowin Papers, b. 4707, f. [no label].

1010 For the Southern tradition of folksongs about train wrecks, see Cohen and Cohen (2000), pp. 169–274; Lyle (1983).

1011 Joe Cook, 'Joe's Jingles,' *The Butler County News*, Sept. 28, 1978, McGowin Papers, b. 4674, f. [Clippings, etc. – Folder 7]; for the typescript of 'The Wreck of Number Five,' see McGowin papers, b. 4707, f. [no label].

1012 'A Veteran of the Rails,' McGowin papers, b. 4707, f. [no label] (proof sheet from *Lumbering Along*).

1013 Joe Cook, 'The Saddle Horse Coon,' McGowin papers, b. 4707, f. [no label, first folder after Family history book] (typewritten manuscript).

silence. A ballad maker would have risen to the occasion, versified the event in couplets, embroidered it until it was nearly unrecognizable, and raised Webb to the status of a folk hero. I have found no such ballad.

No Trial

An undated document in Poole's file lists five potential witnesses for Webb, including his wife and daughter, while eleven were prepared to testify for the estate.[1014] Perhaps a couple of Webb's co-workers or a former supervisor would have come forward to recall Webb's bravery and testify about McGowin's promise. Since the case did not go to trial, we cannot know. As things stand, in all of the massive documentation of life in Chapman while the McGowin's owned the mills, the only suggestion that Webb saved McGowin from death or serious bodily injury is found in Powell's amended complaint, a pleading artfully drafted by a savvy lawyer as he attempted to dodge the argument that the alleged promise was not supported by consideration. Those were only pleadings. The case never went to trial. Powell never had to prove any of it.

Temporary Conclusions

I was usually the one who drafted the complaint in Bill Brown's commercial practice. It was my job to interview the client and craft a coherent account of the events. Most of the time when the client said something happened, it actually happened. But I knew I was only getting half the story. When discovery came back from the other side, the case often looked different. Today whenever I hear only one side of a story, I know enough to withhold judgment. Powell's version of the accident resonates especially strongly because it seems to offer the only explanation for McGowin's promise. Webb must have done something commendable to earn a lifelong pension. But a modest pension is not the kind of gratitude one would expect from a wealthy man, and besides, as we will see, there are better explanations for the promise.

I am not trying to convince anyone. I just want to be honest with myself as I work my way to a resolution. At this point, I note that I am skeptical about the canonical account of the accident. I will therefore leave open the question of how Webb was injured and whether Webb saved McGowin's life. I am thus not going to be able to base my decision on McGowin's gratitude or his sense of moral obligation. As paradoxical as it may seem, I choose this path because I feel a strong tug in Webb's direction. I want to decide the case in his favor, but I do not want to rely on

[1014] See *Webb* File, f. 8 (Trial Court: Witness Lists).

allegations supported by no contemporaneous evidence, not subjected to cross-examination, and that are now beyond our ability to prove or disprove. The task that I now set for myself is to decide the case in Webb's favor even if he did not save McGowin's life and without employing the notion of moral obligation to provide consideration for McGowin's promise.

Workers' Compensation

Workers' compensation is the kind of grand political bargain that impressed Hart and Sacks as the central work of government. All American states and the District of Columbia have passed legislation guaranteeing employees basic compensation for workplace injury and in exchange barring workers from suing their employers for the harm.[1015]

The Alabama workers' compensation program was enacted in 1919 and took effect the following year.[1016] The statute allowed employers to insure against the risk of these payments, but W.T. Smith chose to self-insure.[1017] McGowin favored the system and preferred it to the common law.[1018]

Reports

Within fifteen days after Webb's accident, W.T. Smith was required to send a first report to the Alabama Compensation Commission. A final or supplementary report was to be filed after not more than sixty days.[1019] The Alabama Compensation Commission long ago discarded the reports filed in Webb's case. The only documentation that survives is in Calvin Poole's case file, and the only workers' comp report there is a carbon copy of what appears to be the final or supplementary report. It is unsigned, but I assume that the original was signed and submitted to the commission. It was dated fifty-six days after the accident, and for that reason I believe that it *was* the supplementary report—even though it was recorded on the form designated for the *first* report. The file also contains the original of what I believe was the physician's supplementary report. It was of the same date as the employer's report and completed on the form designated for the surgeon's *first* report. I find it

1015 For the relevant statutes, see Johnson (2022).

1016 Alabama Workmen's Compensation Act, No. 245, 1919 Ala. Laws 206 (codified as amended at Ala. Code secs. 7534–7613 (1923)).

1017 See Letter from J.G. McGowin to The E.E. Jackson Lumber Co. (Nov. 12, 1930), WTS Presidential Files, b. 6, f. Ja-Je; Letter from J.G. McGowin to Charles S. Keith (June 29, 1928), WTS Presidential Files, b. 6, f. Ke.

1018 Letter from J.G. McGowin to Southeastern Products Association (Oct. 28, 1926), WTS Presidential Files, b. 5, f. Sm (brown).

1019 Alabama Workmen's Compensation Act, secs. 35, 38.

likely that the description of the accident in the employer's report was copied verbatim from the first report.

Dr. Watson decided that Webb's disability was total but temporary. For the total disability of an employee temporarily unable to work, the schedule mandated payment at the rate of fifty percent of weekly wages for the period of disability, not to exceed three hundred weeks (about five years and nine months).[1020]

Webb was confined to bed for a month after the accident and remained in the clinic for another two and a half weeks. Dr. Watson's final report was issued about ten days after Webb was discharged. The doctor predicted that Webb would remain unable to work for another six to eight weeks,[1021] which would mean a total disability of between fourteen and sixteen weeks.[1022] The employer's report noted that Webb was earning fifteen dollars a week. W.T. Smith satisfied its obligation by paying Webb his full weekly salary every other week for a period significantly longer than was required.

Promise

McGowin visited Webb in the infirmary on September 1, 1925, Webb's first day out of bed. Webb's wife, Lessie, was there with one of their daughters.[1023] The workers' comp report would not be finalized for another month, but Dr. Watson probably shared his prognosis. Even if Dr. Watson thought that Webb would be permanently incapacitated, he might not have wanted to say so. Webb was still in pain, could not walk, and was surely hoping for encouraging news. Dr. Watson wanted to reassure Webb, but unless he stated on the comp form that Webb would never work again, Webb would not receive his full benefits. The good doctor did the best he could in the circumstances.

As they were chatting in Webb's hospital room, McGowin confirmed that the company would pay Webb's medical expenses as well as the workers' comp benefits.[1024] The legal dispute was about what else they discussed. Nothing was put in writing.[1025] Webb's amended complaint alleged that McGowin 'agreed with plaintiff

---

[1020] Alabama Workmen's Compensation Act, sec. 13(a).

[1021] 'Surgeon's First Report,' para. 15, *Webb* File, f. 1 (Workers' Comp Claim).

[1022] For reasons that remain unclear, the employer's form lists the total period of disability as ten weeks from the date of the injury. 'Employer's First Report of Injury' (Sept. 26, 1925), sec. D para. 4, *Webb* File, f. 1 (Workers' Comp Claim). Perhaps the original estimate in the employer's first report was copied without adjustment into the supplementary report.

[1023] Letter from [Calvin Poole] to T.M. Stevens (Jan. 11, 1935), p. 2, *Webb* File, f. 19 (Correspondence: Lawyers).

[1024] Id.

[1025] See Letter from [Calvin Poole] to T.M. Stevens (Jan. 11, 1935), pp. 1–2, *Webb* File, f. 19 (Correspondence: Lawyers). In his responses to interrogatories, Webb conceded that the promise had not been reduced to writing.

to care for and maintain him... for the remainder of plaintiff's life.'[1026] On behalf of the executors, Poole responded that no one had promised Webb anything, and if a promise had been made, it was certainly not for a lifetime pension. Instead, he argued, McGowin had simply instructed the company's bookkeeper to pay Webb's comp benefits. But Poole's account cannot be the whole story, for it does not explain why the payments continued for eight years.

Poole had likely interviewed McGowin's family and employees and heard nothing of a promise. Poole decided that the payments had continued due to McGowin's well-known capacity for empathy. 'When the time was out, it seems that Mr. McGowin felt sorry for [Webb] and continued to pay the compensation.'[1027]

I think we will eventually conclude that a promise was made, but two facts give me pause.

One is that Poole put W.H. Nall on his witness list. Nall, the company's auditor, served as McGowin's principal assistant and alter ego. He was a fellow board member of McGowin's church and witnessed the codicil to McGowin's will.[1028] If McGowin had made a significant promise, he would have mentioned it to Nall, if only to make sure that the payments were made. Poole would not have put Nall on the stand if McGowin had promised a lifetime pension.

The second troubling fact is found in a letter that McGowin's son Floyd wrote to his lawyer shortly after Webb filed his lawsuit. It seems that McGowin himself had considered suspending the payments. 'Papa continued payments to him out of sympathy, but each year when it came up questioned the advisability of doing so.'[1029] If a person of McGowin's integrity questioned the payments, that means that whatever legal or moral obligation there might once have been had by then been satisfied.

Lumber Barons

And yet I cannot end the discussion there, for the foresters I have consulted have not the least doubt that McGowin made exactly the promise that Powell alleged in his complaint. These professionals explain that lumber barons spontaneously make promises of a lifetime benefit: 'You will have hunting rights on the island forever,'

[1026] Amended Complaint para. 4 (Apr. 8, 1935), *Webb* Record 768, pp. 4–5.

[1027] Letter from [Calvin Poole] to T.M. Stevens (Jan. 11, 1935), p. 2.

[1028] There are undated witness lists for both parties in the *Webb* File, f. 8 (Trial Court: Witness Lists). For copies of McGowin's will and will codicils, see Probate Records. For Nall's role as McGowin's auditor and assistant, see Letter from J. Greeley McGowin to H.S. Aldridge (April 22, 1926), WTS Files, b. 1, f. 1 ('I usually turn these matters over to Mr. Nall, and he will do all he can to help you out.'). For Nall as a church board member, see Unitarian Universalist Association, State Convention Records, p. 64, McGowin Papers, b. 4725.

[1029] Letter from N. Floyd McGowin to Calvin Poole (May 23, 1934), *Webb* File, f. 20 (Correspondence: McGowins).

'You will have this house for the rest of your life.' These promises are always honored. Displaying largesse of this kind is what it means to run a lumber empire. McGowin managed W.T. Smith for twenty years before he became its president some months before the accident. There is nothing about the promise to suggest that McGowin did not make it.

But I am not convinced. McGowin was not a typical lumber baron—or a baron of any kind. He did not call attention to himself or make extravagant gestures. When Earl boasted to his father that he had made the acquaintance of British aristocrats, McGowin responded that members of British high society 'don't represent the class of people that you should get your ideals from.'[1030]

What Might Have Happened

Since Webb was convinced that a promise was made, and since it would not have been unlike McGowin to have made one, I find it likely that McGowin did indeed promise something. McGowin was a generous man, had not forgotten his humble origins, and had a personal connection to his workers. He was 'a citizen of the quiet American type little known to the public, as a rule, for the reason that such citizens are too usefully and helpfully busy to court the plaudits of the multitude.'[1031]

I have grown to admire McGowin, and I find especially appealing his unwavering effort to lead an honorable life in an imperfect world. McGowin was especially solicitous of employees with families,[1032] and it makes sense to me that, out of sympathy for Webb's family, McGowin would have allowed the payments to Webb to continue. However, since we also know that McGowin eventually reconsidered the payments, I believe that McGowin did not expressly promise to take care of Webb for the rest of his life.

Let us imagine the moment. McGowin was visiting with Webb and his family in the infirmary, and Webb was out of bed for the first time since the accident. Dr. Watson had just explained that Webb would have to stay in the hospital for another couple of weeks and would likely miss a further six to eight weeks of work. Though Webb might have felt encouraged, Lessie could see that her husband was not recovering, and she may have doubted the doctor's optimistic assessment. As I imagine it, she asked McGowin what would happen if the comp benefits ran out before Webb could to get back to work.

Help of the kind she was implicitly requesting is just the kind of assistance that McGowin was used to providing. McGowin's grandson remembered that he 'routinely gave jobs to people with physical infirmities, lost limbs, and so forth,

[1030] Letter from J.G. McGowin to Earl McGowin (Feb. 20, 1922), McGowin Papers, b. 4675, f. 7.

[1031] 'J. Greeley McGowin,' *The Greenville Advocate*, Jan. 5, 1934, p. 2 (reprinted from *The Mobile Register*).

[1032] See Letter from J.G. McGowin to Rev. A. Arnold Ross (Jan. 1, 1931), WTS Presidential Files, b. 5, f. Ross, Rev A.A. (brown).

so that they could make a living.'[1033] McGowin had no reason to doubt the doctor's pronosis and almost surely would have promised to continue the benefits until Webb was back to work.

As we know, Webb never healed sufficiently to make it back to the mill. No term was stated, and McGowin let the benefits run. After payment had continued for several years, however, McGowin must have wondered whether he had satisfied his obligation. The benefits were not a problem when business was good, but as the Depression deepened and it became difficult to make payroll, McGowin took a closer look at every expense. What was McGowin to do? As I now see it, this story is not about Webb wrestling with a pine block. It is about McGowin wrestling with his conscience.

On Whose Behalf

If McGowin made a promise, was it on his own behalf or was he acting for the company? The appellate opinion addressed the question without resolving it: the promised pension was either 'paid or caused to be paid' by McGowin.[1034] McGowin probably never thought about it. He probably just instructed his bookkeeper to make sure that Webb received his benefits.

A company president assures an employee that his comp benefits will continue. When put that way, it is clear that McGowin was committing the company's resources and not his own. There can be no doubt about this, unless we confuse ourselves by assuming that the promise was made to reciprocate for a heroic act. Moreover, the payments were all made from company funds.[1035] The payment ledger survives, together with its meticulously recorded biweekly payment entries. Each of those pages is labeled 'W.T. Smith Lumber Company, Joe Webb Cas[ualty] Ins[urance].'[1036] When the time comes to interpret a contract, courts may rely on how the parties performed it.[1037] By this test, it was a company obligation.

There is another reason to think of the promise as company debt. McGowin would have thought of the obligation as his own only if Webb had saved his life. But if a wealthy man like McGowin had wanted to show meaningful gratitude, he would have made a single gift of a substantial sum, one that provided a nest egg to support Webb's family and that also allowed some benefit to pass to the next generation.

[1033] McGowin (2015), p. 7.

[1034] *Webb v. McGowin*, 168 So. 196, 197 (Ala. Ct. App. 1935) (quoting [Brief for Plaintiff-Appellant] (May 8, 1935), p. 2, *Webb* File, f. 10 (Appeal: Briefs)).

[1035] Letter from [Calvin Poole] to T.M. Stevens (Jan. 11, 1935), p. 2, *Webb* File, f. 19 (Correspondence: Lawyers).

[1036] See [payment ledger], *Webb* File, f. 1 (Workers' Comp Claim). Payments were recorded from Sept. 16, 1925, to Feb. 1, 1934.

[1037] Restatement (Second) of Contracts § 202(4) and comment g.

McGowin thought it enough for the company to keep paying Webb's comp benefits. That was the response of a company president.

Legally Binding

There is good reason to believe that McGowin did not intend to be legally bound. Though a self-made man, he had a surprisingly exact understanding of the law, including contract law, and particularly of the consideration doctrine. A couple of months after making the promise to Webb, he signed promissory notes in another matter and wrote to his lawyer to ask whether the notes should state a consideration. 'The thought has occurred to me that there is no consideration set out in the transfer of the Chapman Mercantile Company's stock.'[1038] McGowin knew how to create a legally binding contract. If he had wanted his promise to Webb to be legally enforceable, he would have reduced it to writing and stated a quid pro quo. In the law, we tend to think of legally enforceable promises as more dignified than those that rely on good will, but McGowin thought differently. His promise was governed not by Alabama contract law but rather by the code of honor of Southern gentlemen. Jurisdiction for breach was not in the Butler County Courthouse but rather in the tribunal of conscience.

When Payments Stopped

The benefits were paid regularly until a month after McGowin died on January 1, 1934, somewhat more than eight years after the payments began. Webb had not worked since the accident and was never to work again. In Webb's final years, Webb was bedridden and could barely move. When the payments stopped, Webb and Lessie were likely living in a nearby township together with a son, three daughters, and a grandchild.

Webb must have found a way to transport himself to the company's office and remind the new owners of McGowin's promise. The brothers had college degrees and no longer enjoyed McGowin's intuitive connection to millworkers, let alone to an older employee they did not know and who had not worked in the mill for nearly a decade. They also knew that McGowin himself had come to question the payments. At that insanely difficult moment, the brothers weighed their sense of obligation to Webb against what they owed current employees and shareholders. Since no comp payments were due, the brothers decided not to reinstate the disbursements.

It seems that the Webbs then dropped by Dempsey Powell's office in Greenville to ask for advice. Powell accepted representation and filed a claim against the

[1038] Letter from J.G. McGowin to T.M. Stevens (Dec. 31, 1925), WTS Files, b. 1, f. 5.

estate.[1039] When the claim was denied, Powell had to decide whether to bring suit, and if so, for what and against whom.

Lawsuit

Because the workers' comp statute bars claims against the employer in tort,[1040] Powell's only option was to sue McGowin's estate on the promise, and that meant he would have to come up with consideration. Dempsey Powell was one of the most experienced lawyers in Alabama. He would not have filed a pleading that he did not believe in, and the fact that he prepped for trial means he thought he had what he needed to convince a jury. I am now wondering whether we can reconcile what I think we know about the facts of the case with Powell's allegation that Webb saved McGowin from serious injury or death.

I regularly sat in on the discussions that Bill Brown, my trial lawyer friend, had with his clients, so I think I can imagine Powell's conversation with Webb. Powell might have asked why Webb thought that McGowin would make him a lifelong promise. Webb had never thought about it, never had reason to. Maybe Powell then asked whether anyone was walking around on the ground below where he was working. Workers, contractors, and supervisors were often standing together and talking down there. What about McGowin, Powell asked, was he there? Mr. Greeley was always somewhere around. What about on that morning, was McGowin there that morning? He was there every morning. And that pine block, Powell asked, might it have hit someone? Webb nodded. That was a possibility. And as he fell, was he trying to keep those standing there from getting hit? Webb nodded again as he thought about it. Powell continued to poke at the scene, and at some point Webb told him the story he needed to hear.

That is about the best I can do to explain why Powell's complaint does not jibe with what I think we now know about the facts of the case. I will be the first to admit that it is not satisfying—but to be honest, it never is. Doubts remain, even after the verdict. The parties have lived different truths, the documents support two stories, and both perspectives make sense in the circumstances. As we packed up at the end of trial, I was often still uncertain about what had actually happened years before. In those moments, Bill reminded me that the law is not concerned with 'metaphysical truth.' All that matters is what can be proved to a jury.

[1039] See 'Deceased Estate of J. Greeley McGowin' (May 19, 1934), *Webb* File, f. 2 (Claim against McGowin Estate).

[1040] Alabama Workmen's Compensation Act secs. 9–11.

Settlement

Calvin Poole, the estate's lawyer, challenged the sufficiency of Powell's complaint on several grounds, including that the alleged promise lacked consideration. The circuit court dismissed the complaint, but the Alabama appellate court reversed and remanded, and the circuit court set the case for trial in 1936. The jury would have had to find that it was more likely than not that McGowin promised to take care of Webb for life and that McGowin made that promise in his personal capacity.

Poole believed that he would win at trial, but time was not on Poole's side. Though McGowin died with no outstanding debt, a significant estate tax was due, and since most of McGowin's holdings were in land and company stock, the executors lacked sufficient liquidity.[1041] The company's lawyers wanted to close the estate before the end of 1936,[1042] and Webb's was one of the claims that had to be resolved before the estate could be distributed.[1043] In November 1936, the executors settled with Webb for a lump sum payment of $900.[1044] The sum was less than the value of the three years of payments that were due since McGowin's death. In their internal discussions, the executors had budgeted $1200 to settle the suit.[1045] If the court had awarded Webb all the unpaid installments—retroactive from the last benefits paid and continuing to his death nine years later—he would have collected between $3500 and $3900.

The McGowins, 'a clan that stands for character, inspiration, enterprise and courage,'[1046] did not celebrate the settlement. Family members are still troubled by the case and the implication that the McGowins are not as good as their word.[1047] As *Webb v. McGowin* became the leading American case on the question of moral consideration, Calvin Poole regretted that he had not taken the case to trial to vindicate them.[1048]

[1041] Letter of J.H. Lehmann to H.C. Kilpatrick (Aug. 27, 1936), p. 1, WTS Files, b. 7, f. 8; Letter of Earl McGowin to Nick McGowin (Jan. 14, 1934), in Miller (forthcoming).

[1042] 'Memorandum of Conference in Connection with the Estate of J. G. McGowin, Deceased' (Sept. 9, 1936), p. 1, WTS Files, b. 7, f. 8.

[1043] Calvin Poole, [memo to the file] (n.d.), pp. 3–4 (following Letter from Calvin Poole to Tom Burke (Mar. 7, 1980)), *Webb* File, f. 21 (Correspondence: Professors etc.).

[1044] See Letter from Floyd McGowin to Calvin Poole (Nov. 14, 1936), *Webb* File, f. 20 (Correspondence: McGowins) (enclosing a check for $900 in full settlement); [Settlement Agreement] (Nov. 16, 1936), *Webb* File, f. 14 (unexecuted carbon copy of apparent final agreement); Letter from [Calvin Poole] to N. Floyd McGowin (Nov. 20, 1936), *Webb* File f. 20 (Correspondence: McGowins) (acknowledging receipt of $900 and enclosing the signed settlement agreement).

[1045] 'Estate of J. G. McGowin, Chapman, Alabama: Proposed Plan for Termination of Administration of Executors,' (attached to Letter from J.H. Lehmann to N. Floyd McGowin (Oct. 27, 1936)), WTS Files, b. 7, f. 8.

[1046] 'The Passing of a Ducal Figure,' *The Montgomery Advertiser*, Jan. 2, 1934, p. 4.

[1047] Letter from Calvin Poole to Tom Burke (March 7, 1980), *Webb* File, f. 21 (Correspondence: Professors etc.).

[1048] Letter from Calvin Poole III to Norman F. McGowin, Jr. (July 26, 2000), p. 1, *Webb* File, f. 20 (Correspondence: McGowins).

Proof Difficulties

I do not see how Webb could have proved a promise for a lifetime pension—or a promise of any kind. My speculation about what McGowin and the Webbs discussed in the infirmary does not count as proof. A jury would have decided the question, and juries like contemporaneous documents. Since Powell had no documents, Webb and his wife and daughter would have taken the stand, as well as the three others he named on his witness list, perhaps Webb's co-workers. The company's auditor and four of its bookkeepers would have confirmed that W.T. Smith made the payments directly to Webb and that none of the funds came from McGowin's personal accounts.[1049] The testimony would have referred to events that had taken place a decade earlier. Webb and his family would have made sympathetic witnesses, but on cross-examination, Poole would have been able to cast doubt on their self-interested recollections.

I am no longer worried about the consideration doctrine. As deserving as Webb was, and as needy, I do not believe that the estate was the proper defendant. And given the proof problems, it seems to me that Webb would have lost at trial. Powell wisely used the estate's pressing need for closure as leverage for settlement. He probably got Webb the best deal available in the circumstances.

Promissory Estoppel

What if Powell had sued the company? There would have been no claim for workers' compensation. The maximum permissible duration for benefit payments for temporary total disability was three hundred weeks, less than six years, and W.T. Smith had regularly made the payments for more than eight.

But there might have been another path. As I think about the human reality of the situation, I notice that the one provable fact—really the only one not in dispute—is that benefits were paid without interruption for more than eight years.

The persistence of those payments makes me ask whether they might have implied a promise. I am not thinking of the original promise to extend Webb's comp payments for a few months until he was back on the job. I am wondering instead about the promise that a court might construct from the long history of payment. Webb was paid for years beyond what the statute required, every two weeks like clockwork. It seems to me that regular payment made it reasonable for Webb to infer that the payments would continue for the rest of his life—and also made it

---

[1049] Poole's case file includes a list of witnesses slated to testify for each side at trial. See *Webb* File, f. 8 (Trial Court: Witness Lists). The estate's witness list is also separately included in Poole's correspondence. See Letter from Calvin Poole to N. Floyd McGowin (Nov. 2, 1936), *Webb* File, f. 20 (Correspondence: McGowins).

reasonable for him to rely on them. And Webb relied in ways it would be difficult to prove many years later.[1050]

My promissory estoppel argument may seem like a stretch, but it relies on a familiar idea in the law, one that helps explain a peculiar feature of the statute of limitations. A debtor's partial payment on an outstanding debt tolls (extends) the statute on the creditor's claim for non-payment[1051]—the limitation period begins to run again from the date of the last payment.[1052] Why is that? For one, it makes no sense to ask a creditor sue a debtor who is making payments.[1053] But there is another reason as well. The law treats part payment 'as the legal equivalent of a promise to pay[1054]—it means that 'the debtor recognizes and signifies the intent to honor the obligation.'[1055]

Thanks to this principle, I think that Webb could make out his claim entirely on the basis of the company's history of regular payment. Those payments would have conveyed to Webb the company's understanding that it was obligated to provide for him and his family and would also have implied a promise that the obligation would be paid in full.[1056] The analogy would need some retooling, but I think I could get it to work for Webb.

Anchor in the Law

So *Webb* turns out to be a case of promissory estoppel after all. But thanks to the several books that we have now read together, we know that finding a cozy niche in the law is not enough to decide the case—many factors beyond legal doctrine play a role as well. So why then have I spent decades looking for a suitable legal construction, and why does finding one that I think I can live with give me such pleasure? In fact, now that I am asking, why do we need legal rules at all? We know how troublesome they can be. Why do we not ignore the rules and just decide the cases?

[1050] After the case settled, Webb leased a four-room dogtrot on sixteen acres north of Georgiana. The annual rent for the weathered clapboard house was fifty dollars, and it was paid in 1939 with a bale of cotton.

[1051] See, e.g., Ala. Code § 6-2-16 (2023); Fla. Stat. § 95.051(1)(f) (2023).

[1052] *Cadle Co. v. McCartha*, 920 So.2d 144 (Fla. Ct. App. 2006).

[1053] *Greer Limestone Co. v. Nestor*, 332 S.E.2d 589, 596 (W. Va. 1985).

[1054] *Cadle*, p. 146. See also *Hickerson v. Vessels*, 316 P.3d 620, 625 (Colo. 2014).

[1055] *Cadle*, id. See also *DeCoursey v. Am. Gen. Life Ins. Co.*, 822 F.3d 469, 474 (8th Cir. 2016).

[1056] Part payment tolls the running of the statute only if the debtor, when making payment, 'intends to acknowledge and admit the greater debt.' *Howard v. Pritchett*, 92 So. 782, 783 (Ala. 1922). The main challenge, therefore, would be to prove that the W.T. Smith Company recognized that it was bound by an obligation to Webb. However, since the law interprets the payments as promises, they are interpreted from the point of view of a reasonable promisee. See Restatement (Second) of Contracts § 200 comment b (1981); *Real Est. Loan Fund Or. Ltd. v. Hevner*, 709 P.2d 727, 731 (Or. App. 1985). Webb might reasonably have believed that those payments were intended to satisfy an existing obligation.

Our readings in the great tradition would turn anyone into a rule skeptic—someone who believes that the rules play no meaningful role in the decision process. I read our texts differently. Holmes thought of the rules as an element of the *form* of the law. Though they are not the whole picture, they remain essential. We resolve a dispute legally when we find a convincing argument and formulate it in the law's traditional concepts.

That may be true, but putting it that way does not explain why searching for an appropriate legal construction is worth the trouble. If the rules are only a matter of housekeeping, if their only purpose is to provide a legally acceptable vocabulary for reporting decisions that are usually made on other grounds, then legal construction is nothing but a parlor game.

Looking at rules that way misses their point. One way to see the role they play is to notice when we consult them. As we are setting out, we ask them to set the agenda. They let us know which factors earlier jurists thought of as important, and they also list some questions that we should put to the facts. Their guidance is not less important because we are free to add further factors and questions. We consult the rules at the beginning because we find them shrewdly observant.

We return to the rules when we have settled on an answer. We are then trying to ensure that our legal construction convincingly anchors our decision in the law. We pay particular attention to the outer boundary of the law's universe, for the totality of its resources defines the limits of the law's intervention in social life. The rules thus express a view about how to balance the concerns of the individual with those of society—another definition of freedom. These limits are flexible, and that is because the common law's extraordinary resources allow us to formulate pretty much any solution in terms of legal concepts.

And yet there are constraints—constraints, not barriers—guidelines that synthesize the wisdom of the tradition. If after much effort, judges are unable to justify their preferred result in terms of the law's conceptual structure—if they 'discover that the opinion won't write'[1057]—the court will want to think hard about whether to impose it on the parties. That does not mean that the court should go the other way. As always, judges, not rules, make the decisions. 'Rules guide, although they do not control, decision.'[1058] Judges can use the structure of the rules to understand the reasons for the limits the law has placed on itself, and they generally do not go where the common law has not been. But the structure is always in dialogue with the circumstances, and judges know that they can make an end run around the rules when they need to, but they also know to do so only when they have to.

[1057] Llewellyn (1936), p. 21; see also Kitch (1995), p. 99.

[1058] Llewellyn (1931b), p. 90; see also Llewellyn (1933), p. 79.

Social Circles

There are a few more details to mention about *Webb*, even though they will not help with the legal analysis. McGowin was acquainted with two of the appellate judges who decided the case. Judge Charles Bricken (1867–1951)[1059] was the appellate court's presiding judge, and McGowin knew him well enough to appreciate his foibles: 'Judge Bricken is a very likable fellow; his only fault that I know of is that he will drink a little too much sometime.'[1060]

Ten years before *Webb* came up for decision, McGowin wrote to Judge William Samford (1866–1940), the member of the appellate panel whose concurrence quoted Justice Marshall.[1061] Samford wrote back to express his gratitude. 'I appreciate the fact that you have felt close enough to write to me relative to the situation.'[1062]

Since both judges voted to enforce McGowin's promise and both wrote opinions, I am wondering whether their esteem for McGowin's character may have played a role in the decision. If McGowin had made a promise, as the complaint alleged, the honor of a Southern gentleman was engaged. Those Alabama judges may have felt that McGowin should be allowed to keep his word—consideration or no consideration.

Defense

The McGowin brothers long annoyed me. My irritation began when I learned that they all studied in Oxford, one as a Rhodes Scholar. I did not have a chance as a student to study in Oxford, or even to spend time there. Nonetheless, my reading of British fiction has left me with a clear sense of the opportunity that an Oxford education affords. Oxford students gain a deep understanding of the human condition, and when they later achieve positions of responsibility, they naturally help others pursue their goals, without fear, envy, or pettiness.

And this also seems to be what it meant to the McGowins. As Earl later wrote, 'the simple fact of our going to Oxford had completely changed the course of our lives in viewpoint, in depth of understanding, in knowledge of other parts of the world, in our day to day lives, and in innumerable instances that were apparent to us

[1059] Letter from G.E. McGowan to J.G. McGowan [sic] (Dec. 18, 1924), WTS Files, b. 1, f. 8.

[1060] Letter from J.G. McGowin to L.G. Leonard (Aug. 28, 1924), WTS Files, b. 1, f. 8.

[1061] For the correspondence, see Letter from J.G. McGowin to Judge W.H. Samford (Jan. 1, 1925), WTS Files, b. 1, f. 10; Letter from W.H. Samford to J.G. McGowin (Jan. 2, 1925), id.; Letter from J.G. McGowin to Judge W.H. Samford (Jan. 3, 1925), id.; Letter from W.H. Samford to J.G. McGowin (Jan. 5, 1925), id.

[1062] Letter from William H. Samford to J.G. McGowin (Jan. 2, 1925).

at all times.'[1063] I am continually trying to live up to the image I have of the person I might have become had I had the chance to study there.

And there is something even more painful. I did not have an even minimally acceptable relationship with my father. The McGowin children, in contrast, were respected, encouraged, and given 'every advantage which a wise and cultured father and mother could procure for them.'[1064] The advantages that their devoted parents provided to them, it has always seemed to me, imposed responsibilities. I long wanted to decide the case against them because, when they refused to continue the payments to Webb, they failed to live up to the standard I set for them.

I am not thinking of the executors but rather of McGowin's three eldest sons. They ran one of the largest lumber operations east of the Mississippi and easily could have instructed the bookkeeper to make sure that Webb got paid. Given their personal fortune, this would not have been burdensome. Viewing the case through this lens, I never cared enough about the brothers to ask whether their decision to discontinue the payments might have been justified.

The human situation that most needed clarification was my own. 'Into our past have been woven all sorts of frustrated ambitions with their envies and of hopes of preferment with their corruptions which, long since forgotten, still determine our conclusions.'[1065] My envy got in the way as I tried to put myself in the shoes of the McGowin brothers and to ask whether they might have had a good reason for stopping the payments. And my resentment prevented me from taking seriously one of the critical features of the case, the central concern not only of the McGowin brothers but of pretty much everyone alive at the time, and that is the Great Depression.

Changed Circumstance

The American economy was booming in 1925 when McGowin made his promise,[1066] but the thrill did not last. By the time McGowin died in January 1934, the demand for housing had plummeted, and the lumber industry was hit hard. The production of Southern pine declined to levels not seen in fifty years,[1067] lumber was sold below cost, and mills cut back production.[1068] Demand had come back somewhat by 1935, but even then it had reached only half of the pre-Depression level.

The contract defense sometimes available in these circumstances comes under the heading of *impracticability* or *changed circumstance*. As a rule, courts will not modify contracts when circumstances change. And yet when an event occurs that

[1063] Letter from Earl McGowin to Arthur K. Burt (Feb. 13, 1973), McGowin Papers, b. 4706, f. Pembroke College – Correspondence Re: McGowin Library.

[1064] Ward (1934).

[1065] Hand (1939), vol. 39, pp. 10–11, vol. 52, pp. 362–363, vol. 48, pp. 380–381.

[1066] Kennedy (1999), pp. 10–42.

[1067] Hair (1958), p. 16, Table 16.

[1068] Collier (1965), p. 101.

makes it extremely difficult to perform, a court may excuse performance, provided that the contract did not allocate the risk of that event to the party seeking relief.[1069]

Since W.T. Smith was having trouble making payroll, it might have argued that it should not be required to divert resources to a retired worker whose comp benefits had been fully paid. Though the company's argument looks strong, the case law goes the other way, and the answer is pretty uniform throughout American jurisdictions: even a widespread business depression generally does not excuse performance.[1070] And the Alabama courts have been—and remain—especially unreceptive to the defense.[1071]

Let us put the case law aside for a moment. If we take the calamitous collapse of the lumber market into account, was it too much to ask of the brothers that they continue the payments to Webb?

In May 1932, the manager of a Mississippi lumber company shut down his mill and wrote to McGowin to ask how things were going at W.T. Smith.[1072] 'The wages we are paying look as if it is ridiculous,' McGowin wrote, 'still it is either that or shut down, and if we shut down there is nowhere for our men to make a living.[1073] The company skipped dividend payments for the first time in twenty-six years.[1074]

At the moment two years later when the brothers were deciding whether to continue the payments to Webb, Floyd described the firm's situation to his youngest brother: 'We have had very little business since the first of the year; in fact, none of the mills have had enough business to mean anything.'[1075]

It was in these dispiriting circumstances that McGowin questioned the wisdom of continuing the payments to Webb. In the end though, it seems to me that McGowin's decision cuts the other way. Yes, McGowin considered terminating the payments, but it is more important that he chose not to. No one was better able to weigh the competing factors, and it makes no sense at this late date to argue with him.

[1069] Restatement (Second) of Contracts § 261 and comment d (1981). Because promissory estoppel is generally treated as a contract claim, *Board of County Comm'rs v. DeLozier*, 917 P.2d 714, 715 (Colo. 1996) (en banc); Restatement (Second) of Contracts §§ 1, 90 comment d (1981), the same defenses should apply.

[1070] Corbin (1962a) § 1333, pp. 369–370. For the lumber business, see *Marionneaux v. Smith*, 163 So. 206, 208 (La. App. 1935), rehearing denied, 164 So. 456 (La. 1935).

[1071] *Greil Bros. Co. v. Mabson*, 60 So. 876, 878 (Ala. 1912), cited with approval in *Sumter Cnty. Bd. of Educ. v. Univ. of W. Ala.*, 349 So.3d 1264, 1274 (Ala. 2021).

[1072] Letter of S.E. Moreton to J.G. McGowin (May 3, 1932), in Maunder (1977), p. 123.

[1073] Letter from J.G. McGowin to S.E. Moreton (May 10, 1932), WTS Presidential Files, b. 5, f. Mo (brown), reproduced in Maunder (1977), p. 124.

[1074] Letter from J.G. McGowin to Mrs. L. Keville Larson (Jan. 18, 1932), WTS Presidential Files, b. 6, f. Senator John Bankhead (gray).

[1075] Letter from Floyd McGowin to Nick S. McGowin (Feb. 3, 1934), in Miller (n.d.), pp. 32–33.

Who Should Win

I first read *Webb v. McGowin* as a bewildered student a month into law school, and though I understood little about the consideration doctrine, I was sure that Webb should win. I have now thought about the case for fifty years, and my opinion has never wavered. My quest has instead been to find a legal construction that might get me to my goal. Since I have now found a legal theory that satisfies me, this is the moment to address the question that remains. Unfortunately, it is also one of the most difficult I have run into in the law: *why do I feel so strongly that Webb should win?*

I will now have to confront the question without my props. I no longer believe that Webb rescued McGowin. I also no longer assume that McGowin promised Webb a lifelong pension. Those factors were always only makeweight. Even when I erase them, my mind does not budge. I still want Webb to win. But what then is doing the pulling?

Taking From the Rich

When I probe further, I sense that I have other thoughts about the case, some buried deep inside. I know it will embarrass me to talk about this, but since we have now been through a lot together, it is easier to confess what I find: I do not want to abandon Webb. He and his family should be able to lead a dignified life, and if the workers' comp legislation falls short, the common law should find a way. The McGowins were one of the wealthiest families in Alabama. Those small biweekly payments would do a lot of good for Webb without seriously impacting the McGowins' lifestyle.

I know. These are outrageous thoughts to find in the mind of a law professor. The common law is not Robin Hood. No one has given it a roving commission to take from the rich and give to the poor. 'To strip Richard in the interest of John for no better reason than that John's need is the greater would affront the sense of justice.'[1076] And yet these are my thoughts, and if I were the judge, they would play a role in my decision. I am now asking myself what this means for our work. If our legal system cannot protect its process from prejudicial thinking like mine, maybe we should insist that judges mechanically apply the law.

So yes, my belief that the poor should be able to lead dignified lives plays a role in my decision. But I am now thinking that this view may be a feature of the common law. As we were setting out, we found something like it in Blackstone's book. 'For there is no man so indigent or wretched, but he may demand a supply sufficient for all the necessities of life, from the more opulent part of the community, by

---

[1076] Radin (1935), p. 48.

means of the several statutes enacted for the relief of the poor.'[1077] Since our statutes for relief of the poor are not fully effective, I understand why I want the common law to find a path.

The Great Tradition Today

The *Webb* case has always been about how to assist an injured worker who was no longer able to support his family, but that core challenge has long been obscured by the more beguiling controversy surrounding the doctrine of moral consideration. The tradition as it is today responds directly to the underlying task. That human reality calls attention to itself and demands a solution. Since legal tools are available for pretty much any outcome, the law no longer presents much of an obstacle.

But our recent authors may lose sight of the limits that the common law has long imposed on its own reach. Judges can find a home for nearly any solution, but that does not mean that courts should intervene in every case. Since the Holmesian virtue of judicial restraint seems to have lost some of its appeal, it is not easy to see which factors can today maintain its balance. Perhaps it is enough that social expectation today does not include the redistribution of wealth as a factor that common law judges may consider.

Good Decisions, Bad Decisions

I have one last question before I let this go:[1078] can we tell a good decision from a bad one? A few works of art end up in museums while most others do not, and though art curation is a complicated matter, the existence of museums suggests that there are criteria to help us decide which pieces are better than others. Could we create a pocket museum of judicial decisions? And which decisions would we include?

We would certainly include a few of Cardozo's decisions. And I think we would also include *Webb*.[1079] How would we decide? If I were to think about judicial decisions the way I think about works of art, I would have two criteria. I like art works—and decisions—that are masterly in terms of craft and that teach me something new about myself.

The craft question concerns the legal construction. To compete, the decision does not have to convince me. It need only strike me as an unusually meaningful approach

---

[1077] Blackstone (2016), vol. 1, p. ☆127. See above, p. 72.

[1078] The question was suggested by Crescente Molina.

[1079] Even though the decision has been included in a list of 'the worst of contracts cases.' See Burnham (2018), pp. 961–964.

to integrating a challenging decision into the structure of the law. Perhaps my main criterion is difficulty. A great common law decision overcomes obstacles with finesse. Cardozo's decision in the *Allegheny College* case is great in this way. His opinion is a stunning work of the imagination. In contrast, the decision in *Webb* is not great, or even good, in terms of craft. The cases the court cited are irrelevant, and the opinion does not even try to distinguish conflicting precedent. It neither defines the problem nor explains the real nature of the challenge, and it creates an awkward niche in the law without addressing the obvious objections.

The genius of the decision in *Webb* lies elsewhere. It is great in terms of result. The court saw the goal and got the case to come out as pretty much everyone expects it to—'Everyone wants Webb to win.'[1080] It is a *good* decision because it captures social expectation. It is a *great* decision because the way it confidently pushed past doctrinal limits reveals a deep understanding of the human condition. The decision teaches me how badly I want this result. Though poor in terms of craft, its ultimate resolution is sublime.

I pause to take stock. Though we now have a clearer picture of the world in which Webb's claim arose, together with a fuller understanding of its two perennial companion cases, no reason suggests itself to abandon our initial tug. *Webb v. McGowin*, one of the most perplexing decisions in Kessler's casebook, has at last opened its heart to us. This would make a great Hollywood ending and a perfect way to conclude our discussion. But we are not quite done.

A Lot Going On

Our goal as we set out was uncommonly ambitious: we were hoping to come to some understanding of the entire process that we call the *common law*. But lately we have devoted most of our time to finding acceptable solutions to our three favorite cases. And yet some common law decisions are far more challenging, even doubtful, while it must be admitted that others are completely unsuccessful. The question that remains is whether the great tradition has what it needs to come to terms with these disappointing cases?

For me, the hardest cases are not those I read in the reports but rather those that I know much more about because I have had to litigate them. I am thinking now of an argument I presented to a trial judge about a jury instruction. It was a commercial matter, and the question was one on which I had published. I offered a balanced view of the opposing positions and explained why the Code section is best interpreted as I was suggesting. The judge listened politely and denied my motion. I was sitting second chair with Bill Brown in that case. He noticed that I was disappointed and took me aside at the break. 'It means we're ahead,' he said smiling. I did not understand. 'The judge thinks we'll win.' I still did not understand. 'She doesn't want to give the other side grounds for appeal.'

[1080] Burnham (2018), p. 961.

There is a lot going on whenever a judge decides. To lecture a judge for failing to give weight to any particular factor trivializes the challenges inherent in the judicial process.

System Failure

And yet the system does occasionally fail. When it does, I can sometimes console myself with the thought that it failed for the right reasons. Now I am thinking of a case involving an aircraft lease.[1081] At trial, both sets of lawyers, all from distinguished firms, argued the case on the basis of the common law of contract. They were unaware that the case was governed by the Uniform Commercial Code, which would entirely have reframed the discussion. Sound decisions can sometimes result even when the system is flying on a single engine, but awkward landings are then more likely. As Llewellyn put it, these are moments when the courts 'teach justice to shiver and shake.'[1082]

As much as I revere the common law, I am not claiming that every decision can be defended—'not even its most zealous advocate... will assert that it is perfect.'[1083] The argument in its favor is that it is flexible enough to provide the opportunity for a subtle evaluation of many relevant factors. It is that social process that I have come to admire.

Whenever I encounter a thoroughly unsatisfying decision, I try to see the case as Cardozo might have understood it. From the point of view of eternity, judicial errors do not matter. 'They may work a little confusion for a time. In the end, they will be modified or corrected or their teachings ignored. The future takes care of such things.'[1084] As Cardozo contemplated the common law from that great and silent distance, he concluded that few decisions matter to anyone but the parties: 'The world would be little better or worse if every case that had come before our court during the last fifty years had been decided differently.'[1085]

References

Anderson D, Huber P (1999) 'The Log Train': Hank Williams's last song. Tributaries: Journal of the Alabama Folklife Association 2:9–39

Appleyard J (2000) The W.T. Smith Lumber Co.: A chronicle. Pace, Pensacola

[1081] *Wells Fargo Bank Nw., N.A. v. Taca Int'l Airlines, S.A.*, No. 01 Civ. 11484 (GEL), 2003 WL 21878794 (S.D.N.Y Aug. 7, 2003).

[1082] Llewellyn (1939), p. 702.

[1083] Cardozo (1921a), p. 116.

[1084] Cardozo (1921b), p. 179.

[1085] Lehman (1942), p. 7 (quoting Cardozo).

Blackstone W (2016) Commentaries on the laws of England, Prest W (ed), 4 vols. Oxford University Press, Oxford

Bourke-White M (1963) Portrait of myself. Simon and Schuster, New York

Burnham S (2018) *Webb v. McGowin*: The perils of 'result-oriented' jurisprudence. In: Arnow-Richman R et al (eds) The best and worst of contracts decisions: An anthology, pp 961–964. Florida State University Law Review 45:887–1020

Cardozo B (1921a) A Ministry of Justice. Harvard Law Review 35:113–126

Cardozo B (1921b) The nature of the judicial process. Yale University Press, New Haven

Carmer C (1928) Riding the carriage: Lumber mill, Chapman, Alabama. Poetry 32(5):246

Childers J (1927) By the way. The Birmingham News, May 11, p. 8

Cohen N, Cohen D (2000) Long steel rail: The railroad in American folksong, 2d edn. University of Illinois Press, Urbana

Collier J (1965) The first fifty years of the Southern Pine Association, 1915–1965. Southern Pine Ass'n, New Orleans

Collier J (1986) Earl McGowin of Alabama: a portrait. Faust, New Orleans

Comstock J (1836) A system of natural philosophy, 31st edn. Robinson, Pratt, New York

Corbin A (1962a) Corbin on contracts: A comprehensive treatise on the working rules of contract law, vol. 6. West, St. Paul

C[rosby] D (1972) Hubert E. Olive, Sr. In: Annual of the Baptist State Convention of North Carolina, Willams T (ed). Baptist Convention, Wake Forest, pp [6-7]

Danzig R, Watson G (2004) The capability problem in contract law: Further readings on well-known cases, 2d edn. Foundation, New York

Dowd J (1888) Sketches of prominent living North Carolinians. Edwards & Broughton, Raleigh, pp 296–299

Drake F (1879) Dictionary of American biography including men of the time, supplement. Houghton, Osgood, Boston

Ellis R (1850) Memoir of the Hon. Samuel Howe. Crosby and Nichols, Boston

Escott C et al (2004) Hank Williams: The biography. Little, Brown, New York

Feldman G (2015) Politics, society, and the Klan in Alabama, 1915-1949. University of Alabama Press, Tuscaloosa

Fickle J (2014) Green gold: Alabama's forests and forest industries. University of Alabama Press, Tuscaloosa

Fuess C (1930) Davis, John. In: Johnson A, Malone D (eds) Dictionary of American biography, vol 5. Scribner's, New York, pp 133–134

Giles H (1839) The Christian view of retribution hereafter. A lecture delivered in Paradise Street Chapel, Liverpool, on Tuesday, May 7, 1839. Willmer and Smith, Liverpool

Goldberg V (1986) Margaret Bourke-White: A biography. Harper & Row, New York

Graves J (1934) J. Greeley McGowin. Greenville Advocate, Jan. 5, p. 2

Hair D (1958) Historical Forestry Statistics of the United States. US Dept. of Agriculture, Forest Service, Division of Forest Economics Research, Statistical Bulletin No. 228

Hand L (1939) Mr. Justice Cardozo. Columbia Law Review 39:9–11, Harvard Law Review 52: 361–363, Yale Law Journal 48:379–381

Hoar G (1902) Charles Allen of Worcester. Charles Hamilton, Worcester

Holland I (1991) Olive, Hubert Ethridge, Sr. In: Powell W (ed) Dictionary of North Carolina biography, vol. 4. University of North Carolina Press, Chapel Hill, p. 394

Howe S (1834) The practice in civil actions and proceedings at law, in Massachusetts, Fay R, Chapman J (eds). Hilliard, Gray, Boston

Hutchinson J (1998) No ordinary lives: A history of Richmond County, North Carolina 1750–1900. Donning Co., Virginia Beach

Ingram C (1994) Stevens, Henry Leonidas, Jr. In: Powell W (ed) Dictionary of North Carolina biography, vol. 5. University of North Carolina Press, Chapel Hill, pp 445–446

Johnson J (2022) Workers' compensation laws by state (2023 Guide). https://www.forbes.com/advisor/legal/workers-comp/workers-compensation-laws/

Johnson R (1995) Through the heart of the South: The Seaboard Air Line Railroad story. Boston Mills Press, Erin, Ontario
Jones W (2005) The tribe of Black Ulysses: African American lumber workers in the Jim Crow South. University of Illinois Press, Urbana
Jones W (2010) How Black 'folk' survived in the modern South: Industrialization, popular culture, and the transformation of Black working-class leisure in the Jim Crow South. In: Reed A, Warren K (eds) Renewing Black intellectual history: The ideological and material foundations of African American thought. Paradigm, Boulder, pp 53–79
Kelley E (1956) Chapman, Ala., a feudal outpost: Smith Lumber balks Woodworkers Union. The Gulf Coast News Digest, May 9, pp 1, 2
Kennedy D (1999) Freedom from fear: The American people in Depression and war, 1929–1945. Oxford University Press, New York
Kessler F (1969) Arthur Linton Corbin. Yale Law Journal 78:517–524
Kessler F, Fine E (1964) Culpa in contrahendo, bargaining in good faith, and freedom of contract: A comparative study. Harvard Law Review 77:401–449
Kessler F (1975) Some thoughts on the evolution of the German law of contracts—a comparative study: Part I. UCLA Law Review 22:1066–1082
Kinnicutt T (1854) Notice of the life and character of Hon. John Davis. John Wilson & Son, Boston
Kitch E (1995) *Gustafson v Alloyd Co.*: An opinion that did not write. Supreme Court Review, pp 99–124
Knapp C (2013) Cases and controversies: Some things to do with contracts cases. Washington Law Review 88:1357–1394
Lehman I (1942) The influence of Judge Cardozo on the common law. Law Library Journal 35:2–10
Llewellyn K (1931b) Law and the modern mind: A symposium, I: Legal illusion, review of Frank, Law and the modern mind. Columbia Law Review 31:82–90
Llewellyn K (1933) Präjudizienrecht und Rechtsprechung in Amerika: Eine Spruchauswahl mit Besprechung. Theodor Weicher, Leipzig
Llewellyn K (1936) On the why of American legal education. Duke Bar Association Journal 4:19–25
Llewellyn K (1939) Review of Prausnitz, The standardization of commercial contracts in English and continental law. Harvard Law Review 52:700–705
London I (1963) Attorney F. W. Bynum dies: Was Civic Leader, U. S. Commissioner. Rockingham Post-Dispatch, Nov. 21, pp. 1, 7
Lyle K (1983) Scalded to death by the steam: Authentic stories of railroad disasters and the ballads that were written about them. Algonquin Books, Chapel Hill
Maunder E et al (1977) James Greeley McGowin—South Alabama lumberman: The recollections of his family. Forest History Society, Santa Cruz
McGowen F, McGowen P (1971) Flashes of Duplin's history and government. McGowens, Kenansville
McGowin F (2015) The forest and the trees: A memoir of a man, a family, and a company: The McGowins of Chapman, Alabama, and the logging and lumbering business. New South Books, Montgomery
Miller B et al (forthcoming) Earl: McGowin family letters and photographs: A selection from 1916 to 1947: Letters of Earl Mason McGowin. Privately printed
Miller B et al (n.d.) Floyd: McGowin family letters and photographs: A selection from 1916 to 1947: Letters of Norman Floyd McGowin. Privately printed
Owen T (1921) Powell, Dempsey Monroe. In: History of Alabama and dictionary of Alabama biography, vol. 4. S. J. Clarke, Chicago, p 1381
Parker I (1828) Address of Chief Justice Parker to the Bar of the County of Suffolk at a meeting held for the purpose of testifying their respect for the memory of the Hon. Samuel Howe, one of the justices of the Court of Common Pleas for the Commonwealth. Hale, Boston
Penningroth D (2022) Race in contract law. University of Pennsylvania Law Review 170:1199–1302
Posner R (1990b) The problems of jurisprudence. Harvard University Press, Cambridge
Pound R (1931) The call for a realist jurisprudence. Harvard Law Review 44:697–711
Powell L (2013) The fleeting fame of Henry L. Stevens Jr. North Carolina Miscellany. https://blogs.lib.unc.edu/ncm/2013/10/26/22020/

Radin M (1935) The chancellor's foot. Harvard Law Review 49:44–67
Rankin A (1949) McGowin: Sees a mountain from an anthill. Alabama Journal, June 6, p. 3
Rich A (1891) Henry Giles. Unitarian Review 36:276–290
Simon B (2017) The Hamlet fire: A tragic story of cheap food, cheap government, and cheap lives. University of North Carolina Press, Chapel Hill
Simpson J, Swan E (1937) Improvements in the lumber industry. Annals of the American Academy of Political and Social Science 193:110–119
Smith B (1959) N. Floyd McGowin: Lumberman of the Year. Crow's Lumber Digest 37:5, 27
Spratt J (1955) The road to Spindletop, economic change in Texas, 1875-1901. Southern Methodist University Press, Dallas
Story J (1852) Sketch of the character of Isaac Parker, Chief Justice of the Supreme Court of Massachusetts. In: Story W (ed) The miscellaneous writings of Joseph Story. Little & Brown, Boston, pp 812–816
Sutherland A (1967) The law at Harvard: A history of ideas and men, 1817–1967. Belknap Press, Cambridge
The New South (1949), Bourke-White M (photographer). Life, Oct. 31, pp 79–90
U.S. Department of Labor (1949) Occupational outlook handbook. Bureau of Labor Statistics, Washington DC
Walthall J (1980) Prehistoric Indians of the Southeast: Archaeology of Alabama and the Middle South. University of Alabama Press, Tuscaloosa
Ward L (1934) J. Greeley McGowin: A tribute. The Universalist Herald, Jan 20. In: Appleyard J (2000), p. 293
Watson G (1997) In the tribunal of conscience: *Mills v. Wyman* reconsidered. Tulane Law Review 71:1749–1806
Williams C (1914) The life of Rutherford Birchard Hayes, nineteenth President of the United States, vol. 1. Houghton Mifflin, Boston
Williams J (1828) A sketch of the character of the late Hon. Samuel Howe. Griffin & Morrill, Worcester
Williams R (1981) Sing a sad song: The life of Hank Williams, 2d edn. University of Illinois Press, Urbana

Chapter 18
The Place Inside

The discussion in the *Republic* was winding down when Socrates remembered Thrasymachus, who, as we read him earlier, was suggesting that judges should disregard other factors and just apply the law.[1086] That suggestion presented a challenge to both Socrates and the common law. Both have tried to come to terms with the suggestion, and they give something like the same answer: though we have to take book learning into account, guidance in the end comes from within.

Inner Human Being

The insight is often presented in the form of a cryptic metaphor, one that points to a space inside where we work to integrate the different factors that contribute to the decision. To Socrates, for example, there is within us a rational human being who is able to unify our competing impulses.[1087] For Blackstone, the law is 'deposited in the breasts of the judges.'[1088] Cardozo suggested that the personality of the judge is what guarantees justice.[1089] I have tried to summarize these images with a metaphor of my own—a place inside where we do law. As we conclude, it may be worth asking what more there is to say about that place.

It is not a place of pure interiority—a space so hidden and unexplored that little or nothing can be said of it. The central thrust of these images is that a judicial decision requires work, that the work is complex human work rather than a single simple process, and that much of it can be described. The idea is that there is a space in

[1086] Plato (2004) 588b1–4, p. 292, 590d1–5, p. 295. See above, p. 14.

[1087] Id. 588b-590d, pp. 292–295. For Plato's tripartite division of the soul, see Cooper (1984).

[1088] Blackstone (2016), vol. 3, p. 380.

[1089] Cardozo (1921b), pp. 16–17. See above, pp. 117–118.

R. Hyland, *Common Law Judging and the Great Tradition*, Ius Gentium: Comparative Perspectives on Law and Justice 100,
https://doi.org/10.1007/978-3-032-02307-0_18

consciousness where we process many concerns before we reach a decision. Some of the elements exist only below the level of consciousness. But the place we are thinking of also involves the conscious coordination of whatever concerns our legal training and experience have taught us to consider. The legal sources play a role, as does our sense of what society expects. And for those who have studied them, the factors suggested by the books we have discussed may also prove enlightening. Each element surfaces when needed and is integrated with the others in a creative process that resembles the work of an artist.

Since I find abstractions unsatisfying, I am always looking for a helpful image of the process. The one I have settled on for the moment is the procedure I follow when I decide it is safe to make a left turn.

The rules of the road play a role, as do the stoplight, the crosswalk, and the left turn lane. But they are not the heart of the matter. What matters most is my safety and the safety of those around me. I am always trying to guess what the approaching pedestrians, cyclists, and motorists are about to do. I take account of the time of day, the visibility, the weather, and the road conditions. I also try to access the lessons I have learned from decades of making left turns. And sometimes my decisions depend on whether I am running late for a meeting—or even on just how late, and how important the meeting is.

The common theme in all the images is that there is no hierarchy of factors. Each plays a role when its time comes. And despite the complexity of the matter, in just a few seconds, I am usually able to weigh the elements and choose a good moment to accelerate. To me, this is all happening at a place inside that takes over when I am driving and that disappears as soon as I leave the car. That space—where factors and inputs are integrated, often without my conscious intervention—is the image I have for the somewhat similar place inside where judges decide cases.

Kessler's Path

Kessler too gave thought to that inner human being, and I believe what set him on his path was a sentence he heard as he listened to Max Weber. As we know, Kessler was in Munich during Spring term 1920 to attend Weber's lecture on *General Theory of the State and Politics (Sociology of the State)*.[1090]

Weber's explanation of how the civil and common laws differ must have fascinated him. In the civil law, the codes look forward. They are continually being revised to respond to changing social conditions. The common law, in contrast, is concerned with the past. Its goal is to preserve traditional wisdom. Common law judges do not create law, Weber said. They try instead to recognize the law that exists for all eternity ('*von Ewigkeit zur Ewigkeit*'[1091]), Weber's enchanting translation of the common law

[1090] See Weber (2009) (MWG III/7) (translation). See above, pp. 44, 46–47.

[1091] Weber (2009), p. 84 (MWG III/7) (notebook of Erwin Stötzl).

notion of 'time immemorial.'[1092] Seventy years later, as Kessler began to write his last published piece, he was still thinking of those lectures and that sentence. 'It has sometimes been suggested that the common law embodies eternally valid principles.'[1093]

Weber's suggestion inspired Kessler's lifelong research agenda. As he read advance sheets and the latest issues of American law reviews in Berlin, he discovered the flaw in Weber's hypothesis and used the insight as he wrote his second doctoral dissertation.[1094] He described with admiration how American law overcame the limits of privity of contract—which still constrained German law at the time—to create the concept of *products liability*. Kessler was rewarded for his insight by the challenge of an even greater difficulty: why does the country that serves as the model of economic rationality continue to resolve commercial disputes by means of an unsystematic muddle of obscure legal concepts inherited from the Middle Ages?[1095]

In our final minutes together in the Berkeley Hills, Kessler hoped that I would grasp both the question that animated his life's work and how he had resolved it. That is why he opened his casebook and pointed me to Weber's suggestion that capitalist markets do well under both the civil and the common laws.[1096] But characteristically, even after all those years, he was still unwilling to explain, and I still did not understand. Fortunately, as I later discovered, he had published the answer long before in a German festschrift: 'The lawyers charged with keeping the common law up to date successfully infused it with sufficient rationality to allow it to regulate the capitalist economic formation.'[1097] The common law's trademark judicial tinkering continually reorients the common law toward socially useful solutions and allows it to govern the modern capitalist market. That means that the common law too is rational and both it and the civil law are elements of modern legal legitimacy. Kessler also immediately recognized the next question, and he spent his career trying to answer it: how do common law judges settle on the proper adjustments?

The Law Society Needs

Kessler found the answer in the books of the great tradition. As society advances, it signals the law that it needs. As courts resolve disputes, they recognize and verbalize those impulses and recalibrate the common law to receive them. The genius of the common law is that it clears the way forward without calling attention to itself. The process becomes perceptible only in cases where the appropriate result fails to fit nicely into the law's habitual categories—and it is precisely those cases that

---

1092 See, e.g., *Hodgkinson v. Ennor*, 4 Best & Smith 229, 232–233, 122 Eng Rep 446, 447 (1863).

1093 Kessler (1988), p. 109 (translation).

1094 See Keßler (1932).

1095 See also Llewellyn (1929), pp. 234–235.

1096 Kessler et al. (1986), p. 8 note 31 (quoting Weber (1978), vol. 2, p. 890). See above p. 44.

1097 Kessler (1952a), pp. 67–68 note 3 (translation).

Kessler chose for his casebook. Even today, the results of those cases remain difficult to anchor convincingly in the law, and Kessler thought that, by pondering them, we might escape the misconception that judges simply apply law to facts. He hoped that we would instead turn to 'our inner experience,'[1098] set aside the court's foreshortened explanations, and try to recreate the decision process in our own minds.

True Justice

What common law judges seek is 'the sense of justice of the community'[1099]—our implicit understanding, however elusive, about how society should be structured.[1100] And yet though a judge's decisions are socially meaningful, we should not expect them to coincide with justice: 'True justice is just as inaccessible to the law as truth is to all other fields of scholarship.'[1101]

That is the message that Kessler left with us as he concluded his final publication. All knowledge is supposition. Whether a legal solution is proper is a matter of judgment. This idea is both the great tradition's central insight and a basic understanding of Western civilization. To make the point, Kessler lent his final published sentence to the pre-Socratic philosopher Xenophanes of Colophon (c. 570-c. 478 BC).[1102] 'For even if someone were by chance to utter an ultimate truth,/ he would not know it, for he would not be able to distinguish it from opinion.'[1103] Each decision channels a highly concentrated intuition about momentary social needs, one that, because its sources are both plentiful and unfathomable, will always remain individual. The power of common law decisions is due precisely to their personal character. They are legitimate because they are authentic. The mechanical application of a rule to the facts could never command the authority of a decision that a judge personally guarantees.

Fables

That is why Kessler urged us to remain open to the thoughts that flood our minds. The cases we read in the casebooks are there for practice. They offer dilemmas to be rethought across generations, timeless fables for contemplation by the legal

[1098] Kessler (1941), p. 111.

[1099] Kessler (1943), p. 638.

[1100] Hyland (2018), pp. 471–472.

[1101] Kessler (1988), p. 116 (translation).

[1102] For Xenophanes, see Lesher (ed.) (1992).

[1103] Kessler (1988), p. 116 (quoting Xenophanes of Colophon, fragment 34). The passage is found in Sextus Empiricus (1935) 1.49, pp. 24–25. Kessler quoted from a German edition. The translation here is an interpretive rendering of the Greek.

mind. We have been working with one of these fables—the tale told about Webb in the casebooks. Joe Webb was given but a magical instant to reconcile his individual interest with the common good. No one would have faulted him for allowing the block to slip from his fingers. What thrills us as we read is that he chose to hang on. His decision to sacrifice himself for a fellow human being remains as inspirational today as it was on the day he made it. And the law knows how to respond. It does not compel self-sacrifice, but it will not stand in the way if someone wishes to reward it. By reinstating Webb's complaint, the court conferred on him the lasting renown that befits a figure of legend.

Next Time

Cases are not decided by applying law to fact or by any of the theories or methods that we have examined here. Those are only factors and approaches. The decisions emerge instead from a judge's personal sense of what society needs. The cases help us explore their intuitions, which would otherwise remain inaccessible. They offer us the opportunity to examine what we do not yet fully understand of ourselves and our society, particularly of that place close to the throbbing of the human heart where we do law.

I have for the moment come as close to that place as I am able. I will let it go for now, but I know that I will explore it anew the next time I teach contracts. The course usually begins early on the first morning of the school year and provides to a new generation of law students their first encounter with the law. They know nothing of the questions that we have discussed, nor do they in any way suspect what awaits them. My task, as it has been for several decades, will be to initiate them into these mysteries. After a few weeks, we will talk about the consideration doctrine, we will read a couple of cases, and then the time will come for *Webb v. McGowin*. I will request a show of hands, and I will ask those who believe that the case was rightly decided to explain the result. At that moment I will think of Kessler, and I will smile, and if I am doing my job, years later, if my students happen to remember our conversation that morning, they will smile too.

References

Blackstone W (2016) Commentaries on the laws of England, Prest W (ed), 4 vols. Oxford University Press, Oxford

Cardozo B (1921b) The nature of the judicial process. Yale University Press, New Haven

Cooper J (1984) Plato's theory of human motivation. History of Philosophy Quarterly 1:3–21

Hyland R (2018) On rereading The king's two bodies, review of Lerner, Ernst Kantorowicz: A life. American Journal of Comparative Law 66:458–473

Keßler F (1932) Die Fahrlässigkeit im nordamerikanischen Deliktsrecht unter vergleichender Berücksichtigung des englischen und des deutschen Rechts. De Gruyter, Berlin

Kessler F (1941) Theoretic bases of law. University of Chicago Law Review 9:98–112
Kessler F (1943) Contracts of adhesion—some thoughts about freedom of contract. Columbia Law Review 43:629–642
Kessler F (1952a) Freiheit und Zwang im nordamerikanischen Vertragsrecht. In: von Caemmerer E et al (eds) Festschrift für Martin Wolff: Beiträge zum Zivilrecht und internationalen Privatrecht. Mohr Siebeck, Tübingen, pp 67–78
Kessler F (1988) Metamorphosen im Amerikanischen Vertragsrecht. Juristenzeitung 43:109–116
Kessler F et al (1986) Contracts: Cases and materials, 3d edn. Little, Brown, Boston
Lesher J (ed) (1992) Xenophanes of Colophon: Fragments: A text and translation with commentary, Lesher J (trans). University of Toronto Press, Toronto
Llewellyn K (1929) Ueber den Rechtsunterricht in den Vereinigten Staaten: Ein Vortrag. Jherings Jahrbücher für die Dogmatik des bürgerlichen Rechts 79:233–266
Plato (2004) Republic, Reeve C (trans). Hackett, Indianapolis
Sextus Empiricus (1935) Against logicians, Bury R (trans) (Loeb Classical Library). Harvard University Press, Cambridge
Weber M (1978) Economy and society: An outline of interpretive sociology, Roth G, Wittich C (eds), 2 vols. University of California Press, Berkeley
Weber M (2009) Allgemeine Staatslehre und Politik (Staatssoziologie) (Unvollendet) (Mit- und Nachschriften 1920), Hübinger G, Terwey A (eds) (MWG III/7). Mohr Siebeck, Tübingen

Archives and Case Files

b. = box, f. = folder.

Allied Van Lines, Inc. v. Bratton

Allied Record:

> The court record is available at the Florida State Archives in Tallahassee. It is stored in series S 49, b. 3504, f. 49517.

Allied File:

> Reinald Werrenrath III represented Allied. The Ackerman Law Firm in Orlando, Florida, has preserved his case file.

Joseph Williams represented Ila Bratton. His case file has not survived.

Harrington v. Taylor

The records on appeal for the contract and tort cases are available from the North Carolina Supreme Court. They are located in the file North Carolina Supreme Court, Original Cases File, 1940–1981.

Harrington SC Record 593:

> Case No. 593 (Tort), Microfilm reel no. S.110.1021.

R. Hyland, *Common Law Judging and the Great Tradition*, Ius Gentium: Comparative Perspectives on Law and Justice 100,
https://doi.org/10.1007/978-3-032-02307-0

Harrington SC Record 594:

Case No. 594 (Contract), Microfilm reel no. S. 110.996.

The trial court records from the Richmond County Superior Court are available at the State Archives of North Carolina.

Harrington Trial Record (Contract):

Civil Action File # 1103-A (1945).

Harrington Trial Record (Tort):

Civil Action File # 1321-A (1946).

No police report of the altercation has survived, nor have the case files of the two lawyers.

Icar v. Suares

In the caption in the Louisiana Supreme Court, the defendant's name appears as *Suares*, but his name is regularly spelled *Suarez* in the court record.

Icar Record:

The court record is included in the Historical Archives of the Supreme Court of Louisiana. It is available from the Earl K. Long Library at the University of New Orleans and is catalogued as Docket #2649, Eastern District, January 1835.

Friedrich Kessler

Emergency Committee:

Correspondence by and about Friedrich Kessler for the period between 1933 and 1944 is available in the Manuscripts and Archives Division of the New York Public Library. It is located in the Records of the Emergency Committee In Aid of Displaced Foreign Scholars, MssCol 922, b. 18, f. 'Kessler, Friedrich.'

No general repository of Kessler's papers has been identified.

Mills v. Wyman

The Archives of the Massachusetts Supreme Judicial Court, now in the Massachusetts Archives on Columbia Point in Boston, preserve documents from both the trial court and the high court.

Record books: Official case summaries created after final disposition.[1]

Mills CCP Record:

Court of Common Pleas, Worcester County, records, 1824 Dec., pp. 224–226, *Mills v. Wyman*. JU-SJC/CCP.WO/series 002. Massachusetts Supreme Judicial Court Archives, Massachusetts Archives. Boston, Massachusetts

Mills SJC Record:

Supreme Judicial Court, Worcester County, records, 1826 Apr., pp. 470-473, *Mills v. Wyman*. JU-SJC/SJC.WO/series 002. Massachusetts Supreme Judicial Court Archives, Massachusetts Archives. Boston, Massachusetts

File papers: Documents filed in court. The CCP files contain the originals. The fair copies in the SJC files copies are easier to read and are cited when available.[2]

Mills CCP Files:

Court of Common Pleas, Worcester County, files, 1824 Dec., *Mills v. Wyman*, no. 97. JU-SJC/CCP.WO/series 003. Massachusetts Supreme Judicial Court Archives, Massachusetts Archives. Boston, Massachusetts

Mills SJC Files:

Supreme Judicial Court, Worcester County, files, 1826 Apr., *Mills v. Wyman*, no. 26. JU-SJC/SJC.WO/series 003. Massachusetts Supreme Judicial Court Archives, Massachusetts Archives. Boston, Massachusetts

Webb v. McGowin

Records from the Alabama courts are preserved in bound volumes in the Alabama Department of Archives & History in Montgomery.

Webb Record 768:

The record in the Court of Appeals can be retrieved as *Joe Webb v. N. Floyd McGowin and Joseph F. McGowin as Executors of the Estate of J. Greeley McGowin, Deceased*, 768 3 Div. (Ala. Ct. App. 1935)

Webb Record 170:

The record in the Supreme Court is retrievable under the same case name, located at 170 3 Div. (Ala. 1936)

Other archives also contain information relevant to the parties, the setting, and the case.

[1] For the record books, see Menand (1987), p. 130.

[2] For the file papers, see id., pp. 130–133.

WTS Files:

The Alabama Archives preserve the records of the W.T. Smith Lumber Company.

WTS Presidential Files:

The Presidential Files, a later accession by the Alabama Archives, contain copies of McGowin's correspondence from 1925 to 1934.

Webb File:

Calvin Poole was litigation counsel for the defendant, the Estate of J. Greeley McGowin. The law offices of Poole & Poole in Greenville preserve Poole's original case file. With the authorization of Calvin Poole III, the file was organized for purposes of scholarly citation and a file list created.

Probate Records:

McGowin's will and will codicils are preserved in the Probate Division of the Butler County Courthouse in Greenville and can be found in Probate Records, 5 Butler County Will Record, pp. 188–195 (Nov 1, 1919) and pp. 196–197 (Feb. 28, 1927).

McGowin Papers:

The papers of Earl M. McGowin are preserved in the W.S. Hoole Special Collections at the Library of the University of Alabama in Tuscaloosa.

Dempsey Powell represented the plaintiff Joe Webb. His case file has not survived.

Thomas M. Stevens represented McGowin's estate in probate matters. His case file has also not survived.

Reference

Menand C (1987) A Research Guide to the Massachusetts Courts and Their Records. Supreme Judicial Court Archives and Records Preservation, Boston

Index

R. Hyland, *Common Law Judging and the Great Tradition*, Ius Gentium: Comparative Perspectives on Law and Justice 100,
https://doi.org/10.1007/978-3-032-02307-0

H

Kolibri 360 GmbH
Ferdinand-Jühlke-Straße 7
99095 Erfurt, Deutschland
produktsicherheit@kolibri360.de